Happy Anniversary
Barb & Terry

1985
Mother & Dad

ONE
of a
KIND

Printed by
The Kutztown Publishing Co., Inc.

Published by
The Derry Literary Guild
PO Box U, Hershey, Pa. 17033

Library of Congress Number 83–073169

ISBN 0–9612586–0–8

Printed in the United States of America

ONE
of a
KIND

MILTON SNAVELY HERSHEY
1857-1945

by Charles Schuyler Castner

Dedicated . . . .

to the unsung heroes, the hardworking
men and women whose unflinching loyalty
built a showcase for The Great American
Dream in Hershey, Pennsylvania

FOREWORD

A Chain Word

These stories deal with the life and times of Milton Hershey. They were chosen to recreate some of the most precious moments of an age that is faded and gone. We had to handle them carefully, for they are like the fragile remnants of dusty rose petals once pressed away in the pages of an almost forgotten book.

A haunting fragrance still clings to the yellowing leaves that confined them. With it comes the wispy memories of yesteryear to remind us of the days when life moved at a gentler pace, when people still felt they could take the time to be kind to each other.

Come back with us to an enchanted garden of not so long ago. Come back and meet this different kind of man—a fellow who gathered a handful of beloved companions and then went on to compile one of the most hopeful epics in the annals of this dreamland called America. These are the stories of small folks and small dreams grown tall, and they tell about how these people found a way to live and work together for the sheer love of the work and the unspoken faith they had in each other.

Without the boundless vision of the man who led them, there would be very little to see but rolling cornfields in the place now named Hershey, Pennsylvania. But if his visions had not been matched by the wholehearted respect and the unswerving loyalty of his people, there would have been very few lines ever written about the man.

He was one of a kind. He dreamed the dreams and he worked shoulder to shoulder with his trusted friends to spin all their hopes into the durable fabric of reality. Together, they cast a timeless anvil that rang out with the bright sounds of undaunted optimism, and they hammered out an unbreakable chain that linked their faith and their works to their genuine feelings of affection for each other.

They forged a chain that brings back the meaning of an almost forgotten word called *devotion.*

TABLE OF CONTENTS

Foreword: A Chain Word

PART ONE:

A Child Went Forth

Prologue: Springtime and Movement

PART TWO:
A Man Still Growing

PART THREE:

The Planter at Rest—The Harvest Assured

The Final Leaf—

    Milton Hershey Believed. . . .

PROLOGUE

~·~

Springtime and Movement

The keynote to the saga of Milton Hershey was struck about one hundred and eighty-five years before his birth, and it comes straight from the pages of Swiss national history. It all began on a cozy little farm in the valley of the Berne Canton resting beneath the shadows of the Jungfrau's icy peaks.

On a quiet springtime evening in the year of 1672, the central figure of this narrative stepped forth in the person of Christian Hirschi, the Anabaptist Swiss Brethern farmer. His ancestors had been landholders in the general area of the Bernese Oberland since early in the fifteenth century. The members of his clan were tillers of the soil whose farms lay on either side of the winding ten-mile stretch of road between the villages of Schangnau and Interlaken.

That evening Christian Hirschi stepped out of the past and into these narratives when he left his home to attend a meeting of freeholders assembled in Emmental, the political hub of the Berne Canton. He was a man with many concerns to bother him on his way to the meeting, because his troubles, just as those of most of his Swiss countrymen, had been a long time abuilding. And the seat of those troubles was contained in the single word—war.

The hardy Swiss folk had organized a League of Cantons all the way back in 1412 because they had an eye on proclaiming their independence and they had hopes of keeping foreign invaders away from their soil. But the proclamation earned little more than passing attention, and the only real deterrent to the influx of foreigners had been provided by the rugged harshness of the landscape. The Alps made tough battlegrounds, and the toughness of the Alpiners who lived there didn't help, either.

Nevertheless, wars swirled all around the Swiss frontiers. The Bohemian Wars (i.e., the Thirty Years' War) had wound down almost fifteen years earlier in 1658, but that hadn't kept the Hapsburgs from retaining control of the Franche Comte districts of Switzerland, and it hadn't deterred Louis XIV of France, who had been marshalling troops on the Bernese borders.

Up until this time the Swiss Brethren confreres of Christian Hirschi had led something of a charmed life following the years in which they had embraced the doctrines of Netherlander Menno Simons by becoming Mennonites. Even with wars swirling all around them, their more militant Swiss leaders had let them pretty well alone to "do their own thing," farming and dairying and the like. The simple logistics of Swiss survival had dictated that course, because Switzerland even in those days was an overcrowded land, and its meager resource of arable acreage had to be worked down to the last inch, or its people would starve.

The crux of the internal disturbance stemmed from the real differences between the Catholic and Protestant ranks of the native Swiss. But neither faction, two-thirds of whom were Protestant and one-third Catholic, was cheered by the presence of the Austrians (Hapsburg and Catholic) to the east and northeast, nor by the French (Louis Bourbon, equally Catholic) to the west, who were constantly hammering their Protestant (Huguenot) subjects. The consequence of this led to an outbreak of internecine civil war that raged between 1668 and 1672 and pitted members of the separate cantons (states) against each other.

Then two of the largest cantons, Berne and Zurich, formed an alliance in order to set a course for Swiss national unity. The meeting in Emmental had been called to tell the clockmakers, the textile weavers, the woodcarvers, the embroiderers and the farmers what roles they would be required to play in the newly adopted scheme of allied cantons.

The mere calling of the meeting was felt to be an intrusion in the minds of Christian Hirschi and his fellow Mennonites, the Swiss Brethren sect. After all, the warming sun of springtime had come to the icy peaks of the Jungfrau and the melting runoff from the snows above the frostline had started, and now tiny freshets would nourish the

Menno Simons 1496-1561

grass of the upland meadows. The season for greening foliage and calving milch cows had come, so Christian Hirschi and his fellow dairymen were eager to get their winter-thin brown herds up the hill to feed on nature's lush provender.

Something more than a delay in plans awaited Hirschi and his fellow husbandmen. The elected magistrates of the Berne Canton had drawn up a proclamation to spell out the requirements that would be thrust upon the shoulders of all Swiss nationals. A nation that would subsequently earn international acclaim for its peaceful stance of neutrality had gone on the books with a law calling for military conscription. Every man in the Swiss population was henceforth required to register for military service.

The Emmental edict was inflexible. When Christian Hirschi and some two hundred other families of the Mennonite and Swiss Brethren faiths voiced their dissent, they were given a choice.

Either sign up for military service or get out of the country!

There is good reason to believe that the more temperate arbiters of the Berne Councel never expected the Mennonites like Hirschi and his Swiss Brethren friends to give up their holdings and leave. But they were wrong, because they had had no way of measuring either the depth or the intensity that Menno Simons, the famed religious pacifist from the Netherlands, had impressed on the hearts of these stoical Swiss herrenvolk.

In the Teutonic parlance of authorities, Hirschi and his Swiss Brethren fellows were "hartnackig," i.e., stubborn. But in their eyes, they believed they were something else.

They were Mennonites. They would *leave* Switzerland.

It all began there, in the shadows of the glacial crown of the Jungfrau in the alpine Swiss Canton of Berne in 1672. For that was the year in which Christian Hirschi resolved to pack up his family and his portable possessions and get out.

He simply acceded to the demands of a government that would confiscate the lands that preceding generations of Hirschis had managed to earn for themselves and their heirs across the span of several centuries. They could *take* his beloved fields, his home, and his livestock; and they could *remove* him and his family from the scenes that had sheltered and nurtured them through years of greening springtime and the dazzling whiteness of wintry snowscapes. They could *take* everything that had been home and birthplace to the generations of God-fearing Hirschis who had preceded him. And they could *keep* it.

But they couldn't *keep him.*

The stolid determination of Christian Hirschi was clearly defined and positively resolved. There was no government of men that could keep him from holding fast to the beliefs he held within his heart. His faith in his Father God and his faith in himself were at the very center of his life. He reckoned that for those who believe, there is no death. For those who don't, there could be no life.

Thus, in 1672, a man named Christian became the spiritual patriarch of the stubborn clan Hirschi.

*   *   *

One hundred and eighty-five years later a great, great, great great-grandson of Christian Hirschi would come along to add his own qualities of tenacity to this logbook of familial stubbornness. And from his earliest days of childhood, Milton Hershey would be told the legendary stories of his famous forefather, Christian.

From boyhood, Milton Hershey was curious about the spelling of the family name and he wondered about the strange and antlered deer design that was stamped on certain family papers and belongings. The explanations led to a spate of juvenile puzzlement, especially when his folks told him that the antlered deer symbol was really a coat-of-arms.

The answer came subsequently when he learned that the Swiss (Teutonic) word for deer was "hirschi." The terminal "i" of the Swiss spelling denoted the masculine gender; hence a buck deer was chosen for the device. But that didn't stop him from wondering what a family of pacifists and peacelovers wanted with a coat-of-*arms*?

In later years he came to feel as though he had committed some kind of sacrilege when he'd said, "The deer in the Hirschi (Hershey) coat-of-arms was chosen because they scattered and ran every time they heard gunfire." But in those later years, he would gain a wider point of view and would get a much better grip on the values contained in the old legends. He called it a matter of "growing up."

When Milton Hershey became seriously interested in the history of his predecessors, he started to see some of the relationships that tied the documentary records of the family to the reasons these people were *what they were* and *why they did* the things they did. He was also to learn that the same old man, Christian Hirschi, had come to America along with early contingents of Mennonites who settled in Pennsylvania near Lancaster.

It was all in the records and Hershey was to find that Christian Hirschi, along with his friend, Hans Brubaker, had taken out a warrant for a thousand acres of land near the Little Conestoga Creek (which later embraced the site of President Buchanan's home, Wheatland) back in 1717. Thereafter Bentz Hirschi, Christian's son and Milton's great, great great-grandfather, became a Mennonite bishop.

In later years, the son of Bentz Hirschi, another Christian Hirschi, became the father of Isaac Hirschi who purchased the three hundred and fifty acres that later became The Hershey Homestead in Dauphin County. Sometime following the move into the Derry Township area where The Homestead was to stand, the spelling of the name was changed from Hirschi to Hershey, possibly as a consequence of the Scots-Presbyterian influence that had existed there prior to the influx of Swiss Hirschis.

So in the eighty-eight years following the birth of Milton Hershey on September 13, 1857, he frequently turned back to the legendary deeds of his great, great, great great-grandfather, Christian Hirschi. As he grew older and wiser with the passage of time, he found himself warmed by feelings of reverence and fond affection for the memory of his ancestral grandsire.

During his own lifetime, Milton Hershey journeyed several times to the valley of Switzerland's Emmental to look down the winding road that strings its way between Schangnau and Interlaken. There, in the shadows of the towering Jungfrau, he would stand again on the beloved land that Christian Hirschi had left behind in order to hold onto the beliefs that made of him the man he was.

It all began in the springtime of 1672, when a newly united Swiss nation made its first move in the direction of self-determination. In the years after that, the tiny country gained worldwide acclaim for a continuing record of keeping the peace and maintaining a stance of enviable neutrality. But history also shows that when those beginnings were made three centuries ago, the start was made by running some of the most peace-loving and industrious members of the population out of the country.

Christian Hirschi went on record back then when he made his own decision by asserting his belief in *another kind* of self-determination. Two hundred and seventy-five years later, when all the sands had run through the hourglass for his great, great, great great-grandson Milton Hershey, the spelling of the name was changed, but the legacy remained intact.

They were both Hersheys. They were both Christians. And they were both stubborn. The Swiss patriarch fled from his native village in order to find a place of sanctuary and freedom where a man could be himself. Then his American descendant came along to earn a fortune that would be pledged to securing every good thing his famous ancestor had sought.

And while he still lived, he would give it away.

PART ONE

~·~

A Child Went Forth

Chapter I

❤·❤

From the World of Yesterday

On the fifteenth day of January in 1856, a trio of Mennonites were gathered in the parsonage of Holy Trinity Lutheran Church in Lancaster, Pennsylvania. Their somber garb contrasted strangely with the sporty attire of the late to arrive fourth member of the group who had journeyed to this neutral parsonage for a wedding. The Mennonite party consisted of Abraham Snavely, the father, and his two daughters, Martha (called Mattie) and Veronica (called Fanny) Snavely. The fourth member of the wedding party was the intended bridegroom, Henry H. Hershey, a flashy young sport who carried a golden-headed walking stick and an airy notion that the world was illumined by a series of rainbows that kept beckoning him from one pot of gold to another.

His prospective father-in-law and Mattie, the bride's elder sister, had a more pragmatic notion of what the workaday world was all about. But youngest sister Fanny had been entranced by her betrothed, and so her father and elder sister put aside their demurrers and accompanied her to the scene of the nuptial ceremony. Mattie's prevailing sentiments at the time were akin to those held by Napoleon as he departed from Waterloo. Papa Abraham's presentiments were also similar to those of Le Grande Bonaparte, but his thoughts were more recollective of St. Helena. Sister Martha, who had formerly been courted by the perennial swain, Henry Hershey, viewed the upcoming marriage as a crushing defeat. Fanny's father, Abraham, was more inclined to think of it as a terminal disaster.

Nonetheless, Henry H. Hershey and the bride, Fanny B. Snavely, were joined in holy wedlock on the morning of January 15, in the year 1856. The wedding had been scheduled at the neutral site of a Lutheran Church, for the Snavelys were Mennonites and one of their clan could not be married to "a free thinker" (i.e., Henry H.) at their meeting house, not to "such a one."

And he was "one such," was Henry Hershey. Aside from the "free thinking" name he had earned for himself, the avant garde of his day also considered him "a very promising young man." Folk gossip enhanced the claim to the latter *nom de plume* by recalling that the wedding scheduled for early morning had taken place later in the day, nearer to noon. The reason for the delay was later ascribed to the fact that Henry had been summoned to Harrisburg on the morning of the previous day by a court action. 'Twas said that the "promising young man" had lived up to his name by being required to settle an old breach of promise claim prior to making any nuptially binding new contract.

But he finally arrived and he did take young Fanny Buckwalter Snavely for his bride. The "fait was accompli'd" to become "prima facie'd" for the record, with the sentiments and presentiments of the attending Mennonites, father and sister, notwithstanding. A year and a half later, on September 13, 1857, the fruition of their union and the opening of this saga would begin with the birth of their only son, Milton Snavely Hershey. Some of the events that transpired before the birthdate of our prime subject are worth repeating, for he was shaped in the mold of his forebears, just as they were mightily influenced by the portentous events which befell them during their lifetimes.

The yesterdays of his progenitors and the ways in which they responded to the pressures in their lifetimes played a big part in fashioning Milton Snavely Hershey into the kind of person he was destined to become.

These were the yesterdays that shaped *them* and *him*.

*   *   *

Menno Simons (1496 to 1561), the Dutch-born evangelist and subsequent founder of the Mennonite Church, was the confluent center in the backgrounds of the Hershey and Snavely families which produced the child Milton S. Hershey. The upstream tracery is a study of progressive pairs. It began with a jointure of two families, the Hersheys and the Snavelys, and they, in turn, were ethnically and geographically native to the same general area comprised by the Northern Swiss Alps and the German Palatinate sector of Bavaria.

The point of origin for both families was indistinct prior to Menno Simons' appearance on the scene because the general regions of the German Palatinate and the Swiss Alps had been a veritable crossroads of military conflict for hundreds of years before and after his arrival. So, although the Hersheys were from the same general area in which Simons preached and travelled, like him they may have begun in some other place, for Simons was born in Witmarsun, in Friesland, a Netherlands province bordering the Zuider Zee.

The Swiss family Hirschi with their stag deer coat-of-arms had been inhabitants of the Berne Canton in the middle 1550's when Menno Simons had begun shaping his followers to a new creed. It would seem that they were waiting for him because his creedal text, although subsequently issued in Lubeck, Germany, was largely structured on many of the tenets of faith held by an elementary group called the Swiss Brethren.

Whatever the date of the conversion, the Hersheys joined with other Swiss Brethren to become his followers and thereafter they would be known as Mennonites. Meanwhile, across the border that divides Switzerland from Bavaria, the Snavely family had also begun to rally 'round the banner of the evangelistic Netherlander.

The jointure of Hersheys and Snavelys as practicing Mennonites awaited the appearance of yet another religious figure, the timeless Quaker, William Penn. In 1677, Penn was on one of several recruitment tours through the Palatinate, mostly centered in Emden, and he was proposing to start an emigre movement to the New World, where he would found a settlement that would be dedicated to religious freedom. The date of persuasion that marked the Snavely family's beginnings as members of the Mennonite faith is so profusely recorded that it, like the Hershey record, is profoundly indistinct. "Obscured" would be a better word.

It matters little whether the Snavelys were Quakers who became Mennonites, or Mennonites who stayed Mennonites, when they came to Lancaster County's Conestoga Valley in Pennsylvania. The Hersheys were already there in the persons of the Christian Hershey family which had arrived in September, 1717.

By 1796, one of Christian Hershey's great grandsons, named Isaac, had moved to the Derry Church settlement named for the Scotch Presbyterians who had begun their church there in 1724.

Isaac and his wife Anna built the limestone farmhouse that became the family homestead in 1826 (the cornerstone is inscribed, "Gebaut von Isaac und Anna Herschy, 1826"). Then Isaac and Anna had a son Jacob, who in turn married Nancy, the daughter of Christian and Susanna Hershey of Salisbury Township.

And so it was the cousins, Jacob and Nancy Hershey, who became the parents of Henry Hershey Hershey, the father of Milton Hershey. Although the Hershey and

Snavely families were nominally to become fellow travellers in a cortege under the standard of Menno Simons, a considerable span of time would pass before their paths would cross. Nevertheless, the century and a half of scrambling about which occupied both Mennonite families in the interim were as nothing to those that awaited the next confluence: the marriage of Henry Hershey Hershey and Veronica Buckwalter Snavely.

When Papa Abraham Snavely beheld the young Benedict who had claimed his daughter Fanny, he found solace in the reflection that this cane-carrying, buggy-whip dandy came of "good stock." The Hersheys, after all, had been men of the cloth, and both Christian and his elder son, Andrew, had been distinguished members of the Mennonite Church. Indeed, Andrew had been a bishop.

But Henry Hershey Hershey was something else.

He had some cardinal aims but none of them was church-inspired. Abe Snavely had been alternately refreshed and dismayed by the events which turned on elder daughter Mattie's initial refusal of Henry Hershey's marriage proposal, and younger daughter Fanny's subsequent acceptance of his next offer. But that was after HHH had made some thoughtful adjustments prior to making his second offer to a Snavely.

True, daughter Martha did like Henry Hershey better in the role of a prospective brother-in-law than she did as a husband, but not much. The love she felt for her younger sister constrained her to remain silent. Nevertheless, the Mennonite Snavelys, Abraham and daughter Mattie, were party to the wedding of Henry Hershey and daughter/sister Fanny. Then they gathered up their misgivings and returned to their farm near Lancaster.

The young couple set up housekeeping at The Hershey Homestead at Derry Church, and Henry readied himself for the spring plowing. He had resolved to follow in the footsteps of his ancestors, Grandpapa Isaac and Papa Jacob, the soil tillers who preceded him in tenure at the family homestead. Neither the intention of becoming a gentleman farmer nor the rental lease by which he eventually hoped to gain title to the family diggings at Derry Church lasted very long.

Henry H. Hershey was not a man of the soil and he wasn't much for putting down roots. Within a short span of five years, he was to let the farm "go back to seed," and his rental contract on the homestead fell into default and caused it to pass into other hands. Then Henry, his wife Fanny, and the three-and-a-half year old Milton were forced to move to a Lancaster farm near Nine Points, where they became tenants of a farm belonging to the three remaining members of the Snavely family, Fanny's sister Mattie and her two brothers, Abraham and Benjamin. In the year after they moved to this farm, a daughter, Sarena, was born.

The Lancaster site was expected to provide a new start for Henry Hershey and his little family, and he had high hopes for the Hershey Trout Farm and Nursery which he began there. He knew nothing about trout and even less about raising trees and shrubs so he failed again and moved on to greener pastures and other pursuits.

Thereafter, for the next forty years, the gadabout sire, Henry Hershey, became a career man in the business of chasing rainbows. His little family accompanied him on the first two of these moves, to western Pennsylvania and back again to Lancaster. But after that and beginning in the late 1860's, he was rarely seen in locales that were close to either his family or to his native soil. He was in and out of Philadelphia, Titusville, Denver, Chicago, New Orleans, Lancaster, and New York; and he was several times in each of these places on a peripatetic series of adventures that beckoned him to be off on a variety of quests.

Henry Hershey was a chronic and obsessive entrepreneur. He was constantly compelled to try new things. His perennial quests led him to the oil fields in Pennsylvania, the gold fields in Colorado, and to a variety of merchandising exploits in Chicago, New

Orleans and New York. Along the way he became a designer of vending machines, a canner of various fruit and vegetable juices, and an off-again, on-again innovator who sought to perfect the designs for a perpetual motion machine originated by a man named Wohlgast. A perpetual motion machine that almost worked, but never did.

Yet Henry Hershey kept trying. And he left his mark. Somehow, it always seemed that his symbol would be fixed only to failed experiments: to canned tomato juice (first ever) that exploded because he didn't add a fixative (about which he knew nothing) to prevent fermentation, and to vending dispensers that neither vended nor dispensed. But he came pretty close to improving the motion part of the perpetual motion machine for himself, for *he* was *always* in motion.

In 1904, when Henry Hershey passed to his reward, he left a legendary record that attested to his willingness to go anywhere and to try anything. He travelled along the scintillating arcs of endless rainbows. He composed a litany of failures and an unbroken string of defeats in a saga that bespeaks a lifetime spent in searching for elusive pots of gold that he never found and treasures he never held in his hand. Until the end, he was fated to remain unfulfilled and just as fully undaunted.

On September 13, 1857, his only son Milton was born in the Hershey family homestead at Derry Church in Dauphin County, Pennsylvania. Another forty years would pass and a whole new century would begin before son Milton and Papa Henry would be reunited on their natal soil. They would come back together after Milton regained title to the family homestead and they would begin again. They would put down new roots in the old grounds, and from this fresh beginning they would write the name of "Hershey" across the blazing arc of their own personal rainbow. In time, their name would be stamped on an unbelievable treasure that would extend from the slopes of Pat's Hill to the western fringes of the Lebanon/Lancaster border.

Henry Hershey lived to see only the early beams of the portending rainbow, but that would happen after his son brought his own pot of gold, a half-million dollars, to lend new color and substance to the sequestered Derry cornfields. Henry never saw the treasures that would pour forth from the chocolate barony his boy would establish. He never perfected the perpetual motion machine. But from within his tireless and endlessly optimistic soul, he passed along one priceless trait to his beloved son. Henceforth, it would be the common bond that marked Milton Snavely Hershey as a real chip off the block of Henry Hershey Hershey.

The son would make over the new village into a veritable Camelot of ambitious enterprise. He would fasten the dream of his rainbow arcs to the pots of gold that sprang from hard work and tenacity at either end. And he made sure that his ship would come in by building a snug harbor for it that continued to grow by staying in place.

It all began with the example that a restless, free-thinking, gadabout man named Henry Hershey had set for his son. And it was all contained in the meaning and the meter of the way he had lived his whole life.

He never stopped trying.

The Penny Bush

The chariot of the sun had burned its way across the copper sky of Crawford County, Pennsylvania, and the late morning hour of ten on that historic Wednesday, the first day of July 1863, brought with it more than the promise of heat. In a cluster of scrubby trees off to the side of the quarter-acre garden, little six year old Milton Hershey sought refuge in the shade.

Mama Fanny Hershey had gone back into the clapboard house to see about Sarena, his tiny sister. The tot was sickly, and the thought of her pained the little boy. Nevertheless, he welcomed the brief respite that Mama's absence afforded him. They had been working this scraggly patch of stringbeans and potatoes since shortly after sunrise. Nearly four hours of going down the rows pulling weeds had kept him in plain sight of his lace-capped Mama, who followed him, chopping at the hardened topsoil with a hoe. When she came back, she would be wearing the traditional sun bonnet she had brought along from the Nine Points home they had left back in Lancaster County. And when she returned, he would have to get back to work.

In the meantime, he sat in the shade and reflected on the sorry turn of events that had transpired in the past year. He had only a slight recollection of The Homestead, for they had left the ancestral seat when he was just past his third birthday. But the place to which they moved in nearby Nine Points came vividly to mind. When he turned five, Sarena was born, and after that the wanderlust had seized his father, Henry, and the elder Hershey had become almost like a stranger to them. Then Papa came back and brought them to this place.

The tow-headed, blue-eyed little gardener pulled a man-sized kerchief from his overall pocket and mopped his sweaty brows. It was almost two years since they had come here to this Godforsaken wilderness, and he had spent much of the time since their arrival wondering *why?*

Later he would get to know Papa better. And, on the basis of a wanderlust that in distant years would stir within his own breast, he would understand him better. But on that morning of Wednesday, July first, in 1863, he was a puzzled and unhappy child. He was with his parents and his little sister and yet, somehow, he felt like a stranger, alone in an alien land.

Mama and Papa had changed, but to a little boy just two months shy of his sixth birthday, some inner sense of optimism sustained the hope that one day his beloved parents would change again. On that day they would become the loving and kindly people that he recalled so fondly from his toddler days. But for the moment they were strained in their manner toward each other, and he knew why. *It was this place.*

He knew it only as Titusville, however, and aside from that, he knew only that there were no lush green hills, no rolling meadows filled with milch cows, and no barns filled with hay, no clear bubbling brooks, no root cellars packed with preserves and smokehouse hams. This barren upland plateau had only turgid streams glazed with greasy oil, and the horizon was dotted with the rickety stilettos of oil derricks pointed upward against a sky made gray-orange with smoke.

The siren song that had lured Papa Henry Hershey to this awful place had been compounded by a strange assortment of charms that were invisible to little Milton. And he neither knew nor cared to know anything about Colonel Edwin Drake, the erstwhile railroad conductor who had come to this place some five years earlier to capitalize on the greasy scum that befouled Oil Creek.

In 1859, the Hershey family had been together back at The Homestead in Derry Township. There were just the three of them then, for Sarena wasn't born until 1862. But out here in Crawford County, just forty miles southeast of Erie, Edwin Drake had chosen in 1859 to apply some innovative methods to exploiting new dimensions in lubricant and fuel sources. Colonel Edwin Drake saw beyond the days when whales could supply the expanding needs for oil, and he did something about it. Instead of skimming seepage oil from streams like Oil Creek, this far-sighted man drilled into a subterranean pool of the black, greasy stuff and pumped it into barrels.

Henry Hershey was a man with both eyes on the future, and the black stuff of Edwin Drake beckoned him. When the War between the States broke out in 1861, it

became apparent that vast new quantities of lubricants would be needed for the locomotives, the engines, the caissons and all the machineries of war. There weren't enough
whales or whalers, nor was there enough seepage-processed petroleum to fuel the lamps
of Union homes or to supply the blue-clad Federal troops afield. Colonel Edwin Drake's
"gushers" were summoned to gush full time. And the clarion call to an opportunist like
Henry H. Hershey came loud and clear from the oil fields of Titusville in 1862.

He gathered up his bride, his five year old son and his infant daughter and headed
for what he believed would be their treasure trove. It would later turn out to be the
beguiling song of a deceptive Lorelei, beckoning him to the rocks upon which his marriage would sustain a splintering crash. Thereafter, the close-knit togetherness of the
little Hershey family would be irreparably sundered.

To the small soon-to-be-six year old Milton, under a blazing sun in the scraggly
garden, none of this was known. But he did know that he hated the place, and he missed
the verdant farmlands, the well-stocked larders and the kindlier ways that prevailed
in the old Pennsylvania Dutch country from whence he had been dragged. His current
station simply reeked with an abundance of things he hated, and every time he looked
about him, he continued to wonder why? *Why* had they been brought to *this?*

They no longer trekked off to market with hams and preserves and baskets of fruits
and vegetables to mingle with the straw-hatted men and the sun-bonneted women who
gathered, ruddyfaced and smiling, in the place he called "back home." There, back in
Lancaster County, they had swapped some of the good things they had aplenty for the
wonderful sweets and the cloth the happy little family needed. Now, he sighed, they
were driven bone-tired and rock-hard to wrench from this sterile soil just enough of the
jaded string beans, the stringy carrots and the shrunken tomatoes and potatoes that
provided the Spartan fare that was their mealtime lot. No pies, no jams, no doughnuts
or hams . . . just string beans and pork fat, fried tomatoes and potatoes, mashed turnips
and stewed carrots. Of smiles there were too few; of laughter, there was none.

He pushed his wide-brimmed straw hat back on his head and looked up at the sun
and asked himself, "Why?"

Then he heard the back door creak and saw Mama coming back into the garden.
Her attention was diverted as she tied the ribbon bow beneath her chin to hold the sun
bonnet in place. A staccato of crunching sounds came from the side of the house to
announce the arrival of Henry Hershey in his buggy, followed by a two-seater with four
other men in it. The vehicles came to a halt and the men entered the house.

Mama Hershey lifted her eyes and looked up at the red-orange ball in the leaden
sky. She pushed her bonnet back on her head and waved to Milton, summoning him to
the house. He trundled off toward her as she shook her head. Then she looked down at
him and said gently, "It's too hot out here, Milton." Sighing, she tapped his shoulder
and led him inside the house. It was somewhat cooler inside, but not much. And he
knew that even the slightly cooler difference wouldn't last.

He took off his hat, and she motioned him toward the side room settee. It didn't
take any further prompting as he watched her scooping coal into the stove in prepa-
ration for the midday meal. This bit of action promised to make the kitchen hotter than
ever, and he was hot enough as it was.

The shades were down but the windows of the side room were open and fetid waftings
of oil-scented air drifted across the room. He sat down, leaned back on the settee in the
darkened room and tried to put these recent developments together. For a late morning
hour in midweek, these were strange goings-on. But he savored his escape from the
weeds and sun; whatever the reason for the parole, he welcomed it.

Mama had taken a pitcher of mint tea into the sitting room where her husband and
his companions were gathered. After the tin cups were filled, she brought him a cup

and withdrew to the kitchen to resume her cooking chores. The conversation from the five men gathered in the next room drifted over to him. The side door was slightly ajar, so he got up and opened it a bit more. Then he folded his straw hat and used it to cushion his head on the arm of the settee at the end nearest the open door. He leaned back and cocked an ear toward the excited talkers.

Someone named Lee had broken into Pennsylvania and the people with him—they called them "rebels"—had overrun a town called Gettysburg. There were some people on the Union side of the battle named Buford and Meade and Schimmelpfennig who were trying to fight off the terrible hordes of invaders. The name Schimmelpfennig sounded like "home folks," and the awful truth that his former home country was in danger soon became clear to him. The blue eyes widened as he heard that a hellion named Jeb Stuart had ridden roughshod through the village of Hanover. Then he remembered the visiting Snavelys on Mama's side of the family from those far distant days in Lancaster County. Some of them had come from Hanover.

He had no concept of miles or distance, but he recognized the compelling sounds of excitement and the tones that bespoke a rampant fear. Even to a small boy who had not yet arrived at his sixth birthday, the impact of realization was not late in arriving and it came on the wings of fear. Papa and his friends were very excited. And scared.

He tried to put the scraps of their conversation together, but most of it was beyond his ken. Key words like "the border" being crossed, and the death and pillage the "rebel" raiders were threatening to visit on his friends and his family were all too real. While he was puzzling over those fragments of fresh knowledge, one of the visitors from the adjoining room absented himself for a trip to the outhouse. A draft caused the open door to the parlor to slam shut, cutting off the eavesdropper's pipeline of information.

The youngster sat up on the settee. It was no use opening the door again. Someone would probably see him if he tried. That possibility was accompanied by the prospect of his being sent back into the garden and his weeding chores, Mama or no. That prospect forestalled any door opening. He got up, sidled past Mama in the kitchen and slipped through the door into the garden. Then he headed down the road toward the railway station at the west side of town.

He was familiar with the station and the lines coming into it, from Erie to the north and Pittsburgh to the south. But mostly he was acquainted with the trackside areas where he had come so often to gather pieces of coal spilled along the right-of-way. The homes and cook fires in the area burned coal, and he'd found he could get a penny a scuttle for gathering the solid black fuel. Mama and Papa didn't know about that. Indeed, they never would have allowed him to go anywhere near the dangerous tracks alone and unattended. But today he hadn't come to collect coal; he already had a jar at home under his bed with seventeen pennies collected from that effort. Today he wanted more news about Lee and Stuart and those awful rebels. He was a man of property and he meant to protect it.

There were quite a few other people in town who had the same idea. Dozens of oil field hands, farmers and townspeople were gathered outside the telegrapher's office at the train depot. The news about the rampaging rebels and the frightening prospects of invasion had brought the war home to this distant corner of northwestern Pennsylvania.

On his way to the depot, he had crossed paths with another sojourner, a fellow who sometimes helped Mama as a general handyman around the place, not just when she needed help, which seemed to be always, but when she could afford it, which was seldom. Nonetheless, the man Zeb was known to little Milton Hershey and they walked several hundred yards together before Zeb turned off to another home where his services were required. In transit, however, Milton managed to ask him how far it was to the border.

Zeb was no cosmopolitan font of information, but he had been to Erie and he knew that it was on the border. So, for lack of adequate description as to which border concerned the little Hershey boy, the handyman answered by giving him the distance to the only one with which he was personally acquainted.

"Forty miles," he said.

That was close! The youngster's eyes flew open wide, especially when he recalled that his family had gone further than that on trips to Philadelphia, back in the days when they lived at Nine Points. They'd made the trip during the hours between dawn and dusk, and Philadelphia had been much more than forty miles away.

The trip to the depot was rife with excitement, but it provided very little hard information. The names of Lee and Stuart came up again, and there was talk about cemeteries and seminaries; but apart from the scare quality deeply impressed on his consciousness, nothing really new was learned on the trip. A glance at the clock in the railroad station told him that he had less than ten minutes to scurry home in time for the noonday dinner bell.

However scant or distasteful the fare, a late arrival or a missed noonday meal meant the prospects of scoldings and/or pant-dusting reminders. He headed home.

During the return trip he travelled at a pace midway between a lope and a scurry. Perhaps his excitement was heightened by twin reminders provided by the physical input of exertion and the errant mental recollection that the border was only forty miles away. And Lee's rebels had crossed the border! To him, the disparate identities of the New York border and the Maryland boundary lines were unknown. Had Gertrude Stein propounded his belief in literary form, the extrapolation would have read: "A border is a border is a border . . ." He reached the same conclusion without the benefit of such literary guidance.

He had to do something, but what? The only things of worldly value he possessed were the seventeen pennies in a jar beneath his bed at home and his Sunday go-to-meeting clothes, and he'd outgrown those in the year since they had come to this awful place, without having worn them even once. No Mennonites other than his Mama had come to the oil fields.

Mama, Papa and Sarena, of course, were dear to him, but he was confounded by feelings of helplessness when he tried to puzzle out what he could do for them.

The pennies were all he had. The family didn't know about them because he'd earned the money by gathering coal from the forbidden grounds near the railroad tracks. What to do?

He reached the pump at the back of the house and got himself scrubbed and combed with just enough time to report with the punctuality required for his mealtime appearance. Papa and his friends were gone, so he and Mama ate alone. Then Mama hurried upstairs to tend little Sarena, but she had nothing further to say to him. He was, however, excused from the afternoon weed-pulling because of the extreme heat.

Nothing much happened for the rest of the day, but in the evening after supper he was again consigned to the shady hour chore of weed-pulling. Just before mealtime he had slipped into his room and retrieved the seventeen pennies from the jar beneath his bed. He wrapped them in a big red kerchief and slipped it into his pants pocket. But the burning bulge of the coins kept him from enjoying a supper of string beans and bacon, and sliced tomatoes. He was even served a rare treat of bread pudding, but the worrisome thoughts about concealed contraband kept his appetite out of tune.

He had found a matchbox and put his pennies in it. When he had weeded his way to a far corner of the garden some two hundred feet from the back door of the house, he picked out a berry bush in the fading twilight and buried his treasure beneath it.

Now, let 'em come! His treasure was secure and now he could give full attention to what he was going to do when those awful rebels came.

They didn't come, of course. But right up until Saturday afternoon when the church bells rang and the people began cheering, he was in a quandary about what to do next. On Saturday, July the Fourth, there was a double celebration. Lee and his rebels were retreating from the lost battle at Gettysburg and were headed back across the border. At the time, little Milton Hershey still didn't know they were back across the Maryland border and not the one nearby that worried him (the New York border), but that was a trifling detail. A border was a border, and they were back across it where they belonged.

Mama and Papa and Sarena were safe. So was his treasure trove of seventeen pennies, buried in a matchbox at the far end of the scrubby garden. He hurried out of the house to retrieve it.

He didn't have to cover his move. Mama was in the kitchen getting set for the Saturday gathering they had planned with some of Henry's oilfield friends. The garden had been fully divested of its weeds, and he headed for the distant bush where he had buried his trove. The time was just after nine in the morning.

By noontime, he came to the realization that bushes by twilight look different from bushes at midday. He had spent three back-breaking hours digging, and all he had to show for it was a collection of holes in the ground. His treasure was lost!

Mama noticed that he was disconsolate when he came back into the house for the noonday meal. Motherlike, she decided to have a word with him later on, when the press of midday duties had passed and she had time for it. She knew the signs and she also knew that quiet little six year old boys' problems are seldom dealt with in an offhand manner nor are they quickly resolved. Time begat patience and both were essential in such cases.

After lunch, young Milton added another dozen holes to the rim of the pock-marked garden's edge. Meanwhile, the house was beset by a bustle of activity when several of the neighboring families gathered to celebrate the Gettysburg victory and the nation's birthday. He slumped to the ground, nearly defeated by the sense of having lost something he couldn't complain about. The pennies were, after all, the ill-gotten gains of labors performed in forbidden territory along the railroad tracks.

But more than that. Those seventeen lost pennies represented more than an hour's pay for a full grown man of those days. It was, as he saw it, the beginning of his own personal fortune, and it was most important to him because of what he wanted to do with it, and that was to get Mama and Papa and little Sarena back home again.

Back to Nine Points and the smiling-eyed people, the lush green fields, the root cellars bursting with preserves, and window sills loaded down with cooling fruit pies. Back again, home, where Aunt Mattie and Uncle Abraham would be nearby, where Papa could start up his trout farm again, where Sarena would get well with the good Dr. Atlee attending her.

All these things were represented by what he had, almost unconsciously, been trying to do when he put the first several pennies together and started his nest egg. Now he would have to begin all over again! He gritted his teeth and, blue eyes flashing, he pounded his fist against the ground.

There was a resounding "crunch."

Something had broken under the impact of his hand. It didn't take long for him to realize what it was. In a matter of seconds, he had scooped away the earth and gathered up the smashed box and the seventeen pennies it contained. He hugged it to his chest and looked upward with an earnest impulse to say, "Thanks." Someone up there had made it possible, but his upward look didn't reach the skies.

Mama was standing over him and she was smiling.

She was instantly relieved by the happy look written all over him. She realized in a moment that whatever had been bothering him had passed. With the sage intuition

that comes only to mothers without any need for words, she smiled and spoke his name.
   "Milton."
   He got to his feet and pressed close to her.
   "Mama."
   She put a hand atop his tousled head and gathered him close with the other arm.
For a few unmeasurable moments, they clung to each other.
   The whole misery of a sorrowful year and the fearfulness of the past few days melted
away, and a feeling of warmth flooded the void between them. The eyes of both mother
and child were shining bright as they beheld each other. Only warm silence prevailed.

Before going back to the house, Milton handed over the smashed box of pennies. He began by asking her to keep them for him. Then he told her the whole story, confessing the forbidden way he had sought to earn the pennies and the things he wanted to do when he had earned enough of them. She said nothing. She was unable to speak.

In the twilight of the memorable fourth day of July in 1863, Mama, Papa, and their little son Milton were gathered beneath the wispy boughs of the stringy grape arbor behind their Titusville home. Mama told Papa about what Milton had done and what he had intended doing for them with his secret treasure.

Henry Hershey pulled at his stubbled chin and thought about it. Nothing was said at the moment but the story would have its effect. A few months later the little family of Hersheys found itself back in Nine Points in Lancaster County, where ruddyfaced people smiled, where pantries were fully stocked, and where Aunt Mattie and Uncle Abe were once again gathered around and about them.

There was no pot of gold awaiting Henry Hershey at the rainbow's end he sought in Titusville, Pennsylvania. But he found a real treasure there and it would last him all his life. Mama Hershey had her own feelings about these events, but she was not one for speaking out when the good and simple things of life were so evident.

In a moment of silence spent clasping her only son to her bosom in that pitiful garden near the grimy little village of Titusville, she had come home to a wonderful realization. She found she was proud to be the mother of the most unselfish person she would ever know. Down through the corridors of time in the next three-quarters of a century, she would hold fast to what she had learned. And she would live to share this feeling of deep appreciation with other thousands of people as yet unborn.

In a faraway place and under almost forgotten circumstances, Milton Hershey had begun showing signs of the kindness and unselfish concern that would move within him throughout his life. A few pennies in a crushed matchbox marked the beginning of a sentimental journey home, back to the bosom of the Hershey clan's native heath, where he would return again and yet again. Where, one day, he would write his name across the pages of history by building his own kind of openhanded homestead, always to be shared with his fellow man.

This is how it began—with a sad little boy and his treasure of seventeen tarnished bits of copper, gathered from beneath a penny bush.

Proofs and the Printers' Devil

In a tranquil valley a few miles outside of Lancaster on a farm watered by the spring-fed stream called Pequea Creek, the Reformed Mennonite, Sam Ernst, had established his domain. The big, gruff man in his plain clothes attire and broad-brimmed black hat was a miller by trade, but an enterprising one. On his streamfront property he had set up a grist mill and the barns back of the house were filled with farm produce and dairy cows, so he was pretty much of a farmer, too.

The house itself was divided between living quarters and the rooms in which he had set up a printing press and type cases. From there he engaged himself in the publishing and job printing businesses. His leading publication was *Der Waffenlose Waechter*, a pacifist newspaper in those days of the early 1870's. But Sam Ernst was not always a pacified man on any given day. His evening hours were spent giving singing lessons to students who also received some sharp pointers in discipline when he applied the stick to those who failed to pay attention.

When young Milton Hershey reached the age of twelve, he had already been weighed and found wanting as a scholar. So it was under Mama's guidance that he was ushered into first the presence and then the employ of miller, farmer, publisher, printer and singing teacher, Sam Ernst. He was to begin as a printers' devil (i.e., printers' apprentice) with an eye to becoming, at some future date, a full-fledged newspaperman. Having an earlier acquaintanceship with some of Ernst's singing pupils, the neophyte Hershey chose to forego the pleasures of vocal instruction from a short-tempered man who wielded a stick.

The immediate tasks of printers' devils are manifold, as young Hershey was to learn early in his career with the Ernst conglomerate. His first job was to clean up the press after each job was run and then to clean the type faces and return them to the font boxes in the job cases. The word "cases" proved to be plural because the newspaper *Der Waffenlose Waechter* was a mixed grille of German and English articles, so he had to "distribute" (replace the right letters in the right case boxes) in two languages. Earlier, at school, he hadn't exactly covered himself with glory in the matter of reading English right side up, and now he not only had to learn to read upside down, he had to do it in two languages.

The learning process was to come slowly, beginning with his first lesson in translation. This came about when he was told that *Der Waffenlose Waechter* meant "The Watchman without a Weapon," and this appeared to be a classical misnomer because the guy watching him ofttimes came into the shop still carrying his song director's stick.

All of which made the youngster nervous, and nervousness has never been a prime requisite for anyone being trained to perform type distribution or brain surgery. So, young Hershey repeatedly spilled type and Sam Ernst petulantly rearranged the devil's dandruff with the trusty stick by which he lent emphasis to instruction.

Each time the youngster spilled the type or placed it back in the wrong case boxes or failed to clean the press properly, Ernst would command his attention via the stick. Then he would point to the back door and consign young Hershey to the cow barn where the youngster could help with the milking chores until he regained his perspective. The routine did little to improve the diligence and dexterity of the lackadaisical lexicographer but it did bring him a good deal of knowledge about milk and the cows from whence it came.

The recognition of his innate clumsiness and a hearty distaste for printing work came early to young Milton Hershey, and so did the realization that he was entirely unfit for the trade. But the realization was accompanied by the hard fact that his parents had paid good money for the apprenticeship he was to serve under Sam Ernst. He was often to recollect the frequency with which Mama had reminded him, "A Hershey never quits," and that made his duty plain, although it did set him to wondering why she never said anything like that to Papa. She had, of course, but not within earshot.

Nevertheless, the young man stuck to his fonts and sticks and presses and stoically submitted to the role in which he had been cast as an ink-stained galley slave. Then there came a day when, by some miracle of coincidence, he was left alone in the shop and all the scheduled work had been completed. The press had been cleaned and the last stick of type had been distributed, so there was nothing pending for him to do.

He took a last wipe at the press and walked over to the job case and looked down into it. He picked up a capital "H" but it was a German font and too ornate, so he put it back. Then he went over to the English wood-type case they used for headlines, and he found a clean Gothic "H" somewhat more to his liking. So he armed himself with a compositor's stick and proceeded to set up the name "HERSHEY."

It looked good, even upside down.

He carried the stick of type over to the bench where he slid the line from the stick and tied it with string so the letters would stay together. Then he gathered up a sheaf of offal sheets (slips of paper cut off from another job), got an ink roller, and returned to the bench.

The tranquil hours of the summer afternoon passed as if by magic. He had locked up the block of type with his name on it and then passed the roller, wet with black ink, over it and hammered out a proof. The process had to be repeated several times, but when he finally got it right, he felt rewarded for the effort. It still looked good. Then he went over to the shelf where the colored inks were stored and got a packing box to stand on so he could reach them. This done, he returned to the bench and continued his proofing experiments by changing inks on the roller and hammering out proofs one after the other.

Blue ones, red ones, yellow ones . . . and then by essaying a kind of palette mixture, he found he could make green ones and brown and purple and orange ones, too. They all looked good, especially the red ones.

He had spread a display of different colored proofs on the bench top and stepped to the side of the block when twin disasters struck him. The first came as the roller in his left hand pushed a galley from the back of the bench where it tumbled off the edge and hit the floor. The galley contained the newly set front page type for tomorrow's *Der Waffenlose* et al., . . . but with the "furniture" broken loose, all the type had fallen apart to become a meaningless heap of fragments on the floor.

All of this happened just about ten seconds before the erudite publisher, Sam Ernst, made his appearance behind him.

"Vas gepps, Junga (What gives, youngster)?" he exclaimed.

The young printer's apprentice had no answer. But he silently gave praise for the fact that the "Watchman," true to his name, was this time without a weapon. There was much in the way of explosive verbacity, but it was all one way, despite the fact that the orator tended to alternate between German, English, and rage-garbled expletives. The words "Gedt oudt!" however came through with a pristine clarity that Shakespeare would have envied and Goethe could have lyricized.

He got out.

Force of habit led him to the cow barn, but it was still more than an hour until milking time. Once there, he threw off a spate of sulkiness and turned his thoughts to the immediate need for a workable decision. He could not stay here. That much was obvious and yet it was almost suppertime, and he was a good five miles from Mama and family. Chances were that Herr Ernst wouldn't be disposed to feed him that particular evening. But, on the other hand, chances of his getting a sound thrashing bordered between the extremes of good probability and those of near excellence.

He turned it over in his mind for a while, and the more he thought about it, the more he knew he had done something wrong. So he began slowly trudging back to the printshop to apologize. Once inside the door, he approached Ernst with his hat in hand and began trying to make amends.

The booming voice of the "Watchman" began all over again, and he grabbed the stripling by the scruff of the neck and ordered him to clean up the place and to begin gathering the multi-colored proofs. Then he was told, "Shtay out of the way undt be kvick aboudt it." To which was added the ever-popular, "Then you can gedt oudt, undt shtay oudt!"

It took nearly an hour for young Milton to clean up the proofs and place them in the neat pile Ernst had demanded. Meanwhile, the proprietor, still as angry as only a militant pacifist can get, went about the business of locking up one of the unbroken *Der Waffenlose* et al. forms and was running it on the press. The cleanup lad, in the process of gathering up the fragments of his errant work, had tucked away several of

the better-looking proofs in his pocket. Then he approached Ernst and said he was finished.

The bull-like countenance of the angry proprietor was still flaming crimson, and his eyes narrowed as he glared at his guilty apprentice. Then, without warning, he went over and put a match to the pile of papers that young Hershey had gathered and, without a word, grabbed him by the back of his neck and pulled some of the selected proofs from the culprit's jacket pocket. These were added to the flaming heap as young Hershey was propelled less than gently toward the door.

The heat was excessive and the roughness was unwarranted in the mind of the erstwhile printing trainee, but the size and temperature of the boiler was quite enough to suppress all thoughts of respondent comment on the part of the boilee. In an off-balance moment of struggling to maintain an upright stance while being shoved, he made a grab for his falling hat and missed. Whereupon it fell into the open maw of the moving press.

Singing Sam, the music teacher and editorial entrepreneur, was aghast. His "Watchman without a Weapon" form remained unharmed but now it was also bereft of motion, what with an errantly spilled hat now enmeshed in the works. It became quickly apparent that the multitudes of those waiting publication of *Der Waffenlose Waechter* would be subject to an unscheduled delay in getting its message. There was one exception—a hatless and ink-stained youngster who somehow didn't feel constrained to wait. He had gotten the message.

The door was open so he popped through it. He didn't look back. He really didn't need to. A momentary pall descended, but it didn't last more than a twinkling. Before the fugitive reached the main road some fifty yards distant, the vociferous miller, printer, farmer and singing teacher was bestowing voluminous invectives on the ambient country air that ranged from tones of cerulean hue to tones of deepest navy. All blue.

He had five miles to go and shame was his only travelling companion. The latent feelings of anger quickly subsided when his thoughts turned to the grim prospect of facing Mama. An uncomfortable chill splashed over him, and he just knew he was going to get another lecture about how *"a Hershey never quits."*

"Well," he thought to himself, "they do get fired."

The steps of the fourteen year old lad began slowly as he started on the road back to Nine Points to face a surprised and disappointed Mama. But after he had gone about half a mile, something made him change his pace. He had absently thrust his hand into the deep folds of his jacket pocket where he found a slip of paper. He withdrew it and saw that it was one of the experimental proofs he had been turning out moments before the heavy hand of Fate fetched him a memorable clout. Herr Ernst had missed some of the objectives of the search that had preceded his exercise in homegrown arson.

By the light of the late afternoon sun he looked at one of the still-wet ink proofs he had hammered out after making one of those queer blends of colors he had mixed. It was a strange reddish-brown and had an almost iridescent quality in the slanting rays of the late afternoon sunlight. There seemed to be glinting tones of changeability ranging from red to purple to brown as he turned the paper this way and that. Then he carefully folded the proof and put it back in his pocket.

The feeling of guilt began to subside a bit as young Milton Hershey trudged toward home and Mama. He thought to himself: My name looks good in print. And colors made it look even better.

He clutched the pocket with the proof in it, and a warm feeling swept over him.

"Someday," he said to himself, "I'll get my name in type again, and when I do, it's gonna be in *the color I want* and on *the paper I pick.*"

But for the moment he was faced with another problem. When he got home to Nine Points, Mama and Papa would be waiting for him, and they were going to be surprised to see him. Surprised, indeed they would be, but far from overjoyed. Try as he would, he couldn't come up with any sort of reasonable explanation to put the prospect of Mama's upcoming cross-examination to rest. When he arrived at the front gate, he saw Mama in the yard and a new wave of panic beset him. He still had no answer.

She had evidently seen him coming when he had been some distance down the road. Even though a hundred feet separated them, he could see the look of bewilderment in her eyes.

"Here I am," he announced, trying to get a spark of brightness into the greeting. He failed.

A moment of ominous silence descended, followed in turn by several moments of heavy quietude ranging from the quizzical to the deadly. Then Veronica (called Fanny) Buckwalter Snavely Hershey grimaced at her only son.

The stripling thought his mother was at a loss for words, and for the moment he was right. But down through the years to come, the erudite matron would find the words to fit this occasion. The chronicles all agree in the matter of Fanny Hershey's reticence, for she was a lady of few words.

The words she chose to mark son Milton's ejection from the Ernst conglomerate were, for the record, few in number. But like a record, she played them back to him a dozen times a year for the next half century.

This proved that she had another conversational attribute. When she found a topic worthy of her attention, she had a way of making her point.

"She could stick to the subject," Milton Hershey was to reflect in later years, adding, "and in this case, the subject she stuck to was *me.*"

Chapter II

~·~

The Dunkard's Disciple

In the summertime of 1872, a youthful Milton Hershey had come to a rather decisive bridge in the hectic career he was putting together. At that particular time he was looking forward to his fourteenth birthday, and he had very little behind him that would commend him to even the most optimistic employer. For the past six years, his education had been peripatetically pursued in no less than nine different geographic locations, and very little of academia had rubbed off on the transient scholar.

Up to that time, his most significant achievement in the annals of scholastic attendance had come when he was physically removed from the student body of the Nine Points seat of learning because of an untimely exposure to the oil of skunk. The erstwhile trapper of pelts had sought to earn some money after school by collecting the furs of sundry weasels, muskrats, and skunks. But the net consequence of this effort resulted only in his being sprinkled by the unseen mist with which one of his quarry had sprayed him while he was making the rounds.

This had marked the high point in his career as a student, for it proved to be the only time that he contributed anything of distinctive value to the classroom by virtue of his attendance. But as soon as his scholastic companions noted his presence, they threw him out.

Thereafter, Mama escorted him to the shop of publisher Sam Ernst, but the apprenticeship he served as a printer's devil became a matter of classic brevity, because, as he later put it, "I stunk as a printer, too."

So it came about, on one of those summer days following his ejection from the Ernst establishment, that Mama took young Milton to Royer's Confectionery and Ice Cream Parlor on West King Street in Lancaster. The boy had been there before, on happier occasions, for this was the realm where, in 1868, the famous Joe Royer, one of the leading merchants of sweetness, featured a wonderful new concoction know as the "ice cream soda." But on this particular occasion, he was not transported to the spot for purposes of imbibing the frothy stuff that emerged when ice cream, syrupy flavorings and carbonated soda water were mixed together.

Mama took him straight to the big man with the spotless white apron who ran the place and came directly to the point.

"Mr. Royer," she said, "my son wants to make candy."

The reply of Mr. Joseph R. Royer has not been recorded, but the respondent action taken that day was probably the most important episode in the professional career of Milton Snavely Hershey. He was hired to become an apprentice confectioner, a student of candy-making, if you will. And quite a student he would subsequently prove to be . . . to Mama, to Mr. Royer, and to all the world.

In the next five years, young Hershey learned a lot about making candy from Joe Royer, but that wasn't all he learned. For, in later life, he was destined to become, first a miniature copy of his mentor and later a much magnified version of what Joe Royer himself had set out to be.

Joseph R. Royer, the Lancaster confectioner, had been born on a family farm in Manheim Township, Lancaster County, on March 5, 1835. He was the son of Dunkard parents, Joseph Royer, father, and Catherine (Royer) Royer, mother. Not only were his parents both Royers, but both his maternal and paternal grandfathers were named Joseph Royer. And both families were members of the Dunkard Church in Manheim.

In the years prior to opening his Lancaster shop, the man Royer had compiled quite an odyssey of his own. He had risen to commissioned rank during the Civil War as a Quartermaster and he also managed to get himself captured by rebel soldiery and spent the last year of the war in Libby Prison as guest of the Confederacy. After being returned to the Union forces in a prisoner exchange, the war ended and thus he collected quite a bit of back pay upon discharge from the service.

Thereafter, Royer the entrepreneur swapped the money for surplus Union horseflesh and commenced to run up his personal holdings at a remarkable rate. Consequently, Joseph Royer was no novice in the field of capital ventures, and before coming on the scene in the City of Roses (Lancaster), he had already been an innkeeper, a postmaster, a hostler, and a man with a good grasp on the base equities and values from which new enterprises are sprung.

He would teach some of these values to his new charge Milton Hershey, but it would, however, take some time before *those lessons sank in.*

In 1869 with the savings built up from these ventures, Joseph Royer purchased the confectionery store of Charles Eden, located at the corner of Prince and West King Streets in Lancaster. His new business flourished and, after two years, he had enough money to buy the Whiteside property on West King Street. His first move was to rebuild the store, and with the renovations came some measure of notoriety, for he became the first Lancaster merchant with a plate glass front on his store. It was to this property that Mama Hershey brought her son Milton in 1872 to start his apprenticeship.

There was so much to learn. In fact, to young Hershey it seemed almost impossible for Mr. Royer to have learned so very much himself in the few short years in which he had been engaged in making candies, ice cream sundaes, sodas, and a whole host of other confectionery delights. The novice candymaker was amazed as, day after day, the head man achieved all sorts of wondrous combinations of sugars, fruits, berries, biscuits, creamcakes, and every sort of indescribable flavoring by alternately or endlessly beating, stirring, chopping, cooking, freezing, mixing or baking to produce exactly the tasteful quality he desired.

Every new flavoring potion was a source of excitement and curiosity, and every new mixture, blending, or cooking procedure was a new adventure. So young Milton Hershey began his career as an apprentice candymaker with the startling realization of what great fun it was to make things that were pleasing, first to his taste and then to the tastes of all the young and old folks around him.

This big realization came home to him on the first day of his apprenticeship as a student of candymaking under the tutelage of Joe Royer in Lancaster, and it became more important with each passing day of the nearly three-quarters of a century he was destined to devote to it.

One of the first things he learned was that everything had to be clean before one started making anything. And, by everything, Joe Royer meant the candymaker first, before routine inspections were given to utensils, ingredients, floors, walls, sinks, ceilings, and even the attire of those who either worked on, or merely passed through, the premises where candy or ice cream or cakes were going to be made. Everything and everyone was checked before anybody made anything in Mr. Joseph Royer's shop for Mr. Joseph Royer's customers.

"Crazy clean" is the way Pennsylvania Dutchmen typify it. Crazy *not to be clean* is the way Mr. Royer impressed it on the mind of his young pupil. Thereafter, everything the pupil did was done with almost fanatical devotion to cleanliness.

The second thing that Joe Royer emphasized to his young charge was the matter of giving honest portions of each item that was mixed and served. He insisted that if the measure was honest and always precisely the same, you would not only please a customer, you would keep him pleased and thereby keep him as a customer. Everything in honest measure always the same—that was the credo of Mr. Royer, and it became the scriptural guide for Milton Hershey.

He not only paid respectful adherence to the teachings; he maintained a lifelong posture of respect for the teacher. Throughout all the years of Milton Hershey's lifetime, he always referred to him as "Mr. Royer."

In the four years between 1872 and 1876, Milton Hershey learned his craft and learned it well before removing himself to Philadelphia in time to open his Spring Garden Street business for the great Centennial Exhibition. He memorized the flavorings derived from berries and beans, and barks and roots and seeds . . . the blackberry and strawberry, the coffee, the vanilla and chocolate . . . the sarsaparilla and birch and sassafras . . . the licorice and anise, and more. He began experimental taste trials and noted the peculiar ways in which cross blends and mixtures of these flavorings either went together or fought each other, and sometimes masked each other, without contributing anything more than wasteful expense.

Like Joe Royer, Milton Hershey wasn't on speaking terms with words like "synergistic," "compatible," "incompatible," etc. In his view, mixed flavorings either helped each other, hurt each other, or they simply erased each other. But both the teacher and the pupil were of virtuoso caliber when it came to their consummate skill as food-tasters. They would taste things and they could tell whether or not others would like the new flavors they tried in their experiments, and both earned a niche in confectionery history for their contributions. The teacher, Joe Royer, made his early breakthrough by being one of the first to serve up an ice cream soda in 1868.

The student made his contributions in somewhat greater measure at a later date.

In the files of anecdotes that refer to those days of Milton Hershey's apprenticeship with Joseph Royer, there are some which provide a kind of harbinger of things to come. When Hershey started his apprenticeship, he was told that he would be expected to work ten or twelve hours a day, so he worked fourteen or fifteen or sixteen. In fact, there were times when he would have to be ordered to quit because he was burning up too much precious gaslight after the last customers had gone.

He not only found that the work was more fun than anything else he'd ever done, but he also learned something about the work ethic as a consequence of an early question to his boss.

For one reason or another, he wanted to work a bit later one evening, so he asked Mr. Royer how late he, the boss, was going to work.

"Until I'm finished, Milton," he replied. "That's one of the rights that comes with being a proprietor. Nobody can tell you when to begin working or when to stop. You just come to realize when there's work to be done, you've got to start it early enough to finish before the customer shows up with his pennies. When you're your own boss, you don't work for any one person—you work for everyone who comes into your shop."

The matter of cleanliness in his work had been drilled into young Hershey before he began working for Joe Royer. Mama Hershey had seen to that. It was, in fact, an obsession for cleanliness that once caused Royer to remark that Hershey was always extra busy because he was so fussy about working with clean utensils. It seemed that whenever he wanted to combine two containers of bakery or confectionery ingredients, he poured the contents of each container into a clean third one. Royer thought this was unnecessary but said nothing, because he really admired the young Hershey's penchant for cleanliness.

He did, on several occasions, remark that Milton was twice as busy as necessary, mainly because he could dirty more dishes than anyone the veteran confectioner had ever known. This, too, became a Hershey trademark in later life, a life in which he left a trail of wall-to-wall used utensils throughout the kitchens of hotels, his own mansion, the homes of his friends, the amusement park stands, and virtually any spot where he managed to find ingredients, pots and pans, a few mixing bowls, and a sink.

Down through the years after Milton Hershey had departed the scene of his early instruction, a strange similarity seemed to stamp both the student and his tutor. Joseph Royer had been born into a devout family of Dunkard churchgoers and, while he held strictly to the tenets of the faith he inherited, he never became really active in church affairs or membership.

Milton Hershey had been born into a Mennonite family and he, too, practiced the creedal maxims of his parents, but he never showed up as a regular church attendant, nor did he seek any status as a member of a congregation.

Both the teacher and the student were men of peace, but both were blessed with quick flashes of high temper, and both were inquisitive, perennial inspector types. Hershey ofttimes recalled the way Joe Royer went tiptoeing about as he kept a glinty eye on the workings of his employees. This practice of spying on the ranks of those who might be lax in their duties was labelled in Pennsylvania Dutch as "schnuffling around," a phrase generally used to describe a hound, with the sniffing and snorting at the ground while it followed a culprit's trail. M.S. Hershey later picked up the quality of being a "schnuffler" too, but it remained for him to build his own establishment in which to "schnuffle."

Through the last years of the nineteenth century and on through the early decades of the twentieth century, Milton Hershey would look back and fondly recollect the lessons in cleanliness, honesty, carefulness and rock-hard dedication to work that he had learned from his respected mentor.

And in the last years of his long lifetime, when he looked out over the vast estates and community development that life as a confectioner had brought him, he paid a final tribute to the Lancaster County Dunkard who had made it all possible.

"I wanted to make candy," he said, "and Mr. Royer taught me how. Yes, and Mr. Royer *taught me good.*"

The record clearly indicates that Joseph Royer, like his protege Milton Hershey, wasn't given to the practice of handing out flowery compliments or verbal adulation. But the record also shows something else, and it has to do with the importance that succeeding generations of Royers showed in their preference for the name of Joseph.

As might be expected, Joseph R. Royer named one of his sons Joseph, too, and thus perpetuated the line. But tacit adulation came with the recorded fact that Joseph C. was Joseph R. Royer's *second* son.

He named his *first* son Milton.

Centennial Road

In the spring of 1876, young Milton Hershey was in his eighteenth year, approaching one of the many crossroads he would face in his life. The four-year apprenticeship to Joe Royer was about to be completed and he had to make a choice. He reasoned that it was time for him to strike out on his own.

He remembered that as a child he had stood by the gate in front of the Nine Points farmhouse, and looking down the lane to where it joined the big road, he had often asked himself, "Where does the big road go?" In subsequent years, after he learned that the big road wound its way eastward to the great city of Philadelphia, he decided that he would one day see the place for himself.

Now he could do it. He had learned his trade and, along with Aunt Mattie and Mama, he would have the money and the help he needed to set up a candy business of his own. According to the newspapers, this promised to be a very good year for starting a business in the Quaker City that William Penn had founded so long ago.

The youthful Milton Hershey was not destined to be alone when he went to the big city. He had been invited to stay with his Uncle Christian and Aunt Barbara until he got settled, but that turned out to be a visit he limited to one overnight stay. And he wasn't exactly penniless when he arrived in town because he had managed to save up a few dollars (about fifty) from his years of apprenticeship with Joe Royer, plus a "starter" loan his Aunt Mattie had given him, amounting to another one hundred and fifty dollars. It would be the first of many loans from the staunchest ally and the most silent partner he would ever have.

This initial move, therefore, was made in concert with an arrangement whereby he would make his start by "keeping things in the family," and that arrangement soon became routine. For the next twenty years, he would be almost solely dependent on family members for starter loans, keep-going loans, and sometimes even for his own personal shelter. But this practiced routine that began with the invitation from the Hershey side of the family (Uncle Christian and Aunt Barbara) was later sustained almost entirely by the distaff side of the family, the Snavelys. He would later reverse the procedure again, but that turnabout was still many years down the road.

He began that spring in Philadelphia by renting a small shop at 935 Spring Garden Street. His first helper was his little ten year old cousin, Stoner Snavely, the son of his Mama's brother, Uncle Abraham, and he set the youngster to work pulling taffy on a hook. Then after getting his first candy-cooking machinery set up, he rented a pushcart for street vending sales and set out for Fairmount Park.

In 1876, the City of Brotherly Love at the junction of the Schuylkill and Delaware Rivers was chosen as the site for a great international industrial exhibit. This early-day version of a world's fair was known throughout the United States and the rest of the world as the Great Centennial Exposition, being held on the one hundredth anniversary of the birth of the United States, and it was taking place in the city where the *Declaration of Independence* had been drawn by the founding fathers of the republic.

The big event attracted industrialists, showmen, and entrepreneurs from every corner of the civilized world, but the rental of exhibit space at the fair was beyond the reach of the towheaded candymaker from Lancaster. So Milton Hershey settled into a shop at 935 Spring Garden Street and began setting up the cooking and packaging facilities he would need as a base for his operations. As soon as he got his product line in motion with a variety of taffy and caramels and the like, he purchased a pushcart with an eye on the distant gates of the exposition.

Hershey was an avid newspaper reader, and he learned early that the theme of the Centennial Exhibit was to proclaim the wondrous powers of steam. So he gave some thought to sales promotion and began working out a way to make a connection between his line of candies and the newly developed steam energy that had become the talk of the times.

His first effort surfaced in an array of imaginative business cards that were posssibly holdovers from the clandestine color-proof experiments he had assayed during his short-lived apprenticeship with printer Sam Ernst. The cards featured the exposition's leading attraction, Machinery Hall, a building that was 1402 feet in length and 360 feet wide; but the rims and borders of the cards were festooned in splashes of color largely devoted to carnations, blue birds, rosebuds and butterflies. But that was merely the busy front of these exciting cards. The other side was something else. It read: *M.S. Hershey, Wholesale and Retail Confectioner.* Later, he capitalized on the Machinery Hall picture on the front of the cards by having that particular illustration captioned, *M.S. Hershey, Manufacturer of Pure Confections by Steam.*

There was a smack of prosaic license in the copy, of course, since there wasn't a steam pipe within a mile of the Spring Garden Street emporium when he started. But then he reasoned that the sellers of salt water taffy were making their products many more miles distant from the ocean's salty tides shown on their boxes than he was from the steam with which he claimed association. Later, when he added steam-driven mixers and cookers, he remarked that "the taffy people still don't put sea water in their stuff."

As June approached, he became keenly aware of The Exposition and that the grand opening of the gates was scheduled for the first of the month. He knew that exhibit space inside the fence was out of the question, so he thought about the fence and the gate and reasoned that everyone coming onto the grounds had to enter someplace. And when they were on the way to the exposition, they would still have all the spending money they had brought with them.

So Hershey had a giant billboard made, a sign that featured an enlarged view of the Machinery Hall exhibit and a design which prominently displayed the name of Hershey as the manufacturer of pure steam confections. Anyone looking at the sign would very likely conclude that the dynamic candymaker, Hershey, was not only a thoroughly modern Milton, but he was also doing business out of a pretty big shop.

The sign was covered and carted to the main gate of the exposition grounds a few days before the grand opening. Once there as a non-exhibitor with no rented site inside the fence, he was peremptorily denied admission both for the sign and for himself. He implied that he was negotiating for exhibit space, but the refusal stood, although the guards were quite impressed by the good grace with which he took the rebuff. Thereupon he asked for and gained permission to lean the sign, with its message concealed, against the fence some distance from the gate, ostensibly until such time as he could arrange for a suitable place inside the grounds. The sign itself was covered by a drab blanket of striped canvas that seemed to be badly faded, but it did conceal the artistic effort that lay beneath it.

The centennial summer was to slip away before a suitable place was found inside the grounds. In fact, the summer might have stretched into infinity with the same result. He never got a space inside the fence because he never tried to rent one. But all things considered, he managed to remain a good sport about the entire situation and the guards felt they had to commend him for that.

He hadn't rented the inside space because he couldn't afford it. On the other hand, he probably couldn't have afforded the fence space his sign and his "stand" occupied for those three months of the centennial summer either, but nobody asked him for that. He was the very model of a gracious, albeit highly motivated entrepreneur throughout the season in which he sold his wares in the most heavily trafficked area in the vicinity of the fairgrounds. The patience he displayed in the face of having been denied entrance for himself and his pushcart became a source of wonderment to all who beheld him.

Meanwhile, his "in-town" business began picking up to the point where he and little Stoner couldn't cook, pull, cut and wrap the taffy and caramel volumes they were selling. Mama came down in midsummer, and she brought along some more help in the form of a wizened, string bean of a man named Harry Lebkicher. This gaunt personage was a Civil War veteran who had been a former clerk in a Lancaster lumberyard. He didn't say much, but he impressed everyone, even Mama, with the amount of work he could do.

So then there were four of them—Milton, little Stoner, Mama, and the man they called Lebbie. Milton cooked and sold the candies and tended the pushcart stand at the Exposition fence. Little Stoner pulled taffy and acted as a general errand boy, while Mama cut and wrapped the taffies, and Lebbie acted as "the man in between." This called for his making deliveries, wrapping, cooking, cutting, or doing whatever else was to be done when Milton either wasn't around or was too busy to do it.

In later years, Hershey would say, "Lebbie was the only man I couldn't outwork. But I could out-talk him. Anybody could. He didn't say much, and when he did, he usually snapped at you."

Things were getting warm in Philadelphia by midsummer, and especially at The Exposition pushcart stand. The guards down the line scarcely noted it, but Hershey's little stand had added a new feature along the way. By July, he had a brightly striped awning that rested on poles he'd placed between the entrance gate (and the guards there) which pretty well obscured his venture from their view. He did seem to be doing a pretty good business, and the guards liked him, so even they felt good about that.

The men at the gate got quite a kick out of the towheaded young man who kept parading his pushcart to the same place each day and kept setting up shop there under that awning-shaded "stand" along the fence. It turned out not only to be a very hot summer, but for Milton Hershey, it proved to be a very busy one. By the end of August, none of the men at the gate had taken any interest in the awning he had placed alongside his pushcart to ward off the summer sun, and it was then that the laughter about the way they had treated him during the past months died down. This came about one day when a guard walked down to chat with him, only to find that he hadn't put up an awning—he had taken the canvas covering from a giant billboard and was doing business under an immense free sign.

Until then, Hershey had been too busy to laugh. Indeed, in the beginning, the merest trace of a smile would have given away the whole ploy whereby he was doing a land office business, on a spot where he had no license to sell and beneath a sign for which he had paid no rental.

Later, when the chill of winter came along, the memory of a mysterious awning in the heat of that centennial summer kept coming back to warm him.

Chapter III

~·~

Together They Stand

The Philadelphia venture grew too large for the 935 Spring Garden Street shop, so Hershey made arrangements to move into larger quarters at 925-927 Spring Garden Street just down the block. He and Mama rented a house at 1003 Ridge Avenue, but by that time they'd sent little Stoner back home to Lancaster, and Lebbie had taken up residence with them as a boarder.

After The Exposition closed, the taffy-making trio began paying more attention to over-the-counter sales in the store that fronted their little plant. The sun rose several hours after they started work each morning, and it had long since gone to rest before they turned in for the night, sometimes after midnight.

They tried everything in order to meet the gargantuan sugar bills that kept mounting. They kept the store open until nine, and then ten at night, for fear of missing a single customer. They even expanded their penny goods inventory to include fruit and nuts, and before long they whiled away the hours between taffy-cooking, pulling, and peddling by cranking away on an ice cream freezer. By summer of the second year, Hershey began staging special promotions. On several occasions he hired a German band to play on the sidewalk while he served the gathering crowds ice cream at five cents a plate.

But the penny goods were not rolling up enough profit to pay the bills, so Hershey introduced a line of fancy items. The first of these was a new kind of taffy called "caramel," and instead of selling so many for a penny, he had the temerity to charge a whole cent for the tissue-wrapped confections called "French Secrets." This titillating bit of sweetness came individually wrapped in tissue paper, and each one contained a risque motto of lyric poetry, which read, "Roses are red, violets are blue, sugar is sweet, and so are you." The identity of the original author of these lines was omitted, and so the name of another immortal bard was lost to history.

Sales and production kept increasing. Milton and Lebbie alternated between cooking, cutting and making pushcart deliveries, and Mama wrapped, sorted, boxed, and tended the busy store-front counter. They hired a team of boys to patrol the Shackamaxon district with baskets of candy on their arms, and they even started cooking and packaging a kind of mush, much like the Pennsylvania Dutch scrapple that was indigenous to their home county. This non-confectionery staple went over so well in the neighborhoods between Race Street and Vine Street that they had to open a wholesale office at 532 Linden Street.

Everything was up except profits. Somehow the increased volume of income couldn't keep pace with the mounting bills for materials—sugar, milk, flour, and flavorings. The outgo just seemed to treble every time their income doubled, but Milton Hershey took heart in the certain knowledge that he had gained public acceptance. Yet, somehow it seemed the harder they worked, the more they lost.

So it was time for him to go back to the family again, and first of all to Aunt Mattie. She had helped him make his start in Philadelphia with the one hundred and fifty dollars he needed to spark the venture, and since then, every few weeks, she had sent along parcels of food and flavorings for the business in the hope that this would give his spirits a lift. Whenever she had a few dollars, she sent them along too. But the time came when he needed more than a few dollars, so he turned to her again.

The appeal apparatus began in the fall of 1878, and it rang with prospects of good and bad. The good part of it came with Aunt Mattie herself, for she had chosen to visit her sister and nephew in Philadelphia so she could be there in person. The bad part of it came when Milton told her that he needed four hundred dollars, and she told him she didn't have that kind of money.

But she didn't put him off. She merely said, "We'll see," and then she sat down to think about it. The first thought that came to mind told her that brother Abraham, Milton's uncle, *had that kind of money* in a crock pot under his bed, where it wasn't doing any good. This was reason enough for her to write the following letter, dated November 30, 1878:

Dear friends,

This was a long Sunday for me but boy if you would of saw the pile of fine candy I had laying before me you would of saw a fine site. I was wishing all last weak for Rohrer and Soner to help to fold French Secrets with those fine papers. We are all well at present. Milt burnt his hand with hot candy but it is getting better. He had to get a man to work for him. I haven't much to say for I was looking all around the place. All seems to be right enough and all goes all right. So far he makes very fine candies and he also sells. And Harry puts it to the places. But the trouble is now he is in and scared. But he wants four hundred dollars more.

I don't know what to do. He must stop if he don't get it— for he don't get anything on trust. He is afraid if he don't get more money he must disappoint his customers and he don't want to do that. I must say things look favorable in the line of selling his goods. So you send him four hundred dollars the beginning of next month. The money I brought all went for sugar and will only do till next month. I said to them that we will sell the Ridge Avenue store if we possibly can before Christmas and they are agreed to sell. I don't want to talk in his favor but the people all like his candy and his taste pleases. Send it as soon as you can so that he knows what to do wether he can go on or not. Answer this as soon as you get this.

Love to you

M. Snavely

This kind of letter invites all sorts of interpretive explanation, but they won't be forthcoming in this tract. The bare facts are self-evident.

Milton Hershey needed help, and Aunt Mattie saw that he got it, and so did Uncle Abraham. This was the first in a regular calendar of exchanges that would read like a timetable across the coming span of years.

It was a family matter. Milton Hershey would go to the Hershey and Snavely families (mostly to the Snavelys) for help when he needed it, and when he couldn't go to them, they came to him. That was the way of things for the next several years and, strange to say, when he had to go outside the family for help in a later time, the man who helped him was already in the fold in 1878, in Philadelphia.

One of those not in the fold and not readily accessible to appeal was Papa, Henry Hershey. This was not so much because of any unwillingness on Henry's part. It was just that when people wanted him, they could never find him. But on the other hand, when Henry had a new idea, he could pop up anywhere. Anytime.

In 1881, Milton Hershey's paternal sire blew onto the scene like a breath of fresh air, but this only presaged an oncoming hurricane. He came with high hopes and a more than welcome willingness to help Milton sell his candies. From those who had no use for him (and their names were both Legion and mostly Snavely), there was criticism because they said he overcharged Milton by getting four dollars a week for his services. Later, when it no longer meant anything, his detractors would learn that he had forsaken a venture in New Orleans that had been paying him many times more than that. But Milton knew it all along.

Nevertheless, HHH came in like a storm and he came in trumpeting the oft-repeated slogan, "If you want to make big money, you gotta do things in a big way!"

He showed up with the advice and the way to do things, lacking only the means with which to do them. Down in New Orleans he had captured a fairly sizeable market for the HHH Medicated Cough Drops for which he had worked out his own secret recipe. When a latter-day pundit, seeking to ridicule him, asked for the secret ingredient in the not-so-tasty cough pellets, Henry Hershey replied with a sly wink, "castor oil."

This, of course, set up a round of queries by his detractors who wanted to know how that particular medicant helped soothe the throats of his lozenge buyers. To this he replied, winking again, "Anybody who takes cough drops with castor oil in them is *afraid* to cough."

He wasn't really serious about the cough drop stories. But he was a "tyger burning brite" with another idea about which he was quite serious. He had designed a combination showcase carton and vending machine for the cough drops that he said would be just the ticket for son Milton's candies. As for other ideas, he was like a Jimmy Durante of that day—*he had a million of 'em.* They ran the gamut from a whole new food preserving and processing system that would enable industry to package cereals, can tomatoes and various fruit juices, to a method of packing them in air-tight boxes and cans that would prevent spoilage. Everyone laughed. But perhaps that was because he always topped himself with a discourse on how he would turn farmers' fence wires into telephone lines, and about the new scheme he and a man named Wohlgast had devised for a perpetual motion machine.

His prophecies went aglimmering because of the leaden patina of wool-gathering he laid atop them. Nevertheless, his 1881 sojourn to help son Milton in Philadelphia was evocative of one hard fact: the patent office recorded the designs for a "Transportation and Exhibit Case" in the name of Milton S. Hershey, Patent No. 242,319, dated May 31, 1881.

The patent was awarded to son Milton. But the idea and the designs were the product of Henry H. Hershey's peculiar genius. Somehow, the innovative strain that would make a huge impression on the marketplace of the world in his son's name had not come to full bloom in Papa, the elder innovator. He was a wool-gatherer, and even if there had been a great demand for wool, he just couldn't get it in shape to sell. But he did help to shape someone who could.

Between the two of them, father and son, they hit on a scheme of putting things together, as they essayed to build wooden vending cabinets (not based on the patentable design) and to combine them with a mass marketing program for HHH Cough Drops.

This scheme turned out be about as crisp as a sponge pretzel, but they tried it anyway. And like all failures, it was quickly forgotten.

Thus, Uncle Abraham, who was not at that time an ardent member of the Henry Hershey Admiration Society, became the recipient of one of the few letters Milton Hershey ever wrote:

> *Dear Uncle,*
>
> *I hate to bother you but cannot well do without as it takes so much money. Just now Aunt Mattie wants you to send 600 dollars, and she will stand good for it. She just wants it till the first of the year. So you will greatly oblige me by sending it as soon as possible on Monday. Do not fail as it will save us some trouble.*
>
> > *Yr. Respct Nephew*
> > *Milt*

He got the money, but this letter initiated a less than cheerful exchange that continued for the better part of another year.

There was one prevailing sentiment shared by the participating correspondents at either end of this mailing campaign which exchanged the same old Philadelphia letters of request for fresh supplies of Lancaster money. Uncle Abraham in Lancaster was always good for a loan, but he critically noted that the frequency of the requests had begun accelerating from the moment his brother-in-law Henry H. Hershey came back on the scene.

Early in the year, January 27, 1881, Milton wrote to Uncle Abraham, saying,

> *I can not promise anything for the present, as we are trying to make things smaller and straighten things out a little and then we can tell you better.*

And he followed up by writing on February 18:

> *I am sorry we had to disapot you with the money as being very dull through this bad weather and other difficulties.*

This letter induced Aunt Mattie (who had been hopping back and forth between Lancaster and Philadelphia) into staying with them fulltime. She was determined to straighten out things and she was on the scene when Milton wrote again on March 7:

> *We cannot possible give the money back this spring for it is badly needed for the Cabinet business.*

Meanwhile, as Aunt Mattie saw it, the time had come to retrench. She began by suggesting that they get rid of Henry Hershey. But when Milton wouldn't hear of doing that, she stayed, but she fell silent. A week later, on the twenty-eighth of April, another letter came to:

Dear Uncle

*Aunt Martha arrived safe and we are all well. She wants
me to write to you if you could give or get her five hundred
dollars. For we are going to move in a rent of 20 dollars, a
month and have more room to make candies and fill our
cabinets, and our rent is now 86 dollars a month which is
a save of 66 dollars a month and we have a very good show
to sell our cabinets. So you see that by saving this much
money every month it counts up very much. Now I wish you
could get the money as I would like Marthia to stay down
until we have moved and she thinks it advisable to move
and is going to put 5 hundred dollars in it. So if you can
get it it will save her coming up. So let us know at once as
it is important.*

> *Your Respct Nephew*
> *M.S. Hershy*

Evidently the harried M.S. was at that time also hurried into dashing off the letter
so fast he'd dropped the letter "e" from his name. A few days later the pressure was
off and he did better. The check had arrived, and he wrote:

Dear Uncle

*Your letter and check came all right and we have moved
and are all fixed up in our own place, would like if you
could come down and see us.*

> *Yrs. Respectfly*
> *M.S. Hershey.*

The fresh funds gave the floundering firm a new breather, but it also stepped up
the pace to where the already overworked Milton Hershey had to work even longer and
harder. Then, aside from the physical strain, his Mama and Aunt Mattie began fussing
about getting rid of Papa to the point where they said flatly, "Either he goes or we do."

Milton loved both his parents and this final ultimatum cracked the last beam. He'd
borne up until the continual strain of indebtedness, along with twenty or more hours
a day of cooking, delivering, and running about in all kinds of weather got to him. He
collapsed and was confined to his bed for most of November and early December. Upon
his return just before Christmas, on the eighteenth of December, Aunt Mattie wrote
from the new business address, 1217 to 1225 Beach Street:

Dear friends,

*please excuse me for not writing sooner but I did not know
what to say till now. Milt say he can pay that bill till the
time is up, providing he gets his money in. I think he had
done well so far since he has been up in the summer. Us
three cant turn thousands of pounds of sugar out. There is
only us three that works. Business was rite good how it will
be after Chrismus I cant tell. I dont want to say too much
for the present. I think Milt has changed since he was sick.
I could say much. I dont think I will come home until February. We are all at present, hope you are the same and I
hope you all enjoy your Chrismus dinner and I wish you
all a hapy Chrismus. I will send you some candys if I can
some time. I wish Pap and his 2 boys could hich up and
come see us. And bring us 40 quarts of milk.*

The letter revealed more than the words spelled out, for it would appear that with three people working (Mama, Aunt Mattie and Harry Lebkicher), Milton was still not up to par, and Papa, wherever he was, had lost his membership in the table of organization.

Truth to tell, Henry Hershey had seen the hand that was writing his exit visa in big red letters on the wall. He had begun laying plans for his departure by late summer, but he had delayed shoving off until his boy had survived the illness that felled him. During the autumnal season of deep trial and scary illness, Mama and Aunt Mattie came to center stage. They fussed about, and between them and the faithful Lebbie, they saw to it that both Milton and the business were tended to around the clock.

Henry Hershey was no good at that sort of thing. He was not one for standing by or rallying around; he was a starter. Nevertheless, he hung around until Milton regained his feet and was able to show up for work. Then reluctantly he told the boy that he would be heading west.

The sight of the dispirited, skinny youth who climbed out of a sickbed that winter in Philadelphia had put the final crush on Henry Hershey. Now he *had* to get out. But before leaving, he managed a put-on smile and a cheerful word of his own.

"There's gold out there in the Rockies, my boy," he said, as brightly as he could manage. "I'll get on out there and make a claim. You just get well now, you hear?"

They hugged each other and Papa started for the door. Before leaving, he turned around.

"You get well, boy." Then he cocked his head and winked with that sly little smile and before he walked away he said, "We're gonna make it, boy. Just you and me. You'll see."

Then he was gone.

With Papa gone, Milton tried to get back into harness, and the records show still another flurry of letters between Philadelphia and Lancaster. Aunt Mattie pledged her word and Uncle Abe sent the checks on each occasion. Some latter-day rationales claim that Uncle Abe *had* to send the money because both he and Mattie (and possibly Mama Fanny) had been shareholders in their father Abraham's estate. And that estate included the farm from which Uncle Abe derived most of his income. That may be. Or it may just as well have been the consequence of Uncle Abe's having been a good-hearted Christian gentleman and a loving uncle in his own right.

Records never show the answers to questions like that. But the records do show that by February 1882, a tired and beaten Milton Hershey threw in the towel and left Philadelphia.

He was off for the golden west where he knew his Papa would be waiting for him.

A Choice of Arms

The first two weeks after Milton Hershey joined Papa Henry in Denver turned out to be something less than golden. Each day was spent in a fruitless search for the young candymaker who yearned to apply his expertise in the local trade. But from first light to dim dark, the bright-eyed young Easterner failed to impress the local tradesmen, most of whom treated candymaking as a sideline to their mainstay baking establishments. Nobody seemed to be in the confectionery business for the sake of making only candy.

Then, on a day which was later to prove quite memorable to young Hershey, a series of remarkable events occurred. And each of the incidents seemed to have been spun off an article reported in the headlines of *The Rocky Mountain News*. The banner head of the paper he was reading at breakfast one morning proclaimed

Jesse James Shot to
Death by Man Named Ford

Hershey, who had already noted that most of the local citizenry went about their business with six-shooters strapped to their hips, decided to arm himself. So, before embarking on another day of searching for employment, he dropped into a local hardware store and bought a Starr revolving pistol. It was later revealed that he bought no ammunition for the weapon, but he dismissed the seeming oversight by explaining that he "had bought the weapon so I would *look like* I was able to defend myself."

The rightness of his reasoning prevailed. Later that same day he found himself threatened by a "press gang" group of toughs who were dragooning footloose youngsters and trail derelicts for mining crew work in Leadville. Whoever it was that tried to drag young Milton Hershey off to forced labor in the mines eventually took their places in the long line of march consisting of those who were yet to learn that this tow-headed Pennsylvania Dutchman could not be easily roped in.

Fact is, he had pulled the weapon and bluffed his way out of what promised to be a rather nasty situation. In later years he would ofttimes be asked where he had found the courage to face down a bunch of heavily armed brutes when he was wielding only an empty weapon. His standard reply was quite simple and it was usually accompanied by a knowing smile.

"*I* knew it was empty," he'd say, "but *they* didn't."

Then he would add a rejoinder that seemed frequently to be tinged with an innate kind of smugness.

"You only bet on what *you* know. That's all you'll ever *need* to get the job done. But it usually helps when the other fellow *thinks* you know something he doesn't know, even if you don't."

So it would appear that even though the westward journey wound up being devoid of intrinsic gain, the education and the maturation of young Milton Hershey was still abuilding. Even though he was in the company of his highly mobile and ultra-transient sire, Papa Hershey.

A Choice of Work

At breakfast one morning, the Hersheys, father and son, began comparing notes on what the future held for them in Denver. Milton said that there just didn't seem to be any work for an experienced candyman in Denver. In all the places where he had applied for work the proprietors were hard put to keep their present help busy. Then Papa made a rather surprising point.

He told Milton he had been wrong in the way he had chosen to look for a job. First, he said, he should have gone to the established businesses in Denver that were catering to the local trade. Then he told him he had made a mistake when he tried to impress potential employers with the fact that he had completed journeyman training and that he had also operated his own business back in Philadelphia during The Centennial Exposition.

"The trade here in town doesn't amount to much," observed the elder Hershey. "When people come in here, they are either on their way through to some place else, or they are here to spend their time in the saloons and pleasure palaces after long days on the trail with cattle drives. Either that or they come in from hard times digging the mines, or panning the streams for precious metals.''

"Those people aren't thinking about sweets, Milton,'' pronounced Papa Henry. Then he added, "Besides that, you keep telling the people you expect to hire you that you know more about their business than they do. Nobody hires someone who could take over their business.''

Then he went on to tell his son about the mining camps and the cattle stations that dotted the surrounding countryside in all directions. He carefully detailed the workings of the hucksters who plied their trade by carrying wagonloads of goods to the miners and drovers on all sides of Denver. A lot of those goods were made in town. But they weren't sold in town.

Henry Hershey chose that moment to cite the example of Henry Brown, the former Ohio entrepreneur who was even then making his mark on Denver's (and Colorado's) annals of mercantile history. He mentioned how this man Brown had organized the trail delivery system that hauled Denver-made merchandise to the wagon trains carrying the incoming tides of westerly bound travellers.

He also noted that Henry Brown's cows were even then grazing on the plot of land the venturesome Ohioan had deeded to Colorado as a site for the state capitol. And, at the time of this exchange, the Hersheys, father and son, were gathered across the street from another triangular plot of ground where Henry Brown would make another kind of mark: that site would later become famous when the Brown Palace Hotel would arise to become one of the most luxurious hostelries on the American continent. (The Brown saga and the hotel were destined to reappear in the Milton Hershey chronicle again and again, but at much later dates.) For the moment, however, Papa Hershey seemed to have been a good deal more impressed by the fact that Henry Brown was even then insisting that Colorado's state capitol dome would be wrought from sheets of pure gold. And it would seem Henry Hershey's ideas were in solid consonance with Henry Brown's, for they both liked to project their plans *on the grand scale.*

It didn't take long for the message to sink in. In the next few days, Milton reorganized his approach and it wasn't long until he found a job with a Denver caramel maker. He zeroed in on the place by watching the flow of vending wagons making their way in and out of the city. Thus, he located the shop of a man tending his caramel cookers in a quiet corner of town, whereupon he went to his prospective employer with his papers from Joe Royer to show he had completed his candymaking apprenticeship. That was all. And that did it.

In the following weeks and months, he found that Papa had been right on another count, too. The vending wagons were doing their selling out on the trails, back in the distant hills, away from the glittering lights of Denver. But the equipment prices for setting up such a business came high. He knew he wouldn't be able to get together enough money to buy the cooking vessels and the wagons it would take to haul his wares to the places where they could be sold. Money may have been cheap, but he had virtually none of it. Equipment was high, and he couldn't afford it. So it was back to the taffy tubs and the caramel cookers for the former Pennsylvania candy man.

In a way, he was really an apprentice again, and as such, he began learning some new tricks in a trade he had once believed he had mastered.

In those dreary months of backbreaking labor, he learned quite a bit. Back in Philadelphia, he and Mama and Aunt Mattie had worked until the wee hours of late night and early morning to cook up the batches of caramels and sweets they would wrap to sell fresh next day. He had headed out each morning, first with a pushcart, and then later with a wagon, just so that he could get his wares into the hands of customers while they were still fresh and tasty. Later, after he had built up his delivery service to handle the retail trade through a series of confectionery stands and shops, this need for delivering fresh goods became even more imperative.

That was all changed in the Denver shop however, because most of the merchandise had to be cut, wrapped, and loaded into wagons that were heading out into the hinterlands. Nevertheless, the caramels they made tasted even fresher than the ones he had made and sold in Lancaster with Joe Royer and in Philadelphia. This, despite the fact that several weeks had sometimes passed between the time they were first cooked until they were delivered to the customers. This was when his backroom duties taught him how the extended shelf life had become a mainstay of the caramels his Denver employer concocted.

The answer was milk. His new mentor had learned early that whole fresh milk when added to the caramel base not only made the finished candies smoother and tastier, but it also helped them retain their flavor for a much longer time. This, of course, was vital when a good part of the merchandise was being delivered to people who were located several days or weeks distant from Denver, along outlying trails and in the mining camps. It also gave a sampling of the confectioner's wares to the incoming trade, quite a number of whom were on their way to Denver to eventually stay there.

Milton Hershey knew there was something special about the whole milk additive he had learned about during the days of his employment in the Denver caramel maker's shop. In subsequent years, this bit of knowledge would have a mighty impact on his efforts when he turned to making other and different confections.

During his brief sojourn in Denver in the early 1880's, young Milton Hershey came across quite a few things to think about. He had come to the town with an illusory idea of quick riches and then had turned to thoughts of ensuring his own protection. The notion of quick money quickly faded when he tried to overwhelm people with his vast background as a candymaker. Penniless experts were a dime a dozen, so he had had to step down a notch and work to learn more about a trade he thought he had mastered.

He had spent money for an empty gun, and he had wasted time on an even emptier notion that he "knew it all" when it came to candymaking. If that notion had had any validity, he would still have been in Philadelphia. But he wasn't in Philadelphia; he was in Denver, and he'd left one town a failure and bid fair to becoming another one in another place far from home.

On the wintry train ride across the plains and eastward to Chicago, he thought about it a lot. He had gone into a strange land unarmed and had essayed the choice of arming himself with a gun. But both the gun and the venture had proved to be empty, simply because he wasn't prepared to compete in that sort of arena.

"I am a candyman," he said to himself, "and one day I will be the best one around, but first I must learn more about it. Much more."

Milton Hershey had made his choice of arms. He had chosen to learn more about his chosen profession of candymaking before trying anything new.

It turned out to be a pretty good choice.

Chapter IV

～・～

Big Town—Bad Time

By the end of 1882, some of the golden promise of Denver had faded in the eyes of the Hersheys, father and son. Papa Henry found that schemes were a dime a dozen in this western El Dorado, be they golden, leaden, or whatever. And he was brought face to face with a cold reality that smote him several times daily: *a fellow had to eat.*

Son Milton had readjusted his sights, too, and after spending several months learning more of the rudiments of caramel-making, he'd come to pretty much the same conclusion. He knew he'd painted himself into a corner and he realized that life in The Mile High City required too much climbing. So he came to the hard conclusion that although the town had been great for men like Henry Brown, for a young Pennsylvania Dutch candyman it was too hard for a fledgling business, it was too expensive for supplies and equipment, and it was much too far from home.

Papa had lit out first in the fall of that year. He simply packed his woodworking tools in a chest, slung his personal garb into a carpet bag and boarded a train for Chicago. Milton stayed on until early winter and then he too quit his job and set out to rejoin Papa.

By the time the pair were reunited, Henry Hershey had set himself up in the carpentry business and was feverishly engaged in building bars for a myriad of saloons in the Windy City. In subsequent letters back to his prime funding sources in Lancaster (Mama, Aunt Mattie, and Uncle Abe), Milton carefully omitted the mention of any facts concerning either his father's schemes, or even his presence. The gist of some of his later recollections concerning this period seem to indicate that it may have been Papa himself who wrote the letters requesting sustenance and funds for a new business venture. If this was true, Papa had assiduously maintained his stance of anonymity, because he knew that with the Snavely family, he was about as popular as Casey had been in Mudville on the day *after* the game.

Nevertheless, the Hersheys, father and son, set up a new partnership. Part of the funding and maybe even most of the money for their new candymaking venture was derived from Henry Hershey's labors as a bar-building carpenter. So most of the street vending chores for their taffies and caramels were handled in the off-duty hours of the journeyman carpenter, inventor and rainbow chaser. Milton busied himself buying supplies, cooking the confections and then cutting and wrapping them for sale.

For however well they may have worked together, they still racked up another failure in the record time of less than three months. So Milton took off again, this time for New Orleans. Papa Henry stuck around long enough to settle the outstanding sugar bills and then followed. But before departing, Milton had time to reflect on the one most consistently recurring debacle that seemed to mark every one of his failed ventures. He was beset by the gnawing realization that he always managed to drown in a sea of bills for one item—sugar.

"One day," he resolved to himself, "I'm gonna *do something* about *that.*"

Meanwhile, Milton learned another valuable lesson. In a strange city, far from home and family, there was nowhere for a youngster to get credit. The very thought of going into a strange bank and asking a complete stranger for a loan sent chills up and down his spine.

On the train ride north, he made another resolution.

"One day," he again said to himself when he thought about those unapproachable bankers, "I'm gonna *do something about that, too.*"

Thus it was within five months that the Hershey and Son combine added another pair of failures to the sorrowful litanies of disaster they'd begun compiling in the previous summer.

Three failures in three of the noisily booming and yet the most promising cities on the continent, and all of them accomplished in less than half a calendar year. What was left to them? The very thought of Lancaster and home (particularly for Papa) with the Snavely clan was scarcely beckoning. Perhaps this was when Papa's earlier rejoinder came back, and they recalled what he had proclaimed so many times in years past.

"You gotta do things in a big way," were the incarnate words of HHH. They never were carved in rock, but they surely worked some sort of influence on the duo when it came time to choose their next port of call. It just *had* to be the biggest city on the continent—New York.

Henry Hershey was undeterred, possibly by the gambler's notion that his string of hard luck was about to end. Son Milton, on the other hand, was buoyed by the belief that the secrets in caramel-making he'd learned in Denver were way overdue to pay off their biggest dividends. Where else but in O. Henry's "Baghdad on the Hudson" could he find the "open Sesame" to the biggest treasure of them all?

So he resolved to make one stopover in Lancaster to secure his interior lines of attack. First, he would get Mama and Aunt Mattie to work with him, and they, in turn, would provide him with twin channels of conduit to Uncle Abe's savings jar.

He made the stopover and the plan worked. By spring of 1883, the trio of confectionery entrepreneurs made an appearance on the Manhattan scene. Papa was somewhere out of sight at the time, but Milton knew he'd be back. Whenever he needed them. Or whenever they needed him. The latter prospect, however, did not seem to be a likely one in the eyes of the long suffering Snavelys (Abraham and Mattie) and one former Snavely, Fanny Buckwalter Hershey. Nevertheless, with Papa *out of the picture* for the moment, *they decided to come back into it.*

*   *   *

The twenty-five year old young man from Hockersville got off the ferry in New York and found employment with the candymaking firm of Huyler and Company on the day of his arrival. Then he found a room with "kitchen privileges," an attractive rental feature which his new landlady was soon to regret bitterly, but one which proved to be right down his alley. Thereafter, the concierge of his new quarters was to lament the way her previously tidy kitchen and pantry area had been transformed into a back alley miniature of Armageddon.

Nevertheless, he worked by day for Huyler and cooked candy all night for himself. His landlady fumed 'round the clock for all to see. But this happened after she'd embarked on a series of attempts to evict him and long after she'd burned the sign that offered "kitchen privileges" as a rental gimmick.

She probably went to her grave wondering how such a nice, cleancut young man could invade her domestic life to a point where the breathable air was filled with steam and the very wallpaper reeked of sugar and spice and a number of other things she didn't think of as nice. But her wonderment stopped with one compelling judgment. For whatever good this dish-dirtying, steam-generating dervish from Pennsylvania had done, he'd also speeded up her passage time on the way to the grave.

He was forced to move, of course, but by the time he found new quarters for himself on West 43rd Street, he had already rented space for his taffy and caramel-making enterprise at 742 Sixth Avenue, between 42nd and 43rd Streets. This spot marked his original business site in Manhattan, sandwiched between a Chinese laundry on the uptown side and the Hippodrome Theater on the downtown side. He would continue to manufacture in this place for the duration of his stay in New York, but he would subsequently move his main storefront and storage warehouse to 441 West 42nd Street. Eventually, living quarters were set up at a midway point between both places at 265 West 43rd Street. But these quarters did not include "kitchen privileges" and they were later shared with Mama and Aunt Mattie.

By the fall of 1883, the permanent party membership of Hershey's Fine Candies (742 Sixth Avenue) numbered Milton, Mama, and Aunt Mattie. These were the front line troops in a cooking, vending, cutting, wrapping, and hustling delivery routine that featured caramels, taffies, fruit and nuts, cakes, and whatever else a mercurial Gotham clientele seemed likely to buy. Uncle Abe remained in Lancaster and became the recipient of continuous appeals for money. Each of these urgent requests was predicated on the everpresent and always-on-the-upswing need for sugar money. But some of the sweetness went out of the exchange when Uncle Abe learned that Papa was back on the scene.

Indeed, the ubiquitous HHH was on hand again. But instead of trying to "boss" things, he took his place in the disciplined line of march. While Mama and Aunt Mattie pulled the taffies, cut the caramels, and wrapped everything they sold, Milton cooked, peddled, and bought supplies for the feverishly engaged foursome. Papa showed up every morning and headed out with a basket of candies on his arm selling whatever they had made and given him to sell.

They started on cough drops again, and by the following year, Papa had graduated to driving a team of horses and making wholesale deliveries. This job was turned over to him after son Milton fell asleep at the reins one day at just the wrong time. As he dozed off, someone threw a firecracker between the legs of the unmatched team of glue factory rejects pulling the wagon. They bolted, and the somnolent entrepreneur was flung atop a pile of trash cans. When he righted himself, he began following a trail of foil-wrapped taffies, caramels, and cough drops down a series of side streets, alleyways, and finally Broadway.

Putting Papa behind the whiffletree didn't make much of a dramatic impact on the delivery scheme either. For when he made his way crosstown or uptown, the bearded sire would find little to command his full attention while driving the aged set of unmatched steeds. So he would take along a book to read.

One day he happened to be particularly engrossed in the pages of an unnamed classic as he was crossing the newly completed Brooklyn Bridge. Just as he departed from the span with no jumpers of the Steve Brodie persuasion to watch, he became so deeply absorbed in his reading that he accidentally knocked down a youngster playing on the street.

Henry Hershey was terrified, for whatever shortcomings he may have had, he leapt from the wagon and rushed to see if the child was seriously hurt. He wasn't. But by the time HHH caught up with the team of otherwise sluggish horses, they had meandered several blocks, and another representative group of Brooklyn natives had pilfered every last item from the wagon.

The child hadn't been hurt, but Henry had been. He lingered a while, still making his famous HHH cough drops and continuing to help in whatever way he could, but it wasn't enough. Mama, too, and Aunt Mattie, and the hard-driving and harder-driven Milton hung in there and tried to make a go of things.

But the overwhelming competition of the Smith Brothers with the HHH Cough Drops and the unalterable opposition of the Snavely sisters, Mama and Aunt Mattie, proved too much for Papa. When the end of 1884 came, Papa folded his carpenter tool chest, his cough drop formulas, and his precious books, and stole away into the night.

He would not be seen again in the company of his beloved son and his estranged wife for another fourteen years. He would keep on trying, of course, but he would do it on his own, and elsewhere. He had done his best to help both his beloved son and his disenchanted wife, but it hadn't been enough. Even when he did things their way. So he made his way out of town and west again.

*   *   *

So 1884 was tucked away in the books, but even with Papa gone, the debts kept piling up. Somehow it seemed to young Milton Hershey that the harder he worked, the deeper he got into debt. The whole thing was a puzzle to him. Everybody seemed to like what he made; his volume of sales kept climbing all the time.

His sales pitch to Uncle Abe back in Lancaster was wearing pretty thin, and the thrifty Mennonite patriarch began retrenching. He knew something had to be wrong. How could these people keep working harder and harder, selling more and more goods, and still keep losing more and more money? And the one big bugaboo in all the urgent notes exchanged was the constant shortage of money to pay sugar bills. Before Uncle Abe threw in the final demurrer in summer of 1885, his trenchant refusal was accompanied by the painful observation, "You people ought to own a sugar mill."

Neither the refusal nor the rejoinder was appreciated by young M.S. Nor were they ignored.

He was beaten and he knew it. There was a ten thousand dollar note due on equipment, and he'd exhausted his last line of credit with the sugar and flavoring supply houses. He was out of everything except bills.

Long before the leaves started to fall he would be out of business. So he decided to bid farewell to Mama and Aunt Mattie and pack them off to their home in Lancaster. He resolved to stay on awhile to retrieve whatever he could from the wreckage before the foreclosure notice fell due.

He had come to the big city after three successive failures in less than six months. Here he had managed to hang on for nearly three years, and he had built a business which was at its peak when the bubble burst. But he didn't waste any time wondering what had happened. He knew what had happened—he'd failed again. But he wondered why, . . . why had he failed? And why was it always the same story, and always so painfully true that he never seemed to have enough of the two things most needed in a candyman's surge for success.

Sugar and money.

Those were the two things he never could find in sufficient quantities, and he spent the last hours of his stay in Manhattan musing about these disasters and how he could deal with them.

"I'd better get back home and think about this," he said to himself. But he took no cheer from the idea that things would be any different in Lancaster.

Maybe the folks would help him again. Maybe he could make a go of it back where things were familiar and folks and scenes were friendlier. But the one biggest advantage the place afforded him was also the source of a most painful reminder. The folks would come around again, Mama and Aunt Mattie; he knew it for sure. And sooner or later, Uncle Abe would, too. But only on one condition—that Papa wouldn't be around to antagonize them with his schemes and his books. With him out of the picture, they were bound to rally 'round again. The very thought of Papa's not being there distressed young Milton.

Later, he said, "If I'd had a choice I would have gone west and joined Papa. But I didn't even know where he was. All I did know was that I had failed again, and he wasn't with me to cheer me up with another scheme and another adventure."

In a word, wherever Papa was, Milton missed him. One day, *he would do something about that, too.*

A Thorn Among Roses

September, 1885.

The day was damp and the Jersey City railway station was a steamy mixture of oily engine smells, perspiring passengers hurrying to their cars, and smoke from the chugging shift-locomotives in the yard.

A young man of middle height and clad in a threadbare suit slung a battered carpetbag onto the platform of a glistening wet passenger car and pulled himself aboard. Then he paused and pulled a big handerchief from his pocket and mopped his sweaty face. He sighed wearily; then he picked up the bag and made his way through the door to slump into the first seat on the right.

He leaned back and looked through the window, studying the nearby freight room where he had just checked in the last of his shopworn possessions. A bundle of oddments, consisting of different sized pots and pans and spoons and bowls, all consigned to his Lancaster destination "Collect." Every bit of it was pretty well worn, but all of it was spotlessly clean.

A wave of weariness swept over him as he looked at the window, studying the autumn rain. The tiny droplets collected into spattering streaks that came flashing down the pane. They looked like tears.

There may have been tears held back in his own blue eyes, but the bulldog chin was set and he wasn't about to let them spill over. A grimace flitted across the young man's ruddy countenance as he leaned back in the seat.

A scattering of other passengers had settled in their seats, a last "All aboard" sounded and the outer door behind him slammed shut. Then a whistle tooted, and with a few chugging snorts, the midday train made its struggling departure from the station.

The young man propped an arm on the window sill and leaned his chin on the half-opened palm of his hand as he peered through a window splashed with raindrops. When the car cleared the shed and headed out of the yard and through the dismal suburbs, his eyelids drooped and a moment of saddened reverie descended on him.

It had all begun yesterday morning in Milton Hershey's candy shop on Sixth Avenue in Manhattan, just above Forty-third Street. He had been watching the rain then, too, as he stood in the little shop that nestled between the Hippodrome Theater and the Chinese Hand Laundry. He had been there awaiting the arrival of a formerly pleasant machinery salesman, but when the man showed up he wasn't alone. Nor was he pleasant.

He came with some constables, and he came brandishing a neatly folded piece of paper. His harshness of attitude was paired with an insistent threat—"You either pay up, or else!" Somehow the memory of this man as a pleasant salesman had been washed away by the torrent of threats he poured on Milton Hershey that day.

There was no way he could pay the bills, so a wild tumult of sickening events had showered down on him in the hours that followed. Mama and Aunt Mattie had said goodbye just before noon, and Papa had already departed on the previous day. Just about the whole family knew the venture had failed, especially after Uncle Abraham had refused to send them any more money. So Mama and Aunt Mattie had headed back to Pennsylvania at this same hour on yesterday's train, and he had no idea where gypsy-like Papa had gone.

There had been so little time to get the bundles of pots and pans together and to summon the drayman. Then he spent all but his last few dollars for train fare, paying to have the furniture and utensils carted off to the Jersey City freight station.

By the time he got back to the store to get his clothing and recipe books, another constable from the sheriff's office was there. In a matter of moments, a big van arrived, and some rough-looking strangers began carrying off the mixers and candymaking machinery. They also took the cash box, but by that time it was quite empty.

They had allowed him to keep the recipes and paper files, so he spent most of the night sorting them and carefully placing each one in the one big wooden packing case they had left. The previous evening he had slept in the empty storeroom with his head propped on the carpetbag. He had filled the bag with his spare stockings and underwear, his most precious recipe formulas, and a few extra aprons. This was all that had been left to him following his eviction from the boarding house two days earlier. After that, he had slept in the storeroom at the rear of the shop.

He breakfasted on milk and some scraps of sugar and nuts from the leftovers that had sustained him for most of the week. This morning he had spent tugging and straining with the carpetbag and the heavy packing case to get them on the horsedrawn trolley, the ferry, and the final jitney he had been forced to hire.

At least that part of the struggle was over. The packing case with the pots and pans had been shipped by collect freight to his destination in Lancaster. The carpetbag with his collection of precious recipes was on the floor in front of him.

He watched the afternoon rain slash harder at the dingy window as the grayness slowly absorbed the reflections of flickering gaslight. He had failed again, but all that was behind him now.

Lancaster would be different.

By early evening, the sky was still gray but the rain had stopped falling as the train came into the rolling green countryside of rural Lancaster County. Young Milton Hershey sat up in his seat and shrugged off the torpor of the dull spate of events that had, until then, enfolded him.

He went back to the washroom and scrubbed his face and hands, neck and ears, to the burnished cleanliness that young Pennsylvania Dutch farmboys have impressed upon them from toddling days. A whisk broom from the carpetbag and the well-worn suit was brushed and the "pully" threads either tucked in or bitten off. Failure or no, he wanted to look at least clean and presentable in case anyone was waiting to meet him at the station.

The vestibule was empty as the train slowed, buckled and made its final stop. He hesitated a moment after the stop to survey the platform. He could see a lot of people, but he didn't recognize any of them.

He got off the train and walked along the platform. Then, at a slower pace, he went through the station still looking for someone to greet him. Finally he stepped through the door to the street and came to a halt, still halfway hoping he would see someone he knew. Anyone.

There was nobody. Nobody in the passing throngs, nobody amid the standers-by, and nobody among those sitting in or milling about the station. A jitney driver hailed him when he came to the street, but he fingered the few loose pennies in his pocket and hurried on. A strange feeling of emptiness settled over him as he left the dismal shadows of the station behind him and headed toward Queen Street. From there he

could walk out to Uncle Abraham's farm where there would at least be some members of the family on hand to welcome him.

A chilly drizzle set in, so he pulled up his suit collar and, carpetbag in hand, he hurried down the street through the evening mist. He was wondering about what he would say when he got back to the bosom of his family; then his thoughts returned to the freight goods he'd shipped in from Jersey City. They were probably already here. In any case, his first need was for enough money to get the working gear and cookware from the freight office.

Then he could set up a new business and start again. He'd done it before, right here in Lancaster. He would need help, of course, but here he had friends and family. In a week or two, he would have Mama and Aunt Mattie to help him with the cutting and wrapping. He'd even thought to pack enough labels and wrappers in with the utensils and some more in the packing case, so at least he wouldn't need money for printing for a while.

Head down, he paid no attention to the spray of drizzle and, lost in his thoughts of what to say when he arrived at the farmhouse, he didn't notice any passersby until he felt a tap on the shoulder. Then a big hand grasped him and a voice boomed at him.

"Milton!"

He turned to see the spare figure and the bright, hard eyes of Harry Lebkicher.

Nonplussed, he stopped and said, "Hello," but in a very subdued tone. Of all the people he could have run into, it had to be this one! The skinflint, sharp-tongued Harry Lebkicher, who had formerly been a clerk with him in his Philadelphia venture.

"What are you doing here?" asked the lanky one, in tones that smacked of an accusation.

"Oh," the young man replied, "I finished up in New York and thought I'd come back here and see how things are going."

"They ain't good," snapped Lebkicher, adding, "no money around."

This was typical of him, and young Hershey was not inclined to extend the conversation. He shifted the carpetbag and began to turn away. But then, not wanting to offend the older man, "I'm on my way to Uncle Abraham's," he said, implying that he was already late. "Are you still staying at the old place?"

The other man squinted, possibly struck by the inner recollection that he was not a person who was exactly welcome at Uncle Abraham's, nor at most places that had to do with Milton's family. He'd exchanged some pretty sharp words with just about every member of that clan in times gone by.

"Yeah," he said. "I'm back clerking at the lumber yard, and I live at the same boarding house across the street."

He retreated a step, as though to signal that Hershey was free to depart.

"Well," the younger man responded. Then momentarily ill at ease, "Mr. Leb, . . . er, . . . Harry, . . . they are expecting me. Can we get together, maybe tomorrow?"

"Well, whenever," came the laconic reply. "But now go on about your business."

He turned away, but something inside young Hershey told him to hold up a bit. Hershey took a hesitant step and put a hand on the older man's arm. "I may be starting in business again," he blurted, "right here in good old Lancaster. Would you be interested?"

"I don't know," came Lebkicher's short response. Then he looked up. "But you better be on your way. If you show up late for dinner at Uncle Abe's, you'll go to bed hungry."

"Can we talk later?"

The other man's face tightened, and the mist began to thicken into a real rainfall. "Maybe," in flat tones of dismissal. Then he flicked a hand, turned, and headed off down the street in the opposite direction.

The younger man picked up his bag and renewed the trek to the distant farmhouse. He spent most of his journey rehearsing the speech he would have to give when he was back on the scene with the Snavelys. This chance meeting with Harry Lebkicher had been so much like the dull chain of negative events that had befallen him recently that he quickly forgot it in favor of more pressing thoughts.

Darkness had descended, so the farmhouse lamps were lit when the sodden traveler went through the gate and knocked on the door. In former times he had walked right in, but now something made him hesitate. This time he knocked. When the sound died down, he heard the latch being lifted and Uncle Abe stood in the doorway with an oil lamp in his hand. When he held up the lamp to get a better look at the caller, Uncle Abe's jaw went slack.

"Oh," he said, "it's you."

That was all. He let the door stand ajar and stepped back. He looked at the sorry figure standing in the doorway, shook his head, and walked away.

A chilling sensation swept over young Hershey as he gripped the carpetbag and entered. He paused a moment before giving greeting.

"Hello, Uncle Abraham," he mumbled hesitantly. Then he stopped in the hallway. "Weren't you expecting me?"

The other man started to say something, but before he could get it out, a cherub-faced Aunt Carrie came into view. Her warmer greeting of, "Why, it's Milton," just barely covered the chill of the barely audible, "Yeah, I expected you," which Uncle Abe gritted through clenched teeth before he turned away.

The brief warmth of Aunt Carrie's greeting was quickly dispelled, and the chill of the next hour deepened as torrents of night rain pelted on the roof overhead. Perhaps, young Hershey thought, I have been premature. Maybe he shouldn't have begun by pushing at Uncle Abe about money for the freight goods and talking about setting up in business again. Perhaps that was why he had only been given a cup of tea and a few cookies instead of the usual meal. But for whatever the reason, the talk had only prompted Uncle Abe to repeat his earlier refusal by mail: *he would not put any more money into candymaking schemes of young Milton Hershey.* Nor would Aunt Mattie; and if he, Uncle Abe, had anything to do with it, neither would his sister Fanny, young Milton's mother.

"You and your Papa are *one of a kind,*" pronounced Uncle Abe. "All you Hersheys can think of is how to make easy money! What's the matter with farming?"

Milton had no answer for the farming question, but he had one for the word *"easy."* It stung like a whiplash, and his rejoinder had been to remind Uncle Abe how he had sweated over cookpots in Denver and Chicago, in Lancaster and Philadelphia, eighteen and twenty hours a day. And he added that the work had taken many more hours and much harder hours than Uncle Abe had ever spent in his fields and dairy barns.

"And what do you have to show for it? What does Henry, your father, have? Nothing! Why, you don't even know where he is!"

The younger Hershey stalked out angrily and was back on the road as the rain started to fall again. But thoughts of this unpleasant exchange kept drumming into his consciousness. The thoughts pelted him with the same monotonous impact of every drop of falling rain. It wasn't tepid rain by then, for with deep night, there came a penetrating chill not unlike the one he had felt before departing the hearthside where he was no longer welcome.

He went back into Lancaster and down the length of Queen Street and straight to the place where Harry Lebkicher had told him he could be found. It was past eleven, and he knew the old Civil War veteran was one of those early-to-bed and to-rise types, but he decided to chance it anyway. He realized it was the only way for him, now that

Uncle Abe had turned him out and Mama and Aunt Mattie were at a farm with distant friends. Heaven only knew where Papa was.

Lebkicher wasn't overjoyed to see him, but he didn't seem surprised when he invited Hershey up to the shabby confines of his tiny room. The sodden young man had little to say, but the sphinxlike clerk seemed to sense the fact that the younger one was not only wet, he was hungry. And more. When he arrived at the threshold where Lebkicher lived, he was more than lonely. He was all alone.

"C'mon, you," said the put-upon Harry, ushering him to the upstairs bath. "Get in the hot tub and I'll find you some dry clothes. Then come back to the room, but soak awhile first."

An order. But Milton Hershey obeyed and, strangely, some of the warmth that crept over him was not entirely the effect of the hot tub. In a half hour, after he'd scrubbed, soaked and bathed, he slipped into some extra long and very tight underwear, an old pair of work pants and a denim shirt that Harry brought him.

Back in the room, he was treated to a big bowl of beef stew and some still warm crab cakes and biscuits the host had gone out into the rain to get from a nearby tavern. There was even a glass of elderberry wine the lanky clerk had brought forth from a hiding place behind his shabby bureau.

The warmth of the food and the wine . . . the dry clothing and the tub he had recently departed . . . were all welcome. But neither one nor all of these were as warm as the feeling he gained from the silent show of concern that emanated from the old skinflint who had taken him in.

It was a warmth that gained in width and depth, and it came again in the morning when he awakened on the cot that Harry had set up for him. By that time, Lebkicher, who had risen earlier, announced that he had taken the freight receipts from Hershey's sodden pocket and then he had hustled down to the freight office and redeemed the consigned goods. By the time Hershey had awakened, his property was already in a loft at Joe Gable's livery stable, and a deal had been made to sublease a tiny shop space from the stableman.

"There," said Lebkicher, "is the place to set up a new candymaking business."

Hershey mumbled and bumbled about being grateful, but that only made Harry Lebkicher crotchety. Yet he was to mumble a great many more times about his gratitude in the days and weeks to come. And Harry Lebkicher would always get crotchety.

In the weeks that followed, it was Lebkicher's meager savings that went to buy the milk and the sugar, the spices and the flavorings, and even a brownish powder called chocolate that Hershey wanted to mix with milk for their new line of caramels.

By that time, Harry had quit his job as clerk in the lumber mill and was busy setting up machinery, hitching teams and delivering candy. The two of them kept plugging away until just before spring of 1887, when Mama and Aunt Mattie came back into the fold. This new start in the plant next to a stable on Church Street was to mark a humble but very significant turning point in Milton Hershey's career.

In time, Uncle Abe and some of the other Snavelys would warm up to the prospects of helping young Milton again. But hereafter, those ventures would not be jointly sponsored and exclusively shared with members of the family. Henry (called Harry) Lebkicher had broken the Gordian Knot, and the Hershey fortunes would no longer be tied to the apron strings or the purse strings of "the family." But Lebkicher did it by putting up every last cent he had squirreled away in a battered cigar box beneath his bed. Up until that time, Lebbie hadn't trusted banks, but he would later change his mind about that, too. In fact, a lot of things were due to change for all of them. But the hard-bitten skinflint would change the least of any of them.

Harry Lebkicher had only one condition, and he frequently stated it. "I want to be near the place where my money went." So Milton Hershey made sure that he was.

In the next two score years, Harry Lebkicher's nest egg went first into larger buildings in Lancaster, and then progressively into the tiny spot at Derry Church which was made over into the town of Hershey, and thereafter through a whole procession of new adventures, in Cuba and beyond. But wherever Hershey went, Lebbie went along, and the tiny nest egg grew and flourished and expanded, until it one day became a sizeable bit of equity. Lebbie never would have called it a fortune, but it was.

As the Lancaster caramel business grew and diversified, Lebbie was constantly in Milton Hershey's company. In the early days, he was frequently introduced by Hershey as "my secretary," but as the dreams they shared began to grow, so did his title. When the move was made to Derry Church in the early nineteen hundreds, he became known as "the works manager." But even this was changed in later years, when Milton Hershey would more and more frequently refer to him as "Harry Lebkicher, my good right hand."

From the chilly depths of that rainy night in Lancaster, back in 1885, the tiny nest egg and the big helping hand that started Milton Hershey on his way to heights he'd never dreamed of came from this strange man, Harry Lebkicher, the sharp-tongued, tobacco-stained, bearded skinflint who seemed to be everywhere at once. But whether he was playing the role of teamster, clerk, deliveryman, secretary, or bank director, he was always where Milton Hershey needed him.

Once upon a time in the City of Roses, there was a thorn—a sharp-tongued, no-nonsense man who had taken to his heart a rain-soaked and sadly disappointed youngster. He brought a forlorn failure of a young man in from the rain, and he fed and clothed him when even the members of his own family had turned him away. This was the man they came to call "Lebbie," the man who had made of his shabby little clerk's room and his big warm heart the very cornerstone of a dream that was yet to be built.

He stood alone in the ranks of those who helped and loved the man, Milton Hershey. Together they would make a great many unlikely dreams come true for so many people. And in doing so, this veritable thorn from the City of Roses earned the most precious title from Milton Hershey that he had ever been known to bestow:

"Harry Lebkicher, my Lebbie. My best friend."

Chapter V

~·~

The Magic Crystals

The holiday business was good in 1885, and by the beginning of 1886, things were looking up. At that time Aunt Mattie came back and joined the effort by supervising the three girls that Lebbie kept busy in the little factory. Then both Uncle Ben and Uncle Abe came back into the fold with semi-grudging financial assistance from Pequea and Nine Points. Meantime, Mama was back in harness again, cooking and wrapping goods in the candy kitchen. But Papa was elsewhere—out of sight.

Then a series of breaks came, and slowly but surely, Milton Hershey began to get the feeling that the tide had at last begun to turn in his favor. The turnabout came with the introduction of "Crystal A Caramels." Later, it would become a matter of record. The rosy future awaiting this new enterprise had really begun with the made-with-milk caramels, wrapped in tissue paper, and the box-packaged confections that first bore the "Crystal A" name.

The beginnings were made in the penny-a-piece items sold to the children who attended school next door to the tiny shop. But it wasn't long until the sales volume of boxes and cases began building up both acceptance and high demands from the wholesale and retail trades. In later life Milton Hershey recalled that his most rewarding years came in the period from 1886 until 1890. Yet he didn't spend all of this time merely making and selling products. He had Lebbie and Aunt Mattie overseeing those details. By then he was able to plan his ventures and to experiment with the kind of things he wanted to make and sell.

He also found time to get out in the community and mingle with other people—bankers and importers, commodity buyers (sugar and cocoa), and the like. Bit by bit, he was beginning to learn that no matter how hard he worked, there was no way he could build up a sizeable business by doing everything singlehandedly. Milton Hershey was later to recall those times as being "the point where I found myself."

It was quite a finding.

This introspection came after he realized that two of his greatest talents lay in fields he had hitherto regarded as being foreign to him. The first was directly tied to the experimental trials, the cookbook chemistry of trying and tasting new formula samples, and in developing production routines for novel kinds of confections and beverage flavors. The other was a matter of selecting the risks he had to take in order to expand and chart the kind of ventures he would launch. He had to learn not only *how to make money;* he had to learn *how to use it.*

In his earlier projects, he had obsessively pursued the belief that he could make his way by sheer backbreaking work. Then, one drop at a time, in a system not unlike the Chinese torture of water droplets between the eyes, it came to him. He had always worked in accordance with the Biblical remonstrance, "The laborer is worthy of his hire," but finally the time came when he realized that he wasn't meant to be a laborer in those particular vineyards. His mission was one of stewardship, and that meant it was one of owning and managing the ventures.

By this time, he had made friends with a Lancaster banker named Brenneman, and this is when he began to realize that money is made at both ends of the buying and selling cycles. There were times when he would come close to overrunning his headlights again in those days of the late eighties when he faced the problem of running short of funds to meet a bank note coming due. But on this particular occasion, instead of turning back to the family or trying to stall the banker, he went straight to Brenneman and told him the problem.

The upshot of the discussion led him to become acquainted with one of Brenneman's other contacts, an English importer named Decies. This man wound up giving him a trial order for caramels to be sent to Great Britain. Thereafter, he began exporting more and more of his wares overseas, while his banker friend stood by and watched as both the volume of trade and the promptness of note repayments were being accelerated. Meantime, all phases of the Lancaster Caramel Company were being enlarged in both the variety of goods made and sold, and expanded in the volume of goods being produced.

In the midst of the hubbub caused by increased demand, he began feeling the pressure for the additional capital required, so he was forced once again to turn to Aunt Mattie. The orders were being filled and the monies were due for them, particularly for the overseas shipment, but he still needed more equipment and ever greater material supplies to stay in business.

Along about that time, things were beginning to look pretty thin, and once again it seemed as though Uncles Abe and Ben were taking turns being out of town whenever he tried to see them. The last measurable and mortgageable collateral left to him at that moment was the home in which Aunt Mattie lived. She didn't hesitate. She put it on the block for him.

But then the crunch was on. The note had been secured by putting a lien against Aunt Mattie's property and when it came due, he didn't have the cash to pay it. So a very disconsolate Milton Hershey made his way toward the bank.

Oh, how he hated this!

He didn't have the thousand dollars to pay the note, and most galling of all, he had to face his friend Brenneman and tell him that Aunt Mattie's home was forfeit. Tortured by the thought, he pushed through the bank doors and headed for Brenneman's office. The door was open to him, but he later said that he felt like a man stepping off a scaffold when he passed through it. Brenneman sensed his arrival and looked up.

The bank president bounded from his chair and came around the desk with a smile on his face and with his hand outstretched.

Milton Hershey took the hand, but couldn't find enough voice to exchange greetings. Brenneman, happily effusive, led him to a chair.

"Good to see you," said the banker. "I knew you'd be in."

Fat chance of my staying away, Hershey thought to himself. Nevertheless he kept silent.

Brenneman seated himself. Then he picked up an envelope and pulled an outsize certificate from it.

"I guess you know about this," he said, still smiling as he pushed the folded paper toward Milton Hershey. "You have to sign the endorsement, of course, but I've already credited it to your account."

"Eh," said Hershey. He picked up the certificate and saw a picture of Queen Victoria, along with a pair of Britannic Lions rampant, framed in a field of golden swirls. It was a five hundred pound sterling note from the Bank of England, and the letter with it was from importer Decies.

The exchange rate didn't boggle M.S. Hershey. He knew that this lovely square of paper was worth almost $2,500 in American currency.

Brenneman was still smiling when Hershey looked at him.

"I figured you'd want to clear this," and he handed M.S. the note on Aunt Mattie's house. Then he continued, "I deposited the balance to your account. I hope this gives you enough capital to keep going for awhile."

It did. But not for long.

He needed a bigger plant, and he needed some new money, and that requirement was bigger than ever. Brenneman, his banker friend, said that this new need was going to be much too large for his Lancaster bank to handle. He said that Hershey would have to go to the big city for the kind of money he needed—and he could only get it in New York.

Hershey winced. The memory of New York was painful to him, and so was the reminder that he had left thousands of dollars in unpaid bills behind when he'd departed that financial Mecca some years earlier. He figured his chances were next to nil if he went back to Gotham in an effort to borrow money. But he was to change his mind in the next instant when his friend offered to go to the city with him to help plead his case. Bankers, all sentiment to the contrary aside, really do have friends, and in certain cases, they turn out to be other bankers in other cities.

The two men journeyed to New York, each of them beset by quite different emotions. Hershey was sure his prior record of debts in Gotham would do him in. Brenneman, by contrast, was a good deal more optimistic and even had expectations of being able to borrow more than that. Perhaps he could get as much as $150,000. Hershey knew he could use that much, and more. But he never figured to get it.

Both men were wrong. And both of them came away happy.

It has never been resolved as to whether their success was due to the blank check enthusiasm that Brenneman showed for his young friend from Lancaster, or whether it was the real promise of the young man himself with his sheaf of order forms and his packet of product samples. In any case, the Importers and Traders Bank of New York executives found the arguments persuasive, the orders really promising, and the Crystal A Caramels quite delicious. They did some back-of-the-hand muttering while munching on Crystal A's, and their final decision was absolutely astonishing.

They okayed a credit for a quarter million dollars.

Brenneman blinked. Hershey gulped. Then all parties concerned—bankers, borrower, and ombudsman—reached for some more Crystal A Caramels.

How sweet it was!

This proved to be the catalyst for Milton Hershey. With a bank loan for $250,000. the plant was built on South Queen Street, and he was off and running. But a good deal of the running was on the single track that led to and from New York City. By the time another few years had passed, he was in and out of the city on a regular basis, and the targets of his visits were twofold. The Importers and Traders Bank of New York was to continue financing the ever-rising tide of Hershey enterprises, and the long list of debtors M.S. had left behind in 1885 were speedily paid in full.

In the midst of all this bustle and change, Milton Hershey found himself face to face with one of the most surprising and hitherto unlikely prospects he had ever experienced. He was on the threshold of becoming a rich man.

"My goodness!" he was to recall later to one of his business associates. "One day I looked at the books, and there it was. There was over a hundred thousand dollars in the bank, and I didn't owe any of it."

He said that the cold realization of being suddenly wealthy stunned him so much that he couldn't even talk about it for several days. By the time he was ready to share the news with his family, he found himself smitten with one of the most heartbreaking moments of his life.

On April 14, 1894, after a few days of illness, his Aunt Mattie died. The books and balances were forgotten, and somehow on that day he felt poorer than he had ever been in his entire life.

When he composed himself and went back on the job, he remembered the chocolate-making machinery he had seen in the great Chicago Industrial Exhibit the previous year, and decided to diversify the output of the Lancaster plant. But he decided not to install the new equipment (from the J.M. Lehmann Company in Dresden, Germany) on the premises of the Lancaster Caramel Company. He set up an annex next door, and another in Philadelphia and these were the plants where he began making the coating chocolate and the breakfast cocoa that would launch him on so many new ventures.

Little by little, the chocolate end of the operations began commanding more and more of his time, and it wasn't long until it became the focus of virtually all his enthusiasm and effort. Meanwhile, the Lancaster Caramel Company continued mushrooming and it wasn't long until he felt the need for more help at the management level. Poor Lebbie was getting nervous, and he had all he could do to count the dollars coming in and the pennies going out.

Hershey brought in a big, redheaded, Catholic Scotsman named William F.R. Murrie from the Weaver Costello Company in Pittsburgh. He figured the dynamic Murrie would be just the man to handle the plant supervision and to keep the expansion of sales moving along at a high clip. Murrie did both, and since the contract business was growing, they were faced with increased volumes both in buying supplies and in selling products. So he realized the time had come for the company to add the services of a full-time lawyer.

Hershey's friend at the bank introduced him to a man who was Hershey's own neighbor (on South Queen Street), John Snyder, a non-collegiate lawyer who had passed the bar exam by "reading law," just as Abe Lincoln had done. In a short while, Snyder became a full member of the management team. He was later to help M.S. engineer the terms under which the Lancaster Caramel Company would be sold.

The focal point of all this activity in the City of Roses had begun as the Lancaster Caramel Company, but from its inception, it was known as Hershey's Lancaster Caramel Company, then Hershey's American Caramel Company. The latter name came into use in the early 1890's when the volume of out-of-town and overseas shipments grew by leaps and bounds.

He began in modest quarters at 335 Church Street, where his tiny shop was sandwiched between the Lion Brewery on one side and Sam Cox's carriage works on the other. When expansion began, he added a third and fourth floor to the original shop, and then by 1889, he bought out the carriage shop. Two years later he bought out the Lion Brewery's quarters; so then he owned just about half the block.

At the turn of the last decade of the nineteenth century, he'd also done something else. He had begun paying back the in-and-out funds he had been getting from Aunt Martha. Fact is, in 1890, the residential plot at 347 South Church Street was still in his Aunt Mattie's name, so on November 10, 1891, he bought this last remaining property from her. Subsequently, piece by piece, he acquired the rest of the footage on the block to the Midddle Street (now Howard Avenue) intersection, so by then he had a factory containing 450,000 square feet of floor space. This was when he began looking at other sites, both nearby and far afield.

Sometime in the late summer of 1891, he acquired three lots and a small factory in Mt. Joy that had formerly belonged to the Mount Joy Woolen Manufacturing Company. Along about this time, he considered setting up in New York City again, but then shrugged off the idea and began looking westward to expand the caramel business.

At that time, the American midwest and western territories were the private domains for Hershey's leading competitor, the National Caramel Company of St. Louis. On the basis of freight rates alone, the mid-America based plant had a terrific advantage; yet it didn't control the bigger markets that were building in the north central states. Chicago, "the city of broad shoulders," was booming, and so were some other metropolitan centers like Omaha, Milwaukee, Detroit, Cleveland, and Minneapolis.

Hershey saw Chicago as the hub of this giant spokewheel for caramel sales, so he called in cousin Frank Snavely. Frank was Uncle Benjamin's (Mama Fanny Snavely's brother) son, and he was engaged in running a Lancaster tanning business left to him and his brother Abraham. But Abraham had died, and since Benjamin (the father) had also passed on some years earlier, Milton Hershey offered Frank the management of the new plant to be opened in Chicago.

The tanning business was liquidated, and Frank Snavely and Milton Hershey were on their way west in a matter of days after the offer was first proposed. Along the way, Frank Snavely was briefed on the rudiments of what he was expected to do in the new business once a site was selected, staffed, and the new business was underway. Frank Snavely may have had some misgivings about his fitness to handle this charge, but the selection of the site and the organizational set-up were put in motion so swiftly that he scarcely had a chance to voice his doubts. A seven-story structure on Chicago's West Harrison Street was purchased, and while it was being fitted for production, Frank Snavely was brought back to Lancaster for intensive training. Two months later, he was made manager of the western branch of the Lancaster Caramel Company, a Chicago plant employing four hundred people, all of whom were put to work turning out Crystal A Caramels.

Some years later, when Frank Snavely was asked if he hadn't gone to Chicago with some doubts in his mind and if he hadn't been beset by fears that he might fail, he answered, "No."

"With Milt," he said, "you never had time to get scared. He lined up the work for you; then he stuck around just long enough to see if you could do it. Then he took off. From there on out, it was up to you. Sink or swim."

The bustling Milton Hershey then came east and picked up a young fledgling candymaker from Shillington (near Reading) named Abe Heilman, whom he installed in a brief training routine of production and sales at the Lancaster plant. Heilman wasn't on board very long either before he was sent back to his native soil in Berks County.

"M.S. called me in one day after I'd been in harness a while," Heilman later recounted,"and he told me I was going to be transferred to a new plant in Reading."

Glad to hear the news that he would be working in a place near his former home in Shillington, Heilman asked what his job would be.

"You're going to run it," M.S. replied.

Happy as he was to learn of his relocation, the news stunned the young man. He stumbled around a bit and started to explain that he didn't think he knew enough to be placed in charge of such a big operation. The plans called for a plant employing between four and five hundred workers.

"You'll learn,"said M.S. And the matter was closed.

Abe Heilman learned.

*   *   *

But the middle years of the 1890's were fraught with all kinds of change and adventure. They were the years in which the shy farmboy, Milton S. Hershey, came out of his cocoon and became a bright-winged butterfly. In this metamorphic stage from which he emerged as a walrus-mustached, cigar-smoking ramrod with diamond stickpin and cufflinks, he also began acting out the dual roles of field marshal and moderator.

Management came easy to him. He knew what he wanted, and he knew he could get his orders carried out because he knew how he wanted things done. But he had never shared decisions with anyone before, and now he found himself on a teeter-board between a big, redhaired Scotch Catholic and Democrat plant manager in Bill Murrie, and a staid Protestant Republican, the man he came to later call "the Judge," in the form of lawyer John Snyder.

With Lebbie putting in an incisive bid from the sidelines for the three of them to settle down, they perfected a classic balancing act.

Milton Hershey was the Chief of Staff. No doubt about that.

But he did stop, look and listen when his confreres advanced their own ideas; when sometimes, however infrequently, they chose to differ with him. With him there was never any personal preference pulled in from beyond the room where debates were conducted. His own personality defied labelling; even though he had a Mennonite background, he had no real attachment to any particular faith, and his political leanings were Republican, but only in the nominal sense. He belonged to no party, and when he voted, he voted. He didn't talk about *how*.

And so it came to pass that the long, long trail of debts, stupid risks, and debacles Milton Hershey had left behind in the last years of the eighteen hundreds were finally liquidated. He had changed his pace and lifted his sights from the work bench to the driver's seat. He began by learning that he was not only better at managing a team of gaited steeds in pulling a wagon instead of pushing it, but he also got a bead on the footnote item called "money." It was when he learned how to use this little item that he began to see money as an integral part of the machinery that helped to generate more goods. And more money.

Thereafter, fierce loyalties began taking shape in the personal bonds that were forged during this era. When Harry Lebkicher helped him get a new start by bailing him out with every cent of his meager life savings, Lebbie had registered an unwritten claim on him that would grow stronger and stronger down through the years. The odd couple, represented by the redhaired Scotch Democrat, sales chief Murrie, and the sanguine Republican Protestant Snyder, turned out to be an extremely well-matched set of trotters for the long road ahead. All three men would gain status and stature by filling positions of power and trust that would henceforth make them unassailable. Thereafter, this trio would head up the line of march that Milton Hershey would lead to an incredible string of successive victories.

They became the inner circle of friends and confidantes who were closest to Milton Hershey for the remainder of the course. Until the end of either their lifetimes or his, the circle remained unbroken.

It all began in the aftermath of frustations and deadening losses, with a young man's disconsolate return to the town where he had made his humble beginnings, in Lancaster. He had lost everything—his shop, his equipment, his capital, and even the faith of those nearest and dearest to him. Even the aunt and uncles who had backed him in one losing turn after another, had deserted him. And it had happened when his own father was nowhere to be found.

But he remembered what the Old Man had told him in years gone by: *Never stop trying*. And he found another old man, Harry Lebkicher, who believed in him enough to risk everything he had for one more chance for young Milton Hershey.

What happened after that in the brilliant future that opened up for old Lebbie and young Milton didn't come from the legerdemain of some prophetic crystal gazer. It came out of the penny-a-piece candies named Crystal A Caramels and from the open hands of some school children next door.

In the years to come, Milton Hershey would still remember the magic of Crystal A

Caramels and how they had opened the doors to a whole new world of fame and fortune.

And he would never forget the little school children next door whose tiny hands had turned the knob for him.

The Paladins of the Swiss Guard

In 1892, Milton Hershey began to experience some presentiments that made him restless. His Crystal A Caramels and the Lancaster Caramel Company were booming, and not the least of the business was coming from overseas orders.

At first, the onset of this newfound prosperity disturbed him. He would later recount the nervous feelings that swept over him on the day when he began checking the books and found that the profit balances were "more than a hundred thousand dollars in my favor."

The New York City bank loan was well on its way to being satisfied, and that would mean he'd then have an established credit for more than a quarter of a million dollars. Meantime, he'd been progressively buying up properties in Lancaster, he'd expanded the plant to where he now employed several hundred workers, and he'd come to the point where he debated about what to do next.

He had already enlarged Uncle Abe's farm and was beginning to build up the Holstein herds he figured to use as the mainstay of milk supplies for his caramels. But there were several other possible avenues of expansion open to him, and he'd begun debating which of them to study further before making any real move. Overseas the British Import House account opened for him by Decies several years earlier was coming back with more and more big orders for bulk caramels, and he was curious about that. He had begun by writing off the reason for this increased business in bulk confections to the natural consequence of a localized operation that would cut and wrap the retail merchandise to fit the needs of its own immediate custom. After all, *their* name and *their* labels were appearing on the candies they were selling to their customers. Nothing strange about that. But the growing demand for such vast quantities of his wares bothered him. How were these candies being labelled? How were they cut and wrapped, and what was being done to them to make them so popular?

One day he intended to go over there and see what was happening. Perhaps something in their packaging or retailing methods could be used back home in the States?

But these questions provided only half the impetus that kept pushing at him, urging him to make a trip overseas. From somewhere deep inside his inner soul, there was another innate kind of curiosity that kept working on him. He wanted to know more about milk and dairying. Perhaps it was a holdover from his boyhood days and the hours of sanctuary he'd found in the milking chores that Sam Ernst had consigned him to when he'd fallen into disfavor with the Pequea printer. Or it may have been the natural consequence of the milk base for his caramels that he'd learned about in Denver and which had, thereafter, provided the secret behind his Crystal A Caramel success.

Whatever the reason, he still wanted to learn more about milk, and this yearning tied in very comfortably with something else that kept coming to mind. He also wanted to visit the homeland of his Hirschi ancestors. This, of course, would mean a trip to Switzerland and, as he saw it, there was no better place to learn more about milk and dairy farming than in the native land of his forebears.

So off he went—first to England, and then to the continent and the Swiss valley from whence old Christian Hirschi had come some two hundred years and five generations earlier. No specific dates for arrivals and departures or lists of ships taken and places visited during his first trip ever became part of the documentary record. But the things he learned on this trip and the ways in which he used those lessons in later enterprises all became part of the recollections and reminiscences he would share with others in subsequent years.

Upon his arrival in England in the spring of 1892, he headed straight for his old friend Decies and for the English Midlands importing house that had become his best overseas customer. Nothing much survives on the printed record as the consequence of this fence-mending, goodwill tour, but in his later verbal accounts of the trip, he had something more to say.

"I'd been wondering about how they were handling the bulk caramels we'd been sending them for well over a year. The orders kept growing, and it just stuck in my mind that they must be doing something that I should know about. Of course, back home I'd figured that they were probably cutting up the slabs into different sized portions to fit the so-many-for-a-penny or shilling demands in their market. And I knew without being told that they were putting their own name and their own labels on the merchandise they were distributing to the retail trade.

"I was right about those things, of course," he later recounted, "but that wasn't all they were doing, and it was far from the most important thing I learned."

What he did learn was that they were cutting up his caramel slabs into bite-sized portions and dipping them into chocolate. And that was important. But it wasn't even mentioned at the time.

Then he departed from England and headed for the Swiss valley of Emmental, where the already darkened mirror of specific records became even murkier. Yet from his own verbal accounts and from the storied record of some other Americans travelling in Switzerland that same summer, some other events came to light.

He was in the Emmental district in late June 1892, according to his own recollections, and this locale was also to become part of still another account. His own reasons for being there were twofold; first, because the place was historically linked to his own family's past, and second, because it was located in a dairying sector. In fact, it still is primarily a dairying region.

In late June of that year, three American bankers also happened to be in the Emmental neighborhood where they had come to visit the dairy farms of one of their Swiss banker friends. They had just emerged from a barn when one of the visiting trio (who were also bankers) turned to his companions and pointed to a farm hand who had just passed by them.

"He looks familiar," the man observed.

His two companions turned to watch the retreating figure of a walrus-moustached and gallus-bibbed yokel who seemed to be sloshing about with two overfilled milk pails. But the stocky little guy looked just like any other Swiss farm hand they'd seen, so they merely nodded and kept on going.

The three were together again that evening on a train headed for Lucerne when the man who had pointed out the farm hand sat straight up in his seat.

"Hey, fellows, I've got it! I know who that guy was."

His companions looked at him, wondering what he was talking about.

"That guy back in the barn in Emmental," said the excited banker. "I know who he is. He's that Morton . . . no, . . . no, . . . Milton, yes, that's it, he's Milton Hershey, the guy from Lancaster. The one our bank gave the loan to. He makes caramels or something."

And so it had been.

They had seen no one other than Milton Hershey. But they had seen him in the overalls of a common dairyman because that's what he was at the time, and of course he had always been the great, great, great-grandson of a former Swiss dairyman. He'd come to this place within a stone's throw of his ancestral home, but not alone for the reason of making a sentimental journey.

He'd come back to learn the essentials of dairying, and particularly Swiss cheesemaking. And he'd begun by hiring himself out as a worker in the milk barn because he wanted to learn everything from the bottom up.

The men returned to New York where they learned that someone else at the bank had made the connection for Milton Hershey at the same Swiss farm they'd visited. What they didn't learn was that Milton Hershey had also stopped off and made some of his own arrangements prior to leaving New York. He had also seen Papa, Henry Hershey, and they'd discussed plans for going into the cheesemaking business (Swiss type, of course) upon Milton's return to America. Meanwhile, Henry Hershey would close his picture shop on the Bowery and head west to learn more about dairying and cheesemaking in the shadow of the Rockies.

Hence, Papa took off for Colorado shortly after son Milton departed for England and Switzerland. Another joined venture awaited their getting together again after each of them had learned more about the new business they proposed to share.

He learned a bit more about the milk business and cheesemaking before he left Switzerland on that trip, too. He also learned that quite a lot of milk from Swiss brown cows was going out to the larger cities of Switzerland (Basle, Geneva, Lucerne, Berne, et al.) and even across the borders to French and German candymakers. They, in turn, were using it with chocolate to make various confections.

On his return, he recalled feeling it was strange that not only were his caramels being dipped in chocolate by the English, but that Swiss milk wasn't only being used for table beverages, butter, and cheese, it was also being mixed into the ingredients of chocolate candies.

"Might be something to it," he thought, but by then he was back in America with other things on his mind.

He wanted to get into the cheesemaking business with Papa. With expansion plans for both the candymaking plant in Lancaster and the dairying business he would start back home in the Pennsylvania Dutch country, he would need some good, loyal men around him.

Some men with the timeless loyalty and gallantry demonstrated by the Swiss Guard who had defended Louis XVI and Marie Antoinette in the Tuilleries Palace during the French Revolution in 1792.

Some men who would become his own, personal Swiss Guard.

The Inner Circle

The two-part phase of Milton Hershey's activities both on the record and off the record really began with the events which transpired following his acquisition of the larger quarters he needed to deal with the increased volume for "Empire Caramels," the brand name under which his Crystal A confections were sold to the British trade.

By 1893, Hershey had plants going in Lancaster, Mt. Joy, Chicago, and Geneva, Illinois. He also, in that year, went back to Chicago for the Columbian Exposition, where he put in orders for chocolate "rolling" machinery, manufactured by the J.M. Lehmann Company in Dresden, Germany.

Meanwhile, Papa Henry Hershey had gone on the payroll of the Lancaster Caramel Company, and a monthly check for seventy-five dollars was being sent to him at various addresses (beginning with New York City, then Denver, and Greeley, Colorado) where he was ostensibly investigating the prospects for Hershey's entry into the cheesemaking business. In the meantime, Uncle Abraham's farm had been expanded and purchases of additional Holsteins were made. Whether the build-up of potential milk supplies was being increased in anticipation of growing demands for caramel making, or in order to get ready for a venture into the butter and cheese fields is not known. This expanded dairying complex did not appear to be connected with the newly founded Lancaster Chocolate Company because there was no milk being used by Hershey in chocolate-making at that time. But, in retrospect, one cannot be too sure of exactly what was going on in the mind of Milton Hershey when that buildup began.

In later years, he would be called a clairvoyant, and not without reason. Perhaps this is where it all began.

But the cheesemaking plans and the dairying buildup and even Papa's connection with Milton's activities between 1891 and 1894—all of these things were on the dark side of the ledger, and off the record, as was another trip to Europe to the English importers, to J.M. Lehmann in Dresden, and to Switzerland again.

Back in Lancaster a book was published in 1894 called *The Portrait and Biographical Record of Lancaster County*, in which Lancaster's most prominent businessmen were listed. The Chicago publisher described Milton Hershey as "the president of a caramel company that employed eight hundred hands in Lancaster, a hundred in Mt. Joy, a hundred in Geneva, Illinois, and four hundred in the Chicago factory."

It went on to state: "The original business was started in the city of Lancaster and it has grown to wonderful proportions. The machinery employed is of their own invention and is all covered by patents. Their trademark is 'Crystal A.' These goods are shipped to all parts of the world, including Japan, China, Australia and Europe. The capital stock is $600,000, all paid up, and they do over $1,000,000 worth of business per annum."

The same publication went on the record with another observation. "In conclusion it needs to be said only that Milton S. Hershey has made a complete success of life thus far and is the president of the largest concern of this kind in the world . . . and no man stands higher in business and social circles in the city of Lancaster than this man who has been crowned with success."

This glowing accolade came in a most active year for the bustling young, thirty-seven year old tycoon, and it should have made him very happy. But it did not. The first copies of the publication arrived in Lancaster on the fifteenth of April, 1894. Just one day prior to its arrival, his Aunt Martha, "Mattie" Snavely, died in the home she shared with Milton's mother at 222 South Queen Street.

The lady whom he was first to run to in times of need and moments of triumph had passed away without ever reading the lines about his "wonderful success." It was a disappointment that stayed with him for the rest of his life. Even though his closest friends continually assured him, "Aunt Mattie knew you were a success all along," it never comforted him. There are no comparisons to describe the depth of love one person holds for another, and in the heart of Milton Hershey, Aunt Mattie was special in a way that nobody else would ever understand. And that feeling, too, was off the record.

Before the end of 1897, he was off to Europe once more, and then he took another trip west. Back in Lancaster, while Murrie was building up sales for coating chocolate as well as for caramels, John Snyder had been kept busy negotiating contracts for a new plant in Reading and one other property that was close to Hershey's heart. He was buying up the old Hershey Homestead at Derry Church.

By the end of the year, another member was added to the inner circle of the Swiss Guard in the form of Abraham Heilman, a young man from a candymaking family in Shillington, Pennsylvania. Young Heilman was immediately placed in charge of the Reading plant near the corner of Eighth and Penn Streets, at a place formerly occupied by a dance hall known as Gross's Gardens.

Milton Hershey, meanwhile, had been getting a new slant on chocolate in Europe, and he'd also gone west, investigating the grasslands and the forage and fodder requirements that were needed for the goats and cows that would supply his new cheese-making venture. Papa was subliminally and quite anonymously involved in these machinations, too, but son Milton didn't make much noise about that in the presence of Mama or Uncle Abraham, both of whom were vitally engaged in corporate efforts and each of whom retained a Kelvin zero attitude toward Henry Hershey Hershey.

One of the off-the-record and yet best remembered episodes to occur in 1897 came in the late summer when plans were underway to start rebuilding the old Homestead at Derry Church. Milton Hershey acknowledged just how well this fit into his plans with an announcement that warmed the hearts of Mssrs. Lebkicher, Snyder, Murrie, and family members Mama and Uncle Abe. They knew he intended to translocate the chocolate business to another part of Lancaster because John Snyder was already in the midst of a deal to sell the caramel company.

But that wasn't what Milton Hershey wanted to talk about. It seems he'd learned about a certain kind of grass that grew in a sequestered region of the Rocky Mountains, and he figured it would grow well at the Derry Township site. He went on to tell his wide-eyed and almost traumatized listeners that this special grass would sustain the goats he was going to buy.

When asked, "What for?" he seemed to lapse into another world, and his answer came in a word that sounded like an invitation to lunch.

"Emmenthaler" he chirped.

The word, as it turned out, was the name for a cheese he was going to make. Not the Swiss kind, of course, but it would be a close second to the leader in a line of staple and exotic cheeses he would produce right in America.

The audience was less than enchanted with the announcement and the prospects for the new business venture. In their eyes, the cheesemaking projects were, at best, diversions. At worst, some of them thought Hershey's obsessive regard for the butter, cheese, and dairying fields could put the whole corporate enterprise in danger of jumping the track. Meanwhile, a Philadelphian named B.L. Kraft was getting started with some ideas of his own about cheesemaking in America, and he was not to be deterred in his plans. Three decades later, when the paths of Hershey and Kraft crossed, Hershey would recall the days when he had been dissuaded from being a nose-to-nose competitor with Kraft in the early days of cheese marketing in the United States.

Thus, in the years following the 1897 acquisition of the Derry Church property known as The Hershey Homestead, Milton Hershey's initial plans for the place were twofold. First, he wanted to get Mama and Papa together again in the place where they had set up housekeeping forty years earlier, the place where both he and Papa had been born. Second, it was the ideal spot to build up his dairying and cheesemaking business. Cows and goats would thrive on the lush grasses of the little valley watered by the Spring, Manada and Swatara Creeks.

He figured to build up and expand the chocolate business in or near Lancaster. He had several good reasons for that plan, too, the most vital of which concerned the need to retain the native Lancastrians who staffed the plant top to bottom, plus the fact that he wanted to be near his largest customer for chocolate coatings as represented by the caramel company he was negotiating to sell. There was the additional reason of not wanting to move the cumbersome rolling mills, macerators, and other heavy chocolate mixing machines, which had already travelled across the Atlantic from Dresden's J.M. Lehmann.

It wasn't until after several years had passed, just after the turn of the century that M.S. Hershey even entertained the thought of bringing any kind of chocolate works to the remote cornfields of the Derry Church area. Meantime, the suggestion to make this move would await the advice of someone else, and it would cause him to go back to Lancaster to pick up another member of his Swiss Guard.

A man named Harry Herr, a graduate civil engineer fresh out of Lehigh University, would be the man to whom Hershey turned. Lawyer John Snyder had already recommended that Herr be brought aboard to lay out the plans for a milk condensing plant at The Homestead site. The young engineer proved to be something of a Tartar, for the idea of working on plans for a milk farm, which, as he termed it, "was way out in the country somewhere, in a place I never heard of," and it was not too promising. Then, while he was trying to decide whether or not to handle the job at all, Hershey came back again.

This time, the impatient, forty-five year old candymaker wanted him to lay out a factory, a town complete with streets and houses, as well as a grand design for a trolley line. He said that these trolley lines would not only bring in the people from surrounding areas to work in the plant, but they would also bring in the milk from the farms— north, east, south, and west—all of which would serve as the base ingredient of such diverse things as cheese, chocolate, ice cream, and butter. And Herr was told to hurry.

The demand was phrased in such unreasonable terms it bordered on lunacy. Consequently, the Tartar Herr called a halt to his demurrers and accepted the charge on the spot.

In less than two months, the basic ground plans had been sketched out and the original sixty-acre plot of the Hershey holdings in Derry Church had been expanded by another fifteen hundred acres of farmland. Within that short time, Mssrs. Herr and Snyder went to Harrisburg and were granted a right-of-way to construct a Hummelstown-Palmyra Street Railway Company. The plans for a trolley line had been approved on the basis of "connecting two Pennsylvania communities, Hummelstown and Palmyra, with a series of more than a dozen in-between 'stop-offs' at a remote community called Derry Church."

This was the same Derry Church about which Harry Herr had said three months earlier, "I never heard of it," a place with a half dozen farms, one tavern, and a post office, a place where transportation would be needed to a plant site employing hundreds of people in order to serve a village that contained several scores of workers' dwellings. None of the workers had as yet been hired, and none of the buildings, either plant or dwellings, had as yet been built, all of which, even at this late date, might rank between the classic and the epic in the annals of contrived omissions and oversight.

Nevertheless, Mssrs. Herr, Snyder, and Hershey had asked for a right-of-way, and they got it. They set about the business of filling in the blanks, of plants and houses and streets to be built and workers to be hired.

M.S. Hershey resumed his three-fold search for new fields to conquer in the realms of dairying and candymaking, plus the more finite business of adding new members to his Swiss Guard.

*   *   *

In the latter part of the 1890's, Milton Hershey took on more new projects. In 1897 he purchased the Derry Church area Homestead from Levi Gingrich and initiated plans to sell the Lancaster Caramel Company.

Then came the decision to move the neophyte chocolate company from Lancaster to Derry Church. This move would enable him to combine his milk and dairying ventures with a chocolate-making business he planned to change and enlarge. All of these new operations would go into the Derry Church area surrounding The Homestead. Taken together, his checkerboard plans would impose an overall need for new barns, new plants, a new town with brand new workers' homes built on new streets, new railroad sidings along the Philadelphia and Reading Lines, and a whole new street railway system.

Meanwhile, lawyer John Snyder and general manager and sales chief Bill Murrie were hammering away to wind up affairs in Lancaster. That particular plan called for M.S. Hershey to take half of his million dollar sales proceeds for Lancaster Caramel in cash, and the other half in stock equities and/or notes. The liquid part of the buyout money was to be used to build up the Derry Church complex, and the stock/note equity would help him secure the sales contract which would call for his Hershey Chocolate Company to be the sole supplier of coating chocolate to the new American Caramel Company. He later referred to this move as a "daddy-longlegs exercise, in which I kept one foot on first base while I stole second." This sounded like a neat trick and turned out to be both neater and trickier than it sounded.

In the midst of all this activity, Frank Snavely was running things in Chicago, Abe Heilman was bossing the Reading plant, Uncle Abe, Mama, and young Bowman Snavely were watching the store in Lancaster and Mt. Joy, while Harry Herr was drawing up the myriad plans for the big move.

Momentarily, at the turn of the century, his flitting attention came to rest on a pair of youngsters, one in Lancaster and one in Donegal Township. The Lancaster lad was a neighbor's son named Charles Ziegler, a youth who lived near his Queen Street home and who had done an exemplary job of trimming hedges and mowing lawns during the summer and who'd kept the pavements and driveways clear of winter snow. The other youngster was his cousin, Ezra Hershey, the son of Uncle Elias H. Hershey. Neither of these youngsters would rise to prominence in the Hershey hierarchy until another score of years had passed, but they'd been picked early and would ultimately become members of the inner circle he called his Swiss Guard.

This combination of dervish-like multiples in business activities coupled with the occlusive buildups of his personal staff looked like a sure and certain mixture of gunpowder and sparks. He seemed obsessed with the idea of breaking every rule that had ever been written on how to build a business or to run one.

He was doing too many things at the same time and, worse than that, he was placing every one of the separate ventures into the hands of a management staff made up of friends and family members. In the whole set-up, only Harry Herr had graduated from a university and, except for him, only John Snyder had completed high school. The rest of the inner circle had been indifferently schooled to a level short of grammar school, (including M.S. himself) except for Lebbie Lebkicher. When Lebbie was subsequently asked if he'd ever been to school, he cocked his head and said, "Yes." When asked how far he'd gone in school, his answer was, "Far enough." That was all. The record shows that Lebbie had finished grammar school and had served as a tanner's apprentice with H.C. Locher in Lancaster.

So Milton Hershey entered the twentieth century with nothing like the kind of money needed to build a new plant, a new village, and a whole new way of life for a lot of people unknown to him. But he went on to do just that, and he did it by breaking every rule in the book.

Time and time again he was cautioned against spending too much money on nebulous ideas and acquiring too much property against the balance of his liquid assets. Furthermore, he was incessantly told that if he insisted on hiring his friends and family members to run all these new and untried business ventures, there was no way he could avoid the inevitable bust-ups that were sure to explode in bankruptcy.

They exploded, but not in bankruptcy.

His chancy risks in dairying and experimental chocolate-making skirted the rims of failure. But he dovetailed the aborted dairying and cheesemaking ventures by putting his surplus milk into a new kind of chocolate that emerged as milk chocolate. That was the first of the novel explosions, and it showered the Derry countryside with a green manna called money.

The choice of friends and family—the combination of Uncle Abe Snavely, cousin Frank Snavley, Mama Hershey, and then cousins Bowman Snavely and Ezra Hershey—was put together with Lebbie Lebkicher, major domo; Bill Murrie, sales chief and manager; John Snyder, lawyer and counsellor; Abe Heilman, management man-in-motion; Harry Herr, civil engineer and contract supervisor; Charlie Ziegler, as an early ombudsman. Eleven of them, and all of them either friends or family.

And M.S. Hershey made twelve.

He was the commander and they were his Swiss Guard. When he was later reminded that he had set out on an impossible mission with eleven disciples instead of twelve, he smiled and said nothing. But in quieter moments of reflection down through the years that followed, he must surely have taken satisfaction in what this inner circle of friends and family had helped him build. Maybe their numbers came up just one short of twelve because that was all he needed. There wasn't a Judas in the lot.

Once he'd picked them, that was it. Henceforth, they could do no wrong, and in their eyes, neither could he. But their devotion to duty came after decisions were made. Only their faith in him and his faith in them remained a constant factor.

There were arguments galore. But these came as the natural consequence of the M.S. gambler instincts, coupled with the profusion of ideas that flowed from him. The staff members fought, they reasoned, they cajoled, and they pouted, but only *before the fact* of decision-making. They sometimes deterred or actually talked him out of his dice-throwing ventures, but usually they merely managed to get him to go slower with his ambitious plans. It wasn't long until they all began to realize the same thing.

This was exactly what each one of them had been hired to do.

The man knew himself. He had a phenomenal memory, and every one of his past failures were locked in his mind. He knew his own shortcomings, so he surrounded himself with the kind of people who would hedge his bets and get between him and the spears that could bring him down. But there wasn't another real gambler in the whole lot. The way Milton Hershey had it figured, he was gambler enough for all of them, and then some.

He chose people because he had faith in them. Some of them, like Mama and Uncle Abe, he chose because he loved them and he owed them. But the loving and the owing for the rest of the group, that would come. And it would come as the result of doing things together. Perhaps there was something in each of them that told him that he could work with them and that they could work with him. Schooling counted for little, but education as he saw it was something else. He counted a man educated when he knew enough to do the job he was given. But when he handed out assignments, and some of them bordered on requests that demanded the miraculous, he told his minions *what to do, not how to do it.*

In later life, Milton Hershey would observe that schooling really wouldn't have counted for too much in those early days, because, as he put it, "We were starting out to do something new, something that had never been done before, so how could anyone have learned that in school?" He went on to say, "We had to learn by doing things, and when we did them right, we did more of it that way. And what we did wrong, well, you had to remember that, too, so you wouldn't keep making the same mistakes over and over again."

Simplistic? Certainly.

Successful? Positively.

*   *   *

An amazing flood of bountiful achievements would pour forth from the experimental horn of plenty that began in a Pennsylvania Dutch country cornfield at the turn of the century. It would begin with a compulsively motivated risk-taker who was inspired by the faith he had in his God, his fellowman, and in himself. It would be forged by humble hosts of people who were tied to him and his dreams with unbreakable bonds of loyalty. They would write their names in bold type across the pages of the American free enterprise system.

But they did it all together, out of the devotion they felt for their Creator, for the man who led them, for their work, and for each other. The commerce they pursued, the schools they founded, and the community they built were at all times progressive, and yet they were capitalistic in concept, paternalistic in nature, and Christian in practice.

And they all worked.

The whole turnabout began in Lancaster, Pennsylvania, about one hundred years after the mobs of the French Revolution stormed the Tuilleries Palace in 1792. Way back then, a spark in history had been ignited by the mercenary Swiss Guardsmen who had pledged their loyalty to defend the lives of Louis XVI and his Queen, Marie Antoinette. Every last man of those two battalions of Swiss heroes died to keep the pledge.

Then along came a shy, little American, a man of peace and a nominal Pennsylvania Dutchman, even though he had sprung from the same Alpiner stock as the gallant men who had died in Paris. He would show the world that he, too, set the same value on loyalty that his former countrymen had demonstrated so long ago.

How were the lowly risen?

These people, leader and followers alike, were folk of humble beginnings and little schooling. Yet they were destined to become highly educated and superlatively skilled at doing the work they were chosen to do. They began in faith, and they kept that faith by remaining loyal to each other until they had run the good race, fought the good fight, and finished the course.

In the spirit of loyalty, they waited upon their irrepressible leader in a way that sometimes slowed him but still helped him at the same time. They would work their magic by blunting the suicidal pace of his risk-taking, and yet they could not deter him from the headlong pursuit of goals that were unseeen by all but him.

Again and again Milton Hershey was told, "Wait." If the pragmatic paladins of his Swiss Guard were to be given credit for helping him to achieve overall success, some of it would have to be attributed to the patience they forced upon him.

It was a stodgy lawyer (called "Judge") John Snyder who set the example for slow deliberation with his own snail-paced methodology. But it remained for Mama and her Bible training to commend him to the Book of Isaiah, Chapter 40, verse 31:

> *But they that wait upon the Lord shall renew their strength;*
> *they shall mount up with wings, as eagles; they shall run,*
> *and not be weary; and they shall walk and not faint.*

Together, thereafter, the impatient Milton Hershey and the patient members of his loyal Swiss Guard would comprise a tightly-knit inner circle. The circle would remain unbroken for many years to come.

Chapter VI

❥∙❧

Surprise

Springtime of 1897 found the energetic Milton Hershey in Manhattan where he was beset by a rare collision of contradictory thoughts. Hitherto, the "Caramel King" of Lancaster, Pennsylvania, had distinguished himself as being a pragmatist who had chosen to do things one at a time, on an orderly basis. But things were different that May day in Manhattan.

He had come to the city from a trip through the west end of New York State where he had been making the rounds of small confectionery shops. Then, having completed those calls, he had boarded the New York Central and headed for the big city where he still had a number of loose ends to tie up. Eleven years ago when he had left the big town, he had been forced to close the shop on Sixth Avenue with a judgment note for ten thousand dollars filed against him on a pile of candy-making equipment that had been repossessed by the holders of the note. On that rainy day of long ago, he had gone back to Lancaster a defeated young man with the remnants of his possessions consigned "Collect" to his point of destination.

Things were different now. He had long since come back to New York and he had fully paid off those earlier notes. Then he set up a port of entry for the chocolate making machinery he had arranged to bring in from the J.M. Lehmann Company of Dresden, Germany. All these new dealings were made on the refreshing basis of cash on the barrelhead, and that felt good, too. But that wasn't what was bothering him.

He'd finished the business that had brought him to town and had squandered a careless hour in revisiting the site of his failed venture on Sixth Avenue. A bustling rebuilding scheme was changing Old Knickerbocker's Village, and the old candy store was now dealing in flowers. On the uptown side the Chinese Steam Laundry had moved out, and a tobacconist was doing business from the place where he had once drawn steam to heat and run his candy enterprise. The Hippodrome Theater was still on the downtown side.

He felt a strange rumbling in his chest, but that wasn't caused by the nostalgic return to these old diggings. Somehow, even as he looked at the old building, he found that he really wasn't seeing it or even thinking about it at all.

What he was seeing was the heart-shaped face of an impish Irish colleen, framed against the shadowy outline of a tiny sweet shop several hundred miles away. A somewhat clearer picture emerged from his thoughts when they returned to the memorable facade of the A.D. Work's Confectionery Store in the western New York village of Jamestown.

In the midst of this visionary locket of the mind, he saw the reddish-brown hair and the bright blue eyes of Catherine Elizabeth Sweeney. Her parents called her "Kitty," and he had met the young lady on his recent sojourn to the Great Western region of the Empire State. As the patterns of his vision began to take shape in a definable picture, some other details emerged in sharper focus.

Kitty Sweeney was in her twenties; in fact, she would attain her twenty-fifth birthday when the sixth of July rolled around in that year of 1897. Come September 13th, he would be forty. Gee, he thought, I'm fifteen years older than she is. Then he wondered why he thought that. After which he wondered what *that* had to do with *anything.*

But a disturbing turbulence within the chest of the Lancaster candyman would not subside. In fact, it grew with a feeling of warmth that accompanied every thought of the girl he would call a "most beautiful lady" in faraway Jamestown. It just happened to be the way he thought about her then, and it would be the way he continued to think and speak of her for all the years that were left to him.

He had other thoughts that day, because the year 1897 was fraught with all sorts of volatile possibilities. There was real trouble brewing in the Caribbean where Cuban insurrectionists were threatening a War of Secession to free themselves from Spanish rule. He neither knew nor cared much about politics, but he was sharply cognizant of the economic implications as they applied to his own business. Cuba was a pivotal point as the source of the cane sugar that all confectioners required, and it sat at the cross-roads of commerce whence came the chocolate and the vanilla extracts that flowed back to the States from the tropical reaches of Central and South America. An outbreak of war in this particular area could mean real trouble for him and his customers. It par-ticularly spelled a threat to the new plant he was putting together for an enlarged effort in chocolate-making.

He was building up a coating chocolate trade among the independent candy shops (as typified by A.D. Work's in Jamestown); so, if his sugar and chocolate sources were cut off, his contact with them would be cut off, too. That prospect really bothered him.

As he meandered toward his Manhattan hotel, he was assailed by other recollec-tions. He felt reasonably assured that Bill Murrie back in Lancaster would be laying in the necessary supplies of sugar and cacao beans to tide them over any upcoming disturbance in Cuba. But he was bothered by the thought of his recent acquisition of the old family Homestead in Derry Township on April 1st, because it had not helped with completion of another aim.

Papa was still in Colorado, and Mama was firmly entrenched in the home he had set up for her on South Queen Street in Lancaster. But he wanted all three of them together, the way they had started out some forty years ago at the old Homestead near Derry Church where he had been born. His good friend, "Lebbie" Lebkicher, had already moved into The Homestead and was even then busily engaged in getting the place ready for occupancy by the soon to be reunited members of the Henry H. Hershey family.

That wasn't all he thought about. The upcoming move was only a small part of a whole skein of events he had in mind. He and lawyer, John Snyder, had been planning to sell the Lancaster Caramel Company and to start building up the chocolate making part of the business. Later, they would set up a whole new dairy venture over near The Homestead, after which they would pay more attention to making and selling products derived from the cacao bean. He had long ago decided that chocolate was the coming thing, for it was, in reality, a food. In his estimation, caramels were merely a fad, however popular and profitable they had proven to be for him up until that moment.

But other thoughts bothered him more than his business plans, and the constant intervention of Kitty Sweeney's lilting smile both tantalized and disconcerted him. A sharper focus on workaday thoughts became purely impossible. And *that* had never happened before.

His phone call after supper to Bill Murrie was an adventure. In those days, even a call across town on the newfangled "talking wire" of Alex Bell's posed the probability of conversations which began with trying to identify who was to speak and who to listen once the connection had been completed. Then, when a suitable sequence of exchange had been established, there was an onset of unscheduled interruptions and a spate of indistinct reception, which was usually followed by a succession of "receiver" hook janglings and an unpredictable round of shouted queries comprised of those three little words: "What'd you say?"

When he hung up the receiver, he seemed nominally satisfied with what had transpired. But he continued to feel the warm, chest-bubbling feeling that had been troubling him more and more with each moment that passed. He looked at the black mouthpiece and the wired box he had just finished speaking into, and bemoaned the fact that this demon of gadgetry hadn't yet been connected to certain hinterlands of the country. Like a house in Jamestown.

Twilight had fallen, and a few minutes after he returned to his room, he was still bothered by that fidgety feeling. Being alone and unoccupied just wouldn't do. The impish Irish face was there again. He wondered if perhaps the distant lass hadn't gone into league with some band of leprechauns. The Irish called them "the little people," but to Pennsylvania Dutchman Milton Hershey, they were "spooks."

"I've been spooked," he said to himself.

Then he decided to take another walk, but he hadn't gone more than a hundred feet from the hotel when a sudden thought hit him like an express train. He had looked to his left where he saw the big lights that illuminated the railway ticket office. He didn't want to catch a train, but he did want to look at a timetable.

He already had his ticket back to Lancaster on the "Pennsy," and he was scheduled to take that trip on the morrow, but at this moment, he was curious about the New York Central. Maybe he could go back that way? The realization that this would really be going all the way "around the Horn" on his way home was shrugged off. In those days, one could travel westward to Erie and take the trunk line south to Pittsburgh and then east again in order to get back to Lancaster. Or, of course, he could have returned to Manhattan on the eastbound New York Central and still use his ticket on the "Pennsy." Indeed, the thoughts that come to lightly turn the fancies of young men in springtime have always put geographic considerations pretty far down on the list of reasonable priorities.

The timetable dismayed him. The night train had already departed and the next connection with Jamestown wouldn't leave until late the next afternoon.

He growled and dismissed the notion.

Then, even though he had nothing to do until the morning, he sprinted back to the hotel. Somehow he had become obsessed with a silly notion that the sooner he returned to the place where he would start the journey to Jamestown, the sooner he would arrive in that place. This is akin to the mistaken premise of a sprint runner who shows up early at the starting line because he believes that this will somehow help him break the finishing tape ahead of the field.

The thought of a race bothered him. How many other, much younger and more eligible men were at this very moment racing off to see the distant Kitty?

"And what are you going to say when you get there?" he asked himself.

"Hmmm," he mused, adding to the bubbling mass already stirring within his breast. "What will I say?"

As he entered the hotel lobby, a sudden thought struck him like a thunderbolt. He scarcely noticed the bellhop hurrying toward him. But the young man with a telegram on a tiny server tray arrived to be greeted with the surprising words Milton Hershey had blurted out. He thought he'd said it to himself, but he hadn't.

"I love her!" he squeaked.

The bellhop blinked. He remained speechless. For want of something better to do, he proffered the telegram on a tray.

Hershey grimaced and returned to the real world. He tore open the envelope and

Catherine Elizabeth Sweeney 1897

reached in his pocket for a bill to tip the bellhop. Then everything got *bollixed up* as he later recalled.

He put the telegram into a coat pocket and deposited the torn envelope on the tray as a tip. As he hurried off toward his room, he scanned the bill he intended as a tip, but found there was no message on it.

The reading effort proved fruitless. The bellhop maintained an air of circumspect sanity by remaining speechless. But after a moment, Hershey realized that the Treasury Department had printed nothing in the way of a message on the face of the bill he was attempting to read, so he fumbled in his pocket for the telegram.

The message was from lawyer, John Snyder, urging Hershey's prompt return to Lancaster. He growled and looked up again as he turned to face the silent bell boy. With a dollar bill in one hand and the hateful message in the other, he took another shot at undoing the mixup of the previous exchange.

This time the bellhop found himself in possession of a crumbled paper after Milton Hershey went off still growling, because his other hand now held both the dollar bill and the empty envelope he had so swiftly retrieved. The bellhop had been rewarded with the telegram.

Back in his room and next day on the train back to Lancaster, Hershey was still growling about the upset of this untimely intervention in his plans. But the soothing hum of the train's passage back to Pennsylvania gave him time to regain his composure and time to think about some less emotional decisions that remained to be made.

By the time he had returned to the caramel plant, he realized that his presence really was urgently required in his place of business. The overseas marketplaces were in turmoil. There was going to be a war; in fact, the Cuban insurrectionists were already attacking the Spanish forts in Cuba. And John Snyder told him that until the Caribbean troubles were settled, the upcoming sale of the caramel plant was out of the question. The market had fallen drastically on every kind of enterprise related to sugar imports from the West Indies and Central America.

The war didn't come until April the 24th of the following year, but in the meantime Milton Hershey was caught up in a whole round of bustling activities that allowed him little time to think about Kitty Sweeney.

In the summer of '97, he managed to send her a box of chocolates which he had painstakingly made himself. These were dispatched in time for her birthday and he saw to the wrapping and mailing of them personally. He enclosed his business card and a note expressing the wish for her to have "a happy birthday," but that was all. Somehow he clung to his title as the world's most reluctant letter writer, and this would later prove to be an unblemished attribute he would keep for the rest of his life.

He was back in New York City again in the fall of that year. His Lancaster business had settled down, so a few weeks after his birthday, September 13, when the yellows and crimsons of October touched the maples of western New York, he decided to set out again for Jamestown. The train ride was an overnight jaunt. His berth in the sleeper was not made up, but that didn't matter because he never occupied it. He spent the entire trip in the smoking car, perched on the edge of his seat, puffing away on cigars. He still didn't know what he was going to say when he got to Jamestown.

But he did a lot of thinking about what he was going to *try to say* when he saw Miss Sweeney again. In his heart, however, he knew this was going to be the most agonizing string of words he would ever try to put together. It was a time of cruel exacerbation and introspection for a little, forty-year old man who had become keenly aware of his shortcomings as a badly smitten swain.

He was too old for her. He was too short. His voice squeaked when he conducted a normal conversation, and it became positively shrill when he got excited. And he could

almost hear it squeaking and shrilling even when he didn't use it, when the merest thought of her set his chest to burning and his throat into spasms of tightened dryness.

What can I do? What on earth can I say to her? he asked himself over and over again. Good thing he hadn't told her he was coming, he mused, thereby soothing himself. After all, he would be getting into Jamestown at the ungodly hour of four a.m., and that should give him plenty of time to check into a hotel and think things over.

Meanwhile, he took comfort in the thought that when the train back to New York came through Jamestown that very afternoon, he'd be on it again. He was so tortured by these gnawing pangs and thoughts of her by that time that there was only one thing he was absolutely sure about. He just couldn't face her.

He came to the awful conclusion that he didn't know what to say and he was deathly afraid of making a fool of himself. These things he knew for sure, and of his inability to face her he was absolutely certain.

"Jamestown!"

The conductor's call caught him like a spear in the short ribs.

"My goodness," he said, reaching for his overnight bag. "I'm here."

He waved off the porter and walked down the aisle to the end of the car. He put his bag on the platform and studied the passing landscape as the train began slowing its passage through the star-filled autumn night.

"Oh, my goodness!" he said again, as the car stopped and he made his way down the steps.

He looked up as he realized that his Pullman car had stopped well forward of the station. He had been landed several yards beyond the paved area. Then he grimaced skyward at the sparkling canopy overhead and turned around.

"Milton," came the sound of his name.

He turned, and there she was. Catherine Elizabeth Sweeney, at four o'clock in the morning in the Jamestown station, waiting to meet the only passenger who got off the train. And there he was—a thoroughly dazzled little man who had sent no word of his arrival, a man so shaken by surprise that he couldn't crank up his squeaky voice enough to make a sound.

"Grrummpphh," he said, blinking. The very stars were falling on him.

Such was the brilliant caliber of conversational dialogue exchanged on that memorable October morning of 1897 when Milton Hershey arrived in Jamestown. A morning on which he had stepped off a train firmly resolved to return again home without seeing his beloved Kitty. A morning when he had reasoned he would not know what to say to her, and a morning she never could have remembered, for she would have had no way of even knowing he had been there.

But he had reckoned without the knowledge of all those bright and beautiful things that are known to so very few earthlings—and most of whom are Irish.

Milton Hershey hadn't written her. He had sent a card and candies, of course, but never a letter, . . . never a telegram, . . . and never a phone call, for Bell's bells hadn't been strung to ring in the house where Kitty lived in those days.

Just about the only thing that had travelled between his place in Lancaster and her home and the candy shop where she worked in Jamestown were the packages and the merchandise shipped from his plant to her shop. And, of course, there were people.

Ay, there's the rub. *People.*

In Lancaster, they were the people who worked in Milton Hershey's plant, one of whom frequently made the rounds of the customer places on the road when the boss was too busy to make a personal trip.

The people in the plant had been asked at least once a week when the next shipment of goods was going out to Work's Candy Shop in Jamestown. They'd grown used to seeing the boss putting in little business cards and trinkets or mementos addressed to the distant Miss Catherine Sweeney.

And there was also a red-haired salesman. In those days, the top salesman employed by the Lancaster Caramel Company happened to be an outgoing and decidedly vocal type. The man in motion had been early aware of the fact that the boss had a more than passing interest in the young lady in Jamestown, New York, who worked at the A.D. Work's Candy Store.

In a way, it figured, and in another way, it didn't.

Having seen the pert little Irish girl, the attraction for her, in the salesman's judgment, *that figured.* But having worked for Milton Hershey for several years and by being quite familiar with the solid state of bachelorhood his boss maintained, this sudden attraction for one of the opposite sex, *that didn't figure.* At least, not at first.

But when month after month slipped by after M.S.'s return from New York in April, one thing sparked the consciousness of the salesman often enough to make him keenly aware of one sure and certain fact: the boss was in love.

With this boss, this meant it was serious. And it was bound to be one of those things with cupids and hearts and flowers and ladies crying at the church, and all the rest of the stuff that puts death and taxes to shame as hard rock finalities.

The Old Boy had caught Cupid's shaft dead center.

In addition to being perceptive, this salesman also had another trait in common with members of his vocational ilk. He was a doer of the unexpected as well as of the routine things which salesmen are expected to do.

When Milton Hershey was assailed by the short form of effervescent heartburn called love, he had kept his mouth shut, but he failed to keep the secret by the simplest of omissions. He didn't tell his salesman that it was a secret to be kept. That would have done it, but instead he did all the other things, like asking about Miss Sweeney, asking about Miss Sweeney's folks, Miss Sweeney's address, and what Miss Sweeney liked, or wore, or disliked, or whatever. That did it.

More to the point, that is how the salesman Bill Murrie came to do what he did. Like telling Miss Sweeney his boss would be in on the Wednesday morning train. Murrie had known this, of course, since he had purchased the boss's ticket at the same time he'd picked up his own on the preceding Friday.

So the unannounced and unexpected arrival of Milton Hershey in Jamestown, New York, in the wee hours of the morning on that October day in 1897 was unannounced only by him. The unexpected arrival turned out to be solely a matter of his own errant judgment, for it eventually came to light that nearly everyone in the Hershey-Lancaster ranks of workers and confidants knew where he was going and when, and so did the Family Sweeney, as well as the entire working staff of the A.D. Work Candy Store in Jamestown village.

Aside from the collateral note that Daddy Sweeney, Michael William Sweeney, himself, had accompanied daughter Catherine to the rail station on that memorable morning of long ago, virtually nothing else of historical significance occurred on that particular hegira. But the ensuing consequences of the trip and the surprise meeting between the nervous traveller and the expectant greeter were to prove both memorable and historic.

During the seven and a half months between the autumn of 1897 and the springtime of May in 1898, the records and the recollective memories of those who knew Milton Hershey reveal only sparse documentation via factual entry. The most pertinent of these, of course, is the fact that Milton Hershey made many more trips to Jamestown in the time between the memorable October meeting and the following May, and *that date* certainly would prove to be historic.

On the distaff side, Hershey was to learn that his most beautiful lady was the daughter of Michael William Sweeney, himself, who had come to America from County Cork, Ireland. Then Sweeney became an iron worker. He married Kitty's mother, Catherine Elizabeth Maloney, of County Claire, of the Auld Sod. Miss Kitty Sweeney was one of four children, and she had a brother, William M., and two sisters, Agnes and Mary. Her sister Agnes became the wife of Louis Smith and sister Mary was married to Leroy Hambelton, both of Jamestown. The church affiliation of the family Sweeney revolved around the Roman Catholic Church of Saints Peter and Paul in Jamestown, where Kitty had been baptized.

Miss Catherine Sweeney was educated in the public schools of Jamestown, and the neighbors of her family in that distant time found the home life of the Sweeneys to be remarkably congenial and outgoing. There was, of course, some commentary as to the mysterious method whereby the outgoing Irish Catholic lass had remained at home and yet had collected the bustling candymaker from across the border in Pennsylvania.

But the attractive warmth and feminine appeal of Kitty Sweeney was matched by a deep quality of perceptive realism. And it was balanced by a keen, but disarming sense of humor. The manner in which she attracted, warmed, charmed, disarmed, and conquered Milton Snavely Hershey was to prove phenomenal in the ken of those who thought they knew the forty-one year old Caramel King from Lancaster. In the eyes of Mother Hershey, the conquest bordered on the enigmatic, but the lips of that gentle lady remained tacitly sealed in the face of impending events during the spring of 1898.

Nevertheless, on May 25th of that year, Milton Snavely Hershey and Catherine Elizabeth Sweeney were joined in holy wedlock by a ceremony performed in the Rectory of St. Patrick's Cathedral on Fifth Avenue in New York City. With his new bride, Milton Hershey boarded the train back to Lancaster, home, and Mother Hershey on the following day. He was later said to have observed that he believed Admirals Dewey at Manila and Sampson at Havana were less concerned about facing the enemy fleets arrayed against them than he was about facing his Mennonite Mama with a newly acquired Irish Catholic bride.

His fears were unfounded. The stolid, steely strength of Mother Hershey remained silent and unsheathed at the meeting and in the acceptance she accorded her daughter-in-law Kitty. And the easygoing grace and good humor kept the flame of hot Irish temperament dampened and at peace within the tremulous but determined breast of the lovely bride Milton Hershey brought home to Lancaster. There were vast differences in the personalities of the two main female characters in the saga of Milton Hershey, but they were ever to remain in check. There is no doubt that it was the fuller measure of their individual love for him that made it so.

So, while love was conquering all the expected disruptions that portended for the marriage at the outset, the sweep of other events prevailed and no explosions occurred. Mother Fanny Hershey was set up in her own private domicile and Milton kept himself busy with a variety of other plans. He flunked out on several of his schemes, beginning with a honeymoon to Mexico when he had booked some rather Spartan accommodations for bride and self in the possible hope that she would return home early and allow him to deal with more pressing matters. Home she went, but she went home dragging her reluctant and somewhat dismayed spouse along with her. Later he made up for it by taking her on an extended tour of European capitals. There she would get her fill of the sights and sounds, the art and music, which had slumbered for so long in her Gaelic girlhood dreams.

Milton's own dream of bringing Papa back from Colorado to take up residence in the old family Homestead with Mama finally led to his having to go west and collect Papa himself. With the Spanish-American War terminated on August 12 of that year, the impending deal to sell out the Lancaster Caramel Company was back on the front burner again.

In the two years that followed, Papa Henry Hershey was collected from Colorado and moved into The Homestead with Harry Lebkicher. The Lancaster Caramel Company was sold for an overall consideration of about one million dollars, and the new American Caramel Company not only allowed Milton Hershey to continue his chocolate-making enterprise in Lancaster, they immediately became one of the best and biggest customers for his newly expanded product line.

Over in Derry Township, The Homestead was becoming bounded by more and more acquisitions of Hershey property, and it soon contained a quarry and several hundred acres of farm land that had hitherto been engaged in corn tillage. Meanwhile, Milton Hershey was commonly seen scurrying around Lancaster and environs in his newly acquired Riker Electric horseless carriage.

Out in western New York State, Kitty's father, Michael William Sweeney, had become the new proprietor of the Sweeney House, at 703-705 West Eighth Street in Jamestown. It is believed that his newly affluent son-in-law, the former Pennsylvania Caramel King, was to some degree a participant in that enterprise, as well as with the subsequent attainment of larger and more pretentious living quarters for the family Sweeney at One Murray Avenue in Jamestown.

Maybe. Maybe not. But whether or not it was the helping hand of Milton Hershey that was extended to Mike Sweeney in those days was not important to what occurred then, nor is it now.

But one part of this incident was vital to the continuously unfolding and expanding Hershey saga. For by her appearance in the old Jamestown railway station on that starlit morning of October 1897, Catherine Sweeney had provided a whole new direction in the career of the little Pennsylvania Dutch candymaker.

He had stepped off the train firmly resolved to go back to Lancaster without even seeing her. He later acknowledged that he had just been too scared to face her. This went into the record as having been the first time in his life that he had ever been too scared to do anything.

But she changed all that simply by being there. In the future course of events, she would give her loving colleen's heart and her impish Irish soul to him to keep. For it was by her very presence in the old train station that she gave him the biggest surprise of his life.

He never recovered from it. He never tried.

Derry Homecoming

The Hershey saga included quite a string of dramatic and nostalgic episodes in the years that began with the marriage of Milton and Catherine Hershey in 1898. Plans had already been made by M.S. to sell the Lancaster Caramel Company and to start a new business that would be primarily engaged in making cocoa and coating chocolate. Most of the new items were to be initially sold to their big new customer and next door neighbor, the American Caramel Company that was about to become the successor to Hershey's Lancaster Caramel Company.

Following the wedding, Milton Hershey began to look like a juggler who was putting too many balls in the air. His first aim was to get Papa and Mama back together under one roof, and he meant to do that by having them set up housekeeping again at the family Homestead in Derry Township. This, of course, would fit right into his plans for setting up a string of dairy farms to supply the milk needed in his new cheesemaking venture.

By this time, he installed his new bride in the mansion formerly shared with Mama Fanny Hershey on South Queen Street, and by September of that year he had acceded to his mother's wishes and bought her a new home at 143 South Duke Street.

"Two women under one roof," commented Hershey, "will make the man of the house wish for a bigger cellar to hide in."

So, with Mama momentarily pacified by her new home, Hershey and his trusted companion, Harry Lebkicher (and sometimes Kitty and John Snyder), began a regular series of jaunts to the Derry Church site. Lebbie was somewhat less than enchanted when told that after the Hersheys had repurchased The Homestead and a sixty-five acre farm plot, *he* was supposed to move into the place and get ready for the time when Papa Henry and Mama Fanny were to be reunited for another go at connubial bliss.

"Won't work," he pronounced with cryptic finality.

"No, sirree," was Mama's crisp pronouncement.

But by the time The Homestead had been purchased, a dairy herd was being collected and a new milk barn was going up. Over in Lancaster, John Snyder was beginning to get the sellout of the caramel plant completed and the newly expanded chocolate venture underway. In fact, William F.R. Murrie, was already beginning to beat the bushes for customers for the chocolate company.

At this point, Milton Hershey told Lebbie Lebkicher he should take up permanent residence at The Homestead and await the arrival of a new companion to help him run the dairy farm.

"I'm going out to Colorado and bring Papa back," he confided. "Meantime, you see to it that he gets a workshop for his cabinet-making and vending machine projects. Oh, yes, and be sure to set up a library with a lot of books. You know how Papa likes to read."

"Yeah," came Lebbie's retort, through a bitten lip.

Lebbie moved into The Homestead from the Haeffner Tavern to begin getting the place in shape. Mama Fanny Hershey was busily cleaning up the residential building and Aunt Lizzie, Papa Henry Hershey's sister, was brought in from Hummelstown to help with the household chores. Aunt Lizzie hobbled about on crutches since she had been born with a hip deformity, but despite the fact that Fanny Hershey had been estranged in her marriage to Lizzie's brother Henry, these ladies were good friends and worked very well together.

So Milton Hershey was off to Colorado again to bring back his paternal sire. As the train rolled westward across the Pennsylvania hills, the Ohio and Indiana plains, he could not help but think how very different things had become since those days back in the 1880's when he had first headed out to join Papa in the Mile High City of Denver. He remembered having made that earlier trip with everything he owned either worn on his back or carried in a carpetbag valise. Now he had money in his pocket. He owned three valuable properties in Lancaster and had just reacquired The Homestead property Papa had lost earlier, before taking off on his search for the western end of the rainbow.

When the bustling young Pennsylvanian got off the train in Denver, he got quite a surprise. A letter sent on ahead of him had reached Papa, and he found Henry Hershey waiting for him in the station. He had come down from Leadville with every intention of putting off any attempt to drag him back home again. But that resolve was summarily brushed aside when he met his beaming son. Milton quickly gave him the details about the million dollars expected from the sale of the Lancaster plant and showed him a checkbook with a balance of much more than Henry Hershey had seen in capital figures and on bank stationery as belonging to a member of his family. Or any family.

They spent less than a day in settling Henry Hershey's affairs, and the better part of their overnight stay was spent at the Brown Palace Hotel. This provided another chance for Henry Hershey to write more letters on the hotel's stationery, and this time he took satisfaction in knowing that he actually was a guest at the palatial inn.

During that evening in Denver and for the first hours after their departure, Milton did most of the talking. It took a bit of narrative discourse to bring Papa up to date on all the things that had happened in the more than five years since they had parted company back in New York City. Quite a bit of the conversation was devoted to Kitty, Milton's new bride, and perhaps this was not entirely the product of the son's love and enthusiasm for his own happily married state. He probably sought to convey some idea of the happiness in store for his father, should Henry Hershey essay to become reunited

Henry Hershey and Harry Lebkicker

with Mama.

Henry's sharp negation of the ploy was both tacit and final. Every time Milton mentioned the possibility of Henry's moving into residence with Fanny at The Homestead, Papa shook his head from side to side, or he silently looked out the window. It was not to be.

What was meant to happen began before the train had gone a hundred miles down the track on the way back to Chicago. Henry Hershey had listened to his nouveau riche son without interruption for quite a few hours; now it was his turn. And his turn not only lasted all the way to Chicago, it continued during their overnight stay between trains, and he was still at it all the way back to Lancaster.

Henry Hershey delivered a programmed assortment of schemes for new vending machines, new products, new production and canning techniques, pausing only once in a while to ask his son, "Milton, why do you smoke so many cigars?"

The son removed the stubby panatella from his lips and exhaled a blue-white cloud of smoke. Hershey senior shook his head and expounded on another new scheme before his son could launch either a word or another puff of foul-smelling smoke.

But Milton was nonetheless delighted.

He loved Papa. And he loved Mama. So, bit by bit, he became resigned to the satisfying knowledge that *they were going to be where he was going to be.* Not together with each other, but in homes that would be near his home, and in a place where he could get together with either one of them whenever he chose. That, he finally said to himself, will be enough.

At the turn of the millenium and on into the first several years of the twentieth century, the Hersheys were, in a sense, all together. As the Fates would have it, it was to be a period of less than five years, and yet it was a time of new beginnings for all of them. With Mama, Papa, Kitty, Aunt Lizzie, old Lebbie, John Snyder, Frank Snavely, and Bill Murrie clustered about him, these were the happiest years in all of Milton Hershey's lifetime.

Chapter VII

❧

The Way of the Wanderer

The most treasured period in Milton Hershey's chronicle started with the long train ride in 1898 when he brought Papa home from Denver. Until then, the Hersheys, father and son, never really had been given a chance to get to know each other, either because the press of business or the presence of other people always intervened.

Milton may have been spiralling about on a maddening course of business and personal activities, but he kept track of Papa all the while. Beginning in 1893, a monthly check was sent to Colorado (Greeley, Denver, Leadville, or wherever) payable to "Henry H. Hershey, consultant."There is no record of Papa's having *asked* for money, but every one of the checks was marked "Paid."

So when the carriage rolled up to The Homestead and Papa was re-established in the home diggings, he came back with more books, a snappy new wardrobe, including a Prince Albert cutaway, and with all his dreams, old and new, solidly intact.

His arrival inspired a curious assortment of greetings. His estranged wife, Fanny, smiled and remained coolly circumspect, as did his sister, Lizzie. "Lebbie" Lebkicher was reclusive and noncommittal, as always; and Mssrs. Snyder and Murrie were both expectant and somewhat hesitant. But Milton Hershey's bride, Kitty, was instantly fascinated with Papa, and later she became positively entranced.

She loved the old freebooter on sight. And she came to love him a good deal more during the years she would spend in his company. Time and again she would ask her husband, "Are you sure Papa isn't Irish?" For Papa Henry's gay repartee, his quick wit, and his sunny willingness to joke or debate, to tell stories or sing songs, made him seem like a kinsman of "the auld sod" from whence her own forebears had come.

Kitty's delight was shared by Milton. He was later to say that one of the brightest blessings he'd ever received was "the way Kitty and Papa took to each other."

The kids in the neighborhood liked Papa, too. His midmorning and twilight jaunts through the rising community were carefully noted by all the youngsters from toddlers to teenagers. Papa Hershey's itinerary was marked out, and the siblings waylaid him morning and night for the sweets he carried in his cutaway pockets and for the seemingly endless supply of songs and stories he shared with them. When he wasn't walking and talking, he whiled away the happy hours in his new workshop with companion Lebbie, working on strange and exotic new ideas.

The ideas ranged from cough drop formulas, vending machine designs, canning experiments (fruit and vegetable juices), to his favorite, the perpetual motion machine. None of them worked very well, but the companionship he shared with Lebbie did. In less than a year after his return, folks began to notice that the formerly reluctant Lebbie was always either in Papa's company or he was looking for the old guy just to be with him. They were destined to become inseparable companions, and finally they became the best of friends.

The Homestead was a regular beehive of activity in those early days. In fact, Milton Hershey's birthplace was to provide the hub for the renewed activities that marked the

Hershey family's return to the Derry Church home country. But this didn't all come about in a twinkling nor was it the consequence of happenstance.

Back in 1895, when young Milton Hershey was in the midst of his peripatetic obsession for dairying, he'd made several propitious moves within the space of a few months. He'd hired Bill Murrie from Pittsburgh to take over the sales and management chores at Lancaster Caramel Company. Then he'd gone again to Switzerland to explore the possibilities of getting into the butter and cheese business. In the midst of all this, he got wind of the fact that a man named Levi Gingrich had come into possession of the old Hershey Homestead property which Jacob Hershey had sold to Gingrich's father, Henry, in 1867. Levi was now making noises as if he wanted to sell the place. It seems that Gingrich needed the money to satisfy his creditors, and the whole idea of buying the place seemed to satisfy Milton Hershey's most pressing needs, too.

In M.S.'s view, the acquisition would bring him back to the beloved home of his ancestors, and it would also provide an ideal spot from which he could build up his dairying enterprise. The first idea was a dream he'd had for a long time, and the second was part of an ambitious new aim. Both objectives were foremost in his thoughts.

It took the better part of a year before he got newly-hired lawyer John Snyder to begin negotiating for the property (Sept. 12, 1896), with instructions to "buy the place at any price." Thus, with the price removed as a possible bone of contention, the matter should have been quickly resolved. It wasn't. The tangled state of Levi Gingrich's personal financial needs, plus the fact that Hershey also wanted most of the surrounding meadowlands for his dairying enterprise, all intervened to work a further delay. So it wasn't until March 31, 1897, that the Court of Common Pleas cleared the Hershey purchase of a sixty-five acre section, north of the Horseshoe Pike in Derry Township, which included certain buildings standing thereon. These buildings included The Hershey Homestead property; and Milton Hershey's deed became effective on the following day, April 1. The price of the transaction was $10,310.69.

Throughout the two years of negotiations, Milton Hershey made quite a few visits to the place where he had been born. In quiet moments of reflective solitude he stood on the banks of little Spring Creek and looked across the rolling meadow to the ramparts of the building where he had been born. And he recalled that this was the only place in which he and Mama and Papa had been alone together, and the last place he could remember in which all three of them had been happy.

When he told John Snyder, "Buy it at any price," he meant it.

By the time of Papa's return, of course, the place was newly reoccupied and the activities surrounding it were already in high gear. Lebbie had been dispatched to get the place ready for Papa. Meanwhile, a man named Daniel Schlesser had been appointed manager in 1898, and he was already on hand to get the rundown property in shape. The main building and the chicken houses were repaired and sites for a new dairy barn and a milk-condensing plant had been laid out. Papa's new workshop was already abuilding, and his crippled sister, Elizabeth (Aunt Lizzie), was installed on the premises. Mama Fanny either came over from Lancaster on an almost daily basis, or when the press of work required it, she made her overnight stays with the Erbs in Hockersville. She had on one occasion made an overnight stay at the Haeffner Hotel and Tavern, but that one stop-over in the up-stairs rooms of a beverage dispensary had sufficed.

As previously stated, Papa's arrival in the carriage that brought him down Meadow Lane from the train station was an event marked by mixed emotions. Quite a collection of oldtimers were gathered to greet the old gadabout, and they made it very clear that they had missed him. Both his estranged wife, Fanny, and his only sister, Elizabeth, were more restrained. They were both civil and polite to a degree that was punctiliously genteel; yet the chill of their hesitancy also seemed to indicate that they would wait and see before showing him any personal signs of warmth or enthusiasm.

When Henry Hershey, in his dashing Prince Albert cutaway, needed help to carry his cartons of books, the line of sight between him and his bride of long ago seemed to be strung out on a chilly wire draped with icicles. She never said it, of course, but those books had been the biggest cause of their marital breakup. In her eyes, it had been those books which had alienated her husband's affections and, as such, they were the real correspondents in a breakup that had not been unlike divorce.

Henry Hershey, if he was at all aware of this, simply shrugged it off. After all, he'd just returned from Colorado where his occupational mainstay had been as proprietor of a used book store. But he probably had other things on his mind that day, so they went about their own business, in their own way, and that was to be separately and apart from each other. Son Milton was disappointed with the arrangement, but let it pass as the best possible way in which he could undertake to once again try to get them together. In this aim he persisted until the very last, but that didn't happen until long after both Mama and Papa had died.

So it was that Henry Hershey came back to the land of his ancestral beginnings where he was once again to take up the speculative schemes of work and the circuit-riding socializing that had made of him the man he was. There were any number of witnesses and bystanders who would voice their opinions about the Old Man in the months to follow. But, strange to relate, very few of the comments were hostile. Most of them, in fact, were quite laudatory.

Some of the commentators talked about the way in which he had broken off his work and dashed by carriage to the schoolhouse in Hockersville where young Edna Erb had been taken ill. Henry H. saw her home and called in old Dr. Fox (Thomas Fox of Hummelstown), the same doctor whose father had delivered Henry's son Milton, forty-five years earlier. The younger Dr. Fox later told his own daughter, Miss Elizabeth Fox, some other interesting facts about old Henry Hershey.

When the youthful girl was about to marry Ezra Hershey, Henry's nephew and Milton's cousin, her father told her, "You're marrying into the Hershey family, and you're going to hear an awful lot about old Henry Hershey, both pro and con. But I want you to remember this: he was one of my father's dearest friends, and a more splendid gentleman never walked on the face of this earth."

This was more than a mere medical opinion. But there were others, less complimentary. Some folks decried the fact that Henry Hershey had been saved from abject poverty, that he had been rescued from the abyss of being a second-hand book dealer. Whatever the truth of the situation, the rescue and the return of Papa Henry Hershey to the Derry Church, Hockersville and Campbelltown area had one clear effect on one segment of the population. It made the kids happy.

Amos Brandt, the Campbelltown hardware merchant, said something about that. He often recalled how Papa used to come into the freight-handling part of the store on weekdays and Saturday mornings, ostensibly to pick up mechanical devices and spare parts for his inventions, adding that sometimes the old man would bring along sketches or models of the things he was working on and would explain how they worked to the people gathered there.

"There were always some youngsters around, particularly on Saturday mornings when there was no school," Brandt would relate. "You wouldn't believe how the young folks gathered around this man, because he always had time for them, and time to regale them with stories of his own adventures or with bits and parts of the books he had read. Poetry, too."

So the old man in the cutaway Prince Albert coat became a familiar sight on The Homestead grounds and on the highways and byways roundabout. Then, in 1903, the

Henry H. Hershey

whole scene of his rambling domain changed from the already bustling pace of improvement to the explosive one of a dramatic new building program.

All of this new activity began in the office of a man named Harry N. Herr at 108 King Street in Lancaster. Lawyer John Snyder had heard about the young Lehigh University graduate engineer and had inveigled Milton Hershey into consulting him. The fledgling engineer turned out to be quite an eccentric, but there was virtually nothing that Milton Hershey wanted for his new community that the young fellow couldn't do. He'd already gained quite a reputation for himself as a consulting engineer for the railroads, and he had mastered some pretty big jobs in water supply systems and topographical surveying.

Milton Hershey thought perhaps this new acquaintance might be just the man to come over to the Derry Church site where he could conduct surveys for the new chocolate factory and lay out plans for the railroad sidings, the streets and houses, the water mains, sewage systems, power plants, and even the trolley lines he envisioned for his dream town.

Herr was not only an eccentric; he'd never even heard of the place called Derry Church. But he came along anyway, and before the end of January, he'd gotten together with John Snyder and secured a charter for the Hummelstown and Campbelltown Street Railway Company, based on his plans.

Thereafter, the power plant for the new railway line was initiated and the redesigned chocolate company plant was beginning to rise. As it turned out, Harry Herr's peculiar genius would have a marked effect on the streets and buildings of a town that was yet unnamed, but his plans had already impacted on the life of old Henry Hershey.

Everywhere Papa went there was digging or building. New plant, new homes, new streets—everything new. However pleasing his son Milton may have found all this new activity, it positively delighted his enterprising sire. This was his meat! Things were going on, things were going up, and there was hustle and bustle all about him. This, perhaps, was his undoing, for he was no longer a young man. But in his heart, he was bursting with youthful enthusiasm and he felt compelled to be everywhere at once, to see everything that was happening.

One morning after puttering around in his greenhouse, he came back to the kitchen of The Homestead for a midmorning snack. Kitty was there, and he teased her about her parrot. With a sly wink, he told her about a meeting he had attended on the previous evening. The meeting had been held by the Greiner School Adult Literary Society, and the teacher, one Solomon Balsbaugh, had introduced Papa Henry for the presentation of the main subject: "The Village That Will Rise on the Site of This Cornfield Twenty-Five Years Hence."

Papa repeated the predictions he had made to both Kitty and Mama. How a whole new city with thousands of inhabitants would rise up in those cornfields where broad and spacious streets would be lined with trees, and where the trolley lines would wend their way for miles and miles in all directions. He had been a builder of things all his life, and here in this place every last one of his building plans would come true.

He left the starry-eyed Hershey ladies, Mama and Kitty, and headed out into the late morning snowfall that had begun blanketing the February landscape. The first leg of his journey was by a carriage that took him down to the new plant site where the laborers were toiling away, and from there he made the late morning swing by Campbelltown to Brandt's Store. By lunchtime, he was back at Haefner's in Derry Church. He entertained the fellows gathered there with some excerpts from his Greiner School speech, and after lunch, he sauntered up the road to the home of his good friend, Dr. Martin Hershey. For some unknown reason, the carriage had returned to The Homestead, but Papa was a great walker so he made the journey afoot.

He did not mention that he hadn't been feeling too well in the days just previous to this visit, but Dr. Hershey made an express point of the matter. They spent the better part of an hour chatting after the doctor had examined him, but a real argument broke out when it came time for the elderly gentleman to leave. Old Henry Hershey was eager to be off, but Dr. Hershey spoke out against it, urging him to wait until his wife returned with the carriage. A chilling snowfall had begun, but the hard-headed freebooter would have none of the delay the proferred ride entailed. He was eager to be off, so he buttoned up his cutaway and headed out into the snowstorm.

"I told him to take it easy," said Dr. Martin Hershey later, "but he wouldn't listen. I'd have had to knock him down and hogtie him; you know how set he was once he'd made up his mind."

Henry made his way through the swirling snowfall and headed toward The Home-

stead. But he had only gone about two hundred yards down the road to where Derry Road intersects the Meadow Lane path to The Homestead, and there he began feeling faint. He stopped for a moment to catch his breath when Christopher Moyer came along in a spring wagon and spotted him. The old man looked up, and without complaining, accepted a lift back toward The Homestead.

When they reached the path at the end of the lane, he told Moyer to let him off, saying he could walk the rest of the way. Moyer, not knowing anything was wrong, let his passenger depart and resumed his journey. Papa Hershey disappeared into the midst of the white billows and made his way toward the boiler house at the condensing plant. He reached the building, but by that time he had begun to stagger. Then his legs gave way. Harry Tinney, who was inside fixing the fires for the night, spotted him. Just then, Albert Snavely, the timekeeper, came in and said, "Pap Hershey is outside, leaning against the building. I think he's sick. Help me bring him in."

Hoffer Bowman went out with Snavely as Tinney held open the door. In a subsequent account of the incident, Bowman had this to say.

"He was leaning against the corner of the building. His lips were getting blue." Then Bowman added, "He murmured something about his legs, like 'I'm perfectly paralyzed,' and that was all."

Those were Henry Hershey Hershey's last words. They laid him on a sofa and Hoffer Bowman went to phone Dr. Hershey, but in less than five minutes, the old gentleman had passed away.

The Harrisburg *Telegraph* of Saturday, February 20, made the following report:

> *Henry H. Hershey died of heart failure very suddenly at his home near Derry Church, on Thursday evening, at five o'clock. Deceased was born 78 years ago* at or near the place he died. He spent part of his life in Chicago, part in New York and Lancaster and was closely identified with his son and only child, Mr. Milton S. Hershey, in the manufacture of chocolate caramels and in accumulating a great amount of wealth. He was greatly interested in all kinds of agricultural experiments and developments and had a fine exhibit at the Middletown fair last summer. He is survived by one brother, Rev. Elias Hershey, a prominent minister in the Mennonite Church, residing near Lancaster, also by a wife, who was the only relative at his bedside when he died, for the son is in Florida and cannot reach home before today, after which arrangements will be made for the funeral.*

*Actually, it was seventy-five years.

Mama rushed to him the instant she heard he was ill. She walked around and around the sofa on which he lay, wringing her hands and moaning, "Oh, Pappy, Pappy, Pappy." But he could not hear and he made no reply.

*   *   *

Interment took place in God's Acre Cemetery beside the Hershey Meeting House on Tuesday of the following week. Son Milton, wife Fanny, and daughter-in-law Kitty were at the graveside and the Reverend Jacob S. Lehman from Chambersburg, a minister of the Reformed Mennonite Church, preached the final sermon.

Milton Hershey looked down at his father's grave and was heard to question, "I wonder if he's made up his mind about the future life?"

Throughout the entire ceremony the only surviving son of the man being interred stood off to one side and thought back over the years. He had always loved his father, but here, for the first time, something deep inside came back to remind him how very different, and yet how very much alike, he and his father had been.

Old "Pap" Hershey had been enchanted by the spell of new and different things all his life. But his kind of fascination was for most anything different; like the people who "fall in love with love, find they are playing the fool," Henry H. Hershey had fallen in love with anything different because it was different, and for that reason alone, he'd been called a fool.

And yet, by seeming accident, he'd set up trout hatcheries, designed cabinets, formulated cough drops, and planted alfalfa crops—beginnings which would either be credited to someone else or would come to fruition long after he'd gone. The first patent issued in son Milton's name had been based on designs worked out by Papa. And the farmers of the Lebanon Valley would be beholden to him for eons to come for the experimental alfalfa seedlings he'd brought back home with him from Colorado. Such "accidental" things were soon forgotten. His more voluble acquaintances would recall only the failed cough drops, the vending machines that didn't vend, and the perpetual motion machine that fell motionless when nobody pushed it.

Papa had been a rainbow chaser and in his works, he'd remained a loner. Whenever anything different in the way of an idea or an opportunity showed up, he chased it. He just never caught up with it.

Mama went home silently after the funeral and summoned Harry Tinney to The Homestead. She took him to Papa Hershey's rooms and directed him to begin crating and carrying the old books out to the boiler house. It took Tinney several trips, but he moved every one of them across the way in a wheelbarrow. When he arrived with the final load, Mama opened the flaming maw of the furnace and told him, "Throw them in." She meant to burn every last one of them.

According to Tinney, "She just stood there and didn't say anything." But anyone who had known Henry Hershey also knew that if he had been present, they would have heard his tearful voice crying, "Oh, Mama, Mama, Mama!"

Shadows

Her friends called her Fanny, and she had a lot of friends.

Perhaps the least understood and certainly one of the most prominent figures in the life of Milton Hershey was his mother, Veronica Buckwalter Snavely Hershey. Her self-effacing role finally becomes more understandable when the background of this plain and open-handed gentlewoman is brought into sharper focus.

She was the youngest daughter in the family of Abraham Snavely; consequently, her two brothers, Abraham and Benjamin, and her elder sister, Martha, had pretty well dominated her from infancy to maturity. She had the same strange antipathy for colors that she had for any sign of ostentation. In his childhood, Milton Hershey recalled her traditional Mennonite garb as being "mostly gray," and in her middle and declining years, she changed to black. Even her bonnet was black.

Although she had an innate love for the beauty of flowers and the tints of nature in springtime and autumn, she didn't cut or give flowers, except on very rare occasions, because she thought such acts were frivolous. In the late years of maidenhood, she was dependent on her older sister Martha (called Mattie) for her social contacts and for virtually every person she met, other than those of the tightly-knit congregation of the Reformed Mennonite Church near Pequea.

In the late 1850's, sister Mattie had been briefly courted by the Derry Township dandy who turned out to be none other than Henry Hershey. Although she was momentarily attracted to him, sister Mattie quickly disposed of HHH as a potential suitor. But she had no sooner told Henry Hershey to turn in his suit than she learned that he had instantly transferred his attentions to her young sister, Fanny.

Both the Snavely girls shared an early fascination for Henry Hershey. If the storied records of those days are to be believed, it was an attraction widely shared throughout the countryside by a great many folks, both male and female. The elder and more decisive Mattie had not only jettisoned the idea of a lasting relationship with Henry Hershey, but she also did her best to dissuade her younger sister from having anything whatsoever to do with the gadabout son of Jacob Hershey.

Fanny Buckwalter Snavely was at all times a polite and non-contentious listener. So it would seem that, despite the fact that her father, her brothers, and her sister had a good deal to say against her keeping company with Henry Hershey, they were hopelessly overmatched. He could talk, too. In fact, Henry Hershey could inundate anybody with a torrent of words the like of which they'd never heard.

Indeed, few of them had ever heard of anyone like H.H. Hershey.

So they were married. The time of personal trial for Veronica Buckwalter Snavely began with her January 15, 1856 wedding to Henry H., son of Jacob Hershey, at the Holy Trinity Lutheran Church in Lancaster. The young couple moved into The Hershey Homestead in Derry Church, and Henry had a go at tilling the ancestral acres. But from the outset it didn't seem as if he was spending enough time in the fields if he expected to get much out of them. So bride Fanny began to get nervous.

On the thirteenth of September in the following year of 1857, a son, Milton was born to the young Hershey couple. For a while, Henry stayed close to home and work, for little Milton appeared to have given him a new lease on life. With the arrival of her first-born, Fanny Hershey became just a touch more outspoken and less retiring than hitherto she had been. It has been said that with the birth of a first son some women are given a presentiment of something unique, some rare and unusual quality in the child that will fit him to do great things and to become a great person. In the almost forgotten words of Goethe, "The heart of God is gladdened when He beholds the light in a mother's eye—as she looks upon her firstborn child, for in this light He remembers His own."

For years the arrival of little Milton did much to assuage the peripatetic disturbances and the random disorders which marked her husband's shortfall attempts at wedded union. Her affection for baby Milton sustained her through the loss of tenure they suffered when the little family was forced to move from The Homestead and settle on a farm in Nine Points, with thanks due to Papa Abraham and her elder brother of the same name. She could not avoid accepting this act of charity, nor could she fight down the shame of having to accept it. Shy and plain though she was, Fanny Buckwalter Snavely Hershey was, in her way, a proud woman. She was beholden to God, and freely. But the thought of being dependent on someone else, no matter whom, to hold her family together and to feed her child, was so hateful that she could never find words to let off the steam boiling inside her.

Perhaps something of the same spur worked, but just momentarily, in her husband. For a while after they'd moved into the Nine Points farm, he bid fair to get something going with his combination trout farm and tree nursery. Then, in about the fifth year of their marriage, another child, a daughter, Sarena, was born. But once again a whole collage of disasters befell them.

The little child was far too frail at birth, and in the records that remain to spell out her brief odyssey, she was only ever identified as "a sickly child" throughout her short span of life. Despite this frailty and just when it seemed that Henry Hershey had gotten a grip on things at the Nine Points farm, he pulled up roots in the midst of the Civil War turmoil and bustled off to Titusville.

Nearly two years spent in the smoky, sere, and barren land of oil derricks and greasy smelling air, far from home and familiar folks, put more of a strain on Fanny Hershey's marriage than flesh could bear. And when they went back to Nine Points and her little girl died, that was it.

She had been too long watching her little boy getting uprooted from place after place, sent to school after school, and never being given the time to make childhood friends or to spin the memorable stuff that a meaningful life would be built on. She grieved no less for this living son at a tumultuous time of life than she did for the tiny waif, who had died before she really had had a chance to live.

But this Snavely was made of sterner stuff than most. She said nothing, but didn't quit. She returned to her roots and most of her family gathered about to help. Her husband, Henry, in the face of a need to do the small and obvious things, could not come up with an answer. He was an eagle, flying along uncharted paths across the sky, toward goals unseen by others, yet bright with the prospect of treasure and the promise of spectacular success.

Fanny B. Hershey

He sought, not to dwell, but to everlastingly *tread* upon untrodden ways.

So young Fanny and the Mennonite family Snavely gave home and guidance, finance and succor, to young Milton Hershey. All the while, Papa Henry was off again chasing the rainbows that could change it all. But they never did.

Down through the years, Henry Hershey would travel again and again to Lancaster, Chicago, Philadelphia, New Orleans and New York. He would come back to his little family wanting only to help them and to hang on, but he always wound up becoming an interloper and he always seemed to be hurting one after another of his young son's early ventures.

These interruptions were both trenchant and disturbing to Fanny Hershey because they kept dazzling the daring young eaglet who was emerging in her son Milton. It was Papa's disruptive influence that prompted their fledgling son to try his wings in Denver . . . in Chicago . . . in New Orleans . . . and on and on. Yet each of these abortive trials wound up on a record that began to look like a disastrous paper chase, because every time Papa Henry joined son Milton in business, they always left an agonizing trail of debt and failures behind them.

Insofar as parental guidance was concerned, young Milton Hershey had been given widely disparate goal posts. His Mama didn't ask much of life, but Papa, in turn, demanded everything of it. Yet even though Fanny Hershey never saw herself in the guise of a long suffering soul, she seemed predestined to be cast in the graying stone of selfless martyrdom. But she was no crybaby either, for she perceived her role in life very clearly, and she set out determined to play it to the hilt.

She reckoned she had been put on this earth to give of herself, so while she was here, she gave.

Most of the chroniclers who have studied the mother/son relationship of Fanny Hershey and her boy Milton have certainly conceded the physical help she contributed to his early enterprises. But there are also quite a few accounts of how much and how often she rallied around with the money to help fund his ventures. The source of this monetary input remains something of a mystery, although it has been established that Fanny Buckwalter Hershey was, in some part, an heiress and beneficiary who shared in Papa Abraham's estate. But that estate had been probated while Milton was still in apprenticeship training with Joseph Royer in Lancaster, and whatever cash had been distributed following Abraham Snavely's demise had been ostensibly shared by eldest son Abraham, elder daughter Martha, second son Benjamin, and then youngest daughter Fanny.

Following the customary practice of Mennonite landowners, son Abraham, being Fanny's eldest brother and Milton's uncle, held title to the farm properties left to the quartet of heirs, and he continued to work the land. Thereafter, young sister Fanny shared in the profits forthcoming from each year's farm income, and from time to time she prevailed on elder sister Martha for part of her share as well. She would also be asking time after time for part of brother Abe's savings. Sister Mattie, in later years, would take turns with Fanny Hershey in putting the bite on brother Abe.

The records are brim full of those transactions, especially during the decade between 1875 and 1885. But a lot of nickels and dimes fell between the cracks, and it is reasonable to conclude that when the oft-bitten and many-times-twice-shy Uncle Abe demurred or delayed in answering their requests, Mama Fanny filled in the spaces. There are literally dozens of accounts which relate how this stoical matron worked tirelessly in growing garden vegetables for market and how she slaved over washtubs and ironing boards to raise the pennies and nickels her young son needed to keep going. No accounts were kept and not one word ever passed the tightly closed and silent lips of the lady who came to give. When Milton called, she came; when he needed, she gave.

The accounts of this giving are not on the record, but the results of the getting are. Her efforts to keep her son going made a great many of his early ventures possible. But the loving and the giving and the silence which accompanied the early help she gave him were to disappear like verses written on the wind. Only the everlasting mystique, the *lovingkindness* of mother love, could ever explain that sort of thing.

To those who knew Fanny Hershey, and to those who were familiar with the way she helped her son get started and how she kept him going from the day he was born until the day she died, there remains still another mystery. Both on the record and off it, the lady is made to appear as though she knew only how to give, in silence, and that she opposed virtually nothing her son did, nor did she ever buck at the traces by either punishing him or criticizing him. Not so.

In later accounts of his childhood, Milton Hershey would ofttimes reflect on those bygone days when Mama had more than amply demonstrated that she neither intended to spare the rod, nor to spoil the child. He remembered the day when he had been confined to his bed at the Nine Points farm with a broken arm. On that occasion, Dr. Atlee from nearby Lancaster had been summoned to treat him, but the stubborn young

M.S. had locked and bolted the door to his room. He had a deadly fear of being sloshed full of castor oil, and broken arm notwithstanding, he reasoned that the doctor's appearance had automatically slated him for another dose of that awful stuff. Milton Hershey was nothing if not stubborn. Before they could take off the hinges to remove the door, he had leaped out of the second floor window, thus breaking his leg.

He was retrieved, carried back into the house, and suitably splinted, arm and leg. No castor oil. But he did receive a promise of proper treatment for his defiant and dangerous leap. Such treatment, and even the promise of it, faded and disappeared from his mind by late summer. Then one day, long after he was freed of his splints and was happily frolicking in the yard with some neighbor children, his Mama called him.

When he went to her, she looked at him with a strange and unfunny smile.

"You feeling pretty good?"

He said he was. If she had asked him five minutes later, the answer would have been different. In the meantime, he was reminded of the earlier window-leaping act of defiance and the promised treatment for the same. The promise was kept, assiduously, vigorously, and quite painfully, on a late summer afternoon when he was dutifully thrashed in the privacy of the kitchen.

Hershey later recalled only that the disciplinary event took place when the kitchen premises were unduly overheated by virtue of Mama's baking day routine. His memory of the incident was perpetuated by the sure and certain knowledge that the hottest buns in Mama's kitchen were not in the oven that day.

Comparatively though, those infrequent applications of the rod came nowhere near the pain he suffered when she read him out for other misdemeanors. To the last days of his life, he would recall the tongue-lashing she gave him when he was exiled from printer Ernst's conclave in his early teens. This became a programmed dissertation she continued to deliver several times a year for well over the next half century. He kept trying to get off the hook by telling her, "I'll never forget it." Neither did she.

When he said he'd rather take a good licking than to have her keep bringing up this sad event, she shook her head and told him, "The guilty party never gets to choose the punishment."

The steely resolve of this gentle lady was also demonstrated in the ways she retaliated against her errant spouse. This came despite the fact that she clung steadfastly to the tenets of her Reformed Mennonite faith. And yet, in the dozen or so years after they'd parted in New York in the middle 1880's, and following her return to Lancaster, she began sitting in the widow's pews of the Meeting House and she was subsequently known to have worn the gray bonnet denoting lady members whose husbands had died.

She even went a step further, although perhaps it was unwitting at the outset. This came about in the early 1890's when her name appeared in the church membership register as "Veronica Buckwalter Snavely Hershey, Widow of Henry Hershey Hershey, Derry Township." Perhaps she hadn't been instrumental in having her name listed that way to begin with, but thereafter, she also abstained from having it changed for the several years that followed when subsequent reprints of the register were published.

Fanny Hershey was rather unpredictable, too. Just about everybody who knew her stood back and waited for something akin to a Krakatoan eruption when they got news that Milton Hershey had married an Irish Catholic in a Catholic cathedral (St. Patrick's) in New York City. Without exception, and that included son Milton, everybody just knew that when Milton Hershey came home to Lancaster with his new bride, Mama Fanny was sure to blow her gray-bonneted lid.

But she didn't.

They were as far apart as the North and South Poles. No two women were more different than mother-in-law Fanny Hershey and daughter-in-law Catherine Elizabeth

Sweeney Hershey. The onlookers were divided about half and half insofar as the polar dissimilarity that could be applied to this relationship. Half of them expected a collision that would result in a hot flash of clashing temperaments. The other half expected a division in which the chill factor of each distant pole would be maintained and held sacrosanct.

Both persuasions were wrong. Perhaps Fanny Hershey was a trifle cool at their first meeting, but she had never been effusive toward anyone. To the credit of both, they were more than merely civil, and in subsequent years the effervescent warmth of Kitty was to some degree a disarming factor in their relationship. Fanny Hershey, without changing either her silent and stoical mien, nor by assuming a condescending acceptance of her daughter-in-law, showed something else. She had enough love, whether it came from the well-spring of her love for Milton or perhaps from the love she had for all her fellow creatures, she gave of herself to Kitty, too.

She was neither guileful nor cloyingly sweet, and she would continue calling her daughter-in-law "Catherine" for all the years they shared, but that idiosyncracy didn't amount to much. She seldom used effusive words in speaking; she relied more on the things she did, the little kindnesses she performed, to express herself. Somehow, the slight contradiction posed by her formal stance in calling Milton's bride "Catherine" instead of "Kitty" seemed to have been lost in the shuffle that had, for her, changed the name "Veronica" to "Fanny."

Perhaps the most puzzling factor in the personal chronicle of Fanny Hershey was the way she felt about her husband Henry. She had loved him, she had married him, and she had stuck with him throughout the dozen years in which so much had happened. She had borne him two children, and she had buried one of them. She had helped him start and keep up homes in Derry Church, in Lancaster's rural Nine Points, and in Titusville, and again back in Lancaster. She had seen him rise and fall, perennially and peripatetically, on a schedule she could neither predict nor comprehend. When she needed him most, he was seldom there.

Of all the variants in her life—The Homestead residency lost, the daughter lost, the failures of the oil fields, the rack and ruin that claimed the tree farm and the trout hatchery, and the increasingly threatening promise that her young son Milton would take after his gadabout and wastrel father—they all hurt her.

But even though one after the other of these debacles rolled over her, even though her son Milton kept adding another quarter of a century of failures to this early litany of defeat, she stood by him.

Her attitude toward life was that nothing was final. When death, debts and defeats beset her and her son, she picked herself (and him) up and she kept going. In later years, when success finally crowned her boy's efforts, she didn't see anything final in that either. She spent her entire life telling him to "take care," for nothing in this life was permanent. In fact, in the score of years following the turn of the century, when one after another resounding success came to her son, she came as close as she would ever come to being frightened.

She kept working until the last day of her life doing something, because she was persuaded that on this earth of worldly things, nothing was permanent. If anything, she treated affluence with a great deal more distrust and hesitancy than she had ever shown when things were rough and the cloak of livelihood was threadbare.

In her conviction that the life and times of mortals were fragile and fleeting things, she was, in a sense, much like her transient and highly mobile spouse. There was nothing permanent in either victory or defeat for him either.

Fanny Hershey came to give. Henry Hershey came to take. Between them, they struck a happy balance in their son, Milton. He was the fulcrum of their union, and for all the tempests and tribulations that befell them and ofttimes kept them apart down through the years, they met on common ground when they beheld their only son. In him, they were together—invisibly, silently, and yet unmistakably.

Even in the span of more than thirty years that kept Henry and Fanny Hershey apart, there wasn't a moment when love for their son wasn't first and foremost in their hearts. He was the blessed tie that even across vast distances bound them each to each.

In a way, Milton Hershey was the son of probably the two most misunderstood people in the bustling world around him. Most folks in those days thought they had good reason for being mystified by Henry Hershey. He talked too much, and they had trouble sorting out the substance of the real man from the sketchy, almost kaleidoscopic, image he projected. But most of them had even less to go on when they tried to understand the personality of the tall, slender, gently stoical, and usually silent Mennonite lady, Veronica Buckwalter Snavely Hershey.

They called her Fanny. And every time they called her, Fanny *came* and Fanny *gave*.

Secrets

The last ten years of the nineteenth century were known as "The Gay Nineties" for almost everyone else, but to Milton Hershey, they went into the book as the busiest and most rewarding period in his entire life. The proof of this can be found in his business and personal triumphs during this ten year span. But for all the notoriety commanded by the success and then the sale of his Lancaster Caramel Company, the beginnings of the Hershey Chocolate Company, his marriage to Catherine Sweeney, his acquisition of the Derry Church homestead, along with the retrieval of Papa from Colorado and the implementation of his Swiss guard staffing with the hiring of Messrs. Murrie, Snyder, Heilman, Ziegler, etc., the headlines for this time period show only the record of what happened, but not why or how.

The Gay Nineties covered the venturesome years between Milton Hershey's thirty-third and forty-second birthdays. It was so rife with activity and so filled with scrambling about that the reasons for the activities and the impetus behind all this geographic scrambling seem to have gotten lost in the shuffle. Consequently, many of the daily adventures and the motivating influences that worked on the man never found their way into print. But they did find a place in the memory of this bustling dynamo, who, although he never kept a diary and shied away from interviews, also happened to be one of those rare types of individuals who forget nothing and who turn out to be like those nostalgia-smitten oldsters who love to look back and talk about the past.

Graphically, the written accounts of this era are centered on Hershey's activities in the United States. They cover the jaunts and acquisitions that read like a railroad timetable and they show the events peculiar to expansionary moves in Mt. Joy, Reading, and Derry Church in Pennsylvania, in Chicago and Geneva in Illinois, as well as the financial arrangements made in New York City, and the one about a more than incidental romance that centered in Jamestown.

But no more than the kiss of brevity has been hitherto attached to some of the most significant adventures that were engendered by his trips to England and Switzerland. Despite the fact that these trips formed a major part of the things he loved to recount and reminisce about in later years, they fell into secrecy for two of the simplest of reasons.

The first reason was because most of these events weren't genuinely newsworthy. They weren't the kind of things that made headlines, for the most part. The second reason has to do with the other part—those things that may have been newsworthy, but which Milton Hershey just didn't want known.

His first overseas jaunt in 1892 was made ostensibly for mending fences and learning confectionery trade practices from his English customers, after which he went on to Switzerland to visit the home of his ancestors and to learn more about dairying and cheesemaking. As it turned out, the exposure to overseas confectionery trade practices happened to be a good deal more important than the things he learned, but at the time he merely stopped, looked, and listened to see what was going on in candy-making circles. Then he pushed on to the top target center of his dairying interests.

In England, he learned that his bulk caramels were being cut and dipped in chocolate and sold to a carriage trade clientele. When he entered the employ of the Swiss banker, who also happened to be a dairy farm owner, he took the job because he wanted to learn more about milk-handling and cheesemaking. But he wasn't on the job very long before he found that a great deal of the milk being produced in the cheesemaking center of the world wasn't going into cheese.

His follow-up studies soon revealed that milk was being condensed, evaporated, and also being used as whole milk by confectioners. The bulk solids were formulated in a variety of different ways for the Swiss, German, Austrian, and French confectioners, who were making milk chocolate coatings for nuts, cherry cordials, nougats, and all sorts of other exotic center confections.

But every one of the resultant products was a blue ribbon type, too, just like the English ones. To him, this meant they were not only intended for the upper-crust, i.e., carriage trade; it also meant they were expensive. And this meant they were too high priced for the kind of trade he commanded, the so-many-for-a-penny sweets sold to the kids in the school next door to his Lancaster plant. For that matter, it was the siblings and urchins who were buying up most of his stuff in America.

At the time, he made mental notes of these points, and they went into the memory bank of his mind as incidental facts he would file for later use. Before tucking them away, however, he noted something else.

In the family gatherings, the lawn parties, and other continental approximations of picnic get-togethers where the high-priced chocolate delicacies were served, there were children present. That interested him. So he watched the youngsters as they were favored with various offerings of chocolate-covered cherries in cordial syrup, as well as with chocolate-dipped nuts, fruits, toffees, caramels, nougats, et al. He noted that the kids certainly liked the chocolate delicacies, but then he saw something else.

Quite a few of the youngsters would greedily clutch a handful of the sweet rewards and head out of sight before chomping them down. So he followed the little gamins to watch their consumer reactions and thereby found himself in for a surprise. They weren't all chomping them down. Any number of them would duck behind a hedge or a concealing fold of drapery where they would lick or bite off the chocolate coating, and then they would spit out the center of the delicacy.

It was the center that made these exotic confections so expensive. That too-expensive part was too exotic for his kind of trade—the youngsters of America. But these kids liked the chocolate, and that was cheap.

Yet, in spite of this significant observance, he mentally noted it and filed it away for later use. He had come to Europe to learn the dairy trade and cheesemaking, so he went back to that.

In 1892, he had gone to his banker acquaintance's Berne dairy farm near Emmental, and there he'd hired out near the Hirschi ancestral diggings as a lay dairyman. He milked cows and he milked goats; then he followed the milk carts and the milk trains to the cities where the curds and the whey were so variously handled. But most of all he watched the workers and asked questions, and he kept marking things down in either his very small book or his very large memory.

His curiosity was drawn to the most popular of all the native cheeses, the Emmenthaler variety that bears the Swiss appellation of its national origin. This cheese was one of his favorites, too, but he also knew it was just about the most popular cheese in the whole world. He also began paying attention to another kind of cheese that seemed to be literally exploding into front-running popularity.

The other cheese that attracted his interest was the well-known Gruyere, but it was the second name associated with its type that fascinated him most. On the labels, it said "Gruyere Process" cheese, and he wanted to know more about the word "Process," if only because the samples he tasted were so good. On his days off, he began travelling about the countryside to nearby Berne, and then to distant Basle, Lucerne, Geneva, and he kept trying to get on the inside of several of those cheesemaking plants. But he maintained a center focus of interest in the native Swiss and Gruyere Process types.

He didn't find it easy. He may have looked Swiss, but he couldn't speak the patois of the natives and he found that, like him, these natives knew when they had a good thing, and they wanted to keep it secret. Nevertheless, he kept nosing around and, as he later related, he probably drank his weight in Swiss beer and cinnamon-flavored coffee, hanging around in bierstubes and coffee houses, trying to strike up a conversation with the workers and customers of the cheese plants.

Milton Hershey was in no way even a fledgling bench chemist, for he had virtually no training in the academic rudiments of the science. But he was an exceptionally intuitive, seat-of-the-pants cookbook chemist, if only because he was a card-holding genius in the field of applied common sense, and he had a memory that would make a computer bank blush.

His nosing around and tavern/coffee shop small talk gave him quite a handle on what he was proposing to do. But the kind of real knowledge he needed soon became apparent. He would have to get samples of the stuff he wanted to make, so that something beside his taste could tell him when he'd suitably made the match. If he was going to taste and compare his subsequent trial samples against the ideal standards of the Swiss originals, he would have to smuggle half of Switzerland out of Bremen by boat on his way home.

So, wishing to appear as plain as possible, one Friday evening when he finished working, he headed into town still wearing his boots and coveralls. Once there, he figured he would blend into the crowds as well as any other native, and then he could get the process bulk milk samples and the ideal cheese sample needed for subsequent chemical evaluation. He had paid the money for the samples on a previous visit to town, and all he required was the receipt, so that was all he carried with him. But he had overdone his attempt at anonymity to the point where he not only didn't blend into the weekend crowds, he positively shone forth from them.

In short, the stocky walrus-moustached American in the dung-stained, barn-smelling garb of a Swiss milkhand, sauntered into the custom delicacy food emporium and plunked down his receipt for fifty dollars' worth of purchases. The man behind the counter went off into a corner and talked to another man. Then the other man came back and told Hershey to wait a moment until his partner could go over to the warehouse to get the merchandise. Meantime, the clerk asked if he had any identification that squared with the name on the receipt he'd presented.

Hershey had none. All he'd brought with him was a handkerchief and a fistful of cigars, plus a few Swiss francs to cover the cost of a meal. He'd bought a round-trip railway ticket when he'd been to town on the previous weekend. All he had left was his return ticket to Emmental, which he intended using that very evening. Next day he intended going to Lucerne, but first he would have to go back to the farm to change.

But plans change, too, and the awaited clerk came back accompanied by a Bernese gendarme, and Milton Hershey found himself slated for a short trip to durance vile. All the Swiss parties were speciously polite, but they were also insistent to the point of obduracy concerning his lack of identity and his failure to communicate in their native tongue. So off went M.S. Hershey to the Bernese jail where he would be questioned, fed, and housed for the immediate future, or until such time as he could prove who he was and what he was doing showing receipts for foods he obviously couldn't afford.

He spent the better part of the next twenty-four hours proving that he was a highly vocal man who was also endowed with a fabulous quantum of temperament and temper. Interspersed with all the high-ranging, shrill protestations, he did manage to shout the name of his banker/host/employer, but he didn't come up with that part of the aria until the late hours of Friday night had dissolved into the wee hours of Saturday morning.

Later, on Saturday morning, he also learned that Bernese Swiss bankers with farms in Emmental don't come to work in Berne on Saturdays. They stay on their farms in Emmental. And errant Americans, heretofore engaged in studying milking methods, when picked up for lack of proper identification are then imprisoned.

It wasn't until late Saturday evening that word got back to the farm that the American confectionery tycoon had been arrested. His erstwhile host made all possible haste to set his guest free.

In later reminiscences about this episode, Milton Hershey made no mention of what became of the samples of milk process solids and Swiss cheese cultures, other than that they were returned to him. The entire event was recounted to several subsequent Hershey confidantes, but aside from the fact that he had gotten free and had been given the samples he purchased, he made no further mention of what became of those samples.

So this incident of M.S. Hershey's penal servitude remained variously secret in some aspects. The whole event and the fact of his having made an overnight stay in jail was never repeated within earshot of Mama Hershey. Every time he recounted the tale during her lifetime, he cautioned everyone never to let it get out, so Mama wouldn't hear about it. Much later, after Mama had died, he would still look around to make sure she wasn't there before he talked about it. Even then, he kept his voice down to a whisper.

The not-whispered, never-again-mentioned fact concerning those samples was something else. Nobody can say for sure what happened, but there were comparison samples at the condensing plant near The Homestead in the early 1900's, and there were Swiss cheese cultures known to be around The Homestead when Papa returned with Milton from Colorado in 1898.

On the face of it, if those returned samples were brought out of Switzerland after M.S. Hershey's release from the Berne brig, he had broken the law, whether he knew it or not. Chances are very good that he did bring those samples out of Switzerland with him. But he may have learned that the Swiss have age-old laws to prevent smuggling of precious cheese cultures out of their country only after the fact of his return. Then he shut up and stayed shut up.

Another of the behind-the-scenes secrets that emerged from this last decade of the nineteenth century was also connected with Hershey's interest in dairying. This episodial account took shape because of an assignment given Papa in the middle 1890's. In a literal sense, it tells the story of how Papa went to grass—and found it.

Somewhere along his rambling way, Milton Hershey learned that there was a very big difference in the flavor of the milk and cheese products that derived directly from the quality of nourishment given the animals that produced the milk. He learned about a very lush, short-bladed grass that was particularly high in nutrient quality, and it was also indigenous to a certain slope of the Rockies in Colorado. He reasoned that this kind of grass would be just the ticket for the goats and cows that would produce his new cheeses, and since Papa was already out in Colorado, he'd have him gather up the samples and bring them back.

But Papa demurred. He would not come back with the samples. He would, however, gather up the samples and send them on to son Milton. Quite some time passed in the haggling exchange that followed, but the whole thing wasn't clearly resolved until Milton decided to go out and bring Papa and the grass samples back with him.

As it turned out, Papa had been more than merely assiduous in his grass-gathering duties, and when Milton picked him up in Denver in 1898, they had both seedlings and sod divots in cartons as part of the baggage car freight they trundled back with them. Papa hadn't been too choosy. He latched onto just about anything green that he figured cows and goats would eat. So the seedlings and sod samples amounted to several kinds of grasses, clovers, and even some samples of stuff called alfalfa.

The upshot of all this should have gone aglimmering when the dream of cheese-making burst like a bubble. But it didn't. In fact, the one least likely sample, the alfalfa strain, took hold in the Swatara estuary to the point where it later became the most popular forage crop in the Lebanon Valley. Thereafter, it became one of the leading forage dollar crops not only in Dauphin County and the lush Lebanon Valley, but throughout most of the farm country of eastern Pennsylvania.

Henry Hershey had been sent for grass and came up with alfalfa, and he wound up going on record for having planted that particular type of alfalfa for the first time in Pennsylvania history. To this day, it is still the top forage crop for the dairies in the area. Every time the wind blows across the sunny green meadows of Lebanon Valley, it recalls the name of the man who flunked farming and lost his Homestead a hundred and twenty years ago.

The harvest came a little late for Henry Hershey, but when it came, it was a great big one, just as he had always said it would be.

Serendipity

The apparent aptitude of those who are able to make new discoveries accidentally.

A talent for "discovery" comes into play when someone sees something for the first time. On the other hand, the aptitude called "serendipity" emerges when someone recognizes *the importance* of something seen for the first time.

Serendipity began with fables about the Princes of the ancient realm of Serendip (i.e. Ceylon), because they were the legendary benefactors of the unplanned and unusual happenstances which they *caused*. Milton Hershey probably never heard the word but, as events were to prove, he was an heir apparent to the realm of Serendip. The facts in the case rest squarely on several of his better known capabilities. He was, first of all, a tireless practitioner of the trial and error method by which he was forever mixing, stirring, heating, cooling, and tasting so many confectionery recipes that they were almost beyond number.

On the other hand, he had other qualities going for him, too. He was positively pragmatic in the sense of being able to see (or taste) *what was there* when something new turned up in his experiments. Coupled with this, however, was the aptitude to see other potentials in the trial samples when something radically different appeared.

The experiments prompted by his obsessive curiosity and a hard-driven sense of urgency produced a great many trial results, erroneous or not. When the volume of those testing routines is added to the known fact that the man forgot nothing, the reason why his trial and error systems and his cookbook chemistry were so successful becomes easier to understand.

Success is a sure and certain guarantee for those who know what they are doing while they keep hammering away at an endless number of jobs.

Milton Hershey didn't have the scientific knowledge either to comprehend or to explain such terms as "amorphous" or "exotherms" or "centrifugal torque," but he made use of each phenomenon therein defined to the tune of equally phenomenal product sales and unprecedented volumes of consumer acceptance.

He kept finding unique formulas and techniques again and again, but that was because he *saw what was there and knew how to use it* whenever something new showed up in his trial and error tests. He left the business of finding a word for this aptitude to writers and other poor fools who would come along later and try to explain it.

*   *   *

At the beginning of the 1890's, something serendipitous happened in the Lancaster Caramel plant when a boiler room worker named John Brock had stuck his fingers in a bowl where they didn't belong. It happened at the time when Hershey's Crystal A Caramels had begun growing in popularity. The word of the day was "production," and the bustling Caramel King was endlessly and tirelessly cheering on his workers to get out more goods to meet the unprecedented demand. Hershey was in the plant before dawn every morning, long before his people arrived, where he busied himself setting up for the day's work. He was still there when the shades of evening fell, long after the last of the workers had gone home.

One summer day, Hershey took a respite from the grind and headed downtown on business. That was when John Brock sauntered away from his boiler room post and made his way into the adjacent room where the caramel cookers were bubbling away. He had read somewhere that a person could dip his hand in a basin of cold water and thereafter put his wet fingers into a boiling mass of cooking candy and withdraw a sample without getting burned. John Brock gritted his teeth, dipped his hand in the cold water, and reached into the boiling caramel. Then he picked up a smidgen of the bubbly stuff between thumb and forefinger and withdrew it. He didn't get burned.

He did it a couple more times and happened to be standing by the big kettle, rolling one of the cooled bits of hot caramel in his hand, when Hershey showed up unannounced.

But he was unannounced for only a moment. Then he became an interrogator.

"What are you doing in here?" was the question.

Brock's first response was a gulp, followed by an outstretched hand that featured two fingers sticky with caramel residue. The boss looked, blinked, and looked again. He'd seen thousands of fingers sticky with candy, but very few of them on the hands of boiler men, and never on the hand of a guy who was in charge of keeping the steam up.

John Brock had not kept up the steam in the boiler room where he belonged, but he had done a pretty good job of building up the pressure in his boss's kettle. Hershey blew his lid. But Brock didn't respond in the expected manner. Instead, he dipped his hand in the basin of cold water again and then put it into the hot caramel mass. As the wide-eyed Hershey watched him, he rolled the bit of hot stuff between his thumb and forefinger until it became a solid ball.

Hershey blinked several times. In the intervals between blinks, his eyes flashed bright and opened wide. Serendipity was working.

Thereafter, several things happened. First, Hershey dipped his hand in the basin of cold water and repeated the process John Brock had showed him. Then he waited until the little ball of caramel was cooled and rolled it on a piece of wrapping paper. He shook his head and smiled, whereupon he also nodded, with a look that was half adulatory, half congratulatory, and he went back to dipping and rolling.

Following a few repetitions of the routine, Hershey turned to his minion and told him, "This is great, John! You'll find something extra in your pay envelope for this at the end of the week." Then he followed Brock back into the boiler room. When he saw the steam was down, he raised hell with the boiler man again for having been away from his post.

On Saturday of that week (everybody worked six days a week then), John Brock didn't know whether he should expect extra money or a pink slip in his pay envelope. It contained neither. But he found a transfer notice that told him he had been promoted to another job where he would receive a hefty increase in weekly wages. His new station would be in the cooking room, some distance removed from the boiler room from which he had strayed.

The caramel-testing routine was more than a parlor trick. John Brock had read about it in a recipe book, and it was the discovery of a Lancaster housewife who cooked a lot of taffy for church socials. She had found this was the easiest way to test boiling taffy to see if it was ready to pull.

It worked the same with caramels. In caramel-making, it was known as "the crack," and it represented the point at which the mass of boiling stuff in five hundred and thousand gallon cookers could be tested to see exactly when it was ready to be removed from the heat. It was precisely what Hershey needed to gauge when caramels were sufficiently cooked and ready to pour, roll, cut, or whatever. In a sense, it was a simple testing routine that preceded the advent of the sophisticated thermal and density testing devices of today.

But until the technical hardware to measure the "crack" in caramels came along, Milton Hershey had stolen a march on the competition by speeding up production with this simple test, a test that came about because of a boiler room employee's curiosity, a Lancaster housewife's taffy trick, and Milton Hershey's serendipity.

Together, they came up with the "crack" that put the magic in Crystal A Caramel production.

Probably the most portentous example of Hershey's serendipity came in 1902, and it took place in the new condensing plant that had been built near The Homestead at Derry Church. He was, at that time, equally attentive to the new project he had undertaken to develop a new kind of milk chocolate, and he was still fascinated by the prospect of becoming a dairy magnate and cheesemaker.

Daily he would come over from Lancaster by horsedrawn buggy and at such an early hour of the morning that he could get neither a driver nor his wife Kitty to accompany him. Sometimes he would stay over at The Homestead, but that had become a bit of a problem because both Mama (who had taken up residence there) and Papa were on the premises, at opposite ends of the rambling structure.

They would share supper together, and this made Milton Hershey very happy. But when the dishes were cleared, Mama and Papa would withdraw to their separate quarters, and he was left hanging in between. In the balance, so to speak. If he visited one of them separately after hours, one minute longer spent with either of them drew fire from the other one. He couldn't handle this kind of tug-of-war arrangement; in fact, he said, "I felt like a rope, and in a tug-of-war, the rope never wins."

Nevertheless, he was in the new milk condensing plant from before dawn until long after dark for days, weeks, and months, cooking, evaporating, boiling and testing sample after sample of milk. But the tests were still aimed at two targets: first, the milk solids for process cheese, butter and ice cream, and second, the development of a milk base for milk chocolate. Virtually all the equipment and a good bit of the technology had been set up according to the practices Hershey had learned in Switzerland and Bavaria.

By this time, Hershey had discontinued the trials of whole milk and whole cream as the basic ingredients he was testing in open kettles with John Schmalbach handling the cookers in Lancaster. Over at the condensing plant, a former neighbor, Addison B. Grubb, later recalled, "I'd see Milton Hershey every morning, sloshing around in hip boots as he walked into the creamery plant. We lived right across the road from him then. He would go up to the second floor and put up a 'No Admittance' sign, and he'd stay there for hours. Sometimes he'd stay throughout the night and part of the following day, working away on his experiments. He didn't even come out for meals."

A man named McWilliams was in charge of the condensing plant at that time, and Bill Pierce, a Tennessean, was the mechanic. Milton Hershey's young cousin, Monroe, was there, too, and so was Hoffer Bowman, the man who was nominally in charge of the place. As Addison Grubb recalled it, "Hoffer Bowman had an awful time of it. One day the Old Man would come over and have him make butter, but he was just as likely to ask Hoffer to make cheese samples, chocolate milk, or anything else that came into his mind. And Bowman always came up with it."

Quite a lot of ideas occurred to Milton Hershey, but for all the output of strange and different samples that emerged from the experimental building, the most important one never passed through Bowman's hands, and when Hershey found out about it, he didn't even have a name for it.

Before the mysterious new sample came to light, it is necessary to go back about six months, to begin marking the trail of another shadowy figure from backstage in the Hershey drama.

The story begins with a stone mason from Hummelstown named Tinney. This particular gentleman had come down to the quarry site one summer morning on business, and he'd brought along his young son, Harry. The elder Tinney knew the folks at The Homestead, so the father and son stopped in for a visit when Milton Hershey just happened to drop in from the condensing plant. After exchanging pleasantries with the elder Tinney, Hershey turned to young Harry and asked him what he intended to do in life.

"I'd like to work here, Mr. Hershey," said the youngster. "I'd like to work for you."

Hershey smiled. "We need young boys," he said, "and I especially favor boys from the farm."

Young Tinney said he didn't want to be a farmer, and Hershey asked him why not. "I'm afraid of mules."

Hershey looked down at him and said, "Me, too," but he was smiling. Then he went on, "We need a boy in the creamery. How'd you like that?"

"I'd like it," came Tinney's prompt response.

"Okay, young man," replied Hershey. "You come around at five, Monday morning. The young man asked, "At five, Mr. Hershey?"

"Yep," said the boss. "That's when you start, of course. If you want to come over for breakfast, be here at The Homestead at four."

The Tinneys thanked him and departed, but on the half-hour ride back to Hummelstown, young Harry had a feeling that he wouldn't be very hungry at three-thirty in the morning when he'd have to get up for work. Later he would change his mind about that. In fact, later Harry Tinney would change a lot of things in addition to his mind.

He started out by running around doing everything he was told to do. Thereafter, he ran engines, he carried coal, he helped put in the heating system, and by the end of the year they had him working in the condensing plant.

The first of the condensing plant jobs came at the experimental shop at The Homestead. But by the fall of 1904, another condensing plant had been set up at the factory, so he was transferred. Referring to The Homestead and the new milk condensing plant, Harry Tinney had this to say almost fifty years later.

"You never saw such a busy place. And you never saw such busy people."

Fanny Hershey had set up permanent quarters there. She and Milton's Aunt Barbara were running the kitchen. These women were helped by local ladies, Mamie Goodman and Annie Wentling, who came in to cook for the farm workers managed by George "Toony" Horstick. But there were also crews of men from the boiler rooms and from the creamery. In all, there were a half-dozen women scurrying around to feed a crew of twenty or thirty men. For the women, the workdays began at four-thirty a.m., and they weren't finished until after the sun went down. The men had a comparatively easy time of it; they worked only fourteen to sixteen hours a day.

But Milton Hershey was at work before anyone, male or female, showed up. And he was still there, alone, when the last of them had gone. Each day, a load of one-half to a full ton of whole milk was poured through the condensers, and every day one or more new ways of cooking off (evaporating and/or condensing) was tried. Hershey was relentlessly trying to find the ideal way to process milk solids so they would remain stable. Part of his aim was toward his cheesemaking ambitions, but by this time he was also searching for a milk base that wouldn't turn rancid or streak his chocolate when temperatures changed.

In later years, Tinney remembered solid weeks on end when Milton Hershey worked almost around the clock, day in and day out, pushing an endless stream of sample runs through the condensers.

"But only he knew what he was looking for," said Tinney. Then the oldtime worker remembered something else.

"One week I shall never forget," he said. "There was something I wanted to do on a Sunday coming up, but I knew better than to ask for the day off. Then I heard the boss making plans to take his young wife to a picnic that Sunday, so I decided to take the day off and say nothing about it.

"Well, that's what I did. Of course, the milk came in and stood around all day Sunday, so I didn't even go to bed that evening. I went straight to the plant and started working before the boss got back. And even though he showed up about four Monday morning, I'd already started putting the stuff through the condensers, so he just kept himself busy. But all the time I knew he was watching me.

"It was no use. The stuff had gone bad sitting around all day and I knew the Old Man could smell it. Then he turned to me and started ripping me out from top to bottom. He was so mad that at first I thought he was going to fire me, but he was even too hot to do that.

"He didn't fire me," Tinney recalled, "but before he was through with me, I began to fear for my life. I'll bet they heard him over at The Homestead, a quarter mile away. I don't remember how long he lashed me out, but I do know one thing—I never took another day off without his say-so."

Hoffer Bowman also recalled the endless experiments that Hershey had been running in 1903. He remembered the time when cocoa butter was added to the boiling milk base, but that failed because it scorched the pans. They tried adding warm cocoa, but that failed, too, because even the slightest trace of acid in the cocoa would curdle whole milk. But, as they later learned, that was inevitable because the cocoa had a trace of cocoa butter in it, and cocoa butter is a collage of fatty acids.

Late in 1904, a glimmer of light began to show through the experiments, and that, too, came as the consequence of Harry Tinney's errant work. One day, he asked Hershey whether it might not be a good idea to boil the milk more slowly so it could be brought to a higher temperature with the vacuum reduced. At first, Hershey demurred, saying that this would only corrode the kettle. He walked away, but Tinney could tell that he was still thinking about the suggestion. In a few minutes he came back.

"Try it anyway," he told Tinney.

The sample turned out better than any previous ones, and the old Hershey serendipity showed up again. He knew *something different* had happened, but he didn't know what. But he did know what to do about it. He immediately decided to hire a chemist who would understand what was going on, and then he decided to hedge his bet and call in John Schmalbach from the Lancaster plant. John was neither a chemist, nor did he know very much about chocolate, but he was a wizard in caramel-making, and especially in making caramels with a milk base.

With such expert help on hand, Harry Tinney and George Horstick, who was by that time also working in the condensing plant, just stood by and watched the man of science and the caramel whiz go to work. They also watched them burn the first several samples they put through, and they continued watching while Milton Hershey kept running back and forth to get more and more fresh supplies of milk. That was not only the way they spent the rest of that day, but also the way they spent the two-day weekend that followed.

At last they came up with a batch of some stuff that was more acceptable. It wasn't the ideal base that Hershey wanted; it was a bit too lumpy for that. But it was better than anything they'd yet tried, and most of the lumpiness, but not all, could be worked out in the mixers. In any case, it didn't turn rancid and it wouldn't discolor at the slightest change in temperature.

Several years passed before Horstick and Tinney found themselves working together again in the condensing plant where they could have another go at it on their own. They fiddled around and decided to do a bit of reversing. They started out with a low vacuum and a high temperature; then somewhere beyond midpoint they reversed the procedure, switching to a higher vacuum and a lower temperature. The trick to the procedure, as it turned out, was to find just the right time to make the switch. By some form of intuition, they found it. They knew neither what happened chemically, nor why, but they did know a few things. They knew that the process was faster. Former batches, including the lumpier stuff then being used in production, took from three to four hours to process. This new method took between a half hour and an hour to complete. They also found that the chocolate made from the new process was tastier. Of course, with the cut in running time, the resultant chocolate would be cheaper to produce.

"Better, faster, and cheaper," M.S. Hershey mused, when he saw the end product that resulted from their efforts, adding, "That's not a bad combination."

But he kept toying with the new method. In the meantime, however, he'd made both Tinney and Horstick the top foremen in charge of two shifts working at the condensing plant. Yet, from the day he saw what they'd done and long after the process was put into use in the production line, he would not only toy with the phenomenal thing that happened within the new process, he would continue repeating a question in his mind.

"Something happens," he would say. "Something inside that stuff being cooked and pressurized in there—just seems to make it get hotter all by itself. Yet it doesn't burn. Yep, something happens—I don't know what it is, but it gives us what we want. It works. And that's all that counts."

Milton Hershey didn't have a name for what happened, but he knew how to use it.

In later years, the highly sophisticated chemical labs of Hershey Foods came under the directional aegis of Elwood W. Meyers. He had this to say about the remarkable breakthrough that Mssrs. Tinney, Horstick, and Hershey had found.

"The phenomenal change they'd found was the result of what we call an 'exothermal reaction,'" said Meyers. "This means simply that sometime, following the application of alternates of both heat and vacuum pressures, the mixture reached a point where it began making and giving off some heat of its own."

He went on to explain that exothermal change made the mixture hotter, but that it didn't burn because the heat was coming from within the mass. Extra heat wasn't being applied to it.

Back in those days, chemists had devised means of applying heat two ways—by coils within the condensing tanks, as well as the heated shells and bottoms on the outside of the kettles. But that wasn't the same thing. By knowing just when to do two things—when to switch the high/lows of heat and vacuums at the midpoint in cooking and when to stop cooking—those were the determinant factors.

Thereafter, once the mixture had been removed from the heat and vacuumization cycle, it would set up in literally the same way it happens to folks who make the better kinds of fudge at home. The so-called exothermal reaction describes the extra heat that is produced within the mixture after it has been removed from the heat source. It is the consequence of the chemical interaction that takes place within the mixture itself, and it is the same thing that happens before fudge sets up and thereafter makes it stiff enough to cut into squares.

The whole new production routine, however, was based on a timing factor much like the"caramel crack" that had shown up for John Brock at the Lancaster Caramel Company plant years earlier.

The word "exotherm" was unknown to Harry Tinney, George Horstick, and Milton Hershey. But *serendipity*, theirs and his, told them that *this* was *what* they were looking for, and they knew *how* to *use* it. When they used it to turn out a new kind of milk chocolate with the name Hershey on it, the combination of better, faster, and cheaper proved to be just what a lot of people were waiting for.

*　　*　　*

Quite a few years would pass and Milton Hershey would be well into his middle years before another man, named Bill Hibschman, would come along and serve up another ball for his serendipity batting practice. But the groundwork was laid for Hibschman's contribution before his arrival, and it all started with a "kiss." The one that turned out to be the *Hershey Kiss*.

Milton Hershey had started out by considering the youngsters of the world as his prime market from the time they were swaddling clothed siblings until they were short-panted or knickerbockered young ones. From the very beginning, he sought to please the little people with the tidbits they could buy so-many-for-a-penny. But he also had a flair for the dramatic, particularly in packaging, as witness the five and six colors of birds, flowers, et al., which festooned his early caramels and taffies.

This double-edged ambition was realized when he came up with the tiny, round-bottomed bits of milk chocolate called *"Kisses."* The silver paper wrap was certainly dramatic, and the portions were small enough so they could be sold several for a penny. The hooker in this whole scheme, however, was the fact that it cost as much to wrap these things, the cost of the silver paper aside, as it cost to produce the contents, because they were hand-wrapped. The fact that M.S. wanted every one of them to contain a bit of tissue with the Hershey name on it made the cost even higher.

But how could you make a machine to wrap something that was round at the bottom and pointed at the top? *Hershey's Kisses* were modestly popular from the outset, even though they cost him more to package and sell than anything else in the line. He made up his mind early—one day he would do something about that, too.

But the years came and went, and he was so busy doing other things that the problem was set aside until he had passed fifty years of age. By that time, Bill Hibschman had come aboard and so had a pair of fledgling brothers named Phillippy.

Nevertheless, all three men were aboard when another Hershey package was launched. It had to do with the squares of smaller chocolate bars, and then the rectangles, which ultimately led to the development of *Hershey's Miniatures*. The current requirement was to put out little squares of chocolate that could be machine-wrapped. The name, or names, of the designers of the prototype wrapper-cutting machine are lost to history, as is the exact date and time of the first model trials. Records of these first trials carry several notes which attest to the fact that the machine failed.

Along with the machine shop and testing room reports came a story about why it had failed. Someone noted that the cutters, which pushed up through the bottom of the silver paper along the line of chocolate squares to be wrapped, had torque-twisted the squares so much that they were crumpled and the top of the fold-over operation had also been twisted by torque.

In the Milton Hershey view, that wasn't all that had been twisted. Of torque, he knew nothing, but he had seen something else. He was keenly aware of the twisting motion used by the girls, and even his own Mama, when they wrapped *Kisses*. So he told Hibschman and his henchmen to modify the machine so it would work on the round bottoms of *Kisses*, adding, "And don't forget, you gotta put a tissue-tape in there, too. We want our name on them, just like the hand-wrapped ones."

The whole demand and the very assignment itself were, of course, impossible. Nevertheless, it took less than three months until they had the idea worked out, and less than a year before they had machine-wrapped *Kisses* in full production.

Once again, the Princes of Serendip had smiled on Milton Hershey, but that came along much later, long after he had passed middle age. But the time of his "crossing of the bar" from his years as a young man into those middle years was not too hard to pinpoint.

He had reached that moment on Tuesday, February 23, in 1903, at a place called God's Acre Cemetery, alongside the Hershey Meeting House. The family had gathered there to hear the Reformed Mennonite Minister, Reverend Jacob S. Lehman, from Chambersburg, deliver the funeral sermon at the graveside of Henry Hershey Hershey, Milton's Papa.

Serendipity—yes, Papa certainly had had it. But Papa had been a freebooter and in his works, he'd remained a loner. Whenever anything different in the way of an idea or an opportunity showed up, he chased it. He just never caught any of them. And there at his graveside, Milton Hershey realized why.

Papa had always walked alone. Save for one person.

Somewhere along the line, Milton Hershey, after he and his father had parted ways, learned about his own magical touch in a thing called serendipity. He never learned the word or, at least, he never used it, but he did have the aptitude itself. And he knew that his particular capability had to do with *people*. By seeming accident, he had the aptitude for picking just the right person to do the right thing at the right time.

So one of the latter-day Princes of Serendip had died and another survived.

Milton Hershey turned from the graveside vigil with tears in his eyes and a sensation of loss in his heart. He had come here to say goodbye to the one person in all this world with whom he had been able to share his wildest schemes and the exhila-

ration of fanciful flights into the unknown that endlessly beckoned to both of them.

He had come here to bury his beloved Papa. But he walked away from the grave with the awful feeling that the days when he had been known as *the young* Milton Hershey had come to an end in this place, too.

End of Part One

PART TWO

A Man Still Growing

Chapter VIII

⌣·⌣

A Man and His Dreams

When 1905 rolled around, Milton Hershey found himself knee deep in plans for a new factory, a new string of dairy farms, and a whole new product line; he also found himself on the threshold of building a new town. And that was something else.

The town would need streets, and it would need buildings. The streets would be traversed not only by wagons and autos, but by trolleys, too. The building plans would not only be for the places where people would work, but there would also have to be structural plans for the places where they lived, where they shopped for clothing and groceries, where they would be schooled and entertained, and where they could be afforded every sort of service, as well as leisure time and relaxation.

To him this meant classrooms; and it meant libraries, workshops, offices, meat markets, mansions, bungalows and cottages, and it would also mean drug stores, parks and theaters, playing fields, and dance halls. Of course, there would be restaurants and barber shops and hospitals and doctors' offices. All the things that big towns with lots of people had, his small town with somewhat fewer people would have, too. Only one difference—everything in *his town* had to be *better*.

Because this town was going to be built for *his people*.

He stood on this threshold in the early twentieth century and he thought about it. His new plant had opened, the streets for the new town and the trolley lines were being laid out. The Homestead had been remodeled and a new High Point Mansion was being readied for his bride, and now he would have to get down to the real business at hand.

He knew that the town he would build would one day be the hometown of hundreds and then thousands of people. It would be a dwelling place for mothers and fathers, sisters and brothers, friends and lovers, wives and husbands, and there would be children. So many children. A great many of them would be born here, or be brought here, to grow up in the place where he'd been born. He hadn't been able to grow up here, but he'd change all that for the ones coming along. They'd have a hometown the like of which they'd never have to leave. If he did it *right*, it would be the kind of place they'd never *want* to leave.

The man and his works and his dreams would all come together in this place. But he would be gone before the whole dream would be realized. It would await the approbation of millions of people who were not yet born on the day he started breaking ground for the place he intended to become "a nice hometown for the people who will live and work here."

He wanted to do something different. In the years to come, the people who lived and worked together in this place would, in a sense, make a part of his dream come true. By fashioning a pleasant model community that visitors from all over began calling Chocolatetown, U.S.A., he would be pleased in his old age. Yet he had set out to do more than that.

The way Milton Hershey figured, it was based on something he remembered from his childhood. He never had lived in a place he could call his hometown, but that would not happen to the boys who would grow up in the town he intended to name after his father. Henry H. Hershey, the man, *had been different.*

Hershey, the town, *would be different.*

Cornfield to Camelot

By the spring of 1905, "the factory in a cornfield" at Derry Church was operational and M.S. Hershey found himself busier than ever. It proved to be a time in which he spent a great many hours trying to live up to the headlines he had generated by selling out the Lancaster Caramel Company to the American Caramel Company for the much publicized million dollar check.

The point that bothered him, however, was not how to spend judiciously that million dollars because, stated simply, he didn't have a million dollars to spend. On the record, the capital amount of the transaction for the sale of the Lancaster Caramel Company had been one million dollars, but the actual cash in hand was something else again. And the turnover of the Lancaster Caramel Company was a matter of transferring funds from one company to another rather than an outright sale.

In effect, the entire transaction was more in the nature of a banking arrangement whereby an approximate fund of one million dollars was made available to the new American Caramel Company, and part of this capital fund (somewhere between $400,000 and $500,000) was made payable to Milton Hershey in cash. The balance went into the coffers of the American Caramel Company, but these monies were earmarked as "loans, in lieu of stock equities," in the name of Milton S. Hershey. Thus, he became either a major stockholder or the holder of a substantial first mortgage on the very company he was supposed to have sold.

Consequently, it isn't hard to understand why his burgeoning Hershey Chocolate Company, at first in Lancaster and Philadelphia, and later in Derry Church, was given favored treatment as sole supplier of coating chocolate for the American Caramel Company. Later this brought something else into sharper focus when he began running short of money after the move to Derry Church.

Just before the turn of the century, when he started buying up the Derry Church properties, beginning with The Homestead, and breaking ground for his new ventures, the nominal $400,000 in cash on hand had seemed sufficient. But at that time he was still primarily concerned with dairy and cheesemaking ventures on the site of his ancestral diggings. Then, at a time contingent to the turn of the century, several things happened to upset his ordered priorities.

First, he hadn't made anywhere near the expected progress in the dairying venture, and especially in developing a made-in-America version of Swiss cheese, or in the perfection of a domestic brand of process cheese.

Yet while his gears were slipping in the dairying ventures, the chocolate business, both in America and in England, began to expand in grand style. At first, this new boom in coating chocolate was directly tied to the caramel business, because the Empire outfit in England and the caramel company in America had been dipping more and more of their caramel confections in his coating chocolate.

It wasn't long before he realized that the small chocolate plants in Lancaster and Philadelphia couldn't handle the growing demands. There was no alternative. He simply had to build a much bigger and more modern plant, and this brought him to the problem of where to build it. He was drowning in orders for coating chocolate, and since the Lancaster plant was situated right next to the caramel company, its biggest customer, this site was his first choice. Then he got the feeling that the Lancaster people were playing games with him, and he began to look elsewhere. He dismissed Mt. Joy as a logical choice because the factory site was too remote. Then he ticked off Reading because every place he had started there kept burning down.

By 1901, he was continuing to buy up properties in the Derry Church area, and the cash on hand began looking rather thin. The Lancaster plant of Hershey Chocolate piled up a $622,000 business volume in 1901, but even the couple hundred thousand dollar profits from this, when added to the approximate $400,000 of ready cash from the Lancaster Caramel plant sale, would not be enough.

He had set up another combination of showcase manufacturing and import ware-house for German chocolate-making equipment and Caribbean supplies on Chestnut Street in Philadelphia, but he didn't want to get into the high costs of big city real estate and slide rule taxes he couldn't control. Nevertheless, he had to make a move, and he realized that the cash on hand, about three-quarters of a million, was not sufficient to the need. He knew by this time that his upcoming plans would call for something closer to three or four million, and even with the holdover equity of something more than a half million he still held in the American Caramel Company stocks, the cash on hand was not enough.

But somehow, whether by intuition or luck, he had already taken care of that by the way in which he had arranged for the disposition of the Caramel Company in Lancaster and the funding needs he expected would attend the Hershey Chocolate Company in Lancaster, and later at Derry Church. The whole thing had been handled by the Importers and Traders Bank of New York, which had previously arranged credits of a quarter million in 1891 and a half million in 1895 for him. So the capital sum of the transfer had been *their* investment of one million dollars from the start. In the interim since 1897, that capital funding had been substantially reduced, and by 1903, both parties, American Caramel and Hershey Chocolate, were booming and both of them needed new capitalization to go their separate, if companionably joined, ways.

Nowhere has any written record of the precise transaction come to light, but the mystique is somewhat diminished by the actual events which did transpire and did become part of the published record. First, of course, the building programs and the equipment purchases for the Derry Church enterprise went on uninterrupted, at full clip. The American Caramel Company's string of payoffs to liquidate its notes and/or stock reservations had cleared the books by 1907, and the re-equipment of both booming plants went ahead at a pace that seemed to indicate that all the concerned parties had been blessed with "keys to the mint."

They hadn't, of course, but the facts concerned with what did transpire are even more mysterious. Going back in search of records no longer in existence is no help; in fact, it would be easier to unscramble an eighty year old omelet. Yet the rising tide of bank financing that began at a level of a quarter million dollars in 1892 and crested at a figure of fifty million dollars in the early 1920's does provide at least part of the answer. A "key to the mint," in this light, becomes a more reasonable metaphor when compared with the actual dimensions of what must have happened. It is anybody's guess, but the best guessers attribute this funding sleight-of-hand to the solid banking connections Milton Hershey had established in the early 1890's, which he thereafter expanded, honored, and continued to expand during all the years that followed.

There was one flurry of correspondence between lawyer John Snyder and the executive board of the American Caramel Company between 1905 and 1907 that sheds some light on the dollar-juggling routine then in progress. One of the letters carried an American Caramel Company complaint that M.S. had breached his agreement with them "by selling his American Caramel stock elsewhere." This meant that he hadn't sold it back to them. But according to another account, M.S. had offered the stock to the Lancaster outfit several times, but they had not responded.

Having made the offer and in the face of mounting expenses for new buildings, new equipment, and the new properties upon which he would construct a town complete with a street railway stystem, he was, to say the least, somewhat short of cash. In the interim between 1898 and 1903, his liquid assets from the caramel company sale amounted to less than a half million dollars. Yet, within that time frame, the record shows that he spent more than a million, and between 1904 and 1907, he either laid out or went on the cuff for several more millions of dollars.

When a recapitulation is made of the expenses incurred during that period, a million dollars doesn't seem like much. There were land purchases of more than 1,000 acres, along with a right-of-way purchase for the Hummelstown-Palmyra Street Railway Company, and the factory and creamery/condenser buildings at the new plant.

By 1905, there were more than six hundred men working at various jobs, either in the plant or on the new buildings going up, and Hershey had plans for a village that would both employ and house fifteen hundred workers. Of this original work force, there were several hundreds of carpenters, stone masons, plasterers, electricians, plumbers, and general laborers working on factory buildings, the mansion home site, as well as the streets that would be named Areba, Trinidad, Caracas, Ceylon, Para, et al. The main intersection of the new town, however, would come where the main street, Chocolate Avenue, crossed the north-south avenue, called Cocoa.

New railway sidings had gone up along the P & R tracks and the tonnages of chocolate going out were frequently surpassed by the tonnages of sugar, equipment, flavorings, and machinery coming in. By 1907, the total dollar investment in the fifteen hundred acres, the scores of buildings, plus the newly completed mansion, the tons of heavy equipment and the trolleys, power plants and rights-of-way peculiar to the street railway company, and a hefty payroll that had by then passed one thousand workers stacked up to a total investment that was uncomfortably close to two million dollars.

Hershey had originally come to the place with less than a half million in ready cash, and he'd liquidated his American Caramel holdings, by whatever means, for approximately another half million. But by the time the Hershey Trust Company was opened in 1905, he had close to a million dollars on hand to start that venture, having spent in excess of another million along the way. He had certainly recouped some of his money from the booming sales of the Hershey Chocolate Company as he went along, in Lancaster and in Philadelphia. But those plants, boom or no, were in a constant state of turmoil, caused by the almost weekly arrivals of heavy equipment from Germany, from Lebanon Steel, from Bethlehem Steel, and from Textile Machine Works in nearby Reading. There was even a heavy-duty importation of printing equipment for labels during this period, and yet all the time production kept going up and up. Even as machinery was erected, product lines and packaging systems were constantly being changed.

How did he do it? Ask a hundred people and get a hundred different answers. Only the financial records, at first kept by lawyer John Snyder and later consigned to a confidentiality shared only by Ezra Hershey and Harry Lebkicher, could show that. But, like the men who were in charge of them, the records too are gone.

It was perhaps inevitable that some pundit would come along later and suggest that the heavy purchases made in printing equipment may have had something to do with that, thus suggesting that maybe money was being printed, but that explanation fails in the light of the real need for labels as labels. For, beginning with the advent of *Hershey's Milk Chocolate*, this factory in a cornfield could turn out labelled merchandise for faster sale and at a better margin of profit than could have been realized had they been printing money. And among kids, the milk chocolate bars were much preferred to the pennies, nickels, and dimes they exchanged for them.

Somewhere in the background, an unidentified source had been tapped for a capital sum that amounted to at least one million dollars, and more likely two or three million. Even in those days, it would have taken more than a million to build up a plant and a town with fifteen hundred workers, a street railway company, a mansion, a cluster of five or six dairy farms, along with all the other appurtenances a community required for anything less than five million dollars. But just a couple years later, the place had not only doubled in size, but had added a park, a zoo, school buildings, and a department store. By then it was worth twice as much again, and it also had a clutch on property values and capital stock holdings that were worth several additional million.

How much? Who knows?

Among the men who knew, there were three certainly, and possibly four, besides Milton Hershey himself. The first, of course, was lawyer John Snyder because he made the necessary paper arrangements for deeds, stock transfers, loans, etc. Then, too, there was Ezra Hershey, M.S.'s cousin, who handled the actual banking and accounting. And, of course, there was "Lebbie," Harry Lebkicher, the guy who "came along to see what you're doing with my money."

Snyder had "read" the law, never gone to college. Ezra and Lebbie, like M.S., had been schooled either slightly or indifferently to a level approximating grammar school. But among them, they set a new standard for keeping an eye on the buck that was excelled only by one other trait: *keeping a secret.*

Thus the legend of a factory in a cornfield became a royal fiefdom in those sequestered Derry vales. But, like ancient Camelot, who is to say how it came about?

The Builder and the Buildings

The score of carpenters working on the new chocolate plant under general superintendent William Flick were putting the finishing touches on the first phase of their jobs by late fall of 1903. By midwinter, the plumbers and the machinists were pulling out the stops, and by December one corner of the new plant was operational. Most of the workers had been brought over from the Lancaster plant, and the floors were being readied for the transport of heavy machinery.

M.S. Hershey seemed to be everywhere at once.

He was up well before the crack of dawn, still hammering away at milk chocolate production formulas and new milk condensing routines with George Horstick and Frank Tinney at the new creamery on the plant site. But he was also absorbed with every detail faced by building supervisors and workmen alike. He was always on the go, and even though he charged up and down the lines consulting with contractors, straw bosses, and individual workmen, the good workmen were not afraid of him. Fact is, they came to like him and to respect the way he had of dealing with people.

It hadn't taken anyone very long to realize that the boss was quick on the trigger. He was quick to offer suggestions or to ask questions, and he was even quicker to fire the goldbricks and the bullies. He was even less patient with those workers who had a tendency to be careless and those who really posed a threat of injury to themselves or their fellow workers.

Howard Shelley, later nicknamed "Jeff," recalled those early days when he reached retirement age in 1953, after forty-five years on the job in Hershey.

"We were hauling stones from the quarry to the factory, Jim Hyde and I, and as we came up the hill by the side of the creek, two of the fellows who were tying up cement bags began throwing rotten eggs at us. We had nothing to throw back at them except stones, so we threw stones. Then we backed off around the hill, and there was the Old

Man watching us. We kept right on going, and we didn't say anything because we didn't want to get the other guys in trouble. But he swept down on us and kept ragging us every step of the way."

"At the end of the day, our boss, Eli Rhine, called us over and asked what had happened. We tried to explain it, but Rhine would have none of it. He told us that the Boss had left word he was supposed to fire both of us."

Shelly laughed. "Next day Mr. Hershey was off to Europe, and Rhine decided that we had been pretty good workers and that maybe he could move us to some other job without firing us. He probably thought that the Old Man would forget all about it by the time he got back."

"He was wrong. The Old Man forgot nothing. Why, he'd come back to someone with whom he'd been talking months earlier, and he'd pick up the conversation right at the place they'd left off. But he could make allowances for his mistakes and look away from the guys who would override his wrong judgments. He just didn't mention it again."

It soon became apparent to these workers, and to the thousands that followed, that M.S. Hershey just didn't know how to make apologies. Somehow he couldn't find the words to say, "I'm sorry," and yet he would never overlook an error.

Instead, he became known for the way he made restitution. He repaired the mistake, not in words, but by altering the deed. In a quiet way behind the scenes, he made every effort to rehire people in a similar, and sometimes better, job but he never said anything about it. The hair-trigger temper was a surface flash, concealing a shy little man who dwelt beneath the tough facade.

He couldn't say he was sorry, but he knew when he had been wrong, and more often than not he corrected the deed even though words failed him.

During the summer of 1905, as the first several houses for workers went up on Trinidad Avenue, Hershey managed to drop by the building site commissary along about noon every day. He'd sit and have lunch with the plasterers, and he'd joke with them. They were hard workers and that pleased him, so he felt at ease with them, and they enjoyed his company, too. He had one particular favorite in the crew, the head plasterer, Bill Miller, a shy man, but a good workman. One day he mentioned Miller to the supervisor.

"Give that fellow a little push," he said.

This disturbed the supervisor, who retorted that Miller was one of the best men on the job, if not the best.

"I know *that*," Hershey smiled. "But he's too shy in the chow line. Tell him to push ahead and get some more of that good food. He's nothin' but skin and bones, and I don't want it said that I'm starving the workmen. They do too good a job for that."

When the Areba homes were finished, Hershey was in Europe, so "Lebbie" Lebkicher took over the supervision of the next line of houses on Trinidad. These were also completed by the time M.S. returned, and he went downtown to see them.

The houses on Areba all looked alike and he didn't like them one bit.

"What are you doing?" he demanded. "Building slave quarters? I won't have it!"

That ended Lebkicher's brief career as a homebuilder.

By the turn of the year 1906, Hershey had John Snyder draw up a plan that would encourage householders to own their own homes. The dictum amounted to an early version of the rules that are extant in most community zoning laws. The building code reserved the right of the community builders to cross the properties with poles and wires for electricity and telephones, and to lay and repair pipes for water, sewage, and flood drainage. The householder had to build and maintain sidewalks, and when additional buildings were added to the property, they could be of the owner's design, but they had to be a certain distance from the road.

Certain restrictions were laid down—"no taverns, piggeries, glue, soap, candlemaking, or lampblack factories or blacksmith shops were to be erected in the residential district."

When spring came in 1906, there were about sixty new homes being built along Areba, Trinidad, Chocolate, and Cocoa Avenues. The unfailing Derry Spring had been leased a few years earlier (May 13, 1903) from the trustees of the Derry Church congregation, and four-inch mains were laid to serve the downtown community. This arrangement included an unrestricted water supply to the Derry Church for the annual sum of seventy-five dollars.

In the early plans, a lot of street names appeared which were borrowed from the city map of Lancaster. They were slated to be called King, Queen, Duke, Prince, Plum, and High, but M.S. Hershey would have none of that. He chose instead to name the thoroughfares after the geographical spots whence cocoa derived: Trinidad, Java, Caracas, Areba, Granada, and Ceylon.

Plans for the business section of town that would rim the crossways of Chocolate and Cocoa Avenues called for a store, a bank, and a hotel downtown by late summer of 1904. But fully a year before that, in the spring of 1903, M.S. Hershey had climbed to the summit of Pat's Hill to study the vista below him.

He had come there with a Lancaster teamster named Charlie Black, and he pointed to the raw patch of red brown earth that marked the excavation site for the new plant.

"That's a beginning," he said. Then he beckoned to Black to come closer to his vantage point and pointed off to the right of the plant site.

"There's where we'll build the town, with homes and schools and stores," he began. Then he moved his arm in a sweep to the right. "And over there we'll build a park and a zoo for the kiddies," he went on. "But that'll have to wait until the new railroad siding is built."

A smiled crossed his face.

"I'll have to build a house for Kitty, over there along the creek near the Imboden place," he said. "That'll be close enough to the plant so I can walk to work in the morning. And I can go in the back way so nobody can see me coming. Yes, and I guess Mama ought to have a place of her own, right across the street from the new plant we'll build later on." He sauntered down a bit from the crest of the hill. Black followed him.

"What a view!" he mused, looking out across the valley again. Then he turned and went back to the buggy, but he paused a moment to gaze once more at the rolling green panorama. His eyes lit up.

"One day," he said as he nimbly stepped up into the buggy seat, "I'm going to build a hotel up here. Then I'll be able to watch this place grow when I'm too old to work any more."

Chapter IX

◥·◤

The Builder and the Child

Right in the middle of the explosive building program that swept like a storm across the vales of Derry Church, Milton Hershey showed up at a May meeting of the local school board. The old Greiner School was being torn down, and plans were being made for a new seat of learning which would include all grades from kindergarten through high school. His sole purpose in attending the meeting in 1904 had been to announce the gift of a tract of land that would stand in the crescent between Cocoa and Ceylon Avenues.

By the fifth of June the following year, however, the site was changed to the southeast corner of Cocoa and Chocolate Avenues, where the new McKinley School was opened. The Pennsylvania Superintendent of Public Instruction wrote this about the new school in his year-end report:

"An up-to-date four-roomed limestone building was built by Derry Township for the purpose of grading the schools in the locality of Derry Church and organizing a township high school. This building, in addition to the four school rooms, has a principal's room, a director's room, and a supply room. It has hot air heating apparatus, electric light, water, and all the conveniences of a modern school building."

The report was concise enough, in view of the fact that taxpayer dollars had been used to provide the facility described, but it was also rather too concise on some other counts. It failed, for instance, to mention the land grant that had furnished a free building site, and it contained not a word about the excavation work that was done free, or the free limestone rock, and it said nothing concerning the heat, light, water, and sewage services that were charged off at seventy-five dollars a year for all utilities.

When Harry Lebkicher was later asked how they'd arrived at that figure, he replied, "This is what we charged community service outfits," and they had set a precedent by making the same kind of deal with "the Presbyterians over in the valley" at Derry Church. But all this was merely the beginning of a philanthropic trend that would become one of the characteristics of Milton Hershey's work on behalf of education.

It was the first tiny ripple on a very small stream that was destined to become a floodtide.

From the very beginning of a visionary plan for the new community that would bear his name, Milton Hershey had shown that he was almost obsessed with the care of "my children." The reasons ascribed to his concern are several and diverse, but the most meaningful one propably sprang from the fact that no children he could really call "my children" would ever be born.

One of the cherished dreams they had lost and one of the best kept secrets he would ever share with his beloved Kitty came with the harsh news from the doctors who told them their marriage would be barren. Somehow, despite the cruel fact that they both wanted children of their own so very much, they went ahead to plan what they could do for "their children," no matter to whom they were born. In all the years they shared, nobody could ever remember either one of them saying, "We can't have any children

113

of our own." The keeness of their love somehow surmounted the cruelty of the disappointment they shared in being childless.

Together they found a tacit alternative that was to become commendable. Yet, together, it was destined to remain a silent and unspoken resolve that would wield a mighty force in the lifetime of thousands of children unborn at the moment when all this began. Perhaps, too, all these things happened because not even one child was ever to bless their union.

Down through the years, many scriveners, early and late, have explained away this strange predilection for schooling on Milton Hershey's part by attributing it to his own lack of formal education. No way. Not then, not later, and not ever.

Sure enough, he wanted to help children get an education, and he did. But that was secondary to the fact that he wanted them to learn the familial facts of life, the love of people who would be close to them and who could train and guide them before they ever cracked a book. To him, the rudiments of home and family, love and care from people who love you and care for you so that you would come to love them and care for them—these came first. The three R's came farther down the line for people who wanted to read and write and count what thinkers and workers tell them to do.

The upshot of this communion of spirit between Milton and Kitty was destined to appear in November 1909. Newspapers, then and later, have made the trust they set up for orphan boys appear to be nothing more than a sudden impulse. But these accounts ignore the fact that the Derry Township School Board had been rigged from the outset for just this very purpose. The early chronicles state that the Deed of Trust for the Orphan's School "was the all but inevitable outcome of his early experience."

The inevitability may have been partly due to some early experience, but it was just as surely dependent upon the influence of Kitty Hershey. She, by her presence in a barren marriage and as a direct consequence of her clearly spoken resolve, played a considerable part in setting up the Deed of Trust.

Mutually conceived and dually confirmed, the deed was set up by a childless couple who sought to prove that their love for children was not one whit less than their love for each other. They shared a dozen childless years before shaping this move, just as they shared the idea, which was Kitty's, and the enactment of the deed, which was Milton's.

The planned parenthood for this particular move belongs to the Hersheys, both of them. One day a magnificent building would be built by their successors, and it would be called Founders Hall.

Not by Bread Alone

Although the plans for Milton Hershey's model town are sometimes attributed to the outpourings of unbridled ambition coupled with a rich man's whimsy, the perspective from that viewpoint is tilted and the conclusion is false. Yet the man was immeasurably ambitious, and he was subject to an almost insatiable predilection for spending millions on so-called whimsical schemes.

The whole record of his life would be completed before the tallies proved that his ambitions were communal and many of his whimsies were the product of unflagging generosity. Only when the whole ledger was totted up did the truth emerge and the unselfishness of the man became an example that surpassed the classical to attain the epic. Almost a hundred million dollars in equities would be accumulated by the School Trust, yet during the last third of his lifetime, he would not be an outright millionaire because the bulk of this wealth was never held in his own name.

In effect, the focus of his ambitions were targeted on a three-part bull's eye comprised of *his people, his enterprises*, and *his dreams*.

Throughout his entire life, Milton Hershey courted risk with an obsessive ardor. The early chronicle of his town building program provides some of the best examples of the hazardous risks he undertook, and like the town itself, this one began with a church.

The Derry Presbyterians had been on the site before anyone, of course, but by the time Hershey had relocated his new venture in their area, the Reformed Mennonites and the United Brethren had churches on Park Avenue, north of the Berks-Dauphin Turnpike (1843). The Spring Creek Church of the Brethren (1848) stood off to the south of that same turnpike. In October 1903, M.S. Hershey awarded the first plot of land to the Lutherans for a new church in the town, to be situated on Cocoa Avenue (1914). Somewhat later and still before the second really massive community building program got underway, he deeded land on the main thoroughfare, Chocolate Avenue, to the Roman Catholics (1920) and the United Brethren (1928).

He would never become a member of any church body, but he would respect the separate beliefs of each of them without discrimination. In his view, only the churches could mold and shape the one thing his dream town needed most, and that was faith. In reminiscences with Dr. Herman Hostetter, his personal physician during the latter years of his life, he recounted how all the incoming priests and ministers tried to enroll him in their particular churches. None of them succeeded, of course, but one of them did manage to shake him up a bit.

A duo of Catholic priests came to call on him at the Mansion and, according to Hershey, he figured his Irish wife Kitty had "sicked 'em on me." He politely exchanged views with the elderly Monsignor and the young prelate for more than an hour. They shared coffee and buns, and Hershey, according to his own accounts, said he was quite taken by the friendliness and the fervor of the papal minions. He did not specify whether he was influenced by their religious persuasions, or whether, indeed, he maintained his extra cordial stance because of wife Kitty; but he did say that he enjoyed the visit.

On the temporal side, even after the town and the plants began mushrooming, the behavioral problems of the citizenry and its more lusty members were seldom much of a problem.

Possibly the only real concern sprang from the native Pennsylvania Dutch appetite for beer and schnapps. Hershey reasoned that leopards don't change their spots, and beer drinking was, in part, a way of life for the farmers and townspeople in the immediate area.

From time to time, he cautioned his tattle tale minions to refrain from naming names or compiling lists based on the off-duty drinking habits of his workers.

"Every time they did that," he was to complain later, "I'd wind up with almost the same lists of men whose bosses had recommended them for promotion."

Like Lincoln's considering the charges about Ulysses Grant's intemperate habits, Hershey sometimes wondered why the off-duty drinkers were so often the best on-duty workers. Unlike Lincoln he never said anything about it for publication.

Fact is, Hershey said little or nothing intended for publication—*ever*. Neither in the early days of his blossoming dream town, nor in the latter days crowned with triumph, did the shy little man ever declaim for the scriveners or primp for the photographers. Once he was asked why he had always shown a tendency to stay out of the limelight. He remarked "It makes me look green."

When Milton Hershey came down from Pat's Hill on the day he made the prophetic statement to Charlie Black about his new town, he went to work and a chain reaction was set in motion. He started the ball rolling before the first plant building was completed, and he began it with early sessions held with Harry Herr and John Snyder.

Both men were knee-deep in plans for the Hummelstown-Campbelltown Street Railway Company because that had to come first. The time for buying up the rights-of-way had to be completed before the master plans for commercial and residential building were unfolded, and more. As early as 1903, schematic plans were drafted for a park, a zoo, and a golf course. The land purchases for these projects had also been set in motion about the same time the community plans with plot reservations for schools and churches had been resolved.

Mama Fanny Hershey looked askance at some of these ambitious aims, for she kept hearing about such worldy things as dance pavilions, amusement parks, and sport complexes intended for silly things like baseball, golf, and a form of organized mayhem they called football. In her ken, too many of these schemes were no more than exercises in frivolity and were aimed at newfangled ideas that could only bend the future youth of the community out of shape.

Not so in the mind of wife Kitty. Her part in all this planning of what was beginning to appear as a young man's community went into anonymity and remained unpublished. But her enthusiasm for these schemes became well known, and she kept urging M.S. to develop the diversionary parts of a plan that would make sports and entertainment and music an integral factor in community living. At the time, the young matron was still filled with the energetic zest for living that had made her feel so close to Milton's fun-loving father, Henry Hershey.

She was delighted when the first factory employee group organized a brass band in 1905. She was on hand when the first football team was formed too, and in October of that year, she and M.S. were on the sidelines when the Hershey team beat the Harrisburg Pioneers, 16-0.

The playing field was located near the place where a dance pavilion was being constructed and about which the Harrisburg *Patriot* said, "The first building lumber has arrived for the construction of a dance pavilion on a site where Milton Hershey will build a park."

Men, young and old, have been known to be fascinated by the toy trains they buy for their children and play with to the kids' exclusion. This was the way it went when the Hershey Transit Company emerged from the beginnings of the Campbelltown-Hummelstown Street Railway Company.

M.S. himself would get up before the crack of dawn to ride the trolleys that set forth from the car barn at five in the morning. His nickel ride, from terminus to terminus, figured out to a four-miles-for-a-penny fare, but it had been planned to provide cheap transportation, not company profits. Until its last day in operation, it did just that, but in the fifty year interim, it never did make a dime. It did, however, provide for Milton Hershey an absorbing sideline that began with its construction.

He was an unexpected sojourner at all hours, and especially during the early morning runs, most of which came about when the first leg of the run between Palmyra and Hummelstown got underway. In later years, after linkups and other spurs were added, one could travel from Harrisburg through Hershey to Reading and from there to Philadelphia, all by streetcar trolley.

According to the *Hummelstown Sun* of Friday, October 21, 1904, the first run from Hummelstown to Palmyra had been made on the previous Saturday, October 15, and the report stated:

> *"The expectations and anticipations of our citizens were realized on Saturday afternoon at two-thirty when the first car to run over the entire length of the Hummelstown and Campbelltown Street Railway came gliding into*

town. It stopped in the Square for several minutes where it was boarded by
a few of our citizens; then the run was resumed to the terminus of the road
at North Railroad Street. A stop there for several more minutes and the
magnificent car started for Palmyra. Those honored with the first ride had
an opportunity to inspect the car and enjoy the ride over one of the best
ballasted roads in the country. The car is magnificently and richly fur-
nished, and in addition, the majority of trolley cars have a vestibule or
baggage room and an air-whistle instead of a gong."

The initial plans were subject to one slight change when the wayside station at Derry Church was abandoned and the Philadelphia and Reading (P & R) Railroad moved into its new station at the foot of Cocoa Avenue. An old crossing at Cocoa Avenue was thus eliminated, and a new bridge was built over the railroad at a place later called Park Avenue. Derry Church had been a whistle stop, but the new station that opened on Saturday, November 17, 1906, was a scheduled stop on the main line of the P & R, and the name of the place was designated as Hershey, Pennsylvania.

From the very beginning, M.S. Hershey would be a familiar traveller aboard the P & R's *Queen of the Valley* and on the trolleys of the Humelstown-Campbelltown Street Railway Company. To a great many people who saw the interest he took in the trolleys and railway trains, he was said to have looked like a kid with a new toy.

He did, indeed. But, unknown to the folks who shared those rides with him, a firm resolve and another dream were taking shape in the Hershey mind.

"One day," he said to himself, "I'll build a real railroad, not just a trolley line."

He later recalled that he put aside that resolution for a number of years, mostly because he had other priorities to resolve, like the ample sugar supplies; never dreaming that both the priority and the dream would one day become part and parcel of each other.

The Distaff Disciple

No mistake about it. Hershey's dream of a model town, with model homes and a model plant, was conceived, shaped, and delivered in a form calculated to become *a man's* corner of the world. The whole scheme was based on the belief that only men could be trusted to provide the ideas, and the management that would keep things humming. In the days when all this was beginning in Derry Township, women didn't have the vote, and male dominance was generally conceded to be the way of the world.

In subsequent years, the men of the world would look back with a sense of sweet nostalgia and refer to those times as the good old days.

But even then, all the humming wasn't being done by birds in gilded cages, offices and board rooms. There were women aplenty on the Derry Church scene, and they were the ones who were charged with running the homes, teaching the children, and handling the domestic chores that mades homes livable and plants productive. M.S. and his management team concurred on one point. It took a woman's touch to handle the wrapping and packaging of goods meant for people to eat. Their innate digital skills, along with their early kitchen training, admirably suited them for handling tasty merchandise with a deftness and neatness that made for efficient packaging.

Miss Margaret Clark came on the scene in the summer of 1905, when the place was still known as Derry Church and male dominance prevailed in the halls of the Hershey Chocolate Company. She had just passed her thirteenth birthday, and she was hired to work in the wrapping room at a salary of five cents an hour. She was to spend over a year working at this rate, and although her average ten and a half hour day paid only a bit more than a half dollar, she felt lucky. She recalled later that she walked to work, but the girls from Palmyra and Hummelstown, who worked for the same rate, lost two hours of pay each day by taking the nickel trolley ride to and from the plant.

By 1907, however, things brightened considerably for the girl wrappers. The out-of-towners were given tokens for their twice daily trolley rides, and she, in turn, was transferred to piecework. That year was memorable on another count, too. And Margaret Clark was delighted with a chance to more than double her income when she began to earn ten cents a box for each box of candies she wrapped.

The other memorable event that transpired in 1907 had to do with the kind of boxes she was wrapping, for they were *Hershey's Kisses*. There were one hundred and fourteen kisses to a pound, and each box held five pounds of the wrapped in silver paper bits of milk chocolate. This came to five hundred and seventy pieces per box, and she would wrap more than a box and a half an hour, for which she earned from fifteen to eighteen cents an hour; and that was considered a good wage, even for carpenters and other skilled male workers in those days. Eighteen cents would buy a pound of steak, a loaf of bread, and a quart of milk back then, so the exchange value for an average hour's work really has changed. *It has gone down.*

"I felt rich," Miss Margaret Clark recalled seventy years later, and then added, "but I always liked working for Mr. Hershey, and I'll never forget his lovely wife."

The recollections of this beloved lady, who retired in 1957 after fifty-two years in Hershey employ, were fondly reminiscent of M.S. Hershey's daily rounds.

"He was everywhere," she said, "and I don't mean just everywhere in the world. I mean everywhere *around here.*"

She smiled. "Any time you didn't expect him, there he was. And a couple of times when he showed up, he not only surprised me, I also thought for sure I was going to be fired."

One surprise came when she had been on the job for two years, just after she turned fifteen. She had been reassigned to a station on the scale line, counting and weighing out quarter pound bags of chocolate bars. Deeply engrossed in her work, she was brought up with a start when an unseen vocalist demanded, "Wait, girl, you're giving too much!"

The shrill voice pierced her like a spear. She turned to see the boss man hefting the line of bags she had previously filled and weighed. He held up two of them.

"These are only supposed to hold four ounces," he shrilled in an alto key. "Why, I'll bet there must be six ounces in every one of them."

Her eyes grew wide and his kept flashing. Then he scurried over to the next line and planted one of the bags on another scale.

"See!" with eyes grown brighter and voice pitched an octave higher. "See! Why, there's more than five and a half ounces in that bag."

He removed the first bag, placed the other one on the scale, and once again the reading was the same.

"Well?" he demanded. "How about that?"

Margaret Clark walked over, picked up the first bag he had weighed and found lavish, and returned it to her own scale where she weighed it again. The scale's finger pointed to exactly four ounces.

"Mr. Hershey, I'm supposed to be working with *this scale,* not *that one.*"

He looked at her. He looked at her scale. He looked at the other scale with the other bag and the other reading. Then he lowered his gaze and kicked something. But he did it gently, because it was imaginary. When he looked up again, the fire had gone from his eyes, and when he spoke, his voice was in a lower key.

"You're right," he said. "I'll get you another scale."

She thanked him and he went away for a while. Shortly thereafter, another scale was brought to replace the faulty one. But she did not resume work at once; instead she took a handful of bags and weighed them on the scale that M.S. had previously used for his test. She put them on the new scale and found the weights were identical. So she went back to her weighing and measuring again when, out of the corner of her eye, she saw M.S.'s head appear from behind a nearby column. She wondered how long he had been standing there.

He came up behind her and she could see his reflection on the glass face of the scale. He was smiling. He walked around in front of her.

"That's good," he pronounced. "Don't take anybody's word for anything. Check it yourself."

She kept working and said nothing. He, meantime, had turned to leave, but then he hesitated and came back to face her again.

"I was wrong," he said, in a hesitant voice. "You were doing your job, and you were right. I hope I didn't upset you."

She kept working, but managed a smile.

"You didn't, Mr. Hershey."

His face was creased with a big grin. "You're not afraid of me, are you?" he asked.

She was smiling, too, but she kept counting out bars and weighing them. "No, Mr. Hershey, I'm not," she replied, without breaking pace. "Should I be?"

His mouth fell open and he chuckled for a moment in pleasant surprise. "No, no, my dear. Not at all. You were doing your job, and I was doing mine. But this time you were doing yours better than I was."

With that he made his departure, but not before he heard her parting shot.

"That's right, Mr. Hershey."

He was laughing as he walked away.

Chapter X

❦

Hershey's Halcyon Days

In the years between 1908 and 1910, Milton Hershey found himself in a strange reversal of roles. During the previous ten years he had been out in front—leading, guiding, and shaping the various projects he had launched. But by 1908, the tide of events had turned and he found himself reacting to situations that kept popping up as the consequence of his earlier decisions.

The time had come when, following the completion of the Lancaster move and the "all ahead, full" program he'd launched in Hershey, the chocolate business began piling up profits at an unprecedented rate. Hitherto, his spending schemes had been quickly resolved. He either built another building or bundled up Kitty and took her off for another extended trip to the continent. But a twin combination of fate and fortune intervened and changed all that. And both hit him at the same time.

Business fortunes were changing dramatically, and when 1908 rolled around, he found that more income was rolling in than he could judiciously spend on either trips or building programs. But, coupled with the upswing in fortune, he also experienced another change which proved more disturbing because it was completely unexpected. Some of the bubbles had gone out of the wine for his Kitty. She wasn't feeling well, and her discomfiture was becoming progressively more apparent, so on one of their European jaunts that year, he made two moves aimed at making her well again.

First, he took her to the best known doctors in the world who dealt with bronchial disorders, and that meant they were in Vienna. Kitty's chronic asthma which had persisted since childhood had worsened and alternated between severe bronchitis and intermittent bouts of pneumonia. The Viennese medicos assured both Hersheys (M.S. also suffered from asthma) that their common affliction was the product of over-activity—too much working, travelling, and bustling about. Consequently, both were told in essence, "Take it easy. You'll last longer."

Austria provided another palliative influence when the Hersheys met and hired a widowed Viennese lady named Bertha Condoni. This tall, matronly, no-nonsense personality instantly charmed both Kitty and Milton, and they immediately went to work on her in an effort to bring her back to the States. It wasn't easy, for although the lady in question had been widowed in her middle years and had no other immediate relatives in Vienna, like most Viennese, she had an innate love for the *gemutlichkeit* center of Strauss waltzes and the artistic life.

But she must have liked the Hersheys even better, for she was persuaded to sign on as Kitty's travelling companion. This was a move which in later days Milton Hershey was to proclaim as "the best thing I ever did for Kitty." It didn't turn out too badly for him, either.

The inseparable trio came back to the States together and thereafter returned several times to western Europe, to Egypt, and the Mediterranean. But in late 1909, they went back for a few month's stay at their home in Hershey, Pennsylvania. The tides of fortune were piling up too high to be disregarded any longer.

Before setting out for Europe earlier that year, Milton had put lawyer John Snyder to work consulting with the regents for the Russell Sage Foundation and the Girard College for orphan boys. He told Snyder to come up with a Deed of Trust that would be based on the documents and the experiences that had been put into force under the terms of the will of Stephen Girard, a Philadelphia philanthropist. He told them initially that "486 acres of good farmland will be set aside by the Hershey Trust Company for the purpose of building the Hershey Industrial School." That was the beginning.

On the date of this assignment, John Snyder was also given the task of conveying a grant of nineteen hundred dollars to Franklin and Marshall College for the purpose of securing equipment for that school's chemical laboratory. The conveyance was made, and for several years afterwards, Franklin and Marshall College called the site for this gift *The Milton S. Hershey Chemical Laboratory.* But subsequent building on campus erased the name from the records.

On November 15, 1909, (four years *before* Congress passed the first federal income tax law) Milton Hershey and his wife enacted the Deed of Trust "with the purpose of founding and endowing in perpetuity an institution to be known as 'The Hershey Industrial School' . . . to be located in Derry Township . . . for the residence and accommodation of poor, healthy, white, male orphans . . ." The term "orphan" was used to describe a boy whose father had died. Later this definition was broadened to admit boys who had lost either parent, and subsequently it was expanded to include boys and girls, regardless of race or color, who were denied a home in which both parents were present.

At the time, this Deed of Trust did not put the entire Hershey fortune into the school, but it did pave the way for that by virtue of a clause that read, "If it so happens in the future that gifts, bequests, devices of real or personal property may be made to or for the benefit of the School, the Trustees and Managers are authorized to accept all such gifts, bequests or devices, whenever the terms are not in contravention of the objects and purposes of this deed."

The precise course upon which the school's subsequent charter and its administrative guidelines were to be based was left open. At the time, M.S. Hershey and wife went on the record with two oral requests that later became historic. Milton Hershey made both statements.

The first was, "If we have fifty boys, we shall be doing well."

That proved to be one of the most inaccurate shortfall predictions he would ever make. The other remark came with a reminder that achieved greater significance in the annals of the school and its history.

"I want people to remember that this was Kitty's idea."

*   *   *

In 1911, the Hersheys gathered up Mrs. Condoni and set off for Europe. The mobile concierge was put in charge of umpteen items of personal belongings in the usual array of steamer trunks and hand luggage. With it all, M.S. saw to it that his big Packard limousine was dispatched to Le Havre and from there they were driven all over western and central Europe by a French daredevil chauffeur, known only as Freddie.

Thereafter the trio of Kitty, M.S., and Bertha Condoni were either off on various jaunts by exotic European railcarriers or trundled about (in the more suitable climes and more pleasantly disposed days of fair weather) by the ubiquitous Freddie. In Nice that spring, they were joined by Miss Ruth Hershey (later to become Mrs. Thomas Beddoe), daughter of Dr. Martin Hershey, and the trio became a foursome, driven about by the former French race driver.

The year 1912 proved to be a memorable one. They had arrived on the continent in the waning winter months and headed for the Cote D'Azur where they visited Nice and Monte Carlo. But shortly after they settled down by the Bay of Angels in Nice, M.S. got a hurry-back call from the States urging him to return at once. He made the homeward bound voyage in late March, several weeks prior to the time he had planned to return. He had wanted to make the return trip with Kitty on a new superliner scheduled to make her maiden voyage in early April.

He chafed at the bit about having to sail home alone and continued to be disgruntled until a mid-April day when he was gathering himself and his gear for his return to the continent and Kitty. On the day before he sailed, April 15, 1912, there was news about the liner he had missed by making the trip earlier than planned. The *Titanic* had struck an iceberg and was lost at sea, and hundreds of passengers had gone down with her.

Back in Nice after he rejoined Kitty and Ruth Hershey, Mrs. Condoni came to him with news of a great Flower Festival that was about to be celebrated. The gala affair would feature a parade of flower-bedecked floats, and each of them would carry a nominee, a young girl who would be vying for the title of Festival Queen. M.S.'s response was immediate, and he began at once to put his plans in motion.

He rented a big formal carriage, and he began to arrange for the wheels to be wrapped in bunting and gaily colored ribbons. And when Kitty got wind of the project, after bridling a bit about the cost of it all, she entered into the spirit of the thing. Kitty and Milton agreed on only one point: Ruth Hershey would be the logical choice for candidacy in the Festival Queen contest.

M.S. and Freddie had the carriage gilded and readied for the parade. Meanwhile Kitty was busy, too. She arranged for great baskets filled with rosebuds and carnations to decorate the carriage, wheels, side panels, hubs, spokes, and all. She also decided to decorate her Milton.

Festival Day came and M.S. shrank into a state of near palsy when he beheld the outfit his wife had bought for the occasion, a pinkish, pale orange shirt, with a hard white celluloid collar and white linen ruffles on the bosom and sleeve cuffs. When he beheld this violent assault of color, a local tailor was hastily summoned to fit his paralyzed form with a striking blue and white blazer that featured flaring lapels and was topped off with a brilliant crimson rosebud boutonniere.

Kitty beamed expansively. Milton shrank defeatedly. But he smiled, and posturing himself jauntily on his bandy legs, stoically beheld his wife in her pale blue and pink gown and declared, "Let's go."

They went, and the Festival was a huge success. When their prize carriage with its beautiful entrant came down the white alabaster-lined street, they were overwhelmed by the beauty of their handiwork in a measure that exceeded their greatest expectations. The carriage was a medley of gold and white, of rosebuds and carnations, blue ribbons and white blossoms. All the wheel spokes were adorned with strings of rosebuds, exactly like the one in M.S.'s lapel. It was, all of it, just as Kitty had planned.

Somehow M.S. got the feeling that, dressed as he was, if he had been riding aboard the carriage, he would have *disappeared into it*. But when he turned to Kitty, he saw the light in her eyes as she looked proudly from him to the beautifully arrayed carriage and back again. A Tin Pan Alley composer would have called it "the lovelight in her eyes."

M.S. said nothing. He just beamed at her. His Kitty was happy and that was all that counted.

*   *   *

The Hersheys had spent most of the year travelling about Europe, but perhaps their most memorable adventure came in the Land of the Pharaohs. For some unreported

Egypt, 1912

reason, the small party of tourists was delayed in making its departure from Alexandria one evening, and M.S. wanted to get back to Cairo.

Their dragoman warned against it. He told them that after dark no Europeans or Americans were safe on the bandit-infested byways. They would run the risk of being taken and held for ransom or worse, kidnapping and death at the hands of the burnoose-shrouded highwaymen. But race driver Freddie was adamant.

"Get in," he said, pointing to the Packard. "We can make it."

"We made it, but what a way to do it!" M.S. said when he later recalled the details of that wild ride through the desert night. The big cumbersome limousine literally flew across the rock-ribbed, twisting dirt road. Every shadowy crevice, every rock-strewn gorge shining bright in the moonlit silver and black landscape seemed to be a hiding place for the sinister, camel-riding bandits.

They nearly went off the road a dozen times. They lurched and twisted and spun around rocks in the road that could have torn the wheels from their axles. But after several wild hours, they finally pulled into Cairo and at last the passengers began breathing again.

Later that year, after their return to the continent and just before boarding the liner at Le Havre, M.S. summoned faithful driver Freddie to his side. He handed him the keys to the Packard and told him it was his, a gift from the grateful Hersheys.

"Tell me, Freddie," said M.S., recalling that wild night ride across the Egyptian desert, "you sure proved you were a champion driver that night. Why did you ever give up racing?"

Freddie beamed with pleasure. Then he turned shy and looked down at the ground.

"My eyes," he replied. "I don't see so good, Mr. Hershey. Especially at night."

Milton and the Mobile Muse

The most notable series of Milton Hershey's peradventures with the world of classical art began in the memorable year of 1909. It would be more chronologically correct to point out that 1909 marked the beginning of a chain of events that would appear to have been touched with elements of the eternal, for indeed it seems as though the epochal forces set in motion that year have continued to surface and resurface again and again even to this day. This is what happened, or perhaps more to the point, these are the events that started the whole skein of what seems to have been happening ever since.

It all began with Hershey's resolve to do something that would both please and surprise his wife Kitty, in light of her innate love for classical art. In all their travels, he couldn't help but notice the strange and almost rapturous light that came into her eyes whenever she beheld certain rare paintings and beautifully sculpted marble statues. But the moment to gratify his Kitty's unspoken desire to own a bit of classical sculpture was actually delayed until a late February day in 1913 when both Hersheys happened to be in Philadelphia.

They were in the City of Brotherly Love making some last minute arrangements prior to departing for a spring and summer tour of the continent. It was at this point that the 20/20 visual acuity of hindsight reveals that both Hersheys, man and wife, had the same thing in mind. Each wanted to surprise the other and, as subsequent records certainly show, they were both quite successful.

The breakdown of communications that marked this incident from the outset began with a difference in the perspective views that guided their actions. They had come to

Philadelphia with a common resolve to order something decorative *for the front of the house,* meaning the High Point Mansion they shared in Hershey.

To Milton Hershey, the ultimate plan was to get a diminutive bit of sculpture that would grace the mansion's foyer, something on the order of a four or five foot statuette sculpted in pure white marble. A centerpiece, so to speak, that would stand right in front of the crystal torchere that he had purchased back at the Colombian Exposition more than twenty years earlier.

Kitty, on the other hand, had been thinking of a piece of sculpture, too, but thereafter all commonality of location and design held secret in the separate minds of the planners were at one hundred and eighty degree opposition to each other. Kitty, for instance, was thinking about a full-blown statue that would be outdoors, a centerpiece for a new fountain to be built on a small oval island in front of the house. Knowing her Milton, as she thought she did, it would have to be something big and imposing, for her husband was truly a man who appreciated things that were done on a grand scale. The distaff Hershey, Kitty, had gone a step further. She had been negotiating with a renowned sculptor since 1909, and when 1913 rolled around, she decided to take her hubby Milton at least partway into her plans. This bit of artistry was going to require a considerable deposit of cash and, in that sense, hubby M.S. found himself in the not unusual role of being the indispensable man.

So both Hersheys had a brief spate of togetherness insofar as their common aim to surprise each other was concerned. Kitty told Milton all about the sculptor she had selected, and to her surprise he concurred almost at once. The man, Guiseppe Donato, had been born in Catanzaro, Italy, back in 1881, and he had already sculpted classical bits of bronze statuary dedicated to Civil War Generals Reynolds and McClellan that graced the Philadelphia City Hall Plaza.

Thus seemingly in amicable concord, the Hersheys hurried 'round to the Donato Studio and forthwith made the necessary arrangements. M.S., of course confined his part of the visit to viewing other samples of Donato's work and then to forking over a nominal retainer of $5,000 to get the work started. He told the white-maned Guiseppe that he would receive further instructions on the size and the ultimate destination for the work from his chief engineer, Harry Herr. Then he signed some papers and told Donato, "Mrs. Hershey will tell you the designs she wants," and he departed.

Mrs. Hershey, having arranged for a $5,000 retainer to expedite the project and having further received what amounted to a blank check for its completion, remained in the studio to fill in some of the more secret details of her surprise for Milton. The statue, *Dance of Eternal Spring,* which was the result of these arrangements, was not the only bit of classical history that would emerge from the G. Donato Studio as a consequence of her stay.

M.S. and Kitty returned next day to Hershey and made last minute adjustments in the working calendar that would prevail in their absence. Before departing on a six month jaunt, each had a separate session with Harry Herr. The engineer, having been sworn to secrecy by each of the Hersheys, went about his business in a methodical and unruffled way. At that juncture, everything seemed crystal clear to him, and he asked no further questions of his employers prior to their departure.

The highly animated G. Donato was summoned to Hershey for one last round of instructions prior to their departure, but Milton excused himself shortly after the sculptor's arrival, and Kitty's plans for a fountain centerpiece dominated the exchange. For some unknown reason, engineer Herr was not present to meet the Italian sculptor during his visit.

Harry Herr had thereafter expected two pieces of sculpture from Donato, and that is what he got. But the foyer centerpiece for the High Point Mansion and the fountain centerpiece for the lawn driveway were not among those items which arrived in Hershey by flatcar later that summer. With the arrival of this marble treasure, Harry Herr became the fourth member of an ever-growing party of souls who were destined to be surprised by the arrangements made between G. Donato, M.S., and Kitty Hershey.

Late that summer when the Hersheys returned to High Point Mansion, M.S. made it a point to dally with Lebbie Lebkicher and Bill Murrie so that he and Kitty wouldn't arrive at their home until sometime after darkness had fallen. He wanted her to see the new bit of sculpture in the mansion foyer with the scintillating rays of the crystal chandelier playing on it. Boy, would *she* be *surprised!*

He found Kitty to be amenable to his plans and she was equally unhurried insofar as returning to the mansion was concerned. Unknown to him, Kitty of course wanted to delay their arrival so that he would see the new driveway fountain for the first time bathed in the golden light of the following dawn. Boy, would *he* be *surprised!*

Surprise for both of them awaited neither twilight nor dawn, as the record for that evening clearly reveals. First, M.S. was pulled aside by his host, Bill Murrie, and a pair of agitated cohorts, Lebbie Lebkicher and Harry Herr. Before he could even ask about it, all three men were eager to discuss the marble statue that had arrived in Hershey, having been dispatched by G. Donato Studio some weeks earlier. But the hubbub of reunion after nearly half a year's absence prevailed, and Milton Hershey couldn't make a good deal of sense out of the shower of sporadic remarks of Messrs. Murrie, Lebkicher, and Herr.

By the time the handclasping and the furor of greetings had subsided, he barely had time to squeak at Harry Herr out of concern for his foyer statue. But he did it to the back of his trusty engineer and strategic grounds planner. Herr had been beckoned away by Kitty and somehow, in the scheme of things he felt were about to descend on him, he looked on her as the lesser of the two portending avalanches that his immediate future promised.

Finally, M.S. turned to Lebbie and Bill Murrie and asked them pointblank about his marble statuette and whether or not it had been placed in the mansion foyer.

"Nope," said Lebbie. "Milt, it's so big. We have it sitting on a flatcar down at the plant siding. Boy, wait'll you see it."

Hershey meant to do just that and right then.

He snapped a hard look at Bill Murrie and Lebbie and motioned them to follow him. Neither Murrie nor Lebbie said anything, but they fell in behind him, and all three sidled out through the back door. Had any one of them chanced to look at Harry Herr across the room with Kitty, they would have been treated to an additional dab of consternation, which had already become the prevalent sign on the faces of those two.

The hasty trip had not been unanticipated. In fact, Murrie had called the freight yard night crew and told them to get a battery of carbide lamps set up near the rail siding so that Hershey could be shown the statue. On the way to their destination, Lebbie added another note to the already ample supply of consternation.

"Milt," he prodded, "I dunno what you people ordered, but we got a bill after this freightload of stone arrived, and that guy in Philadelphia wants another twenty-five thousand dollars."

"He wants *what?*" Hershey shouted. "You mean he wants another twenty-five thousand bucks just for a five foot centerpiece for the mansion foyer? He must be nuts!"

"Oh, that ain't all," Lebbie chimed in again. "Wait till you *see* it. Why, that thing fills up a whole flatcar. We couldn't even get it into the shed, it's so big."

They arrived at the freight yard, and Hershey nipped from the car and bustled off for the siding. Lebbie scurried away in the direction of the yard crew so he could alert them to light the lamps, but they were ready and waiting. Bill Murrie struggled to keep up with his boss, and then both of them stopped alongside the canopied flatcar. Lebbie returned, and the trio stood in silence as Milton Hershey pulled a match from his pocket and lit up a fresh cigar.

The canvas was pulled off and the lights came on.

Hershey stared up at the life-sized forms of three dancing white marble nymphs. They seemed to be ecstatically gamboling beneath the figure of a cherubic baby boy precariously balanced on their outstretched fingertips. The whole thing weighed several tons, and the cherub appeared to be at least a dozen feet above the lights on the floor of the flatcar.

The cigar fell from Hershey's slackened jaws.

"My God!" he gasped. *"They're naked!"*

Murrie swallowed. Lebbie gulped. The carbide lamp rays flickered against an ever darkening sky and then slowly the whole scene came into focus.

Three splendid white marble nymphs, true daughters of the Muse-Terpsichore, innocent of all vestments and nimbly balancing the cherub resting on their outstretched fingertips. They were, indeed, a hymnal delight to those appreciative of the graceful beauty and symmetrical purity of the unadorned feminine form.

But they were no more than shocking examples of unmasked pubicity in the eyes of the former Mennonite farmboy who had just been billed for them.

Hershey coughed. Hershey choked. Then he almost seemed to have collected himself as he bent over to pick up the cigar that had fallen from his mouth. He looked at the statue again.

"Thirty thousand dollars," came the mournful intonement of Lebbie's voice somewhere in the depths of a shadowy background.

"DAMN!"

Hershey exploded and threw down the cigar again. He jumped up and down on the shattered remnants of the Corona-Corona. The night sky was pierced by a frenzy of ranting that bordered on hysteria.

"DAMN! DAMN! DAMN!"

The last vestiges of the trampled cigar had been ground into the turf of the freight yard siding long before his anger subsided.

Kitty had made her point. Milton Hershey had been surprised.

Meanwhile, Harry Herr had found a somewhat less turbulent but far from amiable audience in the company of Kitty. Perhaps guided by the practical influence of his engineer training, he essayed to go with the plain truth of the situation. But the Irish in Kitty surfaced more than once, and she bid fair to match her absent spouse's explosive renditions elsewhere, until one cold fact emerged to cool the tempest within her Gaelic teapot.

The chill factor set in when she heard the figure twenty-five thousand dollars mentioned in connection with the proportional immensity of *The Dance of Eternal Spring* and the several tons of marble with which Guiseppe Donato had shaped her surprise for Milton. She probably could not hear the rising chorus of "DAMNS!" being emitted in the nighttime amphitheater of the distant freight yards, but something within her bespoke a warning.

Catherine Elizabeth Sweeney Hershey had surprised her husband. But something told her than an eternity of springs would dance across the pages of time before her Milton would recover from this one. And whatever it was that told her *this* told her *right*. He never got over it, and the consequences of this bit of timeless sculpting would continue to unfold long after all the principal actors had made their final curtain calls.

In the months that followed, no one in Hershey's immediate circle of friends and family even dared to mention the incident. But there came a day when the gigantic

item of their summer discontent could no longer be avoided. The distant Guiseppe Donato became increasingly dissatisfied and then he became intensely motivated because of the twenty-five thousand dollars he was owed. His bills, letters, and phone calls were ignored, so he filed suit.

Hershey was all set to oppose him by every legal means at hand until John Snyder showed him a copy of the papers he had signed in Donato's studio on that ill-starred day of the previous year. M.S. looked up at the lawyer.

"It's not the money, Judge," he barked, still full of fight. "But there's that other condition, and there's no damn way they'll ever get me to concede to that."

The "condition" to which he referred was simply this: he had also signed a paper in which he had agreed to "prominently display the sculpture entitled *The Dance of Eternal Spring*, by Guiseppe Donato, in some central location in Hershey, Pennsylvania." It went further to require that the unveiling was to be conducted with all the fanfare and formality usually accorded to some historically significant work of art.

By that time, Donato already had a judgment on the books and Milton Hershey, who had not contested the action, had clearly lost the case. But he was still insistent.

"I won't have it! There is no way they could ever get me to put that damn thing up in this town. Never, never, never!"

But once again the clearer head and the dispassionate view of John Snyder prevailed. He spent a good part of 1914 working on the case, until the following year when he got G. Donato to agree to accept the money on the condition that his sculpture would appear in a park in the city of Harrisburg.

Five years later the agreement was fulfilled. The money was paid, and *The Dance of Eternal Spring* was unveiled at a fountain in Harrisburg's Reservoir Park in 1920.

Milton Hershey did not attend the unveiling.

Eighteen years were to pass before another chapter in *The Dance of Eternal Spring* unfolded. In the meantime, the busy Guiseppe Donato remained restless on behalf of his works of art, and of course Milton Hershey maintained his obdurate stand on behalf of one of them.

In 1931, the gutsy Guiseppe ran afoul of the people in Philadelphia who had allowed his bronze statues of the Civil War generals to become begrimed with a greenish patina of oxidation and mold. He even went onto the plaza and scrubbed the mounted figures of the works with Fuller's earth. Later, he showed up in the mayor's office with a bill for the maintenance. The upkeep of those Donato works of art was in and out of the news for several more years to come. Fact is, the redoubtable Guiseppe even harrassed the W.P.A. into a position where their crews cleaned and polished Generals Reynolds and McClellan rather than face the abrasive insistence of the temperamental chiseler.

But when 1938 rolled around, the city of Harrisburg made another pronouncement that brought *The Dance of Eternal Spring* back into the headlines. The statue was to be moved to the Municipal Rose Garden on the grounds of Polyclinic Hospital. So Guiseppe Donato showed up for another unveiling, and an eighty-one year old Milton Hershey stayed away and said nothing.

His very silence was remarkable. But he really hadn't said anything further about the statue after the matter had been resolved back in 1915. There were some folks who thought that once payment had been made and Donato had given up on his insistence on a prominent display place in Hershey, Milton Hershey had simply dismissed the entire matter from his mind and forgotten it.

But the date of his silence followed *not* the completion of his agreement with Donato; it came after the date of a personal letter he received in the days following his beloved Kitty's death in Philadelphia. The letter read:

Studio, 337 South Broad St.,
Philadelphia, March 26, 1915.

Mr. M.S. Hershey
  Bellevue-Stratford
  Philadelphia, Pa.

Dear Mr. Hershey:

> *The reading of the death notice in this morning's pa-*
> *pers of the passing of your noble wife, Mrs. Hershey, was*
> *indeed a shock to me, as no doubt it will be to many.*

> *I shall never forget the time I had the pleasure of meet-*
> *ing her in your home some time ago, when she showed so*
> *much interest in my work in connection with your Foun-*
> *tain.*

> *Permit me at this sad hour of your bereavement to ex-*
> *press my deepest and most heartfelt sympathy, and believe*
> *me,*

Yours very truly,
Guiseppe Donato

The second surprise surpassed the first one. And, in the face of it, Milton Hershey could only remain silent.

The historic entries tracing the passage of Guiseppe Donato's controversial sculpture *Dance of Eternal Spring* from its point of conception to its current resting place offer a compendium that reads like a trip ticket from the perennial to the enigmatic. It had all begun with the inital plans discussed by Mrs. Catherine Hershey and the sculptor back in 1909, but the juggling that attended the highly mobile, and in M.S. Hershey's judgment, naked, nymphs was still earning headlines in 1971.

According to Paul Beers, columnist of the *Patriot News,* Harrisburg, the original arrangements made between Kitty H. and Guiseppe D. took place in the spring of 1909, and they were aimed at producing "a fountain centerpiece." In his book, *Profiles of the Susquehanna Valley,* Beers affirmed that this beginning then led to the notable trio of dedications that covered a span of fifty-one years.

The first dedication came in 1920 after the statue was moved from a railway shed in Hershey and placed in Harrisburg's Reservoir Park. The second dedication came in 1938 when it was moved to the Harrisburg Rose Gardens, just off the edge of the campus of Polyclinic Hospital's School of Nursing. Then, finally, Guiseppe Donato's *Dance of Eternal Spring* found a new home in Harrisburg's Italian Park in 1971. There it rests today, slowly becoming tarnished by the stains of weathering that in Guiseppe Donato's lifetime were so regrettable; but he has fallen into the silent companionship of his former patron, Milton, and patroness, Kitty Hershey.

The nubile "Dancers of Eternal Spring" were treated to another spate of public attention in the years between 1938 and 1971 whilst they gamboled on the lawn near the Polyclinic Hospital grounds. For most of these thirty-three years, each time the Polyclinic Hospital turned out another class of graduating nurses, the girls would dash from the ceremonial hall and proceed to fasten their brassieres on each of the three dancing maidens. Thereby the nurses established still another tradition while at the same time they provided a measure of decorum aimed at propitiating Milton Hershey's earlier objections.

At least momentarily, each class of graduating nurses saw to it that the "Dancers of Eternal Spring" were in certain parts, no longer naked. Perhaps in those moments,

Guiseppe Donato and Milton Hershey found themselves at last in accord somewhere in Beulah Land. Perchance they finally shared a harmonious state that had been conspicuously absent during those earlier days when Kitty Hershey secretly ventured to surprise her husband.

There is a statue in Italian Lake. And *There Is a Balm in Gilead* which, hopefully, has come to be shared by the trio of mixed-up souls who conspired to bring *The Dance of Eternal Spring* into being. The art world can only remember. And smile.[1]

[1]*On July 16, 1971, there was a little old lady present for the rededication ceremonies for* The Dance of Eternal Spring *statue when it was installed on the island in the middle of Italian Lake, Harrisburg. She had been born Amanda Straw, ninety-six years earlier (back in 1875) at a place called Fishing Creek Valley in Lancaster County.*

The 5'4" former vaudevillian later acquired the stage name of Madeline Stokes, and as such she served as Guiseppe Donato's model for all three of the maidenly statues of the Eternal Dancers. When J.L.G. Ferris immortalized her as the model for his classic painting of Martha Washington, he remarked, "She was simply one of the most beautiful women in America."

In the buff, she had been carved in marble and thereby became one of the biggest surprises in Milton Hershey's eighty-eight year lifetime.

Chapter XI

∿·∿

If Winter Comes . . .

The first years following the marriage of Milton Hershey and Catherine Sweeney were reeled off with such startling rapidity they found no time for an immediate post-nuptial honeymoon. But as they would explain in later conversations, their marriage had been consummated at one of the most critical turning points in the career of Milton Hershey; a career that was marked by a series of turning points, each of which was to be mightily influenced by events that befell someone who was near and dear to the bustling M.S.

Both had a great many plans upon entering into their marriage contract; in fact, they had spent the latter days of their courtship discussing all the wonderful places they would visit and all the wonderful things they would do when they had time. But both had come from years of hard work and their first responsibilities had been based on some rather old-fashioned credos. In those days, it was more obsessive than fashionable to try to "do better" and to work to "make something of yourself" than it has become in recent years. And no *perhaps* about it, the doing better and the making something of yourself were more family matters in those days than in these.

In late May 1898 when the newly married Hersheys departed from St. Patrick's Cathedral in New York City, they were ready to go out to see the world. But the real world demands that had been set in motion before their connubial binding were to prove more powerful than the whimsical notions they shared in moments when the gossamer dreams of first love clouded their vision.

Kitty brought something unique to her side of the ledger. She was no intellectual sophist, but this Irish shop girl brought a strange admixture of Rapunzel-like dreaminess and Gaelic candor to a union that made of each partner something more than either one would have been had they not been joined. They were surprisingly well suited for the union they shared.

The novel adventure of becoming a forty-year-old Benedict with a bride who was still in her twenties and the fact of her Catholicism and typically Irish high spirits, could have been more distracting than compelling to someone less purposeful than Milton Hershey. But these things hadn't happened to a less purposeful man. They had been made to happen by one of the most purposeful men who ever lived. The diarists of his lifetime would, in later years, describe Milton Hershey as a man with tunnel vision, and in the matter of selecting, starting and seeing jobs through to completion, that he was. But he seldom, if ever, had only one thing going at a time, and when it came to tunnels, he was sure of one thing: You can't *turn a train around in them.*

During this time when Milton paid attention to the responsibilities of business, several disappointments were to grow into major frustrations that brought great personal pain to the tireless entrepreneur. The first and possibly greatest setback he was ever to experience came in the early years of marriage when he and Kitty were told that their union was to be barren. They would be childless. They both wanted children, but they found the strength to withstand this loss in the depth and warmth of their love, and thereafter, they became infinitely closer and dearer to one another as a result of the pain they shared.

Then they were stricken by the more telling blow of Kitty's physical frailty. The spirited colleen, for all her sprightly, and bubbling enthusiasm, was not endowed with the sturdy health and durable strength of her bantam spouse.

The first of these physical weaknesses surfaced with the onset of hay fever and other seasonal allergies. Of course, the sneezing, coughing, teary-eyed symptoms of her discomfort did not in the early stages seem to be all that different or dangerous. She and M.S. simply bundled themselves off to the White Mountains of New Hampshire, to the high country of the Colorado Rockies, or to Hot Springs in Arkansas. Perhaps it was the adventure of travel or the change of scenery, but in the early days, these continental American jaunts seemed to help palliate her illness.

Then one day Kitty Hershey swooned in Broad Street Station in Philadelphia, and the severity of her condition became all too harshly evident. M.S. was beside himself with anxiety, and he bustled her off to every specialist he could find. But one after another simply gave him the grave answer that she was, of late, showing the evidence of a congenital nervous disorder which had afflicted her since birth.

Having lived with a chronic form of recurring asthma, Hershey himself would ordinarily have been inclined to regard this spate of debility as something a person had to live with. But this threat wasn't posed to Hershey himself; this was his Kitty who was in danger, his nearest and dearest, his best-loved companion and wife, and whatever in the world *could be done,* he would *have done* for her.

So they were off to see the homeopathic wizards of the world, the best medical men of London, Berlin, Paris and Vienna. They were destined to spend the years between 1908 and 1912 in search of a man who could heal, or a spot that could soothe the painful invalidism of Kitty Hershey. The best healer they found turned out to be neither a medico, nor a man of science. Instead, they found a friend and a travelling companion for Kitty in a Viennese lady, Bertha Condoni, and in her they found a jewel.

The clinics, the spas, and the fashionable watering places were to become regular ports of call for the Hersheys in those years. They alternated between Wiesbaden, Aix La Chappelle, Monaco, Nice, Salzburg, Luxor, Heliopolis, Alexandria, and Cairo. They traversed the bounding mains and wine-dark seas in a never-ending search for the health that Milton Hershey's most beautiful lady would never have restored to her.

Yet in all these ceaseless journeys, from the snowswept ridges of the Alps, the blossomed vistas of Monte Carlo, and the sere, scorched deserts of ancient Egypt, they crowded their days with many a memorable adventure and with the friendship of some unforgettable people.

The irrepressible Bertha Condoni came onto the scene in Vienna in 1908, and she would prove to be not only a close friend and confidante of both Hersheys, but she was also one of those irreplaceable gems who knew her job and did it well. On a return tour to the continent and the Middle East in 1912, Bertie Condoni packed and repacked for excursions that trailed from England to Paris, to the Code d'Azur and Monte Carlo, and from thence to Wiesbaden, Aix La Chappelle, Rome, Berlin, and finally to Cairo and Luxor. For stopovers that totalled more than a hundred, she packed, unpacked, repacked and shipped the seventeen steamer trunks and carry-on valises. Sometimes the travellers rode trains like the *Paris-Orient Express,* the *Vienna Alpiner,* and the *Milano-Roma* lines, and on other occasions, they switched over to their Packard limousine. Each time, Bertie Condoni packed the bags and stuffed them into whatever vehicle they boarded.

Everywhere they went, they bought something, and everything they brought with them from the States was removed, used, and repacked again. But Bertie Condoni saw

to it that nothing was lost. She later admitted she had had a hard time keeping a tally on the things they chose to give away—and there were many—but she kept an eye on every item they deemed either necessary or keepable. And saw that they were kept.

Somewhere in the globe-trotting that spanned the time between Kitty's early discomfort and her subsequent invalidism, a subtle change in attitude began showing in the normally effusive and outgoing Mrs. Hershey. By slow degrees and by almost imperceptible incidents, she became less and less talkative, and the intermittent periods of silence were underlined by the tone and brevity of her attempts at conversation.

She had always been noted for teasingly provocative offerings and for the sharpness of wit, that sparked her responses. But, bit by bit, as their journeys took them to clinics, doctors' offices, and spas in country after country, M.S. noticed that his young wife was not only becoming more and more introspective, but there began to be a good deal more solemnity in the words she shared with him. As the periods of silence became more frequent and of longer duration, both M.S. and Bertha Condoni noticed that Kitty's face was distorted by pain almost every time she tried to walk a few steps.

Then, near the end of 1909, the subtlety of her quiet manner changed in favor of the dramatic. One day, Kitty Hershey told both her husband and Bertha Condoni that she had sought guidance in the doctrines of Christian Science. Perhaps it was the consequence of too much pain for too long a time, or perhaps it was the depressing and numbing sensation that resulted from too many negative nods by an array of medicos who peered at her through fogged monocles or pontifical pince nez.

For her own reasons, Kitty Hershey still held fast to her faith in Catholicism. Her faith in God and in the church which she embraced as a youngster remained intact. But her faith in the professional nay-sayers of medical science had deserted her. Yet, even Christian Science with its mind-over-matter instructional disciplines did little to ease the hurt of her impaired mobility, and it helped very little to ease the painful spasms she suffered with virtually every breath she took.

One tenet of her newly acquired guidance in self-willed discipline did however manage to hit the mark and become a part of Kitty Hershey's outlook. Although it bears more than a passing resemblance to doctrinal Christian Science, she heard it from a dairy farmer friend and brought it to bear on her own weakened condition.

It was almost a parody of the famous line, "If winter comes, can spring be far behind?" and it seemed all too fitting to the young woman as she struggled through the painful hours of each day in the hope that by tomorrow some magical thing would happen to make her feel better. In her case, it came in the words of a farmer who had been telling M.S. and Kitty about the tribulations of near starvation that had visited him and his farm animals during one particularly cruel winter of harsh cold and bitter impoverishment.

"I would go out to the barn," said the man, "and each day I would go to the stall of my one last remaining horse. When he looked at me and saw that I had no hay for him, there was still something in his eyes that told me he knew I cared."

"Then," the man said sadly, "I would say to him, 'Live on, old friend. Spring is coming—there will be grass. Live on . . . live on . . . you'll eat grass again.' "

Sure enough, the winter passed and the spring came again. And the horse lived on to eat the grass and to see many another winter come and go.

Down the painful track of time spinning beneath the personal train that carried Kitty Hershey through the remaining days of her life, she counted the rails by telling herself, "Live on, old horse. Soon winter will be gone and you'll eat grass again."

The span of his Kitty's declining years became increasingly painful to Milton Hershey as he became more and more concerned and yet even more devoted to her with each passing day. But whatever pain stabbed him, never a solicitous smile nor the slightest look of pity ever passed beyond the cheerful face he put on for her. When he showed any sort of concern in her presence, it was about business; and more often than not, he succeeded in getting her attention away from herself and onto problems which hitherto he had seldom discussed with her. And in the years between 1911 and 1915, he began making it part of a practiced routine.

At her slightest wish, he would bundle her off to whatever place she wanted to go, but with the war in Europe, they had to narrow the circle of their travels to the Hot Springs of Arkansas, the Colorado Highlands, and New Hampshire's White Mountains.

Somehow they stumbled onto the fact that her limited breathing capability had a direct relationship to lack of oxygen. In a blessedly simple sense, they found that she breathed easier and better in the seaside air of Atlantic City. It proved to be a happy discovery because they had always loved the place, and Milton, when there, was near enough to return to High Point and Hershey in a matter of hours.

So the lines of travel were shortened to railway or motor car trips from Hershey to Atlantic City with frequent stops, either by rail or car, in Philadelphia. Kitty, even in cold raw weather, preferred to make the trip by car, and she ofttimes chose to keep the windows open even on the coldest and dampest days.

M.S.'s doctors had warned against this, and not only for Kitty's sake. M.S. had, after all, been smitten by onsets of respiratory failure himself as a chronic asthmatic and a frequent sufferer from both bronchitis and lobar pneumonia. His box-a-day cigar consumption didn't help either condition, his or hers. So in 1914 and 1915, he tried to give up smoking in her presence. As he was spending more and more time with her, he had nearly kicked the habit when she made a change of her own. One day she noticed that he was no longer smoking in her presence and she mentioned it.

He could see by the look in her eyes that this really bothered her. Somehow she had sensed that what he was doing was out of sheer regard for her. Then she dropped the other shoe.

"You treat me as though I am dying," she whispered.

He quickly denied it and almost as quickly dashed from the room for a cigar.

Thereafter, whenever he was in her company, he made it a point to have a cigar between his craggy teeth. He seldom lit up, but he did maintain a stance of normalcy and thereby managed to keep her at ease.

Sometimes, when she caught him being too kind too often, she mentioned that, too. She had always known him as a shoot-from-the-hip and fly-off-the-handle kind of guy who let everybody know just how he felt about things, no matter what. But when her life was apparently endangered, everything else became unimportant.

He cared about her and that was all there was to it. But his concern proved troublesome, too, for when she sensed that he was being something other than himself and when he began to hold things in, she told him to "quit babying me."

So even though everything else had paled in importance with the onset of her illness and decline, he began to manufacture little things to pop off about in her presence. He thought he had done a pretty good job of working this ruse at the time, but later he wondered if she hadn't been aware of this bit of play-acting all along and if she hadn't been putting on a show for him as well.

Mrs. Condoni recalled later a great many things that happened offstage to M.S.'s beloved Kitty when he wasn't around. How his wife would sometimes fall into a dead faint and just lie on the floor until either enough strength returned to get back on her crutches or Mrs. Condoni helped her into her wheelchair or bed.

"I never knew," he would sigh.

The kindly housekeeper's eyes would shine as she told him, *"She didn't want you to know."*

The Atlantic City trips also gave Catherine Hershey another kind of sanctuary. Somehow the Irish pride in her makeup could not countenance the pitying looks of her friends and companions at High Point. She wanted to be away from those looks. She chose to be among strangers, for she could not stand the signs of hurt in the eyes of those whom she loved. Milton she forgave, although he did cover pretty well, for she loved and pitied him in direct measure to the love and sense of hurt he felt for her.

They were in Atlantic City in late March of 1915, when M.S. got a call to hurry back to Hershey on business. They drove to the halfway point in Philadelphia, and Kitty insisted on keeping the car windows down even though it was a cold, raw day. She took sick on the trip, so Hershey decided to stop over at the Bellevue Stratford and call a doctor. Kitty was bundled off to bed, and M.S. called in the best specialist he could find. Then he called the plant and told his associates that his wife was too ill to travel, so he would delay his return.

When the doctor came, he told M.S. that his wife had suffered a severe attack of bronchitis and that she should be kept in bed lest it become a full-fledged case of pneumonia. She had a high fever, too, and the numbness in her limbs had fully immobilized her. After the doctor left, M.S. went in to see his wife.

She smiled at him, but said nothing.

"Is there anything you want?" he asked.

There was an Irish pixie's look in her eyes. She pouted, half expecting him to refuse the request she was about to make.

"I'd like a glass of champagne," she coaxed in a whisper.

He cocked his head and started to say "no." But he thought better of it and said, "Coming up."

He left the room and in a matter of minutes returned with a glass and a chilled bottle of champagne.

But she was gone.

Her will had failed her. He hadn't heard her say it, but he could see that she still wore the same expectant and hopeful expression she had always worn when she said to herself . . . ,

"If winter comes—live on . . . live on . . ."

Milton Hershey nearly went out of his mind on that day of March 25, 1915, when his wife Catherine passed away. He ranted and raved, he wept, he threw things about, and he finally went down on his knees, still weeping as he prayed.

"He was like a madman," Mrs. Condoni said later. "But there never were two people who were more in love than Milton Hershey and his beloved Kitty."

On Saturday, March 27, the Reverend Francis J. Clark of Philadelphia said Mass for Catherine Elizabeth Sweeney Hershey at the Oliver H. Bair Funeral Home on Chestnut Street in Philadelphia. The body was interred in the West Laurel Hill Receiving Vault. For a time, the heart of Milton Hershey was interred with it.

*   *   *

Four years later, the mortal remains of Catherine Hershey were removed to a newly prepared cemetery on Owl Hill in Hershey. On April 14, 1919, funeral services were held at Cathedral Chapel in Philadelphia, and a Harrisburg priest summoned by Milton Hershey conducted graveside services in Hershey.

During the years prior to the reinterment there were twice weekly visits, sometimes by Milton Hershey himself, sometimes by a messenger, who put a bouquet of roses and carnations on the casket.

Almost twenty years later, in the late 1930's, Milton Hershey was destined to see festooning roses and carnations again. But these were in the greenhouses and along the slopes of the famous Rose Gardens that his protege, Harry Erdman, would bring into bloom.

On the day the Hershey Rose Gardens opened there was a colorfully organized procession that came over from town and swung around the front portico of the Hotel Hershey.

M.S. had gone down the hill with Cousin Ezra and Doc Hostetter to mark the formal ribbon cutting ceremony that would open a path to a beautifully landscaped scene of bushes, trees, and bowers. Everything was splashed with roses of every color, dotted here and there with brilliant clusters of white carnations.

The ribbon was cut, the band played, and the aging M.S. withdrew from the crowd and struggled to the top of a nearby knoll. Someone had bedecked a float with strands of colorful flowers, and as he stood there looking at the carriage wheels, nostalgic sights of a bygone day returned to him.

He remembered the colorful moments of another day. A matronly Mrs. Thomas Beddoe was in the crowd, and he remembered the day in Nice when she had been Miss Ruth Hershey, a candidate for the title of Festival of Flowers Queen.

He remembered a pink and almost orange shirt with white ruffles and a blazer of sky blue and white stripes, and he remembered the one red rose in his lapel buttonhole.

But most of all, he remembered Kitty.

Chapter XII

～·～

The Yankee Dollar Raises Cane

Cuba, the Pearl of the Antilles, had been freed from Spanish rule in 1899 and the American forces which helped gain that freedom were still there, but nobody seemed to know why. The hostilities had ceased following the destruction of the Spanish squadron at the Battle of Santiago by Admiral Dewey's fleet on July 3, 1898, and the peace was sealed by the Treaty of Paris, signed on December 10 of that same year. So the Spaniards relinquished control of Cuba and began their departure. Starting with the pivotal date of January 1, 1899, the American troops began a period of military occupation that lasted until May 20, 1902.

Three years later the American military occupation ended and native Cubans replaced them. Thereafter, all military and civil offices were held by Cubans, and both factions quickly courted American traders and industrialists to help them build up the island's economy. The educational, sanitary and civil administration offices begun by the Americans began to pay off, and by 1910 the Cubans were beginning to take the initiatives necessary to start getting their agricultural and industrial commerce on a more productive footing.

With yellow fever under control and literacy on the rise, Cuba gave promise of being able to match the skills of its people to the job of making their metalled and fertile land into a productive source of sugar, tobacco, copper, and bauxite. Exchange missions with the United States had taught the Cubans that the good neighbor to the north had the means to buy what they had to sell, and the methods to show them how to produce and sell much more.

Milton Hershey had begun paying attention to the Cuban sources in the middle 1890's when his Lancaster Caramel plant began booming. The Spanish-American War originally posed a greater threat than ever materialized because it was resolved in less than a year; nevertheless, the sugar basket some ninety miles off the Florida coast was early to compel his attention. Thereafter, it was to become first a source of fascination and then an obsession with the little Pennsylvanian who wanted to change his caramel kingdom into a food-producing empire. Sugar wasn't the only reason, but it certainly was the biggest one.

Later, during the waning days of the Great War in 1917 and early 1918, the world need for sugar expanded mightily, especially for the confectioners whose needs were mainly centered on cane sugar. So the point which sparked Milton Hershey's initial interest was ignited by his great *need* for sugar and Cuba's great ability to *supply* cane sugar. The initial spark of his fascination was lit when he visited the island at the turn of the century, when the American occupation had begun and the Cubans were eager to grow, refine, and sell cane sugar anywhere they could.

Hershey was smitten by Havana from the outset. The very flavor of antiquity in the Spanish haciendas and the Moorish gardens cast an instant spell over him. The flowers, shrubs and palms worked another powerful kind of magic, and in later years, he would regale his friends with stories about the "thousands and thousands of different flowers that were native only to Cuba." His remarks were politely accepted with some reservations at first, but when he later built his Tropical Garden Greenhouse in Hershey, Pennsylvania, the custodian of that place, Harry Erdman, would find that he had between 5,000 and 6,000 varieties of tropical flowers to pick from that were uniquely native to Cuba.

During his first visit, Hershey had been able to travel by horse-drawn coach along the newly improved coastal road from Havana to Matanzas, travelling through the lush Yumuri Valley and visiting the tiny halfway port of Arcos de Canasi. This quiet little coastal village lay on the borderline of Havana and the Matanzas Provinces, about thirty-five miles east of Havana and less than fifteen miles from the inlet port of Matanzas. The rolling hills sweeping down from inland mountains to the intervening flatter plains and the elevated coastal plateaus quickly caught Hershey's attention. Tropical heat and high humidity abounded in the cane fields and a splendid proliferation of flowering plants and giant Ceiba trees attested to the sufficiency of moisture, ensuring perpetually bountiful growing seasons for all sorts of plant life. But the cooling brace of offshore breezes and the higher elevations of the coastal regions meant something more than that to the thoughtful sojourner.

People could work comfortably in most of those places because even during the hottest parts of midday, the temperatures in the coastal regions were quite bearable. Here at night, with the cooling effects of the healthier offshore breezes, tired workers could sleep and awake refreshed. Here, too, the calculative mind of the common sense man, Milton Hershey, took account of the most important integer on any production scale—the people.

Milton Hershey loved the Cubans. With prosaic license, virtually every move made by the innovative community builder and Chocolate King could be translated into volumes of proof that his first concern was for people, simply because he loved them. All of them. But the Cubans were special to him.

His contemporaries could only guess as to why he felt the way he did, but the record still stands to prove this belief. A record of the substance contained in the buildings, the raw lands he brought to tillage, the natives that were trained, schooled and housed, the miles of railroad track, and the overall community development and construction he piled up in Cuba as no other man ever did—before or since.

It wasn't until 1918 that his first real move into Cuba took the form that his twenty years of dreaming had shaped. The Great War and his wife's sudden death in 1915 had caused the initial delay in his Cuban plans, and he hadn't brought them into focus until 1916 when he visited his mother in Havana. Mother Hershey had moved down there shortly after the death of her daughter-in-law; and she had established herself in a modest residence which she shared with her friend and companion, Mrs. Leah Putt.

Some earlier journalists ascribe Milton Hershey's Cuban sugar venture to a suggestion made by his mother, but the records show that he had already been a substantial buyer of Cuban cane sugar before the turn of the century when they were both still living in Lancaster. So the evidence of his prior interest in Cuban sugar is substantiated by the record of those earlier purchases, even though the proof of an earlier trip has escaped archival lodgement. Only the fragmentary references to certain exotic Cuban flowers remain to confirm the facts of an earlier visit with his wife Kitty, but they didn't surface until a much later date.

Then when Hershey began building his Tropical Garden Greenhouse in the 1930's, he made a point of bringing in rare orchids and hyacinths that were found only in Cuba. Ostensibly, he had done this "because Kitty loved them so much." So it becomes quite reasonable to conclude that she would have had to *have been to Cuba* to have seen them and to have loved them. Nevertheless, there was still another definitive step taken during an earlier trip that led to the crystallization of his plans in 1918. This came as the consequence of a second meeting with an old friend, Senor Juan Bautista Solo, with whom he had become acquainted some years earlier in the United States. The earlier meeting having occurred after the Spanish-American War when American occupational forces moved into Cuba and Bautista was in the United States as a consular envoy trying to help with the sale of Cuban products. One of those products was the very cane sugar Hershey had been buying all along, and a commodity that would increase in demand as part of his ambitious plans to deal in sugar in unprecedented volumes.

The two friends toured the surrounding countryside between Havana and Matanzas in an early Model T Ford. Their main path followed the old coastal highway from Havana through the Yumuri Valley, past the tiny port village of Canasi and Santa Cruz del Norte on the way to Matanzas. They also made side jaunts over rough roads and timber paths that the Ford wouldn't traverse, so they switched to a Cuban type of buckboard, a springless two-seater called a *volânta* (a name descriptive of the leather swing straps that were suspended between the rockhard seat and the wagon body). Hershey later said he felt sure he was going to get seasick for the first time in his life, even though he was on a springless wagon seat some twenty miles from the nearest ocean.

He learned a lot on that trip, but he was primarily attracted by the geographic lay of the land that stretched between the port of Matanzas and the fifty miles distant capital of Havana. If a man were to build a railroad through such country, the main line would have to follow a straight course, but thereafter spurs could be added which would carry the north-south cargo from the inland cane fields of Rosario and Yumuri to the sequestered ports of Canasi and del Norte. Later, this layout would prove to be of vital importance.

So some speculative ideas were formed in 1916, but they weren't destined to get off the paper and into the hardware of actual works until 1918. Upon Hershey's return to mainland U.S.A. in the fall of 1916, the national elections were held. In November, President Woodrow Wilson, who had campaigned that "he kept us out of war," was returned to office for a second term. Several weeks after his second term began on March 4, 1917, the United States got into the war and for a while this kept Hershey out of Cuba. At first, the German U-boats were considered a threat to the sugar boats which had to carry the raw cane sugar from the Caribbean to the east coast refineries of the United States, but these fears proved ill-founded after awhile, although for a brief moment in 1917 these shipments were sharply curtailed for fear of German submarines that never appeared. Meanwhile, Milton Hershey had some fearful concerns of his own and both of them centered on the people part of his plans for the years of 1917 and 1918.

The first of these concerns was sprung from the fearsome fact that hundreds of young men from his Pennsylvania hometown were being shipped to the battlefields in Flanders. Having known and having worked with so many of these men, he was later to recall that World War I had marked a time of great personal trepidation for him. His Mennonite heritage possibly lent substance to an innate kind of burning hatred for any kind of mortal conflict, but he always regarded the First World War as the one he resented most. He'd always been highly sensitive to conditions that affected him personally, and perhaps this was why he carried an extra degree of resentment during World War I, simply because of the threat it had posed for those who were near and dear to him. Some others called it "the Great War," but to Milton Hershey it was nothing less than a great affront to him personally.

In his Cuban jaunts, something else of a personal nature also bothered him. In the plans for developing the lands of the hot and steamy tropical canefields he was faced with quite another problem. Despite the great works of sequestering yellow fever by

General (Dr.) Walter Reed and the U.S. Army Sanitation Corps, the lowland sugar-producing areas were still dangerously infested by malaria-carrying Anopholes mosquitos. The mortality rates among canefield planters and cutters were several degrees greater than horrendous, and the hard facts of worker health and well-being were so incredibly bad they were virtually non-existent.

In late 1917 Hershey finally figured out what he wanted to do in Cuba when he travelled northeastward from Havana to the crescent of coastlands known as the Canasi and Santa Cruz del Norte regions. After months of beating about in the swampy, malaria-ridden hinterlands, he had returned for a respite to the cooler upland plateaus that rimmed the northern coastline, and one evening he found that the offshore breeze which came to cool his twilight contemplations brought him more than a mere respite.

It also brought him an answer.

For then and there he decided that this fifty-mile stretch of geography between Havana and Matanzas was situated in a livable swatch of land that was sufficiently elevated and so remarkably cooled by offshore breezes that made it more than habitable. It was also workable.

Thus, in 1918 Milton Hershey kicked off his Cuban sugar enterprise by purchasing the plantation and refinery sites he would subsequently build at Canasi and Santa Cruz del Norte.

Then he returned to Pennsylvania to deal with a capricious chewing gum venture that seemed for the moment to be floundering. Somewhere in transit back to the States, he came to grips with the fact that Hershey chewing gum wasn't selling well enough because it simply lacked the flavor to make it popular. Then an idea came to him that eventually led to a mild flirtation with failure, and still another extremely passionate courtship of the perennial Hershey sweetheart called Serendipity.

A whole new epoch began when Hershey went to see a doctor about his sick chewing gum venture. As he saw it, the chewing gum needed more sweetness and flavor, and in Cuba he had just acquired the places where he could soon produce plenty of both.

The doctor Milton Hershey sought out was a man from Yonkers, New York, a Ph.D. chemist, Dr. William Dodge Horne, who was a summa cum laude alumnus of Columbia University. But more than that, Dr. Horne was a dyed-in-the-wool wizard when it came to developing commercial sweeteners for foods and confections.

On shipboard, Hershey had gotten the idea of introducing the highly aromatic flavorings such as spearmint, peppermint, and a variety of fruit extracts right in with the raw cane sugar (to be used as a sweetener) *before* it was refined. It seemed to him that such a process just might help infuse the chicle substance of his chewing gum with more lasting qualities of both flavor and sweetness. And so it was that he sought out Dr. Horne, explained the theory behind what he had in mind, and forthwith the scholarly chemist found himself hired to conduct some experiments which he wasn't quite sure he understood.

Consequently (and almost immediately, subsequently) Dr. William Dodge Horne found himself at sea on board a ship running in the opposite direction to the one on which Hershey had a week earlier gotten the idea which had led to this unexpected voyage. And en route, Dr. Horne ruefully came to the conclusion that he should perhaps have booked double passage because he was doubly at sea about his new assignment.

Upon his arrival in Cuba, the new Hershey minion was greeted by another scholarly missionary from the Hershey fold who turned out to be a down-east Maine Yankee named P.A. Staples. Horne scarcely had time to become fully acquainted with the man of whom Milton Hershey had said, "Tell him what you need and he'll get things set up for you," before the man had done just that.

The newly-arrived chemical doctor found himself ensconced in a fully-equipped experimental lab with cookers, distillate systems, presses, centrifuges, and vacuum chambers, all spanking new, before he even learned that the P.A. initials prefixing his new companion's family name stood for Percy Alexander. This man got his work done so swiftly that when another Hershey worker told him, "P.A. Staples is the kind of a guy who can detail his schematic plans onto a piece of paper falling from a desk—and have them ready for blue-prints before it hits the floor," Horne didn't scoff. And like just about everybody else who ever became privileged to work in the company of P.A. Staples, Horne didn't feel inclined to laugh. Not ever.

Time being of the essence, Doc Horne came up with an awesome string of failures to prove that at once and for all time, there was no way that raw sugar cane could be steeped, boiled, pressed, sprayed, or pressurized in a manner that would impart any lasting flavor to either the sweetening agents or the chicle substances of Hershey's chewing gum.

But here again the pot was sweetened for the Hershey saga by the appearance of another visitor from the realm of Serendip. The good Dr. Horne would never see anything like what Milton Hershey had instructed him to find in the way of a pre-flavored sweetener for the cane sugar destined for use in his chewing gum. But what he did see in the qualitative and quantitative residue assays performed in many of the experimental trials, was an increase in the volume and purity of the refined cane sugar extracted (i.e., defecated or refined) out of the same base weights and volumes of raw cane.

A number of his experimental processes had yielded five per cent more in the weight of sugar extracted and the purity of the volumes produced had been increased from ninety-three to ninety-six per cent. Eureka—Serendipity strikes again, and even though Dr. William Dodge Horne never saw the pre-flavored sweetener Milton Hershey had sent him to find for his chewing gum, he did see something else in what was really there. Something that proved to be even more of a find.

In the years between 1919 and 1921, a number of steps were taken to match the chemistry of Dr. Horne's refining serendipity to the geographic advantages that led Milton Hershey to invest in the Cuban sugar-growing regions in the first place. The third leg of this conceptual design base would emerge from the P.A. Staples' logistical plan to exploit every integer in the system from planting through harvesting, then transport, refining, and packaging. But each of those separate but closely related integers was to become a vital factor in a scheme that enhanced production speed, quality, and economy which made them geometrically expandable.

In short—and in secret—each of the three base components made the other two several times more valuable than each had been alone. Horne's refining methodology, Hershey's selection of a geographically "perfect place," and Staples' systems plan of linking up each of those two basics into a synchronized flow plan would have revived old Pap Hershey's belief in a perpetual motion machine.

By 1921 Staples was put in charge of the whole Cuban shebang, and Doc Horne was at once reported to be both in M.S. Hershey's doghouse while at the same time rumored to have been put on a handsome retainer for a period of no less than seventeen years.

This whole romance surrounding doghouse rumors and fat retainers was affixed to something as real as an official U.S. Patent. But for all of the factuality of U.S. Patent No. 1,486,091 (titled "Process for Defecating Sugar Cane") having been issued to Dr. William Dodge Horne on March 4, 1924, and in view of the fact that Hershey had forbidden anyone to patent or publish *anything* involving Hershey systems, methods, or machinery, Horne really wasn't in his doghouse. Not even Horne's article published in *The Journal of the American Chemical Society* (as related to the "Horne Process" detailed in the patent) had really delivered the bespectacled, van Dyke-Bearded One to

M.S. Hershey's "bowser box."

It was all smoke.

And so it went again on December 24, 1929, when another patent (U.S. No. 1,740,693) was issued in the name of M.S. Hershey himself. This one carried the title "Sugar Refining Methods," but anyone who bothered to get a copy of it would be hard put to figure out what it could do for a sugar refiner, other than getting sticky fingers for the practitioner who followed its guidelines. This was another gem of smoke-sculpting, and it turned out to be no more than a replay of the Hershey "caramel crack" practice that had been found and used long ago in Lancaster back in the 1890's when a boiler room employee had dipped his wet hand in a boiling caramel batch and thereafter, unscathed and unscorched, had been able to roll a firm ball of the mix 'twixt his fingers.

But the real fire underneath this unparalleled production of chemical, geographic, and systems flow lashup was mysteriously combined and no less than marvelously kept in secrecy for nearly a score of years. From the opening of the Roaring Twenties to the close of the 1930's, Hershey, Cuba, grew by leaps and bounds, to reach unprecedented and unbelievable proportions.

Once again the consequences of Hershey's legendary serendipity and the common sense applications that were pressed into use were never patented. Indeed, they were never patentable.

Only the smoke is on the record for patents and publications that were involved in this effort. The one secret Hershey couldn't hide, of course, was quite something else. It popped up in the export-import figures and the sales records which showed that the Hershey-Cuba enterprise had become the largest single sugar-producing operation in the world.

It all began when Serendipity started raising cane in Canasi. And Milton Hershey was there to cut it.

Enter Parsifal

On May 1, 1921, a Yankee from Maine with an engineering degree from M.I.T. was brought up from his staff work on the Cuban railroad and named to succeed Walter B. Gonder, who had begun the whole operation. And when Percy A. Staples came to the table, he brought something like the Holy Grail with him. He carried an extremely keen pencil for drawing up plans, and it was conversely quite as sharp when it came to cutting costs. But his sharpest tool was his mind. His attention to business hovered between the compulsive and the obsessive, and he had one singular conviction that positively endeared him to the heart of M.S. Hershey.

He was a Roman rider who kept things moving while he separated the problems from the work. He made a reputation for getting problems solved at the same measured pace by which he kept the work moving ahead, and he let neither steed interfere with the stride of the other. Sixty years later, Konrad Hartmann, who had served P.A. Staples when he later became a live-in guest at the Hotel Hershey in the l940's, had this to say about him: "He's the only man I ever knew who committed suicide with a briefcase."

But, beginning in May of 1921, P.A. Staples was alive and well, and he made the six "Centrals" of the Hershey enterprise in Cuba positively hum. He organized the hub of the whole complex in a headquarters operation called Central Hershey. He spotted five combination sites, each containing plantations, refineries, railheads, and port facilities, in places named Central Rosario, Central Carmen, Central San Antonio, Central Jesus Maria, and Central San Juan Bautista, which was named for Milton Hershey's old friend.

Working hand in glove with his mentor M.S., Staples planned and built each one of these places around a settlement that provided schools and homes and community buildings to serve the refinery and plantation workers and their families. Each one became a separate and competitive corporate entity, and in each one a local manager and staff were installed. The main settlement in Central Hershey contained the homes, the shops, the stores, schools, theater, library, and post office that any model town would feature. Just as Hershey, Pennsylvania, was becoming a model for well-planned communities in the United States, so was Central Hershey in Cuba.

By 1925, Staples acceded to M.S.'s wishes and completed the Milton S. Hershey School for Orphan Children in Cuba. By that time, the total of Cuban lands under tillage or for the containment of local manufacturing facilities was nearly sixty thousand acres. Later, when the trackage and rights-of-way for the railroad were included, the total land under Hershey ownership in Cuba passed the sixty-five thousand acre mark. The redoubtable Staples had been so busy with his keen mind and his sharp pencil that by the 1930's, Milton Hershey's Cuban holdings were turning out many times more sugar annually than he had tried to control back in 1920.

With Percy Staples in the saddle, M.S. Hershey made tens of thousands of Cuban friends wherever he bought or built. In May of 1924, Milton Hershey became an adopted son and Honorary Citizen of Matanzas. The great Cuban artist, Esteban Valderman, presented him with a splendid portrait, and the humble villagers of Matanzas chipped in to have a gold medal struck in his honor. Nine years later, Hershey was awarded the highest honor the Cuban nation could bestow, when at the Presidential Palace in Havana, he was given the Grand Cross of the National Order of Carlos Manuel de Cespedes.

Cuban President Juan Machado made the presentation on the first day in February 1933 in the Palacia Habana with these words, "With this medal we give a bit of our soul, and with it goes all of our lasting admiration."

The Yankee dollar had come to Cuba, and under Percy Staples it had done better than merely raise cane. It had brought along the doughty Pennsylvania Dutchman whose feisty ways and daring disposition had led him to take the risk.

But on that sunny morning in Havana, a simple Mennonite farm boy sat there, unable to speak. Another orphan had come home to a strange land to some dark-skinned people who would no longer be strangers to him. They had given him a medal, along with a "bit of their souls," and he would always remember that day.

Nor would he ever forget the Parsifal who had brought him this Holy Grail.

Portrait of Milton Hershey By Esteban Valderman 1924

Chapter XIII

~·~

The Epicurean Gulliver

Milton Hershey was a man of many parts, but there were two facets of his character that seemed to dominate during the first twenty-five years of the twentieth century. He loved to travel and he loved to eat. Somehow, his reminiscences were to be heavily drawn from the memorable dishes he had enjoyed in England, in continental Europe, in Egypt, in the Caribbean and Central American regions.

When sharing notes with other globetrotters of that time, his viewpoints differed from theirs. When he shared in reflections with the famous Will Rogers, they spoke mostly about theaters, circuses, and internationally famous showplaces. Later on, in the company of men like Lowell Thomas and Cordell Hull, he was regaled with recollections of famous buildings and landmarks, the notorious and the classical sites where much of written history had occurred. He appreciated their views, for he was as fascinated as most folks by the accounts of romantic history, but he was positively obsessed with the memories of the foods he had enjoyed in strange and distant lands.

His version of a Cook's Tour was spelled with a small "c." His notebooks contained the names of the eating places that he personally preferred; and when he travelled, his destination was more likely to be a famous restaurant than it was to be a battlefield, a museum, a palace, or an opera house.

While others took pride in *having been there* in various cities, historic sites, and scenic centers, he remembered the places where he had eaten. The others travelled around the world; he ate his way around it. In the reflective years of later life, he would recount the round-robin trips to great epicurean centers of the world—Claridge's in London, the Ritz in Paris, Sheppeard's Hotel in Cairo, and so on down the line. A fledgling raconteur in the field of gourmet appreciation named Duncan Hines would cross his path in the late twenties, and later Hines would write a series of articles and a book called *Adventures in Good Eating*. After the Hotel Hershey opened under the eagle eye of Joe Gassler and the percipient palate of M.S. himself, Hines would choose to make glowing references to the cuisine's highlight, broiled squab on toast, a specialty of the house and a Hershey favorite.

Despite ample wealth and virtually unlimited cosmopolitan exposure, Hershey remained both plebeian in his tastes and pretty much of a pedestrian in the field of culinary preferences. His all-time favorites always remained such ordinary Pennsylvania Dutch dishes as schnitz und knepp (apples and dough), pot pie, apple dumplings, and sauerkraut.

But one thing about these adventurous eating habits was more important to his life story than the mere presence of a healthy appetite can explain. He was endowed with an extrasensory taste when it came to discerning the differences in food flavors and aromas. From his earliest years as a candymaker, both as apprentice and journeyman, he had been able to taste the samples and tell whether or not they would be pleasing to the custom trade. For all of his innovative genius and tireless working drive, this hypercritical sensitivity to the differences in flavors was perhaps his most valuable

147

physical asset and his least known secret weapon in the field of confectionery enterprise.

There are quite a few reasons for this belief. Some of them are based on recorded facts, and one in particular is so apparent that it cannot be avoided. By reverse order, the philosophical judgment that matched his taste pitch to the tonal key of the marketplace was always so readily apparent, and yet most of his contemporary candymaking associates and virtually all of his biographers simply missed it. The fact emerges with the knowledge that he had travelled around the world and tasted so very many of its top examples of fine foods, and yet he was left with his preference for apple dumplings, pot pie, and schnitz und knepp intact . . . plain foods—the uncomplicated kinds of things that Pennsylvania Dutch housewives and mothers never had any trouble getting their kids to eat.

So when he cooked up a batch of taffy, caramel, fudge, or a recipe for a chocolate bar, he did it to suit his own taste. The wholesome, uncomplicated quality peculiar to his own appreciation became, for him, the weapon that would command the confectionery field. *If he liked it, the kids would like it.* And this became the proof of the pudding of market appeal. His own taste turned out to be his key to the mint.

Specifically, the proof of his extraordinary taste-testing capability piled up a mile long record. Here are a few instances:

After Joe Gassler departed the Mansion/Club, (in which M.S. had set up residence) to assume Hotel Hershey management, a new chef moved into the kitchen. M.S. took immediate exception to one of the early meals served to him, and it happened to be chicken and waffles. He didn't like the chicken, saying that "it tasted like something made in a factory." Then he included instructions to get a "real" chicken from Prudence Copenhaver, who lived on a farm over at the school.

Later, the difference came to light when the club cook revealed that he had received some freshly killed and cleaned chickens from a commercial establishment. These fowl were "factory chickens" in M.S. Hershey's ken, and he stoutly maintained that "unless a chicken has to root and scrabble around in the barnyard for its food, it's got no flavor."

Over in the experimental labs where confectionery ingredients were constantly being checked by chemical analysis, cooking, and tasting, Sam Hinkle, the chief chemist, and his lab chief, Al Meyers, had learned early about Hershey's extra-keen flavor perception.

Chocolate was ever the hub of the spokewheel in the village that came to be known as Chocolatetown. But the chocolate flavoring came in three varieties of beans, from many climates and many regional differences in elevation and soil condition. The varietal types of cacao beans—Criollo, Arriba, and Forastero—all have different flavor characteristics, and each of these in turn acquires still further peculiarities of pungency, color, and smoothness, depending on the elevation of the tree farm, and of course, the chemistry and the alkaline/acid balances extant in the soil where the trees are grown.

All cacao is grown in latitudes within two dozen degrees north and south of the equator. And that chocolate flavor belt circles the middle of the globe from Guatemala, Costa Rica, Nicaragua, Southern Mexico, Venezuela, Panama, etc., to the Ivory Coast, Nigeria, Madagascar, Ceylon, Ghana, etc. But *each* of these areas grow *all* types of beans, and all grow them at different elevations and in different soil regions. Consequently, each one of these factors makes a difference in the flavor of the powder extracted from the beans. Therefore, the uniform flavor of finished chocolate depends on a seemingly endless string of different blends assayed to meet the need.

There were, and there still are, all sorts of chemical tests made for the pungency, aromatic qualities of the individual cocoas and the various blends, but tasting is still the final determinant in the test. Back in the twenties and thirties, M.S. Hershey would be ceaselessly engaged, and quite frequently engrossed, with these tests, chemical and sensory. But he was the only one who ever came into the place who could tell if the varietal powder was derived from Criollo, Arriba, or Forastero beans, and he could also identify the country, i.e., Venezuela, Nicaragua, etc., from which it came.

The epicure extant in M.S. Hershey also bespoke a man with an obsession to stick his fingers into bowls, beakers, and pans to sample whatever was being mixed, cooked, or assayed. On one occasion he made the mistake of dipping a finger into a beaker labelled vanilla which in reality contained *vanillin,* a synthetic and bitingly bitter concentrated chemical substitute. His reaction was a spluttering dive for the nearest faucet so he could quickly rinse the flaming residue from his mouth.

His explosive trial had attracted attention, but having spent a fountain style moment of slurping and spitting, he finally straightened up and regained his composure.

"I was a little boy the last time I did that," he said. "Mama was cooking lye soap in a kitchen pot. I should have learned my lesson then."

In a way, Milton Hershey was lucky he could taste anything after a couple experiences like that, but his role as a persnickety taster was one of long duration. Even curious cats have nine lives, and this one had at least that many.

He knew what he liked. He knew what the children would like. If he'd had his way, he would have been a producer of milk products, ice cream, cheese, chewing gum, and a whole variety of things other than merely wholesome beverage bases and confections. But he was destined to have his way in only one product, and that was in chocolate.

How broad the way became a matter of history. But his own enchantment with the flavor so irrevocably linked to his name and his works was, in a sense, a matter of history too. The swath he cut for himself—as a world traveller, an industrialist, an educator, a philanthropist, and a culinary aficionado—all stem from the taproot romance, the first love of his working and striving down through the years.

He set out to capture a following of children with a brownish flavoring substance that would make them his very own. And, walking in the steps of the mighty Hernan Cortez, he made the urchins of his time the willing prisoners of a new and enticing brown substance. But he used the weapons of his Mennonite heritage.

A conquistador with a spoon and a mixing bowl, he wrote his name across the pages of history in big, broad letters of milk chocolate. It all began with the simple blessing of having been born with the kind of taste that tells. And with the kind of sense that told him what to do with it.

A Treasure in Brown

In Milton Hershey's mind, the story of chocolate was a strangely mixed chronicle of dashing personalities and fascinating adventures played out against a backdrop of exotic lands and historic times. His entire association with the brown flavoring extract of the cacao bean was one of romance, and his recollections were based on his own peculiar blend of hard facts and fanciful legends.

His fascination began with a trio of imposing personalities who figured in the beginnings of the chocolate story—the Aztec Emperor, Montezuma; the Grand Conquistador, Hernan Cortez; and the last of the Holy Roman Emperors, Charles V, who was also the reigning King of Spain.

The whole story revolved around a letter and a package of samples that Hernan Cortez had dispatched to the Court of Seville in the summer of 1528. And this, despite the fact that even though the letter described the *chocolatl* substance contained in the sample packets accompanying it, the whole exchange was obscured by events that had happened several years earlier.

The events were patent to the Aztec Emperor Montezuma, and they stemmed from the historic date (sometime prior to 1520) when Hernan Cortez had made the Indian potentate pay off his own ransom by filling a temple storeroom to shoulder height with trinkets and appurtenances wrought of pure gold. Gold, then as now, commanded attention. The king's ransom had gained the attention of Charles V, Spanish King and Roman Emperor, when he first learned about it in 1520. He had received a letter and samples on that occasion, too, but then the samples had consisted of great chests of gold. Charles V was impressed with the samples.

So there was a lapse of ten years between the samples that Hernan Cortez sent back to the court in Spain, but quite a bit of history was written in the interim. The three leading personalities in this narrative of an Old World in turmoil and a New World being opened for exploitation provide a key to the events that transpired.

In this era, Hernan Cortez became the Grand Conquistador. History portrays him as a conquering general who marched across Mexico in a campaign to bring the land under Spanish rule and to separate the natives from their treasures of gold. But he departed from Spain with virtually no record of military leadership. He had studied law at the University of Salamanca, but he left school without a degree and his first ventures in the New World began as a farmer and public notary in Santo Domingo. In 1511, he accompanied Diego Velasquez to Cuba, where he subsequently became (alcalde) mayor of Santiago, then the capital of that province. In 1518, he was sent to Yucatan with a force of more than five hundred soldiers to rescue an endangered expedition. He quickly resolved the initial problem, then settled in Tabasco and set about studying the natives and their way of life.

Another year passed before he set up a new base in a port he named Vera Cruz, and thereupon he managed to get himself chosen as Captain General of the king's forces and chief justice of the soldier citizens. This proved to be the turning point of Spanish conquest on the mainland, because it projected a law-trained adventurer into an entirely new role as conquistador. He began by replacing Diego Velasquez as the Spanish commander, and this brought him under closer attention by the Spanish court and forced him into inevitable contact with the Aztec Emperor Montezuma.

Cortez' seat of power was in the Republic of Tlaxcala, a nation in a chronic state of war with the Aztec Emperor of Mexico, Montezuma. But when Hernan Cortez sought to march against the Aztec ruler, the Spanish authorities sent him only a handful of men, precious few of whom were soldiers. Many of his long sought reinforcements turned out to be better trained in religious fields than they were as men-at-arms, for they were padres who had been sent to do the work of the church.

While the new general set about raising and training an army of 1,000 Tlaxcatecs, he turned his evangelistic padres loose to spread The Word among the natives. Thereafter, this split in objective goals was to become the crux of the historic events which occurred on the Mexican mainland, and it was to provide the beginnings for the two kinds of treasure, as well as for the letters and samples that Cortez sent back to the Spanish court.

When Cortez entered Mexico with his tiny force of Spanish soldiers and friars, he was accompanied by a one thousand man troop of Tlaxcatecs. The Emperor Montezuma resisted him at first, then he desisted and made a complete turnabout. He greeted Cortez with great honor and proclaimed the Spanish conqueror as the reincarnation of Quetzalcoatl, the father god of the Aztecs. Then Montezuma went a step further and promised to become Cortez' ally.

A brief spell of quiet ensued. Montezuma retired to his capital in Mexico, continuing to make protestations against Cortez and his forces entering the city. Meanwhile, several token forces of padres, travelling alone or in pairs, began trickling off into the Yucatan and Mexican hinterlands, carrying the symbolic cross and the lessons of the

Bible to the natives. During this interim, Cortez, with his limited force of a few Spaniards and his thousand Tlaxcatecs, kept slowly pushing toward Mexico City.

Hernan Cortez had made a pair of promises, one of which he could not keep. He had promised the Aztec Emperor that he would not enter the capital city of Mexico, but he had also written home to Charles V announcing his intention to seize the Aztec king and, by holding the monarch as hostage, to thereby achieve the political rule and religious conversion of the Mexican realm. In the meantime, he kept slowly but relentlessly pushing toward the Mexican capital, seemingly reluctant to breach the pledge he had given to Montezuma.

The Conquistador was close to his destination when word reached him that a force of Mexicans had attacked his base at Vera Cruz and had slain his chief in command there. Using the news as a pretext, Cortez marched straightaway into the city, captured the palace, and clapped the Emperor Montezuma in irons.

Another period of quiet ensued. But under the surface there were other forces at work. The missionary padres were pretty well dispersed throughout the Aztec, Tlaxcatec, and other Mexican and Yucatanian tribes. And they were speedily becoming familiar with native foods, and this eventuated in a kind of reverse order conversion, whereby the missionaries gained a certain fondness for strange new foods and exotic spices. Several of these flavoring substances were derived from bean pods that grew on shrub-like trees, and virtually all of them found their way into culinary records by way of the cooking expertise of the Mayans. But, by the time Cortez and his band of padres made their way through the jungles and across the mountains of Yucatan and Mexico, the ancient civilization had become an historic memory and Mayan culture ceased to exist.

Nevertheless, the Mayan bean pod extracts for the strange new flavoring substances the padres found so appetizing were still widely in use. These were contained in packets which the missionaries would carry back to their captain-general Hernan Cortez, and they in turn would become the samples Cortez would eventually send along with the letters to Spain he sent at a much later date. They would become the bean powders that would have to await the turn of still another century before gaining prominence under the names of chocolate, vanilla, and coffee. So the discovery of this treasure in food flavorings was launched in a quiet moment of history, and it was destined to be held in secret for a long time to come.

Cortez, meanwhile, was discomfited by several strange turns of political events. With Montezuma in irons, he had become the master of Mexico. But shortly thereafter, he received news that his old leader Velasquez had raised and sent a Spanish force under Panfilo de Narvaez to relieve Cortez of his command. He reckoned at once that he could not afford to keep Montezuma captive and still try to mount any kind of resistance to the new Spanish leader. His immediate forces amounted to a handful of Spaniards and the remnants of Tlaxcatec troops who remained with him. The Mexican/ Aztecs were not likely to join him, not with their emperor in irons. And he had the further problem of doing something to mollify the high command at the court back in Spain if he were to oppose Velasquez' man. He had only a sketchy contact with the powers around a throne some five thousand miles to the northeast. He knew that General de Narvaez' sponsor, Diego Velasquez, had many more friends at court than he did.

Montezuma presented the key to his problems. So Hernan Cortez set a price on Montezuma's freedom that would answer *all three needs*. He told the imprisoned ruler that he could ransom himself by filling a temple room to shoulder height with native gold *and* by allying his Aztec soldiers with Cortez' own forces to oppose de Narvaez. Montezuma agreed, and Hernan Cortez removed the shackles from the emperor's legs with his own hands.

The key worked. The combined soldiery marched out to defeat de Narvaez, and thereupon Cortez enlisted the enemy survivors in his own army. He did it just in time, for when he was on his way back to the Mexican capital, he learned that his garrison troops had begun an aggression in his absence and that the Mexicans were in full revolt. Cortez fought his way into the center of the city, and he arrived only moments after Montezuma had been killed. Later, he learned that his Aztec ally had lost his life while trying to get the Mexican rebels to cease their attacks.

Cortez and his remnant of Spaniards and Tlaxcatecs awaited darkness and fought a bloody exit from the city; they nevertheless escaped with the golden ransom of Montezuma intact. Later, he was greeted enthusiastically upon his return to Vera Cruz. But the level of that particular enthusiasm was as nothing compared to the greetings bestowed on the shipload of gold he sent back to the Spanish court, via Cadiz.

Montezuma perished in 1520, trying to rally his countrymen around the standard of the Spaniard he considered the incarnate form of his native Aztec god. His ransom of gold had taken the curse off Cortez' armed conflict and resulted in the subjugation of the de Narvaez troops sponsored by the previous court favorite, Velasquez.

After that, it was Cortez who was favored at court. But the gift of gold sent home to Spain in 1520 far outshone the letters even then being sent home by the expatriate padres on behalf of their findings in strange new foods and flavorings. A few more years would pass while Hernan Cortez would lead his forces up and down the mainland that would subsequently become Mexico. The gift of gold had convinced Charles V of the value of Cortez' leadership and exploratory ventures.

But he had begun to sense a slippage of his influence at court several years earlier, and that was when he began to listen to the padres and their excited stories about native food substances. So it was in 1528 that he sent home packets of the new food flavoring called chocolatl, and along with them letters testifying to their source of derivation along with instructions for their use.

Back in Spain, the dockside bursars in Cadiz and the courtiers in Seville were still looking for gold. The intermittent arrivals of food and flavoring samples like chocolatl (and coffee, vanilla, cane sugar, and tomatoes) did not assuage them. They still wanted gold. Yet, their hope was inspired neither by the personal greed of the Spanish King nor that of his courtiers.

There were much larger questions of statecraft and politics at stake in the Europe of that era. The problems began with the very identity of Charles V, who was not only the King of Spain, but who also wore a crown as the last Emperor of Holy Rome. By blood lines, he was only part Spanish, having been fathered by Philip of Burgundy (France). His mother had been Joanna, third child of Spain's King Ferdinand and Queen Isabella (the sponsors of Christopher Columbus). By nativity, he was Dutch, having been born in the Netherlands city of Ghent on February 20, 1500.

So the Spanish King and Roman Emperor Charles V ascended the Spanish throne at Seville in 1518. He was only a twenty year old novice king of Spain when he was named Holy Roman Emperor at Aix on October 23, 1520. The ascendancy had been aided by Henry VIII of England, because at that time, King Charles' aunt, Catherine of Aragon, was married to the British monarch. Pope Leo X had been reluctant to bestow the Empirical Roman crown on him, but *something happened* in the autumn of 1520 to make the pontiff change his mind. History records that Pope Leo X was known for his personal greed and as a man frequently influenced by pecuniary considerations.

History also makes note of the "gift of Montezuma," the gold that Hernan Cortez had sent back to the Spanish court in the summer of 1520. Perhaps the disappearance of Pope Leo's hesitancy in naming Charles V of Spain to the throne as Emperor of Holy Rome was merely *coincidental* to the timely arrival of Cortez' shipment of Montezuma's gold in Seville. Both events—the arrival of the gold and the appointment of Charles V—happened in sequence in 1520. If there was a connection between these two events, it has not been established by documentary proof.

But the simultaneous occurence of these events in 1520 does hold some other explanations. They certainly show why a twenty year old King of Spain, who became the recipient of a vast new golden treasure from the New World (shortly before he received the crown of the highest throne in the Old World,) would be disinclined to do anything much about the food samples he had received at the same time.

The gift of gold far overshadowed the receipt of the flavoring samples at the Spanish court in 1520, and thereafter Charles V in Europe and Captain-General Hernan Cortez in New Galicia (Mexico) were busy. By 1528, there were no more treasures in gold being sent back to Seville, and along about that time, Cortez finally acceded to the remonstrations of his padre companions and began sending out the samples and the letters of record that became the starting points in chocolate history.

Charles V was twenty-eight years old in 1528, and he faced a Europe in turmoil. By that time, he had established a highly mobile court, and among the retinue of followers that accompanied him in his journeys throughout the continent, there were some padres who had returned from Mexico. A few of these men had brought samples of chocolatl along with them. Some others, fewer still, had set up a sort of ad hoc conduit whereby further supplies of the foods they had learned to like in the New World could be sent back to them in the old one. So Charles V was off on the business of empire, and he carried along with him the camp-following padres and some of the new foods they had learned about in the lands beyond the Great Sea.

Charles V and his court travelled virtually everywhere. When he wasn't in Austria trying to turn back the Saracens, he had to deal with the royal house of Hapsburg in Vienna. He seemed to be everlastingly caught between the Catholic ranks of his Holy Roman subjects while trying to find a balance between the extremists of the Inquisition and a new sect of Protestants called Lutherans.

With the Turks nearing the Danube, Charles was caught by the petulance of the new Catholic leader, Pope Clement VII in Rome and the dissidence of Luther's followers in Bavaria. Meanwhile, his cousin wanted to be King of Denmark, and he got word from his court back in Spain that he really should do something about an adventurer named Magellan who wanted to explore the Pacific. So Charles went to work.

He argued Luther into modifying his obdurate stance enough to allow a Teutonic peace that would enable Charles to raise sufficient troops to turn back the Turks. He captured and imprisoned Pope Clement VII long enough for the Pontiff to realize that Christians, both Catholic and Protestant, had to unite against the Moslems. Agreement was reached, the Turks were turned back, and Charles put his cousin, Christian II, on the Danish throne. Then he borrowed money from the Portuguese to send Ferdinand Magellan on his way to the first historic sea voyage around the world.

Consequently, the Emperor of Holy Rome did not have a good deal of time to be pushing the popularity of any new food discoveries coming in from the New World. On the continent of Europe, he became the most widely travelled monarch of his time, and everywhere he went, his court, his padres, and their food samples went along. By then, the chocolatl (a name translated into Spanish from the phonetic Aztec, caccuatl) in the hands of his ministering missionaries had been found worthy of the meaning ascribed to it by the originators who had called it *the food of the gods.* In time, some scholarly scrivener versed in Greek came along and renamed the chocolatl beverage *theobromo cacao.* The contraction then became further subject to converse expansion when translated into English as *the food of the gods from a chocolate tree.*

Charles V and Hernan Cortez knew not what was happening to the strange brown powder under the name of chocolatl, cacao theobroma, or whatever. But while the mobile padres of Charles' court travelled to Holland, France, Switzerland, Austria, the Palatine principalities of the not yet federated German states, Italy, et al., they took the beverage base along with them. For the remainder of the sixteenth century, the secrets of chocolatl and its cane sugar sweeteners were closely held by the padres of the Spanish court. It was almost as though the men of the cloth had come to the literal belief that chocolatl really was meant to be *the food of the gods*. Whatever the reason, the record shows that they only served the novel brown beverage within the confines of monastic gatherings, and only rarely did they share it with their royal companions at court.

The seafaring Dutchmen and the Dutch West Indies Company would come along and internationalize the appeal and distribution of cocoa, but that expansion of knowledge and availability did not take place until after 1623, the year in which the Dutch West Indies Company was formed. Thereafter, the history of cacao, cocoa, and chocolate splintered into the dozens of improvements and modifications contributed by whole hosts of European countries. But those changes and the product offshoots they generated were technical in nature. They had little to do with the "romance" of the brown treasure that would later become the bull's eye of Milton Hershey's fascination.

In the last decade of the nineteenth century, Milton Hershey was repeatedly off to visit the hubs of the chocolate-making trade. But again, these were technically inspired visitations and most of them centered around Dresden, the German center for chocolate-making machinery, and of course Switzerland, for the progressively changing methodology that was constantly underway. The "Schweitzers," as Hershey called the kinsmen of his forebears, were not only ingenious in the formulation of new chocolate confections, they were geographically centered in the "mittel Europa" dairying regions where milk chocolate was introduced early and thereafter constantly changed and improved.

His technical interest and innovative input to chocolate development is variously detailed in other parts of this chronicle. But his romance with the cacao beans began with personalities and times peculiar to the Spanish Main and Central American settlement. His fascination was constantly drawn to the personal touches provided by the Grand Conquistador, Hernan Cortez, the Holy Roman Emperor, Charles V, and, of course, the last of the Aztec rulers, Montezuma. Hershey would ofttimes express a childlike sense of wonderment when he recalled the strangely circumscribed lifestyles that had so altered and frustrated the heroes of his chocolate fantasies. And he made a point of visiting many of the places where these historic figures had lived and worked, perhaps hoping to learn how such towering personalities, noblemen all, had each been forced by circumstances to retreat from the very niche that each had seemed destined to fill in the pages of history. But their destinies were thwarted and their life purposes were frustrated by the capricious intrusion of a great many other fateful events.

Hershey's recollections of Montezuma were tinged with a kind of sadness, especially when he recalled how the Aztec king had died while in the act of being loyal to a strange Spanish conqueror whom he had viewed as the reborn figure of his own native god, Quetzalcoatl. He believed that Montezuma had been the one who furnished the roomful of gold that Charles V had used in making his bid for the crown of Holy Rome. But he realized that the padres had been the ones who transmitted the Mayan secrets of caccuatl (chocolatl) to the Spanish priests who had thereafter both kept and carried along the substance of the treasure.

But Montezuma had been slain on the temple steps of his capital in the act of trying to pacify his subjects in armed rebellion against the invading forces of his idol and friend, the Castilian, Hernan Cortez.

Cortez, too, despite his shipments of golden treasure in 1520 and his little-known treasure in brown dispatched in 1528, had fallen into disfavor and then into obscurity at the Spanish Court. He terminated his explorations of Lower California and on his return to Central Mexico in 1535, he learned that the new realm had been renamed New Galicia and he had been placed under the command of Antonio de Mendoza. The King Emperor had chosen a new Captain-General and had made Mendoza viceroy of all the lands that Cortez had brought under Spanish dominion.

Cortez was then replaced in the field by Francisco Vasquez de Coronado, so with no command of his own, he returned to Spain. He reminded the courtiers of his previous contributions and finally in 1541, he was given a "nuisance" assignment to campaign against the Algerian pirates. Once again in his absence, his enemies at court prevailed and, with his mission completed, he returned to Spain, but he never appeared at court again. He retired to an estate near Seville at Castilla de la Cuesta. On December 2, 1547, the Grand Conquistador, Hernan Cortez, passed into history virtually unnoticed by the man he had helped to put on the throne of the Holy Roman Empire.

But Charles V, like his one-time esteemed Captain-General and very much like the deposed Emperor Montezuma, found himself too busy with the confusion of *responsibilities he couldn't avoid* to do anything about the *high purposes and ideals* to which he was dedicated. All the gold in the world wouldn't have quelled the disturbances of the strife-torn Europe of that era, most of which he was nominally charged to rule.

He found himself submerged in a floodtide of commitments, striving to keep peace between the Hapsburgs of Austria, the Burgundian French, the truculent Italians, and all the other Christian nations in a fight for survival against Suleiman and the Ottoman Turks. And when he got that done, he found himself hard put to reconcile the Lutherans and the Catholics in a manner calculated to save Christianity itself from the internecine onslaughts of its own dissident "believers."

But gold was not the treasure carried by the Spanish friars who returned from New Galicia and who accompanied Charles V on his endless missions to bring peace to a strife-torn Europe. They simply tagged along on the series of far flung marches that carried them to the valleys of the Danube, the plains of Pavia, the swales of Aragon, the mountains of the Tyrol, the vineyards of Burgundy, and the dikes of Holland.

For thirty-seven years, Charles V and his gypsy-like court were on the road—fighting, pacifying, cajoling, and trying to reconcile the differences that had put the warlords, the religious leaders, and the peasantry of the European continent at each other's throats. Whatever the aims of his high purpose or the intrinsic values of the treasures in gold he carried with him, they were insufficient to the task. He failed.

In 1557, Charles V, the last of the Holy Roman Emperors, resigned himself to the inevitable. He put aside the crown. He abdicated the throne. Then he retired to his quiet home in the hamlet of Yuste, in the Spanish province of Estremadura, where, at the age of fifty-seven, he would await the judgment of history.

Three of the titans whose names have been written indelibly on the pages of sixteenth century history had lived and fought and worked and died. Each one of them—Charles V, the last Emperor of Holy Rome; Montezuma, last of the Aztec kings; and Hernan Cortez, the grandest of the Conquistadores, and Captain-General of the King—had gone to glory, each one of them a failure in what he had set out to do.

Each of them had momentarily handled a fortune in gold, and yet all of them sought the same goal—*peace.* They found not peace, but a sword. The treasure of gold failed them.

But the butternut-clad ranks of lowly padres with each of their ropelike waist cords dangling a heavy cross had trudged their interminable ways across the searing sierras and the steaming jungles of Central America to mingle with the natives and to bring them The Word of God. They taught and they learned. The cross was the only gold they carried wherever in the world they went, old or new.

They learned the secrets of caccuatl (cacao, cocoa, chocolate), so they became the ones who had found *a treasure in brown*.

Perhaps Milton Hershey doted on these tales of historical romance because he was, at heart, a romanticist. But maybe he had another reason, one that was more closely tied to the Mennonite heritage he was to frequently proclaim, even though it was also the name for a following he would never join.

The unheralded padres were men of peace, and so was he. They found a treasure in brown that later was termed *cacao theobroma*, "the food of the gods from a chocolate tree."

But Milton Hershey shared another secret with those nameless monks who had braved the hardships of a harsh and primitive land where they lived with danger far from home. They *knew*—and he was to *learn*, that all the gold that God put beneath all the lands of the world would never be enough to satisfy the cravings of selfish men. The treasure in brown was different, for it was a treasure that would take its place as part of the vast foodstores mankind depends on for survival. A very *small* part, indeed, but the day may well be approaching when all of it will be needed. A day when all of the food in the world may not be enough.

Once upon a time there was a treasure in gold and a treasure in brown that were brought from the New World to the old one. The pages of history have dwelt ever since on the exploits of the emperors, kings, and conquistadores of that day who made their grand impressions on the minds of men. The names of regal personages like Montezuma, Emperor of the Aztecs, Charles V, Emperor of Holy Rome, and the Grand Conquistador, Hernan Cortez, live on to remind us that each one of them was the last of his kind.

But on the excarpments north of the Elbe, on the streets of Vienna, and in the alleyways of Reggio, some other scenes were later played out in the middle of the twentieth century where once Charles V had gone with his combined treasures of gold and brown. Treasures once known to Montezuma and then sent to Charles by Hernan Cortez. They helped him little, and perhaps not at all in his struggle with Popes and Lutherans and Sultans.

Memory calls much better on a time of not so long ago when someone else came back again to walk across the scenes of these same historical places. The sliver of foodstuffs elicited from that treasure in brown became something else in those days of the middle 1940's. The days when American GI's saw the dirty Calabrese urchins and the hollow-eyed flotsam of Dachau, greedily clutching some brown bits of maroon-wrapped chocolate in their skin-tightened fists.

These liberating soldiers witnessed the tragedy of hunger and saw the kinds of scenes no brush could paint. The thin trickle of butternut brown-robed padres carrying chocolate had long since passed into the pages of history, but in the twentieth century some khaki clad crusaders from the New World had come along with numberless truck-loads of field rations and chocolate bars that were made in a place called Hershey, and with them came yet another page in *human* history.

The most meaningful shipment of the treasure in brown had finally arrived. But to tens of thousands of American GI's who helped make delivery, the memory will last a lifetime. Even though they would never quite be able to find the words to fully describe what really happened.

You had to be there.

Chapter XIV

❦

Something Ventured—Something Lost

The ongoing saga of Milton Hershey appeared to have come to a grinding halt in the period immediately following Kitty Hershey's death on March 25, 1915. In the words of the redoubtable Bertha Condoni "He went around like a man in a dream, and for weeks at a time he just couldn't get his mind off the terrible loss that had smitten him."

Friends and family alike, beginning with Mama and Lebbie, Bill Murrie, and John Snyder, all of them tried time and again to get M.S. back in harness, but to no avail. He had fallen into an abyss of terrible loneliness, and as time went by, it seemed to worsen. He reached the nadir of his misery on May 25th of that year on the seventeenth anniversary of his marriage to Kitty. The entire day was spent alone in his room at the mansion; he wouldn't come out to eat, and he even refused to talk to those who were nearest and dearest to him. It happened on a Tuesday, and it went down in his memory as one of the blackest days in his life.

But Wednesday, the twenty-sixth, was different. He came down to breakfast, read the papers, hustled out of the mansion, and walked briskly over to the bank. On this day of emergence and change, he had a bright "Good morning" for everyone he saw.

Despair couldn't hold him, and records of the booming chocolate company show part of the reason why. By 1915 the newly enlarged plant covered thirty-five acres, and in this boom year, the business grossed $10,331,951 which was for the moment a record. But it didn't stand long, because the company doubled in volume and continued to expand across the next four years (1916—$19,876,415; 1917—$26,698,079; 1918—$35,061,664; 1919—$58,013,280). In fact, by 1920 the company's gross revenues were nearly six times greater than in 1915.

Dividends of one hundred per cent were declared in two of these years, 1918 and 1919, and bonuses of fifteen and twenty per cent were paid to wage earners and salaried employees in each of those four years. Buildings of every type were added to the chocolate plant for roasting, grinding, mixing, moulding, wrapping, etc., and the main building was enlarged to a height of six floors.

But company business alone could not contain his renewed and almost obsessive drive. He turned to building a new zoo, followed that by constructing a Convention Hall, which later became the Ice Palace (now the Hershey Museum;) and so he laid plans for a theater and social hall, which eventually became the theater complex of the Community Building to be constructed in the early 1930's.

This was not enough. Business was up, and the financial lifeline to sustain even greater growth was then assured by the negotiation of an unlimited credit account with the National City Bank of New York. So M.S. Hershey had the wherewithal to accomplish his grandest schemes, but even that wasn't enough.

He turned his attentions to a pair of prospective ventures, both of which were mightily tempting and each just as highly fraught with the dangers of risk. But he had his heart set on getting a handle on the sugar that he had always found to be in short supply, so he looked southward to the Caribbean and Central America. While he studied the cane sugar prospects, someone whispered the magic word "chicle" to him. He would have been better off if the kibitzer had stuck a wad of chewing gum in his ear, but at the time the notion enchanted him.

In 1915, after he returned from a European trip, he tried to ascertain the prospects for a cessation of hostilities in the Great War. The prospects were bad, but on the other hand, most of his continental competition was virtually out of business. Somehow on the homeward bound boat, he came to the conclusion that he wouldn't take advantage of the war to beat down his embattled European confectionery rivals. But he was committed to improving his place in the sugar market, and he had no reservations about opening lines of competition in America.

He began an active search by dispatching a team of loyal workers to investigate the sugar properties in Cuba. Then he decided to disconcert one of his sugar buying competitors, who was in the chewing gum business, by another ploy. This decision brought him a nose-to-nose confrontation with P.K. Wrigley, the chewing gum magnate. He decided to open the assault by having the outcome decided on the ancient playing fields of Baker Bowl in Philadelphia.

Out in Chicago, the Wrigley fortune had been built on chewing gum, and as one of the first manifestations of newly acquired wealth, P.K. Wrigley had purchased the Chicago Cubs, with an eye to installing them on a playing field named after himself. Hershey, with something like this in mind, approached John Myers, who was then owner of the Lancaster team in the Tri-State League, and sent him to Philadelphia to buy the Phillies. The object was aimed at also acquiring Baker Bowl, a prospect which Hershey viewed with double delight, because the name Baker, (also the name of one of his other leading competitors in the baking chocolate field,) would be erased from a stadium henceforth to be known as The Hershey Bowl.

Neither the prospective purchase nor the delight lasted very long. When John Myers came back to Hershey with the news that the Phillies' owner had turned down his offer of two hundred thousand dollars, Hershey upped the figure to a quarter million, but that evoked nothing further than another refusal. The owner, said Myers, wanted three hundred and fifty thousand dollars and that was it. According to Myers the team and the dilapidated field just weren't worth it.

Hershey disagreed. He would have bought the team at any price, but Myers wouldn't let him. He said the Phillies, at best, had a few "fair" players, but most of them weren't good enough to play on his Tri-State Lancaster team.

"And that park, Baker Bowl," he added, "is an absolute wreck. It's too small. It's run down. It's in a bad location. There will be no parking for the increasing number of people who drive automobiles to the games."

Hershey almost waved him off, but his business cohorts, particularly John Snyder, talked him out of it. Snyder later claimed, "He really didn't want to get into baseball that much; all he wanted to do was upset Phil Wrigley."

Whatever the reason, Hershey kept going right ahead with the other facet of that aim. He began by hiring his cousin, Clayton Snavely, son of his former farm manager, Frank Snavely, to develop and market "a chewing gum that will drive Phil Wrigley off the field!"

Snavely began by collecting a check for a thousand dollars and heading for New York. He took up residence in the Imperial Hotel on Broadway, and in a matter of weeks he got things rolling. He spent half the money for rolling machinery, and then he compiled a buyer's guide for the sources of chicle, chucca gum, spearmint, peppermint, sweet birch, and other oils, and whatever else he thought should go into chewing gum flavorings.

The initial effort was set up in Hershey with another Snavely cousin, Joe, the Hershey printer who was put to work on the labels for "Easy Chew Gum." They rocketed right along; in fact, the gum was so superior within the limited trade circles that by 1919 they were doing better than eighty thousand dollars a month. Then M.S. set about to do three things, all calculated to get P.K. Wrigley wriggling.

He began by putting out a six stick package of gum for a nickel retail, and followed that by opening a new plant in New York. No sooner was the new company installed in the six story structure, the O'Neil-Adams Building on Sixth Avenue between Twenty-First and Twenty-Second Streets, than it applied for and got an export license.

Then the hammers began to fall. This began when demand increased to the point where they had to add a flour mill to grind up the extra-fine flour needed to make the gum more chewy. But they had to make these materials in Hershey, so they decided to flavor the flour before mixing it with chicle. The peppermint, spearmint, and other flavorings were so lavishly added to the mix that Bert Black, one of the old-time workers in the mill, said, "I hadda keep my eyes closed. Those peppermint oils were so strong they made tears run down my cheeks all day."

His were not the only tears. P.K. Wrigley came out of the box by writing a letter to the War Tax Office in Washington. The war was over, but the tax was still on, and *Hershey's Easy Chew Gum* was nailed for an extra six cent tax stamp for every carton of twenty packs. The extra stamps had to be put on by hand, and between the extra labor of affixing the stamps and the tax premium, he found his gum priced out of the market.

Not only were tears in abundance, but the chewing gum inventories were becoming a glut on the storage facilities, both in New York and in Hershey. Then a young man named John J. (Jack) Gallagher was brought onto the scene and put in charge of chewing gum sales. He did two things at once.

He began by cutting production to the level of daily orders received and tried to work off the excess inventory. But inventory reduction went slowly, mainly because incoming orders were dropping at a remarkable rate. Hershey called in Gallagher and asked him what to do.

"Drop it," said Gallagher. And they did, but after the smoke and the aroma of spearmint oil cleared and they were unstuck from the gum business, Hershey counted up the score. He figured they had lost four years and two and half million dollars on the venture.

"We couldn't get sugar, we couldn't get chicle, but most of all, we couldn't get orders," Clayton Snavely was later to proclaim. He added, "We were out of business."

Down in Washington, a young Undersecretary of Commerce in the Harding administration declared that "importation of raw materials for non-essential products are still restricted." Chewing gum was non-essential, and Milton Hershey was not at first delighted with the former California engineer whose Commerce Department powers had militated against him.

But later on, he came to respect the man when he headed up the Belgian War Relief Commission and even voted for him in 1928. His name was Herbert Hoover.

Perhaps sensing the hammer blow that was beginning to fall on his chewing gum business in 1920, M.S. Hershey decided to get away from it all by going to Europe in the fall of 1919. He headed for Le Havre, but northern France and Belgium were still so war-ravaged that he turned immediately south to the Cote d'Azur and Monaco. He was beset by many problems.

The chocolate business was booming, and his sugar enterprises in Cuba had risen to the point where he had teams of men busily acquiring cane fields and refinery sites just east of Havana. He had accompanied Mama down there in 1918 and set her up in a comfortable apartment right in Havana. But her health had failed in subsequent months, so she returned to her home on Chocolate Avenue in Hershey, Pennsylvania.

Activity was the byword, and everywhere he looked, the post-war world was changing. But two immutable problems remained. In his personal life, he was deeply concerned about Mama. He had wanted her to accompany him on this trip, but in her eighty-fourth year, the Mennonite matriarch had begun to weaken. He had notes from her telling him, "I haven't been able to wrap any kisses today," and he had to smile, even though the smile was a sad one.

She still distrusted his newfound wealth. She had come out of Cuba warning against "the way you're throwing money around" in his Matanzas and El Centro ventures. Before parting, she let him know she found out about his gambling on the sugar market, and she said, "If you aren't careful, you can lose it all." Then she added the chill reminder, "Remember 1885."

He told himself this wasn't 1885—it was 1919. Now he had property, he had a growing chocolate business that would gross more than fifty million dollars in the next twelve months, and he had a town, a park, and a school. Best of all, he had made some very good friends, and some of them were bankers. He even had a bank of his own, for he was, in reality, a one-man holding company. While in one sense he never really became an outright millionaire by the level of only several hundred thousand dollars he usually kept in cash in his own name, he did control the votes on sixty per cent of the stock deeded to the Hershey Industrial School.

But none of these assets changed the fact that he still needed sugar to meet the growing demands of the chocolate business. In Cuba, land was being developed, railroad lines were being laid out, plantations were being cultivated, and work was underway on the refineries and port facilities being built to meet those needs. But the whole complex of operations wouldn't be in full production for another year or two at the earliest. Meanwhile, he faced product demands *right then*. He knew you couldn't put next year's sugar into chocolate bars you have to ship today.

While seemingly out of touch with business ventures, he became more and more active in the sugar market, particularly with sugar futures. He began buying them up as though they were dollar bills selling for a nickel each. In his ken, sugar prices could only go up, and no matter what the price, he had to have sugar to stay in business.

There is no way of knowing how much Mama Hershey knew of this daring venture, but when someone told her that her boy Milton was buying stocks on margin, she asked them to explain. She gritted her teeth and actually wept when she understood that he was, as she put it, "gambling with borrowed money." Her "boy" was then a sixty-three year old business tycoon, and he knew better. Or, as Mama straightaway told him, *he should have known better.*

Meanwhile, he sought refuge in Monaco and Nice, perhaps because it offered him a sentimental journey away from the cares about sugar futures, and P.K. Wrigley. He needed a sanctuary in which he could once again relive the brightest days he had ever known, when he had gone there with Kitty in 1912.

But when winter came, he returned to Hershey and 1920 brought with it the twin disasters of a falling sugar market and, worst of all, he found Mama had been forced to take to her bed. One day he was told that she was sinking fast, and he quickly dashed to her home on Chocolate Avenue.

He spent the following several days at her side, reassuring her that "the little note I signed" with the New York bank "would soon be cleared." She knew better, for somehow she learned that her Milton had borrowed fifty million dollars. Worse than that, it was to pay for sugar he didn't have. He did his best to console her, but he failed.

On a chilly Thursday morning, March 11, 1920, Milton made his way to Mama's room. He stood for a moment looking at the gaunt figure on the bed, and the tears welled up in his eyes. He walked to the window and peered through the brassy shafts of cold slanting sunlight that beamed across Chocolate Avenue. His memories went trailing off to the hot, oily air of a summer garden in Titusville, the steaming candy kitchens in Philadelphia, and the room downstairs where, until recently, his beloved Mama had been wrapping her daily boxes of *Kisses*.

Her labored breathing came to him as he turned and went back to her bedside. His heart welled up with emotion as he lifted her almost weightless figure in his arms and gently carried her to the rocking chair by the window. Her breathing seemed to come easier as he cradled her in his arms and slowly began rocking back and forth in silence.

He felt tears trickling down to the edges of his moustache as she opened her pain-darkened eyes and gave him the merest trace of a smile.

"Be careful, Milton," she said. Then she closed her eyes for the last time.

*   *   *

Disasters were coming in triplicate for Milton Hershey. His Mama's death hurt him most of all, and not alone because he missed her for herself. It was the time that bothered him. She had died *scared*, the one thing in the world he wanted to keep her from being. The other twin debacles were just that. The failing chewing gum venture was no more than another expensive flight of fancy, and the sugar future bond loan—"What the hell!" he snapped. "I'll clear that thing up in no time at all."

But Mama had died scared, afraid he would fail again. If anything was needed to put steel in a spine that was already tempered with vanadium, that was it.

He stood by her graveside on Sunday, March 14, and saw her laid to rest in the Owl Hill Cemetery next to the spot where Kitty was buried. The Right Reverend Jacob Kreider of the Reformed Mennonite Church intoned the text of John 12:24:

> *He that loveth me not keepeth not my sayings;*
> *and the word which ye hear*
> *is not mine, but the Father's which sent me.*

Son Milton looked down across the vale below, where Fanny Buckwalter Snavely Hershey in her eighty-four years had known it all. From pain and poverty, plenty and generosity, she had remained everlastingly the goodhearted "plain person" she had always been. She had spent a lifetime in accordance with the thrift and the carefulness she always observed. For she had always loved people better than wealth, and plentiful money had scared her more than poverty. The Eternal Galilean came as a carpenter, not a king. And Fanny Hershey kept the faith by always remaining the same humble, gentle, and loving person—just as God had made her.

Second Homecoming

A very determined Milton Hershey faced up to the twin calamities of sugar and chewing gum losses assayed at roughly two and a half million dollars each. But very few people ever understood why he should put everything he had on the line and borrow fifty million dollars when his losses totalled less than ten per cent of that amount.

Aside from the few who did understand, nobody looked at the problem in the same light as Hershey. Others thought of this new credit stretching bond issue as an attempt to cover a loss. He thought of it as an opportunity to keep right on growing at the same unprecedented rate without even taking time to count up a loss, or even several of them.

He was building, particularly in Cuba; he was not filling in a hole. Nevertheless, there was a hole, and it was both considerably large and in urgent need of attention.

The sugar stocks he'd bought were pegged at twenty-two cents, and he intended selling them at twenty-five cents. He was offered twenty-three cents, refused it, and then came the crash. In a matter of days, the stock he thought he'd be able to sell at twenty-five had dropped to two cents per share. By the time he sold, it was down to less than one-seventh of a cent. His man in Havana, Carrera, said the loss was at least two and half million. Hershey sold off, shut up, and blamed nobody. Not even himself.

The Cuban banks closed, with the exception of National City Bank of New York, Chase-Manhattan of New York, and the Royal Bank of Canada in Ottawa. When he ticked off the additional two and a half million he'd also plowed into the chewing gum debacle, the total losses went over five million. Then, as the year ended, the Hershey Chocolate Company chimed in with a deficit of $395,739.

He went out and straightway put the lie to the famous line, "You can't borrow your way out of debt." He not only borrowed, he borrowed five times more than he needed. Then he proceeded to spend his way out of debt—on borrowed money.

But there came a day when a new kind of man was brought into town to do the impossible. It began with the arrival of R.J. deCamp, manager of the Industrial Department of the National City Bank, and he was installed in Hershey to watch and try to direct everything in sight.

Hershey simmered, but he took the heat and kept his silence. The so-called terms of the attachment were indefinite, but Hershey's immediate aim was to "get that so-and-so out of here" before any papers were brought into play. A New York colleague of deCamp's said this about the arrangement.

"They picked just the right man for the job. Mr. deCamp would march into the Hershey bank impeccably dressed and replete with spats and walking stick. Then he would sit at a big desk and start giving orders. And he would tell everybody, including Hershey, what to do and how to do it."

They say M.S. "looked like a pint percolator, fuming with a quart of steam-heated water." He may have sizzled and bubbled, but he didn't boil over. Nevertheless, he was hard put to keep a lid on his pent-up anger. The other work went on, and the longer deCamp stayed, the more M.S. kept accelerating toward the target date of his riddance. In effect, however, the National City Bank had chosen precisely the right man to get the job done expeditiously, however painful it was to Hershey.

The gentlemen was shown every courtesy. In Hershey, Pennsylvania, he was given a home on Chocolate Avenue, a handsome stone dwelling formerly known as the Tea House, just a short walk from the bank. He moved into M.S.'s personal mansion headquarters at Rosario when he was in Hershey, Cuba. Each place he moved into, he rearranged and redecorated to suit his own taste.

Then he tried to do the same thing on the farms and in the chocolate plant. M.S. once again held his peace, and he had to put the brakes on everyone else, especially his old sidekick, Lebbie.

One day, some pigs got sick on the farm, and Lebbie stormed over to the mansion to complain about deCamp.

"Throw him out," he demanded. "You keep him around here very long and we won't have any cattle on the place."

Hershey, going against his primal instincts, pacified Lebbie. He told him that the only way to get rid of deCamp was to "get that damn note paid off, and the only way to do that is by getting the business into high gear."

The shirt-sleeved Hershey set an example by showing up at the bank and getting started by seven a.m., an hour before anyone else arrived. By eight, he had streaked out of the bank and hurried down to the plant. After a whirlwind tour of the various departments, he took off again and began riding circuit to the farms, the store, the school, and the park. It wasn't long until the whole town and all the people caught fire from the sparks spinning off the boss.

They wanted to give his town back to the Old Man. He set an example for them, and they got off the mark like a shot. John J. Gallagher, who had been moved up to assistant sales manager, said M.S. kept telling them, "Boys, don't *rock* the boat, *row* it!"

Back in New York, W.S. Lambie, vice-president of National City Bank, kept a keen eye on these developments.

"If they thought the sugar crisis was dramatic, they hadn't seen anything. And if anyone thought Milton Hershey was licked, they were wrong. But he didn't do it with any sleight of hand tricks; he just got into harness with the rest of his people and they straightway slugged it out."

Everything began clicking with the well-oiled precision of a Swiss watch, and Milton the watchmaker, stood by and ticked off the minutes. He liked what he saw. Fred Pugh was pumping away at sales, and chocolate company profits went up to $3,146,599 by the close of 1921. By that time, P.A. Staples had Cuba humming like a queen bee honeyed up on dextrins, and there was a genial six-foot giant named T.L. McHeffey, comptroller at Hershey, Pennsylvania, working as the linchpin between both operations. John G. Snavely, another cousin, had been sent to Cuba as general accountant, and John Lucas, manager of the New York branch office, was charged with keeping the National City Bank brass hats pacified.

They worked so well that by the spring of 1922, M.S. decided to take off for other parts. His passport application for ports of call in the British Isles, Belgium, France, Italy, Switzerland and Gibraltar told it all. Under the line, "Purpose of Trip," was the word, "Pleasure."

He made a whirlwind tour of the spots mentioned, and it was reported later that it was in this period that he met and became acquainted with Herbert Hoover, who was then working in Europe as Belgian War Relief Administrator. But he was back in New York by the end of May, and there he had dinner in the Waldorf-Astoria with Sam Clark, former manager of the Hershey Department Store.

"Sam," he said, "tomorrow we get our town back. I've paid off the note, and we'll be dealing with the Corn Exchange. Now I've got to get back to my people and kick that watchdog out of the house on Chocolate Avenue."

A few days later, M.S. and John "Judge" Snyder composed a letter:

June 1, 1922

Mr. R.J. deCamp
Hershey, Pa.

My dear sir,

As I desire on July 1, 1922 to have possession of the premises in Hershey, Pa., now occupied by you as a residence, you are requested to remove therefrom on or before that time; the period of your occupancy will end on the day named, when you will surrender the same to me.

Yours truly,
M.S. Hershey

The letter was hand delivered. The departure was made. The next day, M.S. Hershey strolled into the bank and went straight to the vacated desk. He unlocked it and held up the key which he had carried for the nearly two year tenure of the man so recently departed.

Everyone had told him, "It will take a miracle to get that loan paid off in five years," but they all had overlooked the fact that he was a man schooled in the art of working miracles.

He was still a shade bitter about it; in fact, he never again set foot in the Rosario Mansion that had been his favorite Cuban haunt, because, as he put it, "This still smells like a kennel since that watchdog pulled out." But on the bright summer morning when he unlocked his favorite desk at the Hershey Bank, all of this was forgotten. He spun around in his chair and folded his arms across his brown-vested bosom.

His voice didn't squeak even a little bit as he said, "This is one of the happiest days of my life."

Chapter XV

◆·◆

When Jekyll Was Hyde
. . . and Hershey Was Hall

In 1886 when Robert Louis Stevenson wrote *The Strange Case of Dr. Jekyll and Mr. Hyde,* he brought attention to the alter egos and the good side versus bad side struggles that beset most *homo* types of *sapiens*. In that very same year, Milton Hershey was deeply involved in a struggle of his own, but his problem was not concerned with an inner contest between good and evil. Until 1886 he'd been a loser, pure and simple, and as he saw it, he'd arrived on the threshold of his thirtieth birthday with only an unbroken string of defeats to show for his ill-starred business ventures.

The record shows that in the years that followed his thirtieth birthday, he finally managed to turn things around, and he began substituting a chain of victories to take the place of his prior debacles. But one thing, one personal characteristic, that played a big part in both the strings of winning and losing was directly tied to a trait he'd inherited from his Papa. He was a gambler, and he didn't know when to quit.

Some things don't change. Chances are, to coin a phrase, born gamblers live out their lives to become winners or losers, but when "The Roll Is Called Up Yonder" and the last roll of the dice is made below, they simple go to glory as dead gamblers. They may act out their roles in consonance with the scriptural admonition that "we come into this world with nothing, and we go out of it with nothing," but they spend their lifetimes gambling on what they can win—between the times of their coming and going.

The record clearly shows another peculiarity on the part of Milton Hershey. He hadn't quit taking chances when the cards were stacked against him, when he kept piling up loss upon loss in his early life. And he wouldn't quit taking chances in later life either, especially after he'd begun what has since emerged as one of the longest winning streaks in the annals of risky ventures.

But he did alter his style, and thereby hangs the tale. It became an odyssey of calculated risk-taking, but it was kept anonymous. Now it emerges as a litany of trials and errors that hitherto went unrecorded. In the Robert Louis Stevenson book, Dr. Jekyll found himself involved in a terrible struggle with another side of the coin contained within his own personality, named Mr. Hyde.

Milton Hershey had an alter ego, too, and it was this subliminal personality who became the occasional gambler known as Mr. M.S. Hall.

The original date of emergence for the character who functioned under the pseudonym M.S. Hall is shrouded in mystery. But the verity of his existence is based on solid documentary proof. The pile of Traveler Check stubs and Express money orders in the personal file of Milton Hershey were too real to allow room for doubt. Nevertheless, the exact date of Hershey's adoption of this pseudonym cannot be clearly ascertained. The best, and most reasonable, approximations have set the date for the unbaptized emergence of the misty character known as M.S. Hall, as sometime between late 1918 and early in the year of 1920.

This would put the date at sometime after the death of Catherine Hershey, his wife, and a time that came before his mother, Fanny Hershey passed away. It would also fit a time frame in which he would be travelling pretty much alone and on his own, and it would fall within the period when he was to be frequently exposed to the proximity of the gaming tables of the Havana casinos. The particular gambling forms he favored were simple. In the casinos he played roulette; elsewhere, Atlantic City, Belmont Park, Saratoga, etc., he alternated between "the bobtail nag when sometimes he bet on the bay."

The diarists who believe that M.S. could walk on water without getting his feet wet have long since acceded to the fact that he frequently did go abroad under the alias of M.S. Hall. But they have been quick to point out the necessity for such a coverup identity, since he had always been prone to rub elbows with the crowds, even though he had become both rich and famous.

When he took off from Hershey or New York, his record for "other money" purchases in the name of M.S. Hall went from an average low of five hundred to a thousand dollars and hovered at a high median average of five thousand. One of the men who worked in the Hershey Bank during the twenties recalls that there was one check issued to M. Hall that hit an all-time record high of ten grand.

But the instrument had been a wired money order, sent to Cuba, and it could have been spent for any one of a number of things, including a donation to a local charity, or even as an advance security payment to bind some business deal. The facts are obscured by the record of M.S. Hershey's having so frequently donated much more than ten thousand dollars to local charities, in a series of on-the-spot gifts, in any one of so many of the spots where he happened to be. He also had a record for instantly putting money on the line whenever a rare business opportunity came to light and demanded an immediate deposit.

This alter ego side of the ledger Milton Hershey compiled under his other name as M.S. Hall is filled with stories that also deal with two of his other occasional diversions. He liked the ladies, and he didn't always keep his nose dry when in the presence of the cup that cheers. The tales have been recounted by responsible witnesses, some of whom were devoted to the man and some of whom were not. They are all believed to be true, or they wouldn't be part of this chronicle. But none of them is either sordid or seamy, for nothing like that ever came to light in any of the searches made either by the man's devotees or his detractors. The ranks of both are legion.

The following stories were culled from the notes of Dr. Herman Hostetter, Hershey's personal physician from 1924 until 1945, and they were affirmed by the recollections of several former Hotel employees and one former chauffeur.

Hershey had the middling repute for being just exactly midway between the opposite goal lines of teetotaller and wine bibber. He liked a splash of toddy from time to time, but he seldom had more than one or two, and nobody ever saw him sprockled.

The closest near-miss in his personal saga of nose wettings came one evening during the middle 1930's at the Hershey Hotel when he had been scheduled for a dinner meeting with Doc Hostetter. The good doctor showed up a few minutes before the appointed hour of seven, only to learn that M.S. had been delayed at a cocktail party being held by some prominent visitors, including the governor. It was seven-thirty before the prospective host made his appearance, and he was about half a notch west of his ordinarily genial pre-dinner self.

He smiled a little more and talked quite a bit more than usual, so this prompted Hostetter to ask him during dinner how many drinks he had taken aboard at the previous happy hour he'd attended.

"One," he replied, with a funny smile. But he also looked quickly away from the inquisitive medico. He abstained from ordering any more libations before, during, or after the dinner.

When M.S. and Hostetter finished their meal and went into the main foyer of the hotel, it came time for them to part, so the doctor asked him again.

"M.S.," he persisted, "are you sure you only had one drink?"

Hershey grimaced. "Yeah," he replied, drawing his upper teeth tight against his lower lip and looking heavenward, "you could say that. I had one drink."

Then he turned and walked toward the elevator, but as he passed Konrad Hartmann, who had been a witness to all this, he winked and whispered, "One more than I needed."

*   *   *

Doc Hostetter figured in some other events that were part of the continuing routine in the middle thirties, and these were also centered on the Hotel Hershey. Attendance and rentals were skeletal in the early years, but when M.S. was in town, he'd stop in for his favorite cocktail. The afternoon tete-a-tete usually occurred on Tuesdays, and it was frequently held in the company of several ladies, the widows and wives of current or hitherto close friends. The drinks were Bronx cocktails, an M.S. favorite.

But the good doctor, in keeping with the hawk-eyed vigil he always maintained over his aging patient, had rigged the wine list. He had instructed Art Bowman and other bartenders to vary the M.S. dosage, quite unbeknownst to the impatient patient, so that the gin portion of the gin and orange juice drink was tailored somewhat closer to Mennonite than man-about-town standards of measurement. The only gin in the drink came with the slice of orange affixed to the rim of the glass. This slice of fruit was dipped in gin, and although it was redolent with the fragrant aroma of juniper juice, it had somewhat less than half a teaspoon of active spirits contained within it. The whole liquid balance of the libation was straight orange juice, modestly sweetened by a dab of confectionery sugar. So M.S.'s Tuesday afternoon trips to the tippler's trough were medically prescribed to give him a high level of vitamin C and a low measure of spirited octane for his aging fuel tank.

Once again, happiness prevailed in the absence of the exact knowledge that so often tends to diminish it.

*   *   *

Friday morning get-togethers at the Hotel were something else. Roughly, the group was made up of the wives of Snyder, Murrie, et al. M.S. Hershey, of course, was the center of attraction while they met and set up their itinerary at the hotel.

But once they departed, he became the aficionado of fine horseflesh known as M.S. Hall. The destination was usually Atlantic City, but springtime ventures to Bowie, Pimlico, and Monmouth tracks also went on the record. The one thing that did not go onto that record until way late in the game was the unbelievable luck of the host bettor, M.S., (in this case) Hershey. Again and again, the ladies returned from the tracks to tell about the miraculous winning streak of M.S., the wizardous bettor. Again and again he held a winning ticket in *every* race.

This went on for quite some time until the doubting Thomases had heard enough from the ladies about this fabulous all-winning record. It was just too good to be true. So the previously preoccupied spouses, i.e. Murrie, Hostetter, and Abe Heilman, decided that they would see if they could get to go along on one of the jaunts.

One nameless hubby put the request in words and was told to "come along and bring the others." The following Friday, it took the Packard limousine and the big La Salle, to carry the party of a dozen enthusiasts to the track.

Roy Tice, M.S.'s full-time chauffeur, drove the La Salle, and that was the car in which his boss, the incognito M.S. Hershey, chose to ride. Shortly after the party arrived at the track, Tice was dispatched to the betting windows to place the wagers of M.S. Hershey. The others placed their bets one at a time between races, but after going to the window for the first time before the first race, Tice just gave M.S. his tickets and sought diversion elsewhere.

Meanwhile, the races were run off and, aside from holding up a winning ticket after each event, the beaming M.S. awaited the return of minion Tice. Thereupon Tice was dispatched on a mission of collection, following which he came back with a different envelope for each race, and with a stack of bills for a winning ticket in every one of them.

There was a good deal of mumbling about this among the male passengers of the Packard town car on the way back to Hershey. *Nobody was that lucky!* Yet they'd been there, and they'd seen it with their own eyes. Milton Hershey, had indeed, had a winner in every race.

It remained for the diagnostic skills of Doc Hostetter to unravel the note concealed inside the private fortune cookie of one M.S. Hall, nee Hershey. The group had stopped off for a late dinner at the Berkshire Hotel in Reading on their way back to Hershey. Hostetter finished his coffee in record time and went in search of the elusive Roy Tice, who had dined and returned to wait at the car.

"Okay, Roy," he asked in something less than his most soothing bedside voice, "how does he do it? And don't give me any of those blank looks, or your private stock of Havana cigars stops right here!"

Hostetter had delivered a well-aimed shot. But Tice didn't make an immediate reply, because he was probably weighing the alternatives between the poles of being without cigars or the one wherein he would be engulfed by smoke and flame, courtesy of a cigar-smoking M.S. Hershey when he wasn't in the skin of M.S. Hall.

"C'mon, Roy," Hostetter persisted, "how does he do it? How can he pick a winner in every race?"

The chauffeur turned his head away for a moment, then he gritted his teeth and looked straight at the hard-nosed Herman, M.D., Inquisitor.

"It's easy," he grudgingly pronounced. "He picks a winner in every race because he *buys a ticket on every horse in every race.*"

Hostetter gulped. But having closed his mouth, he kept it shut. Not until he wrote his own tract on Milton Hershey more than twenty years later, *The Body, Soul and Spirit of Milton S. Hershey,* would he plan to spell this out as part of the text to be published. But when the time of publication came, he had latter-day misgivings, and the notes remained unpublished. Then Art Bowman and Konrad Hartmann, the Hershey Hotel workers, would come along to confirm the story. By then, the holders of the point and counterpoint named Milton Hershey and M.S. Hall had long since gone to their singular and simultaneous rewards.

But, by then, both Hershey and Hall probably managed a smile between them. You could bet on it.

A Tale of Two Bachelors

The tale began in 1908, when the village of Hershey, Pennsylvania, was coming out of the budding stage with the promise of blooming into a full-sized city. The Hershey Chocolate Company was humming away, the streetcars were bringing people in from the nearby countryside, and buildings seemed to be going up everywhere.

Milton Hershey and wife Kitty were busily engaged in globetrotting in those days, but back in Pennsylvania, the face of their tiny hometown was being changed almost daily. But man doesn't live by bread alone, nor does he thrive on expansive plans for putting up buildings, laying track, and installing utilities. So the erstwhile community planners had to look up from the drawing boards for a moment. The time had come for them to begin paying attention to the social needs of their burgeoning community.

The churches kept pace with the incoming tide of prospective communicants, particularly the Presbyterians who had been there since long before Hershey became Hershey. The town fathers were early to recognize the power wielded by the distaff side of the populace, so they quickly made plans for the building of a Women's Club. Meanwhile, the ranks of the male population were filled by men of every age, many of whom remained unmarried. Some of the middle-aged and elderly ones were still firmly resolved to remain that way, so they moved to start a club of their own. They didn't even ask for one. But they did feel a need to band together, if only to tighten their grip on the single state they prized so much. Thus, a Hershey Bachelors Club was formed and became operable a few years before the Women's Club was opened.

The two most prominent stalwarts in the early day Bachelor Club were the redoubtable Lebbie Lebkicher and the persnickety Ezra Hershey. In the viewpoints of both men, there was communal aspiration to warm the hearts and not the hearths of the maidenly members within the burgeoning center of society. There were some outspoken members of the feminist sect who insisted that the most heartwarming thing that Ezra H. and Lebbie L. could do was to stay as far distant as possible from the ladies' respective hearths.

Of the two flag-waving misogynists, Ezra Hershey was both the youngest and the noisiest. Lebbie, who had been variously linked to virtually every single lady in the Hershey realm, found it somewhat easier to avoid feminine entanglements by simply staying away from women. There were quite a few of those who remembered times when he had not stayed away from Aunt Mattie, and there were even one or two who thought he showed more than friendly concern for widow Fanny Hershey.

He would have been the first to admit his love for both the Snavely sisters, had anyone dared to ask, but nobody did. The affectionate bond on all sides was more familial than romantic. They looked on him as a brother, and he esteemed both the Snavely ladies as sisters of his own. Still and all, Lebbie wasn't very vocal in any sense of the word, and he was perennially voiceless in the presence of members of the opposite sex. Thus, by remaining singularly mute, he remained both happily and silently single.

Cupid's shaft knocked Ezra Hershey from the ranks of the Bachelor's Club on Sunday, September 20, 1910. The date was to become memorable because of two events that transpired within eight hours of each other on that second Sunday of the month. First, Miss Mary Rohrer, daughter of Mr. F.B. Rohrer, had gathered the worthy Ezra Hershey into the viselike grip of holy wedlock that afternoon in a living room ceremony performed in the Hummelstown home of her parents. Later that same evening, the newlyweds retired to their suite in the Cocoa Inn. In the morning, they would be off on their honeymoon trip to Canada, but the night was not yet ready to give way to morning.

Outside on the lawn of the building lot across the way, on the southwest corner of Chocolate and Cocoa Avenues, a band of well-wishers had set up a novel arrangement to serenade the newlyweds. A cluster of partially sozzled bachelors, along with a smattering of some others who would later wish they were bachelors, had trundled a giant new bell across the street to the corner of the lot. The serenaders, who were reported to have been led by Lebbie Lebkicher, then proceeded to beat away on the bell with a variety of canes, sticks, hammers, and whatever else came to hand. The exercise later proved interesting to those who study the manners, morals, and customs of wet-nosed throngs who perform prodigious feats while alternately dipping their noses into the cup that cheers.

Some measure of significance later emerged from this event when it was noted that it took the combined strength of twelve semi-sloshed serenaders nearly half an hour to drag the newly delivered firehouse bell to the concert site. Several days later, a crane hoist and a tractor, complemented by the arduous labors of two dozen men, spent an entire afternoon returning the bell to its original site.

Concertmaster L. Lebkicher and his eleven percussionists gave the newlyweds less than an hour in which to enjoy their performing skills. Then all hands withdrew to Haeffner's Tavern to offer another toast to the happy groom. Nothing remains on the record to show how the happy groom rated their performance that evening. Several weeks later, "Ez" Hershey returned from Canada and said he hadn't noticed anything on behalf of their serenading efforts, whereupon one of the erstwhile revelers made a distinctly lascivious reference to the other concerns which commanded the groom's attention on that memorable wedding night.

Lebbie and his group did not go to Haeffner's in search of sanctuary, and save for him, none found it. But the old Civil War veteran broke away from his companions and settled into a quiet corner. He later told his friends that the recent spate of jollity had set him to thinking about himself and the kind of life he had led.

The old skinflint had caught a Minie ball in the calf of his right leg back at Gettysburg in 1863. A dozen years after being discharged, he had first hooked up with Milton Hershey, in Philadelphia, in 1876. That effort failed, and he was peripatetically engaged otherwise until 1886, when he and young M.S. essayed to give it another go.

And go it did. But twenty-five years had passed, and even though Lebbie found his station in life had been greatly elevated by the success he shared with Milt, he realized that only hard work had dominated his daily life for a quarter century. He also realized, without saying anything, that he was the only one privileged to call the boss "Milt," and the very only one who had ever been known to lecture M.S. like the proverbial Dutch uncle. And M.S. listened.

Something came over Lebbie in Haeffner's that evening after the celebration of Ezra Hershey's nuptial embarcation, and he, William Henry Lebkicher, emerged a changed man. He returned to his own apartment in the Community Inn and, after quietly folding away his Prince Albert cutaway, he went to bed and dreamed of making a new start.

He had to get away from Hershey. Not just the man or the work or the town, but everything that had been a daily grind for the past twenty-five years. He had to see new lands, meet new people, and do new things. And he had to do all of it quickly, because he was past his sixty-fifth birthday.

"I ain't no spring chicken," he said to himself. Then he went to sleep.

Next morning, he got up and set out to prove something that almost everyone who knew him had known all along. He wasn't a chicken at all; he was a hawk. The quanta of spring left in him was about to surprise everyone, even him.

He spent the better part of the year laying plans, and in 1911 he took off. Just before he set out to see the world, some of his closer confidantes were tempted to caution him about staying away too long. Several were of the opinion that Jim Leitheiser had been awaiting just such an opportunity. They feared Leitheiser had been biding his time, awaiting the chance to take over Lebbie's job. This trip, they feared, would give Leitheiser the chance to do just that.

Nobody said anything to Lebbie. They didn't want to spoil his trip with any bothersome worries. Anyway, they figured, the old skinflint would be back in a few months, and nothing much could happen in that time. Besides, M.S. was away, too. So they put their fears to rest. What could happen in a few months?

The guessers were wrong. Lebbie had waited a long time before going, but when he took off, he decided to go all the way—all the way around the world.

The man who decided to get away from it all did a good job of it. He spent the balance of that year and part of the next in a globe-trotting hegira that read like a paper race. Everywhere the old skinflint went, he sent back cards and letters to tell his friends where he was and what he was doing. The Cook's Tour people would have been proud of him, for he touched virtually every geographic port of call on the map. For some unaccountable reason, he set off on a westward jaunt that began in Honolulu, Hawaii, whence he proceeded to the Fiji Islands, New Guinea, the Philippines, Java, Australia, New Zealand, and Tasmania.

Then he went up the coast of China, visited Manchuria, and swung over for a tour of Japan. After sending back some silk prints from Nippon, he was off again to Ceylon and India. All the while, as the *Hershey Press* tried to keep up with the redoubtable globetrotter, the Hersheys themselves, Milton and Kitty, went back and forth between Egypt and the continent. But Lebbie never crossed trails with them, even though he did pass through Alexandria while Milton and Kitty were on their way to that place.

He wound up touring the Mediterranean, visiting Italy and the south of France, before pushing on to Switzerland and then Germany. Somehow, the card collection and the published record of his travels became regular features in the *Press*. These accounts contain no mention of his having visited any part of the British Isles.

By the time he returned, the Hershey from which he had escaped in order to make a change had been pretty well changed itself. The day he came back to his office, he learned that Jim Leitheiser had moved in during his absence, and all his papers had been taken from his desk and put away. He decided on the spot that he could best handle the situation by putting away Jim Leitheiser. A real brawl evolved, but its resolution was deferred until M.S. Hershey returned from Europe.

The Boss called Lebbie the moment he returned, and the entire affair was speedily resolved, although the speed was momentarily offset and the resolution was somewhat delayed by an initial explosion of salty diatribes from one Lebbie Lebkicher.

The declamation began with "Dammit, Milt," and ran some five minutes, during which the recent globetrotter leveled protests that ran up and down the chromatic scale. He went full distance from an indignant posture at the starting point from where he traversed the far regions of outraged hostility. M.S. stopped Lebbie just short of the apoplectic goal he seemed to be seeking.

The boss told Lebbie, "You pick any job you want." Then he went on to say that the estates management, the banking, purchasing, and general groundskeeping jobs "have become far too much for one man." He was told to "pick out what you want to do, and Mr. Leitheiser will help you with the rest."

Lebbie picked his spots, and Jim Leitheiser stayed clear of both them and him.

Henceforth, the odysseys of the two charter members of the Bachelors Club became two of the main struts in the Hershey version of winged victory. Ezra, although he lost his bachelor status in 1910, went on to flesh out his role as one of the main characters in the Hershey saga. During the next thirty-five years, he would become the official signator on most of the paper generated by Hershey deals and acquisitions.

His name would appear on the guest register as the most frequent visitor to the upstairs apartment in which Milton Hershey spent his last year of life. When M.S. died, cousin Ezra would be named an executor of the estate.

Lebbie Lebkicher retained his bachelorhood throughout his life, but he returned from his 'round the world sabbatical a changed man. He also came home to a changed Hershey. The town, the man, and the countryside had all changed. Yet, he returned to a favored niche in the scheme of things that fell under the rule of his friend Milt.

His place in the Hershey scheme of things never changed. But when William Henry Lebkicher, sometimes called Harry and sometimes Lebbie, returned to Lancaster in February of 1929, he went back to another place that had drastically changed. Back in 1885, he had been the first to help a distraught young Milton Hershey get a leg up and start over again, following dismal failure in New York. But on this visit, he faced the kind of change he could not avoid.

He died on the tenth day of February, 1929, in the City of Roses.

When Milton and cousin Ezra Hershey came away from the funeral service for Lebbie, the memories of each went back through the years. Milton was thinking about the days of struggle in the Centennial Exposition year of 1876 in Philadelphia. That was when old Lebbie had first begun working for him. Then it skipped ten years to 1885, when the old veteran had put his life savings on the line just to help M.S. get a new start.

Ezra wore a funny smile. His memories carried back to September of 1910, and he could almost hear again the sounds of drums and dishpans and the eerie gong of a giant bell being hammered on his wedding night. The bell was now hanging in the belfry tower of the Hershey Fire Department, for which it had been originally purchased. But Lebbie would hear it no more.

M.S. broke the silence when they reached the car.

"You know, Ezra," he said, "we've just buried the best friend I ever had."

The funny smile came back to Ezra's face, but the corners of his lips turned down with a hint of sadness. He said nothing to his sorrowful cousin. No use telling him now, he thought. But when he recalled the Van Dyke-bearded face, the Prince Albert cutaway, and the testy manner of their dearly departed bachelor friend, he changed his mind.

"Milton," he said, "you were more than a friend to Lebbie. For more than fifty years, you've been just like a son to a lonely old man who never had any children of his own."

The ride back to Hershey passed in silence. As the car came over the hill and went by a farmyard at the school, the childless Milton Hershey saw one of his Homeboys swinging on the front gate.

"I know what you mean," was all he could say.

Chapter XVI

◆·◆

A Good Night's Sleep

Following the twin near-disasters of Hershey's flop in the chewing gum field and his misadventure in sugar futures, the remainder of the decade to be known as the Roaring Twenties appeared to promise a time of tranquility for him. Once the huge bond issue and its indebtedness had been cleared, M.S. did seem to have pulled his horns in a bit, and there were those who were beginning to think his age had finally begun to slow him down. In 1927, as he approached his seventieth birthday, he seemed to be more excited about Charles "Lucky" Lindbergh's solo non-stop flight to Paris than he was about taking any flyers on his own.

Messrs. Snyder, Murrie, Ezra Hershey, Heilman, and Ziegler kept pretty close tabs on the near and far gyrations of their high-flying boss, but only one of them found a disturbing note in the itinerary.

"He's spending too much time in New York," observed Snyder, but at the time he attached no other meaningful footnote to the comment. He didn't have to; they all knew that M.S. was still dabbling in New York City properties, and for the most part he was still either buying up bad buildings or, at the least, thinking about it.

Come the middle of summer 1929, Ezra Hershey and Abe Heilman went to New York to follow up on one of M.S.'s offhand buys, and when they returned home, both men were disturbed. True, they had gone off to the city faced with the unhappy prospect of closing another bad deal, and their premonitions proved right. The Old Man had bought up another warehouse property, and on the day they got to town, they went straight to the building and met a team of city building inspectors. They got there just in time to see the last of the "Condemned Property" signs nailed to the building walls. One of those walls was caving in under those tackhammer blows when they arrived.

The incident, of itself, while not too unusual, was still a rather disturbing experience. But on that occasion, this was not the real source of their summertime discontent. During the early and middle twenties, they had all too often been dispatched to New York City to follow up on one or the other in a series of bad buys that Milton Hershey had made. But on this particular trip, it wasn't the tumbling edifice that decreed their dyspeptic demeanor. It was something they heard, rather than something they saw. And the word that muddled their mood was even less appetizing than murder.

It was merger.

Everywhere the stodgy Heilman and the hesitant Ezra Hershey went, they heard the same thing. It was being whispered in Wall Street, bruited about in the banks, and it was part and parcel of dinnertime debate and luncheon levity.

The Hershey Chocolate Corporation was going to merge with somebody. That was the gist of the gossip, but the particulars as to *with whom* or *with what* remained unclear.

So the works manager and the reluctant bookkeeper wound up their trip by signing the necessary and highly distasteful documents they had been sent to execute, and then they turned again home. Neither had any real evidence to support the reality of the merger claim, but both knew M.S. well enough not to put anything past him. And neither enjoyed their homeward train ride on the *Queen of the Valley.*

Back in Hershey, they sought out confreres Murrie, McHeffey, Gallagher, Ziegler, Snyder, et al. and they talked. But the discourse was confined to rumination, speculation, and dismayed anticipation, and that was all. There simply were no hard facts to discuss, and the hard factor, M.S. Hershey, was in Havana trying to solve the logistics of turn around shipments of ocean-going vessels—coal to Cuba, sugar back to Pennsylvania. An unusually silent John Snyder having nothing to say—said nothing.

When M.S. returned home prior to the Labor Day closing of the park, the members of his Swiss Guard, old and new, were at the P & R station to meet him. After they'd hustled him off the train, they formed a procession of Model A's, Jewetts, Oaklands, Buicks, Chevies, and one Franklin and followed his big Packard back to the mansion. Once there, a round dozen of them prevailed on him to give them the news. He just cocked his head and looked out again, nonplussed, over the rims of his glasses.

He began to ask them, "What news?" Then he thought better of it and invited them into the billiard room. After he had them seated, he leaned against the edge of a pool table and recounted his recent adventures.

He told them about Rosario. He told them about Havana. He talked about coal that was being shipped from the coal regions of Pennsylvania to fuel his mountain-climbing locomotives in Matanzas and Rosario. Then he mentioned the great job P.A. Staples was doing in Havana.

There was a bit of stirring about, so he lit a cigar and began again.

He talked about Dr. William Dodge Horne down in Matanzas, and the five years that the sugar expert had been working on the process that led to the February 1, 1927 patent on a refining process which produced 99.8 per cent pure sugar. But they knew about that, and they also knew that it was Hershey's mechanical ingenuity that, by its very unorthodoxy, had sparked the working process.

Then he went on to tell them that he'd hired another leading sugar expert in the Caribbean to help them develop flavored sugars. That was news, but not the news they wanted. Nevertheless, Bill Murrie asked him how the new man was doing.

"Oh," said Hershey, "he's doing all right, I guess. But the guy said that my ideas for flavoring a sugar were all wrong. He told me I'd have to do the flavoring before we refined it. I said we had to start with the pure, white stuff or the impurities would interfere. Then he told me I was crazy."

"What happened then?" Snyder asked, somewhat wearily, half believing he already knew the answer.

"I fired him," came the matter-of-fact reply. *"But he is a good man."*

He leaned back and smiled. As he took a deep breath with eyes narrowed a bit, he looked around the room. "He just asked too damn many questions."

There was a bit of throat clearing, followed by a spate of silence before, one by one, each of the visitors got to his feet and walked around to the Boss. He was still perched on the end of the pool table as they filed by, each taking a turn shaking his hand and saying, "Welcome home." Without another word, they went Indian file to the main foyer and out into the summer night.

The same question was still on their minds. Everyone had the same gnawing suspicion. That question may have been just one too many, and with the possibility of a merger still in the offing, none of them wanted to be the one who asked it.

Nothing more meaningful happened in the next few days, but it wasn't long until M.S. was back on the circuit making his rounds of the plant. His mind was still on sugar, and once again he talked about the expert in Cuba. The exchange took place in the Hershey Experimental Sugar Plant with a man who was later to become factory superintendent, Rosario Cangelosi, and he was another one of those who sharply disagreed with Hershey's sugar ideas.

"Trouble with you," Hershey said to Cangelosi, "is you know too much about sugar. You guys know so much you're afraid to try anything new. That's why I keep doing things around here that nobody else would even try."

Cangelosi protested, "But you're the boss, M.S. You can get away with it."

Hershey pushed his glasses up on his nose and grimaced. Then, with an expression halfway between a smirk and a tightly suppressed grin, he looked heavenward as he turned away. "That helps, Rosie," he said, in the tones of a teacher who has just received a nearly correct answer from a none too perceptive pupil. "But it's also the reason *why* I'm the boss."

The merger question didn't come up again until the day before his seventy-second birthday. Meanwhile, virtually every discourse was skillfully turned aside or, at least, was given the same sugar coating that had lately become such a popular topic of conversation. On the evening of the eleventh, he and Mrs. Condoni got on the phone and invited each member of his inner circle to breakfast for the next morning.

M.S., as usual, slept well that night. Both he and the otherwise noncommittal Mrs. Condoni had dropped the line, "We're going to talk about a new company deal tomorrow," and let it go at that. This put a round dozen of his closest henchmen to bed, all of whom were consigned to a sleepless night, save one. The rest learned that P.A. Staples had been brought back to town for the meeting, and that was enough to inspire three more requests for laudanum from the redoubtable Doc, Herman Hostetter.

"I didn't know what was going on," Hostetter said later, adding, "and maybe I was the only guy in town, outside of M.S., who got any sleep that night."

The next day M.S. chomped his way through sausages and eggs, fried liver pudding with onions, and apple turnovers as though he were stoking up for the week. But most of the nervous ones around him merely dabbled. Only the usually high-strung members ate heartily. President Bill Murrie remembered later that he nearly drowned himself in coffee and that, in his words, "only made him *nervouser*."

M.S., having finished his trencherman assault, clicked a spoon against his cocoa cup and beamed at each of them in turn. They had been attentive from the moment of arrival; the spoon clicking earned only their responsively cadenced blinks.

He started by pulling a page from the history of his arrival at Derry Church. He talked about his dairy plans for the area and how he'd gotten Papa to bring back forage samples for the animals, and how he had always wanted to make cheese and ice cream. Then he recounted how Snyder and Murrie had talked him out of it, or thought they had, but they had been wrong.

"Oh, I gave up on the cheese thing, all right," he said, "but it wasn't because of anything you fellows said. No, it was because there was another guy already in the business, and he found the answers I was looking for, before I did.

"His name is J.L. Kraft, and he did something about it. And he's been doing pretty well ever since."

They all looked around, but nobody said anything. Murrie and Snyder seemed on the point of wincing.

"No, Bill, . . ." Hershey remonstrated, "we're not going into the cheese business. Well, not exactly. But we are going to get into harness with this guy Kraft. And with a couple of other guys you may have heard about."

The other guys turned out to be Sidney M. Colgate and A.W. Peet, men who were coming into prominence in a soap and toothpaste outfit that would become famous as Colgate-Palmolive-Peet. He said that the alliance with them would one day provide an outlet for the cocoa butter surpluses which, as he said, they should already know would make "the best damn soap in the world."

But then he said, "There's nothing to worry about," because everything in Hershey—as a chocolate corporation, as a town, a park, a school, or whatever—would remain the same. He explained that, until now, he had been a one-man holding company for all those ventures. The only thing that would be changed was that this would be a new holding company, but each of the subdivisions, the Chocolate Company, the soap company, and cheese company, would remain separate and intact.

Judge Snyder broke the silence. "Who would have most of the stock in the holding company, M.S.?"

Hershey looked down. Hershey looked up. He turned to a sheaf of papers, then picked one out and handed it to Snyder.

The eyes of the men around the table went from the face of M.S. Hershey to that of the grim visaged lawyer.

Hershey was stoical. Then he smiled. Snyder kept on reading, and when he'd finished, he looked across the table to M.S. His eyes shone and he too smiled.

The smiles had it.

*   *   *

For the next five or six weeks, there wasn't much talk about the proposed venture. All of the breakfast meeting attendees had been cautioned to keep it under wraps, and they did. But among lawyer John Snyder, President Bill Murrie, and M.S., there was a good deal of scurrying about. Ezra Hershey sat on the sidelines and watched as Snyder and Ziegler reviewed, rewrote, and took turns running back and forth to the Mansion.

One day, reasoned Ezra, they're going to give me something to sign, and I only hope I'll understand it when it happens. Meanwhile, M.S. sat back. Except for a few haggling discourses on the phone with parties calling from New York, he just kept his mind on the papers that Snyder and the battery of New York lawyers kept shoving at him.

Finally the paper race came to an end, but Ezra found that the big paper would carry the signature of M.S. himself. John Snyder now had all the papers and was awaiting a call from the boss to see if there were any last minute changes in the deal. The papers had been drawn and signed, copies had been made, and so the only thing remaining to be done was to get the documents into the mail or into the hands of a messenger for the New York bank.

Snyder checked the documents at hand. The first paper was the Letter of Transmittal, executed as of October 25th and intended to accompany the Offering Letter and the proxy papers whereby the stock could be reassigned. The transfers were to be made via City Bank Farmers Trust Company, 52 Wall Street, New York City, and Continental Illinois Bank and Trust Company, South LaSalle Street, Chicago. The letter carried instructions on how the transfer was to be made and how the shares of Common and Preferred Stocks were to be listed. It carried the note that the transmittal was being made under a Deposit Agreement between the said corporation, International Quality Products Corporation, and certain other corporations. The certain other corporations were National City Bank of New York, the Hershey Chocolate Corporation, the Kraft-Phenix Cheese Corporation, and Colgate-Palmolive-Peet Company. The agreement carried the names of Stanley A. Russell, W.F.R. Murrie, J.L. Kraft, R.S. Reynolds, Charles S. Pearce, Sidney M. Colgate, and A.W. Peet as personal endorsements.

Accompanying the Transmittal Letter was the offering which appeared on the letterhead of Hershey Chocolate Corporation and was addressed "To the Holders of Convertible Preference Stock and Common Stock of the Hershey Chocolate Corporation." This particular instrument announced that the "holders representing a majority of the voting stock of the Hershey Chocolate Corporation, the Kraft-Phenix Cheese Corporation, and the Colgate-Palmolive-Peet Company have organized a new holding company under the laws of Delaware with the name International Quality Products Corporation, to acquire control of these three companies."

Then the letter further stipulated, "Each constituent company will preserve its identity and continue to operate under its present management." The balances of each of the three companies' total equities were then outlined.

Thereafter, the letter stated that "if the plan is not consummated by January 1, 1930, your stock certificates will be returned to you without cost on surrender of the Certificate of Deposit." The date of consummation for the plan was set as November 15, 1929, and all stockholders were urged to have their stock on deposit before that date. The letter, dated October 28, closed with the line, "We shall exchange all of the stock that we own for stock of the New Company, and we strongly urge you to follow our example." It was signed, "Very truly yours, M.S. Hershey, Chairman, W.R.F. Murrie, President."

Lawyer John Snyder, having reviewed these papers for the hundredth time, concluded that everything was in order. Then the phone rang and he was summoned to the mansion for the final review of the deal which was expected to be finalized by noon of the following Friday. This had been the busiest Monday of any week that Snyder could recollect, but as he drove to the mansion, he still had some thoughts about the way the new plan would work out for the people in Hershey.

Snyder took the long way around town on that unhurried drive, first heading west on Chocolate Avenue, and then turning north at the bank corner and heading down through the park. The circuitous route still only required fifteen minutes to traverse, but during that trip, the lawyer passed by the plant, the homes, the stores, the park and zoo buildings that were part and parcel of a community he had come to love. The community which others believed that Milton Hershey had put on the block and almost gambled away.

But he knew otherwise, and it was subsequently to be revealed that the Snyder input on behalf of the entire scheme had been far more than mere legal counseling or documentary draftsmanship. But more than half a century would pass before the facts concerning this particular bit of knowledge would come to light.

With no graphic notes of directorial minutes or meeting notes surviving for latter-day revelation, John Snyder had something else in his briefcase that precious few people were ever privileged to know about. It was a simple letter that Snyder had drafted and Milton Hershey had signed. All it contained was Hershey's pronouncement that he would not serve in any executive or directorial capacity connected with the International Quality Products holding company.

Since his earlier efforts had constrained Milton Hershey to a limited stance on behalf of the School Trust holdings of Corporate and Estate stocks, he had no reason to worry about M.S.'s predilections to gamble it all away.

He—M.S. Hershey—couldn't.

Snyder had seen to that by two of the most insightful maneuvers and a pair of the most adroit moves ever made on behalf of all things named Hershey, Milton included.

He had managed it by having the real equity, the ownership of the stocks, put into a Trust that was made subject to a Board of Directors' approval. Milton Hershey's proxy rights extended only to the limits of the ability to disburse profits and dividends pretty much as he saw fit. And, of course, he did just that—to the limit.

But when Snyder persuaded him to stay out of the proprietary ranks of International Quality's executive staff, he had ostensibly taken Hershey off a playing field and out of a game in which he could have been hurt.

Fewer people than could be counted on the fingers of one hand knew about Milton

Hershey's letter of abstention from International Quality management, of course, but the letter still reposes in Judge Snyder's files. Prior to that, when Snyder had drawn up the Deed of Trust that placed stock ownership under directorial control, he had done something more than merely remove Milton Hershey from the game. He had, in fact, taken away the ball so there could henceforth be no game played with the stock *by any single individual.*

He had all the pieces in place. He met with M.S. on the evening of Monday, October 28th and they committed the final documents to the mail services. Then John Snyder very probably came to the conclusion that the next place for him in this scheme of things was crystal clear. He went home to bed and got a good night's sleep.

Circles Drawn on Water

The memorable day of Tuesday, October 29, 1929, when the New York stock market collapsed, had a hundred million impacts on the society of the time, as it would have in the lives of other countless millions of people then unborn. The theatrical news tabloid *Variety* said it best: "Wall Street Lays an Egg."

It had indeed. But quite apart from the international floodtide of spectacular events set loose in the world by the crash, there were some immediate and finite consequences that directly impinged on Milton Hershey and his plans. His proposed merger of interests and the establishment of the holding company called International Quality Products Corporation eventually collapsed. The people at National City Company, the brokerage arm of National City Bank, had already paid a half million dollars as an option price put into the Hershey Trust Company account of the Hershey Industrial School. This represented an option to buy sixty per cent of the Hershey Chocolate Corporation's equity. But the option was never picked up, although an extension was granted some time later when Mr. Stanley Russell sent the School Trust account another personal check for $1,000 in order to get a further extension.

But the market crash had put the crusher on Milton Hershey's plan to merge Hershey Chocolate Corporation with Kraft-Phenix Cheese and Colgate-Palmolive-Peet into a holding company called International Quality Products Corporation. Subsequent historians and most of the contemporary and surviving residents of Hershey heaved a sigh of relief. Both in the published opinions and in the sentimentality which prevailed in the hearts of people living and working in Hershey, the town, the company, and the school, they all believed they had been saved from a fate worse than death. Milton Hershey had been prevented from selling any part of their community holdings down the river. But even though it appeared as though M.S. had sought to put the major equities of the chocolate plant in Hershey on the block, in reality he had not done anything of the sort. Judge Snyder had seen to that.

In the estimate of previous scriveners and in the minds of virtually all surviving Hershey workers and citizens, this move would have given the school trust *a third* of the voting powers in a big new holding company, whereas it would have surrendered three-fifths of the chocolate company which it controlled. Therefore, in those judgments, the other two principals—Kraft-Phenix and Colgate-Palmolive-Peet, along with the private investment blocks of stock patent to National City Bank's administrative powers—would have put the Hershey interests into a minority slot with control of not more than thirty per cent of the total voting power.

Had they been right, the changes in everything named Hershey—town, school, plants, et al.—could have become subject to any change that even the most hidebound pessimist may have envisioned.

But they were wrong.*

Sophocles once said, "The recollection of things *as they might have been* are *like circles drawn on water*," and his association was certainly accurate, insofar as the philosophical meaning goes. But in this case, what might have been is a clear case of what Milton Hershey's real intentions were when he essayed *to trade, not sell* off, the sixty per cent stock interest of the Hershey Industrial School Trust in Hershey Chocolate Corporation. From the outset, there were several misconceptions both as to the nature of what was being traded and what was to be received, and those were basic to the fallacy of the entire belief.

When National City Company was prevented from exercising its option to pick up the stock in the Hershey Chocolate Corporation, a total of $501,000 had gone into the Deed of Trust Account of the school. It would, thereafter, become an integral part of the capital funding that would help to sustain Milton Hershey's most durable legacy.

More than fifty years have come and gone since those memorable days, and yet the prospect of something that might have been is still recalled as a scary notion. Many of the oldtimers are still haunted by the belief that Milton Hershey had gone to the edge of bargaining away the town, the school, and the company that bore his name for some mystical grabbag scheme they never understood. Many of them still believe that he had been willing to gamble with the holdings that constituted their very way of life, and a lot of sleep has been lost to the holders of that belief—in those days and in these.

Note:

The Hershey/Snyder part in the plan to establish International Quality Products Corporation as a holding company was never clearly defined for a number of reasons. Up front the plan called for *only* the Hershey Chocolate Corporation (not Hershey Estates, Hershey, Cuba, etc.) to become an IQPC "holding," and as such, Chocolate Corp. stockholders would be vested with an option to acquire about forty per cent ownership of IQPC stock via National City Company. Each of the other part interests were reserved by Colgate-Palmolive-Peet and to J.L. Kraft.

Several parts of the International Quality Products plans for subsequent capital expansion *did not show* on the records. But some Hershey plans *didn't show* either; and they were tacitly bound to the mysterious role being played by Stanley Russell, former National City Bank of New York executive, who acted as the go-between and who had made option payments to Hershey for the Chocolate Company stock reservations.

But there were also the capital expansion plans for IQPC to sell another one hundred million dollars worth of stock on the open market, intended to double the capital base from which the company would operate. Of the three principles, Hershey would hold about forty per cent of the original base equity in the holding company; hence each of the others (Colgate/Kraft) would have reserved thirty per cent of the base capitalization, originally set at 100 million dollars.

Then someone introduced an act of oneupsmanship into the proceedings by doubling the prospective capital base of IQPC to 200 million via stock sales. Under the initial plan with Hershey, Colgate and Kraft each subscribing for the three blocks of original stock, Hershey would have swapped fifty million of Chocolate Corporation stock (only) for forty per cent of IQPC stock. The other Hershey interests—Hershey Estates, Hershey Creamery, Hershey Bank, Hershey Atlantic (Cuba)—would remain unpledged and intact. But Hershey, Cuba, and Hershey Estates (with former as a vested interest of the latter) would be waiting in the wings and occupying a vantage point that would not arise until the second round of IQPC stock would be made available in return for an additional 100 million dollars of investment capital.

In the same wings the IQPC intermediary Stanley Russell, acting for the National City Company, was waiting. Down in Cuba the Hershey unpledged sugar interests were scheduled to be brought under the control of Hershey Estates, and Estates' stock belonged 100% to the Trust of the Hershey Industrial School. At this point an element of speculation intervenes, but the known facts exert a mighty influence on *what might have been.*

The facts are these:

1. Hershey had reserved forty per cent of the initial IQPC stock for Hershey Chocolate equities.
2. Hershey, Cuba, had a negotiable, tangible (and noteworthy) net worth of seventy million dollars.
3. Stanley Russell, having arranged the initial option, was the linchpin who could deliver the additional seventy million for Hershey when the second round issue of IQPC was made available. His designation

He did not take a chance that would compromise the walls of his camelot. He simply wanted to build a deeper and wider moat. And he almost made it.

It is at all times difficult, and sometimes it is well nigh impossible, to define the purposes that motivate intuitive innovators and restless entrepreneurs. They move when others hesitate; they attack when others cast about for the means of defending themselves. And yet their ways are too often a source of bafflement to those who bear witness to their abilities and even to those who may be joined with them when they perform their deeds.

Some thousands of years ago a man named Job wondered about this sort of thing and posed the question,

Why is the light given to a man whose way is hid, and whom God hath hedged in?

(Book 3, verse 23)

Milton Hershey never made any historic declamations; he was cut from plainer stuff than that. He simply reasoned that all of these things had happened before and they would happen again. He had come upon a time when he found he was getting used to

---

as intermediary would then have enabled him to arrange for seventy per cent of the second round stock issue on Hershey's behalf.

Because of the crash the whole thing was called off, but the simple arithmetic of *what might have been* is quite persuasive. Consider the factors: Hershey *would* have held forty per cent of the initial IQPC stock in exchange for Chocolate stock. Hershey *could* have gained an additional seventy per cent of the second issue of IQPC stock by swapping equities or launching a bond issue worth seventy million against Hershey, Cuba. Together the forty per cent initial IQPC holding, when added to the seventy per cent anticipated from the *second round* purchase, would have given Hershey a proprietary stockholder's share of *fifty-five per cent* of the IQPC stock.

The Hershey record for swapping stock equities was already established by the fifty million dollar, five year note that Cuban sugar helped him pay off in two years back in 1922. By 1929, the Hershey, Cuba, project had enlarged its cash-producing volume by five times and was well on its way to not only becoming the largest sugar-producing entity in the world, but it was also a considerable holder of Cuban National Railway bonds, as well as a company trading in tobacco, mahogany, hemp, cocoa (later to become a separate Cocoa Trading Corporation); and (as vested railway bondholder and with major shipping facilities at Matanzas, Canasi, etc.) it also became an exit port for bauxite, i.e., aluminum.

The next decade would witness the generation of much more capital from the Cuban enterprise than a seventy million dollar bond issue or note would have required. Somewhat more than fifty million dollars would eventually show up in a whole series of capital improvements that would mark the 10,000 acre Hershey domain in Derry Township.

Milton Hershey, John Snyder, and Stanley Russell *knew* back in the fall of 1929 that they had the cash-generating wherewithal in Cuba to subsequently buy control of the International Quality Products Holding Corporation. But the crash came and the whole scheme evaporated. And, like circles drawn on water, the motives and the men behind them disappeared behind the mantle of history that forever conceals so many things that *might have been.*

On paper, only one personal check, in the amount of one thousand dollars from the account of Stanley Russell, stands as the indicator of a last-ditch effort to keep this plan alive in the year following the crash. But on the Derry Township horizons, the settlement known as Hershey stands with the landmarks that still act as silent testimonials to what happened after the target for Milton Hershey's new Cuban money was eliminated.

The aims of his original intentions were changed by the crash of '29. And, like circles drawn on water, they disappeared. But the subsequent structures that arose in school buildings, theaters, sports palaces, rose gardens, and the like, became circles that were cast in concrete because they still stand.

it. When the final count came in on his failed plan at the end of the following year (Christmas, 1930), he just sat back with folded arms and sighed, "You'll have this."

Then he went to bed and enjoyed a good night's sleep of his own. He may have smiled a bit before dozing off, for he was living up to his reputation as a man who never forgot anything. Perhaps the memory of two Snyder-wrought compositions wafted through his somnolence from an almost forgotten pair of legalistic lullabies.

A Deed of Trust and a letter of abstention danced like sugarplums through his slumbering head. The good old Judge hadn't drawn any circles on water; he had preserved the castle keep in the traditional manner expected of the heroic Swiss Guard.

As an unheralded legal wizard, John Snyder could have done no more. As a devoted and loyal friend, he would never do anything less.

End of Part Two

PART THREE

~·~

The Planter at Rest—The Harvest Assured

Chapter XVII

~·~

A Final Homecoming

The stock market crash in 1929 marked the beginning of an era in which a whole set of paradoxical values were set loose in the world. It was a time in which the economic stability of most nations would fail because there was too much more of borrowed money and unsecured venture capital in motion than there was in the real values of goods and services being traded. In the United States, there were hundreds of millions of dollars invested in mineral stocks for mines never dug and oil wells untapped, with a great deal of the money being spent on the paper of margin purchases made on the basis of credit, not cash.

Everybody seemed to be obsessed with the idea of buying now and paying later, and people were perhaps more than a little influenced by the speakeasy syndrome that led all too many to wink at conditions they knew to be wrong. It was an era in which bootleggers and gangsters were regarded as naughty, rather than wicked figures. These were the crazy days when former teetotalers and many hitherto modest imbibers would sneak onto illegal premises and fight to pay as much for a glass of bathtub gin as they had formerly refused to pay for a whole bottle of the good stuff when it had been legal.

The warning signs had begun flashing from Europe where social turmoil was beginning to elevate certain elements of the gangster stripe into positions of governmental leadership. People everywhere were scared, and the uninhibited greed of the freebooters was beginning to rub them raw. Little wonder that regulations seemed to offer the panaceas of a well-ordered life to those who were toiling for worthless marks and lire, and especially to those who had no incomes at all. The continent turned itself over to men like Benito Mussolini, who promised to make the trains run on time, and to Adolf Hitler, who was trumpeting about a new order.

Consequently, the leadership of countries in Europe and America was being progressively turned over to a new breed of men who proposed to return all power to the people. But what they really meant to do was to put the government in charge of everything, and then to turn government over to the kind of strong men who had not existed since the days of Napoleon and the Caesars. Bit by bit, the changes wrought by dictators and autocrats began to occur, but the early changes were so subtle and almost imperceptible that the patina of trains running on time and of people going back to work pretty well masked the impending military confrontations and the Apocalyptic chaos that would follow.

Hershey settlements in both Pennsylvania and in Cuba began assuming some of the contradictory dimensions that were directly opposed to the trend of those times. The chocolate business in Derry Township was continuing to grow, and while expansion volumes were at a somewhat slower pace than before, the confectionery company was still thriving at a somewhat better than modest rate.

Beginning in 1929 the whole shape and substance of both the United States and the American Dream would undergo some dramatic and explosive changes. It was in these years spanning the time between the Great Depression and the end of the second

Great War that Milton Hershey would observe his final homecoming. There he would make some dramatic changes of his own, perhaps the greatest of which was to stand pat on some oldtime beliefs in the midst of a world he thought had gone crazy.

His stubbornness didn't allow him to remain fixed in place, however, and the net consequences emerged in the community showplace that became Hershey, Pennsylvania. The following stories offer profiles of some few of the men who helped build this showcase.

The Jacks—Of All Trades

The Right Bower, Harry Herr, was the first college graduate to become part of Milton Hershey's Swiss Guard. The Lancastrian had earned his degree in civil engineering from Lehigh University and had been working as a consulting engineer when he was asked to do some landscape and utility designs for the new dairying venture Hershey had started in Dauphin County. At the outset, he hadn't known Milton Hershey and had never heard of a place called Derry Church. One thing led to another, however, and it wasn't long before he was not only working for M.S. Hershey, but was also busily engaged in changing the face of the place called Derry Church.

When he first came on the scene, he was charged with putting in the water systems as well as the utility lines for the experimental shops and the first working plant near the old Hershey Homestead. The whole scheme mushroomed following the turn of the century, and Harry Herr found himself laying out plans for a street railway line at the same time he was reshaping the watershed potentials by tapping the Spring and Manada Creek confluences. While all this was in motion, he was tagged to lay out the lines for natural gas and to sketch the water supply lines for the new community he would plan. His question, "What community?"—evoked a response that left him in charge of laying out the streets, the power lines, the trolley tracks, and the very landscaping for a town that hitherto had been a figment of M.S. Hershey's imagination.

It was some figment. But it all became Harry Herr's project, a job that called for a full-fledged, card-carrying sorcerer.

In 1924, the sorcerer got an apprentice. A thirty-year-old Lancaster construction foreman named D. Paul Witmer had caught Hershey's eye. The young man was working for a Lancaster outfit on a downtown building project when both M.S. and Witmer's supervisor, Harry Herr, became impressed by his "can do" attitude. They learned that he had graduated from the Stevens Trade School in Lancaster and that he had doubled as both a design draftsman and as a field construction manager.

He was a performer as well as a planner, and both Herr and Hershey concurred that he was just the man they needed. When they offered him a job as Herr's assistant, he signed on immediately and was put in charge of the home building crews that were hammering away on the Para Avenue dwellings.

Meanwhile, Witmer's immediate mentor, Harry Herr, was becoming more and more involved in the overall planning that would reshape the thoroughfares and the contours of the whole Hershey landscape. As the building programs grew larger and became more highly accelerated, so did Paul Witmer's duties.

It soon became apparent that Witmer, like Herr, brought something more than mere nuts-and-bolts knowledge to each of the jobs he was given. Both men had an imaginative spark that surpassed the mundane qualities of run-of-the-mill draftsmen. In many instances, their talents rivalled those of the better architects of their day. Each one could do what was needed to be done at any level, whether it was as the design draftsman, the contract supervisor, or as the construction foremen who directed the men doing the riveting, sawing, wiring, pipefitting, bricklaying, or painting.

When Milton Hershey decided to beat the Depression by getting men to work again, he began by putting the exemplary talents of Harry Herr and D. Paul Witmer in charge. Hershey provided the ideas, the faith, and the money that was needed, while the other two, Herr and Witmer, did the designing and building.

This ability to make anything, build anything, and do anything was patent to Harry Herr and D. Paul Witmer, and nobody knew that better than M.S. Hershey. Consequently, if there is an unmistakable imprint on the buildings that dot the Hershey landscape and the gardenlike atmosphere that pervades the whole place, most of it was put there by Herr and Witmer. Although both of them were quiet, unassuming men who merely did as they were told, M.S., knowing the mettle of his men, told them to do quite a lot. Their stamp is virtually everywhere.

These scenes still recall that old-fashioned card game called "Hassenpeffer" because Milton Hershey had found in Harry Neff Herr and David Paul Witmer his Right and Left Bowers. They were his jacks of all trades.

They went on to prove they were masters of most.

The Topographic Kaleidoscope

In the years between 1933 and 1938, the Hershey Community landscape looked as though someone had broken apart an intricate jigsaw puzzle and then tried to replace the key pieces with some entirely new parts. The center piece, the Community Building in the middle of town, was begun in early 1932, and later that year the Hotel Hershey was launched. But Hershey had given Paul Witmer the site plans for the Hershey Hotel site back in August of 1931. The net consequence of all this turned out to be a veritable explosion that would markedly change the face of the overall topography.

Actual work on the Community Building began before the Hotel Hershey project was initiated, and yet the Hotel was finished and dedicated on Friday evening, May 26, 1933. The Community Building wasn't ready for its formal opening ceremonies until a hundred days later, on September 3, 1933.

Searching the records only thickens the broth of puzzlement as to how many men were put to work in this five-year span when the rest of the country bottomed out in the depths of the Great Depression. There were more than two hundred bricklayers, laborers, carpenters, electricians, stone masons, plumbers, millwrights, draftsmen, and assorted others on both the Hotel and Community Building jobs at the same time. Most of them stayed on to be joined by the additional hundreds of men who worked on the windowless office building, the school on the hill, the Sports Arena, the Rose Garden, and the stadium, which appeared in triphammer sequence on the Hershey landscape.

Meanwhile, the improvements and enlargements of the dance pavilion, the park, the zoo, and the golf links were being carried out as the intown residential construction was booming. The ubiquitous Harry Herr's landscape layouts were but a few scant yards ahead of the structural designs and contract supervision of Paul Witmer and his crews of builders. In the midst of all this activity, M.S. Hershey was to interject a pair of other pet projects. Little items, like a furniture factory and a junior college.

In the middle thirties lapse time, while excavations were being done for the arena and later the stadium, D. Paul Witmer had an average of more than three hundred men making furniture at the lumber company, and in 1938 the payroll at this sideline venture hit six hundred. The result of this five-year building explosion was an economic phenomenon that ran straight at the teeth of the Depression. Subsequent tabulations show that these make work projects wound up providing employment for just about half the people in Hershey. About three thousand of the full-time employees worked for the chocolate company, almost a thousand were employed by the school, the bank, and the Estates, and yet there were between six and seven thousand heads counted on the weekly payrolls, which indicates that by way of landscaping, building, wiring, planting, bricklaying, furniture-making, painting, digging, concrete-pouring, stone-cutting, et cetera, Milton Hershey had found work for just about twice as many people as the chocolate company needed to turn out its ever-expanding volume of goods.

Perhaps this is why the latter-day seers of socialism set up a hue and cry that all this building had been done at the expense of the workers and for the essential purpose of getting things done by cheap labor. This was hogwash of purest ray serene. The record proves it.

The money spent was elicited from operational profits, but well over ninety per cent of that profit was produced by the Cuban sugar wing of the Hershey enterprises. Meanwhile, the chocolate plant workers in Hershey were earning as much as or more on an hourly basis than their counterparts in New York, Chicago, and nearby Reading.

It was in the middle management in the corporation and at second level management at the Hershey Bank and Hershey Park where the incomes were low in comparison to those in Philadelphia, New York, and even Reading and Harrisburg.

The comparative economics are interesting, if not completely applicable, for yet another reason. In Hershey, with the management/ownership control factor vested in the various teams comprised of the Industrial School's Board of Directors and the Township Board of Managers and the Estates Planning Board, there was another factor to be considered. Today we call it the cost of living, and it heads up a whole list of things like food, clothing, rent or mortgage payments, and utilities. For the people living in Hershey, the real break came in regard to school taxes, power bills, and the like, because their rates were considerably less than others were paying in surrounding towns. But even the out-of-town employees could make purchases at the meat plant, the dairy, the bake shop, and/or the department store where they could also buy furniture, clothing and other items at considerable savings.

So the Community Showcase had a cash register behind it, as any sensible venture must. But the money paid, the money shared, the money that built things, gave people jobs and provided good products for millions of consumers elsewhere, as well as the splendid education provided to fatherless boys right in Hershey. These were the straight arrow consequences of the American capital system.

The money didn't come out of anybody's pocket because it never went into anybody's pocket. Nobody took the money from the worker's envelopes, either in Hershey, Pennsylvania, or in Hershey, Cuba. The profits went straight into and out of accounts managed by Milton Snavely Hershey. He saw fit to use them by giving jobs to twice as many people as he needed to employ simply *because they needed the work.*

Chapter XVIII

∿·∿

Open Doors—Key People

The model community Milton Hershey had in mind for the town that bore his name was destined to become a study in contrasts. Like Xenophon, after the Athenian conquest by Sparta, Hershey wanted "a place filled with nice people and offering a variety of pleasant ways to spend one's time." But the methods were different because Hershey was dealing with a resurgent society that believed in itself. Xenophon dwelt amidst the insurgent ranks of a city/empire that had lost its belief in everything before it misused its power and lost all reason for further existence.

"A place with nice people," as Hershey saw it, meant he would have to get the best ones on top of things, or there would be very little chance of his town's "offering a variety of pleasant ways to spend one's time." The places where people lived and worked, the parks, schools, theaters, stores, and libraries would all have to be under the guidance of the kind of men who would make them pleasant—and profitable. They had to be profitable or they wouldn't stay pleasant very long.

The view was clearly autocratic, but it was something more than that. He reasoned that the town would belong to the people. He was merely going to help them get it set up; then they could run it themselves. Meantime, *he* would call the shots.

The social planners of those days argued about the philosophy that motivated his community plan. The liberals called the scheme a company town or a one-man town. The conservatives were more than somewhat aghast at the "freeholder" notions that appeared to them to be socialistic. To Hershey, it was none of the above. He had spent a lifetime studying the ways to do things. When he found the ways that worked, he used them. That was the way he tackled the community planning, and for whatever else the devotees or detractors may have said, one undeniable fact remains:

It worked.

He wanted shareholders in all the enterprises. He had seen this work for the co-operative groups running stores, trade guilds and farmers groups in Switzerland and elsewhere. The people in those places were as independent as any people in the world, and he found nothing wrong with their combining their working skills, their purchasing power, and their actuarial numbers into tightly-knit community efforts. When people worked together, their freeholder or cooperative institutions worked. It was that simple to him, so he went ahead and tried to make the same thing happen in his town.

But he made his plans without taking into account some deep-seated human traits that were foreign to him. As a man with an almost religious bent to work hard, to share, and to build, he never understood greed, envy, selfishness, and deceit. He took charge and held the reins because he had fitted them to his own hands from the first. After finding certain ways to make things happen in business and commerce, he forthrightly set out to do the same thing for his community.

He made it his first point to start building places that would serve the community plan. Then he began the task of picking the men to do the job of making his Community Showplace come alive. He would put up the money for the buildings and for the land-

189

scaping and the equipment, but each place would need the personality of a man who would get out in front, leading and shaping it every inch of the way. The individual quality of this man would henceforth put the stamp on each of the separate entities.

Thus, the whole town and all its parts bear the name of the founder. He began things with a head filled with ideas, a heart full of loyalty, and a pair of most generous hands that were dipped into the bottomless till he had fashioned.

Some of the personal stamps imparted by the men who helped put together this showplace still remain. Some of their individualities are still hauntingly present to the oldtimers who remember them when they pass certain buildings. For fellows like banker Arthur Whiteman and picture framer Frank Edris, the buildings and the very neighborhoods call back vivid recollections of the men who once worked in the offices or walked on the pavements.

Quite a few of the buildings where these men once held forth are no longer standing, and virtually all of those remaining have been remodelled or restructured. Down on West Chocolate Avenue in the general area of the old lumber company, there had been a cluster of facilities that handled everything from tinsmithing, lumber planing, furniture manufacturing, landscape and building designs, even a machinery shop, all in the place where Harry Herr and D. Paul Witmer held forth. This particular complex of shops and offices was the real nerve center for building designs, street layouts, trackage routes for streetcars, power and water company plans, landscaping, and virtually every kind of scheme that went from paper to three-dimensional form and substance.

Strange to relate, however, the two top men who were assigned *to work there* were usually *not there,* because they were so frequently out on the jobs. Conversely, just about everyone else in town had a frequent need to visit that nerve center even if they had no business to transact with Mssrs. Herr or Witmer, because this was the place to pick up hardware, garden supplies, or furniture, and it was also where the people went for sheet metal work, for machinery repairs, and a whole host of other household needs. The people from the chocolate plant would go there for special machine parts, or any one of the thousand and one special needs that arise when there is a shop in town that can seemingly make anything.

The offices in the Homestead where George Copenhaver, school superintendent, lived and worked are no longer there. The so-called Park Creamery where P.N. Hershey had his office has long since been closed down and used for storage. The old Hershey Press building where Joe Snavely held forth was later changed to the Hershey Department store during the time when John Hosler managed both the store and the Hershey Meat Packing Plant. It later became a furniture store.

The Hershey Bank Building is still haunted by the myriad of talents that once performed on the premises, such as Lebbie Lebkicher, John Snyder, Charlie Ziegler, Ezra Hershey, and John Sollenberger. The "windowless" chocolate company at 19 East Chocolate was where Bill Murrie had his presidential office.

Soon after Alex Stoddart came to town, he established his operational center for the "Hotel Hershey Highlights" in a left corner wing in the front of the Community Building just off the esplanade. That particular site was also to become the forerunner of the publicity department which was charged with turning out every kind of copy. If the name Hershey went on a press release about the theater, the park, the hotel, the chocolate company, the golf club, or even M.S. himself, it was Alex Stoddart and his crew that ground it out.

Harry Erdman, the rose grower, head gardener, and sometimes landscaping designer, had a regular itinerary of working places for his first few years. He skipped from a tiny office next to the solarium at the Hotel Hershey, to the greenhouse by the Rose Garden, and for a while thereafter he was seemingly everywhere and nowhere. In the late thirties after the Rose Gardens opened, Harry Erdman had a post office box, but no definitive business address, although he could usually be found either at the greenhouse or at M.S.'s apartment at the country club.

Joe Gassler and wife had been managing the Highpoint Mansion Country Club for a while prior to their installation at the Hotel, but the record does not reveal where they lived during their stay at the club. The imprint of Joseph Gassler, however, remains indelibly stamped on the personality of Hotel Hershey. The continental air, the luxuriousness of accommodations wrought to suit the tastes of those who were *to the manor born*, still lingers wherever Joseph Gassler's blue blood once pulsed.

These men, of course, are representative of only a few of those who gathered around the standard of Milton Hershey and helped to build what became the Hershey Community. The Hershey story in the community sense—of town, school, park, plant, hotel, et cetera—is a story of the ways and the means required to forge a whole new way of community life.

M.S. Hershey got the ideas and provided the means to buy the goods and services that made it all possible. The men behind the doors found the ways to shape all these things into something akin to what Xenophon wanted for Athens so long ago.

A place full of nice people that offers a variety of pleasant ways to spend one's time.
These are the stories of some of the men who helped to build just such a place.

Presidential Caliber

Perhaps it was sheerly coincidental or maybe it was the consequence of a vitally important contribution, but whatever the case, the rising star of Hershey fortunes began growing in magnitude from the day William Franklin Reynolds Murrie came aboard. He started working for M.S. Hershey in 1895 in Lancaster, having served several years as a top salesman for the Pittsburgh confectionery firm of Weaver and Costello.

This son of an immigrant Scotsman had been born March 25, 1873, in the remote village of Mann's Choice in Bedford County. After quitting school and leaving home at sixteen, he had become first an apprentice, and then a full-fledged telegrapher. But by the time he turned twenty, a combination of tireless ambition and the winning ways of a forceful personality swept him into a career that proved to be his inevitable niche in life. Bill Murrie was a born salesman. Weaver and Costello had learned that, and so did Milton Hershey.

Because the Pittsburgh firm was somewhat concerned about the young man's age, they hesitated to entrust him with any real executive status. M.S. Hershey was singularly unconcerned about anything other than the work he wanted done, and he had already become a classic model in the school of non-hesitant personalities.

Murrie was twenty-two years old when he was brought to Lancaster and put in charge of sales for Milton Hershey's Lancaster Caramel Company. He was not yet thirty years old when the Hershey Chocolate Company broke ground at Derry Church in Dauphin County and he was made president of the new venture. He would go on from there to work shoulder to shoulder with the other men who comprised Milton Hershey's inner circle and, aside from John Snyder, he was to become one of the most influential men in the Hershey scheme of things.

William F.R. "Bill" Murrie, the big, red-haired Scots Catholic, would later become a Director of the Hershey Trust Company and the Milton Hershey School Board between the years of 1915 and 1947. All three tenures—Chocolate Company President and directorships on School Board and Trust Company—were terminated when Percy Alexander Staples took charge of almost everything and thus became the only other man who ever wore all the hats once fitted to the crown of Milton Hershey.

The latter-day ascendancy of Percy Staples generated a bookful of anecdotes concerning the inevitable competition and contention that would finally unseat Bill Murrie. Milton Hershey probably knew that this was going to happen, but throughout his declining years, he had steadfastly maintained another point of insistence.

Bill Murrie would keep his presidency until he reached retirement age and he would not be replaced in any of his offices so long as Milton Hershey lived. That was the way the boss wanted it and that is the way it was. The loyalty that bound the Lancaster bunch together was an unbreakable cord, and the men who shared it were unassailable during Hershey's lifetime. But, in Bill Murrie's case, he had something more going for him than the privileged status he enjoyed as one of the original crew who made up the Lancaster bunch.

He had several strong trump cards, not the least of which was the ace constituted by his own skills and talents, for he was more than merely a top-drawer salesman. He was endowed with more than layman proficiencies when it came to technical knowledge, and he also had that indefinable skill of handling people that marks the master administrator. Hershey workers said that Murrie could get more things done by being nice, so this was to become one of the attributes that set him apart from the more abrasive methods employed by Mssrs. Lebkicher, Heilman, and, later, Ezra Hershey.

In subsequent years, detractors would claim that Murrie was nice enough to your face, but that was because he turned the hatchet work over to Heilman and others so that hard-nosed appellations would fall on them. This post mortem appraisal has followed virtually every nice guy who ever once held power to his grave.

The man's appearance and manner were also strong integers in his favor, for he was a six feet, four inch, reddish-towhead, with sparkling blue eyes and an ever-ready smile. Bill Murrie looked the part of the alltime Mr. Affable, and by his warm "hail fellow, well met" pleasantries, he disarmed friends and adversaries alike. But he did not go weaponless himself.

One other, almost indefinable source of strength was in the trump card that came along when Kitty Sweeney became Mrs. Catherine Hershey.

This was not merely an accident of the kinship they shared as fellow Catholics in a land of Protestant Pennsylvania Dutchmen. The bonds of their friendship stemmed from an earlier time when Bill Murrie had undertaken to play Cupid back in the days when Catherine Sweeney worked in the confectioner's shop in her native Jamestown, New York. For Bill Murrie had not only been the one who introduced his boss to the Irish colleen who subsequently became Hershey's bride, but he was also the intermediary who helped expedite the romance that followed their meeting. No proofs exist to link Bill Murrie with the cards and extra goodies shipped to Miss Catherine Sweeney when other packages were sent to the shop in Jamestown in the name of Hershey the man, or Hershey the chocolate company. Nor is there anything to show for the verbal confidences that served to keep Kitty in Jamestown informed about what Milton was doing in Lancaster, or vice versa.

Bill Murrie was an intuitive salesman. As such, he was never satisfied to *let things happen*. He had to *make them happen*. The records of the Hershey Chocolate Company prove how busy was its chief executive. The whole span of Milton Hershey's one year courtship and seventeen years of marriage to Kitty Sweeney were spun out against the many episodes that transpired when Bill Murrie was around. Was it mere coincidence? Did these things just happen when he was around, or did they occur *because he was there to make them happen?*

But of all the things that have been said about Bill Murrie, and those which a better than fifty year record can prove in his behalf, he also had a tendency to perform like a juggler who could keep an awful lot of balls in the air. Without dropping them. Except on one or two occasions.

His mid-1930's sojourn to Europe, spent mostly in England, was to later come under sharp criticism because it culminated in the launching of several products that never quite made it in the market. He and his subsequent ally, Sam Hinkle, were speared with the decline and fall of bars called *Bis-Krisp* and *Aero,* but Milton Hershey had had several shots at a semi-sweet bar which had not made it very big either.

Few people recalled, however, that in 1927—and later—Bill Murrie had been beating the drum for an economy peanut bar, introduced in 1925 and later named *Mr. Goodbar;* which virtually none of the salesmen, or M.S. himself, thought would ever have a chance in the market. It turned out otherwise.

In those same 1920's when Babe Ruth got into the national headlines by asking the New York Yankees management for an unprecedented salary of a hundred thousand dollars a year, the sporting scribes noted, "This is $25,000 more than the President gets." Meanwhile, the usually quiet, redhaired prexy of Hershey Chocolate was folding his bills at better than $100,000 per annum.

By the late 1930's, when FDR was in his second term in office, the U.S. President was still being paid $75,000 a year. But Bill Murrie in Hershey drew a salary pegged at $125,000 per annum. Then some pundit with a pipeline to corporate earnings chided Bill Murrie, "How can you justify making fifty grand more a year than the President?" The big redhead growled, at first, then regained his composure and answered with a winking smile.

"That's easy. This outfit is *making* money. That gang in Washington is *losing* dough every day."

A rather strange remark on the face of it, because Bill Murrie, in addition to being a Scots Catholic in a land of Protestant Pennsylvania Dutchmen, was also a Democrat and a staunch supporter of F. Delano Roosevelt in a place where virtually everyone was Republican. But then he was where he was and he was paid as much as he was because he was also the kind of guy who could keep people happy—workers and customers alike. This unique capability bespoke the fact that he was something more than merely a headliner in the realms of master salesmen.

The mainspring of the sales force was largely comprised of a mechanism Bill Murrie perfected. His bit by bit enrollment of men like Fred Pugh and John Gallagher attested to his perspicacity in selecting men; his record of working with these men and many others, plus his grooming and ultimate dependency on chemist Sam Hinkle, revealed a visionary talent not unlike the mainstay quality of his boss.

But perhaps Bill Murrie's most important asset was contained in the phrase "privileged access," and in his case it was a two-sided coin. As one of M.S.'s oldest and most dependable co-workers, he had more than mere access to the boss. In most things he shared a shoulder-to-shoulder working partnership with him. But, on the other side, in the business and in the political arenas that lay outside of Hershey, is where another peculiar kind of privileged access was accorded him.

His internal access came as the consequence of his great ability to handle his people and to smooth out the personnel erraticisms that so frequently make even great operational schemes sputter and misfire. Bill Murrie was a born conciliator, and in the Hershey corporate machinery, his was the oil that lubricated the moving parts, and usually he applied the old oils before friction and breakdowns occurred.

It is true, of course, that virtually each of the men in Hershey's top echelons of management wore several hats, but Bill Murrie wore quite a few more than most of them. He was general factotum and ambassador at large in Hershey's dealings with banks and brokerage houses, with suppliers and customers, and, when eventually the need arose, Bill Murrie stepped in and became the wheelhorse of the Hershey interests when it became necessary to deal directly with the new kind of government that was beginning to emerge in Washington.

Until the Depression came along, M.S. Hershey had assiduously steered clear of national politicos. He made no bones about his innate distrust of the people who were entrusted with the reins of government. Even though he later came to admire Herbert Hoover, M.S. could look back on a time when a ruling by then Undersecretary H. Hoover of the Department of Commerce had driven him out of the chewing gum business. Later, this same Hoover, as War Relief Food Administrator, had played hob with his two-edged plan to corner some sugar futures at the same time Hershey was planning to plunge in Cuban sugar plantations and refineries. Subsequently, of course, M.S. had reason to smart over the altercations that arose when his plans for a Community High School on Pat's Hill ran afoul of the Pennsylvania State Board of Education's policies.

Murrie had not been consulted and he had not meddled in these earlier debacles, but one can only guess at the reasons for his abstinence. As a registered and sometimes vocal Democrat, he probably figured he could not contribute much in those earlier dealings with Washingtonians who were in those times usually Republicans. The "School on the Hill" plan came about during a Democratic administration in Harrisburg, but the school disciplines were pretty much the charge of the men in Hershey Estates, and he did not choose to cross these lines very often. M.S. Hershey himself held the tiller on *that sled*, so there were not many crossovers into those privileged sanctuaries.

When Franklin Delano Roosevelt swept into office in 1933, Murrie, even though he was happy with the change as a Democrat, still managed to keep a low profile during the first four years of the New Deal. But when FDR was reelected and the number of government bureaus kept exploding in a profusion of lettered designations (i.e., NRA, PWA, CCC, WPA, etc.), Murrie was quick to perceive the importance to Hershey of good relations with the brain trusters in Washington.

He nearly came a cropper on his first move when he invited Agriculture Secretary Henry Wallace to speak at the Community Building dedication on Labor Day in 1934. Otherwise, that move launched Bill Murrie on a round of inner circle introductions and these subsequently earned him a unique angle of access to the people who made the wheels go 'round in Washington.

The first real manifestation of this newfound advantage came about in the same year, 1937, when a strike hit Hershey that was more than somewhat encouraged by the Labor Department wing of the New Dealers in Washington. Even before the smoke had cleared on that debacle, Bill Murrie had set up a Research and Development project on behalf of a new ration bar for the U.S. Army.

Two salient developments were to emerge from the inception of the ration bar project, and they would have a mighty impact on the future of the Hershey image, both corporate and international. On the corporate level, Bill Murrie selected Sam Hinkle, chief chemist of Hershey Chocolate Corporation, to head up the developmental project. But it was from the seeds of the project planted in 1937 that Bill Murrie was to later harvest for Hershey Chocolate some of the most advantageous governmental favors that ever befell an American corporation.

In less than a score of years, Sam Hinkle would rise to the board chairmanship of Hershey Chocolate Corporation. There is no doubt that his successful work in developing the War Ration Bars helped start him on the way upward.

The international image of Hershey and the scope of governmental favor came about in the latter war years, when sugar priorities and production quotas were rearranged by the powers in Washington. But by that time the administrators of the WPB, the OPA, the OPM, etc., were first name acquaintances of Bill Murrie. His phone conversations to "Chet" and "Don" were almost daily occurences, and Chet was none other than Chester Bowles and Don was Donald Henderson.

The inner and the outer workings of Bill Murrie in Hershey Chocolate Corporation's leadership in war and in peace became well nigh incalculable. Indeed—*vital*. For in the near half century of his works with Hershey, Bill Murrie became a big gun. A man of truly presidential caliber.

Dear Old Golden Rule Days

When Milton and Catherine Hershey set up the Trust for the orphans' school in 1909, they cast the die for a key element of the Hershey story. The school would ultimately become the holder of controlling stock shares that made it the primary recipient of corporate earnings and the virtual landlord of all the property holdings acquired by Hershey enterprises. Hence it would become the star emerald in a 10,000 acre tiara and a major funding source for the advancement of education in Pennsylvania.

But before all the ambitious plans for the school could unfold, someone had to get it started. The choice of George and Prudence Copenhaver to set the whole new place in motion was to prove to be more than prophetically sound. It was positively inspired.

Nevertheless, in ticking off the contributions and the characteristics of the various people who helped put together the Hershey story, the focus of the attention is more concerned with their personalities than it is with their achievements. The hard facts of achievement are already on a record that begs no more of repetition.

George and Prudence Copenhaver represented almost as much of a marriage of opposites as did ex-Mennonite Milton and Catholic Kitty Hershey. Both Copenhavers were certified teachers, but like most married couples, they probably learned most of what they knew about life from each other, an unavoidable consequence of spending most of their lifetimes together.

In the man's world typified by the Hershey consortium of those days, George Copenhaver was the principal of the school and a princeling in the royal scheme of things ordained by the Chocolate King. But George had a patient, compassionate and warmly human personality, and he was the very model of a studious senior sentimentalist.

Prudence was made of sterner stuff. She not only taught by the book—she lived by it. She was not only a qualified teacher—she thoroughly meant to see that what she taught got learned, or she would *throw the book* at anyone who might have missed the message. This penchant was not solely confined to the academic arena, for "Pru" Copenhaver kept a book of an ever-present set of rules she thought applied to everyone, save one. The intractable M.S.

She later softened her martinet role in deference to her husband, particularly in her dealings with him. She learned that he had more "give " than she could either regulate or overwhelm. It would appear from this vantage point of hindsight that George Copenhaver was a pretty smart cookie because his wife had learned something from him by assimilation, and he hadn't taken recourse to the stick either as an instruction pointer or as a rudely applied rod.

All of which leads to one of the best-remembered stories about George Copenhaver. Perhaps this is because it is irrevocably tied to the old axiom, "Spare the rod and spoil the child," a long-ago practice that has almost faded from memory, save for those few of us whose aging anatomies still remember the days when smartness was infused into students at both ends.

The Hershey School for orphan boys began as a home and a school. The first order of business in the early days of admission and assimilation of students was devoted to establishing a suitable home life for the young charges. George and Prudence Copenhaver were houseparents before they tried to instruct the squads that descended on them. They were always known as "Mr." Copenhaver and "Mrs." Copenhaver, but in the home they shared with the little fellows, they took on the roles of Mama and Papa. Those appellatives slipped out on many occasions of skinned knees, bloody noses, and skip-a-tooth grimaces.

This brings us to the Saturday morning routine of the paddle. Each week, particularly after the school had expanded its enrollments to several dozen boys, there was a disciplinary session invoked. In summers, it took place on the lawn in front of the house; in winter, in the big front living room at the Homestead.

Each week there was a gathering of the reprehensible, rowdy, or recalcitrant students for a great come-and-get-it day as the boys lined up in alphabetical order and Mr. George Copenhaver sat down in a big, wooden, straight-back chair. Across his knees rested the instrument of instruction.

One by one each boy would approach Mr. Copenhaver and state the nature of the infraction he had committed. The paddling, thereafter, was applied to the seat of those boys who were sentenced to drape themselves either over a sawbuck or across the administrative lap. Smaller recipients were given demonstrations of Mr. Copenhaver's personal handiwork. Bigger ones got the paddle.

Punishment was meted out to fit the breach. The briskness of application was supposedly dictated by the degree of seriousness of the misdeed. But briskness was not a Copenhaver trait when it came to punishment. This gentle man was truly hurt far more each time he measured out the paddlings than were the recipients. When constrained to use the paddle, that hurt him most of all.

Nevertheless, a condensed version of applied crime and punishment was staged and conducted each Saturday for quite a few years. In the early 1930's, however, an event occurred in which the word crime could have been truthfully applied to one of the boys in the lineup of culprits.

Harry Hartman, a school employee, couldn't find his watch. Later the timepiece was found in the possession of a twelve-year-old boy who had been in the shop class when the loss had been first noted. He admitted to the theft and, having been caught, took his place in the Saturday lineup and awaited his punishment.

When his turn came, he approached Mr. Copenhaver and restated the confession that he had made off with Mr. Hartman's watch. As he got ready to bend over and assume the position, George Copenhaver put the paddle aside and touched his hand to the boy's shoulder, fixing the lad with a pitying look.

"Son," he said gently, "this is a bad day for both of us. Right now Mr. Hartman could go out and buy another watch for a dollar or so, and he wouldn't have lost much. But you stole it, and although Mr. Hartman has his watch back, something much more precious has been lost—your good name. Now you're going to have to spend the rest of your life with the hateful knowledge that you are a thief."

He put both hands on the boy's shoulders.

"I can't paddle you," he announced sorrowfully. "You've punished yourself far worse than anything I can do to you. Now get off to the side and think about that."

The boy, who had feared the severity of the punishment he expected, somehow didn't feel relieved to have escaped it. He went off to the side and from that vantage point he set another precedent.

Until that time, it had been an unwritten law among the culprit clan that no matter how hard he was paddled, nobody ever cried. Not ever.

But the unpaddled boy did. Every stroke of hand or paddle to the seat of one of his classmates was accompanied by his choking whimpers and sobs, as though a riveted lash were being struck across his own backside. He cried so hard, and the effect on George Copenhaver was so intense, that the schoolmaster had to stop the punishment routine before he had dealt with the last several boys.

He got up from the chair and threw the paddle across the yard as though it had done something terrible to him. Then he waved off the boys and told them that the proceedings were closed. He walked over to the still sobbing culprit who had received, in his own eyes, the worst penalty of all. He had been denied the catharsis of a well-merited paddling. He was too bad to whip.

George Copenhaver took the boy into the house with him and they talked things over. The conversation turned again to Harry Hartman and his watch. Between them, they resolved a course: The boy promised to make restitution by washing Mr. Hartman's car every week for a year, or any time in between washings when it got dirty and he could get off to clean it up. Copenhaver agreed, phrasing his response in terms gentle enough to soothe the youngster. He later said that the verdict he had pronounced was the cruelest thing he had ever done in his life.

Possibly it was, but it also turned out to be one of the most effective remedial measures ever undertaken in the history of the school. Not alone for what it taught the boy, but for the subsequent and really lasting impact it had on just about every student in the thousands who have since passed through the portals of the school.

The boy kept his promise, and on the anniversary of the punishment date, Harry Hartman showed up and told him the slate was clean. Right there, in the presence of Mr. and Mrs. Copenhaver, he gave the boy a watch. The lesson worked in several ways.

The identity of the boy was known to his fellow students as well as to George and Prudence Copenhaver and to Harry Hartman, but kept secret. Those who have told and retold the story spoke only of the incident, not the name. Everyone privileged to the boy's identity will tell you that he not only went on to lead an exemplary life, but at last report he was one of the most prominent citizens in his community with his name at the top of the company he founded.

The gentle man who fitted the punishment to the crime had at first regretted the decision not to whip the boy and, by making him aware of the outcast status earned by his misdeed, thought for a long time he had been too cruel. He lived long enough to see the effect of his decision and he came to realize that he had saved more than just one boy. He had set an example that bears repeating. It keeps on being repeated among the upwards of five thousand students who have since passed through the halls that George and Prudence Copenhaver opened.

One boy and one man figured in one of the most valuable lessons the school ever taught. The secrecy so assiduously maintained on the boy's behalf was an assurance to him that helped him excel in later life. The keeping of that secret is a credit to all the people who knew it and kept it.

The epoch established something else, too. It became the first in a multitude of events that took place across the next quarter of a century. George Copenhaver was a wise and gentle man. Every year that passed into the annals of his tenure is dotted with proofs that his selection by Milton Hershey to be the first schoolmaster of Hershey Industrial School was an inspired choice.

That never was a secret.

John Was the Judge—But Snyder Was the Governor

Of all the men who were tied to the personal affection and to the decision-making business functions of Milton Hershey, none of them were closer to his heart or more vital to his success than John E. Snyder, the attorney. Snyder's first contact came in the early years of the 1890's in Lancaster, when he had been a neighbor of Milton and Mama Hershey, who lived next door to him on Queen Street.

Snyder had been recommended to Hershey by the banker, Brenemann, when the paperwork generated by the young confectioner's expanding ventures began requiring the assistance of someone trained in the law. Even though they were neighbors, Hershey hadn't known Snyder, and at the time of their first meeting, the young attorney had only recently completed his legal training. His certification as attorney came after spending several years in the role of legal clerk apprentice in the offices of Lancaster attorney David L. Eshelman.

Although Snyder never attended college and hence had no degree, he had been a brilliant student in public schools. He had graduated from Lancaster High at the top of his class in 1878 shortly after his sixteenth birthday.

By the turn of the century when Hershey was ready to move back to the Derry Church locale of his early childhood, John Snyder had become his right-hand man. He had begun his duties with the expanding Lancaster Caramel Company, and was thereafter charged with drafting and filing virtually all the legal papers necessary to each of Hershey's ventures. He had handled the terms of sale for the Lancaster Caramel Company, and he had simultaneously negotiated the purchase of The Homestead. Shortly after that he set in motion the whole scheduled program to buy up the additional Derry Church properties and to prepare the town planning and street railway rights-of-way from which the village of Hershey would one day evolve.

The slow, surefooted manner of lawyer John Snyder earned him the nickname "Judge" that Milton Hershey gave him during those early days of explosive growth and expansive movement. From the very beginning, the stodgy and ultra-cautious pace of Judge Snyder's deliberations were nothing short of maddening to the impatient Hershey. But there were several other conservative and deliberative men in the Hershey camp of those days, not the least of whom was old Lebbie Lebkicher, the only other man to share the personal warmth of Milton Hershey's close affection. Consequently, Judge Snyder and Lebbie became friends and allies from the early days when they began working together.

In the years following the opening of the Hershey Trust Company there was a balcony above the main banking area where Judge Snyder and Lebbie Lebkicher had adjoining offices. These were the rooms where Milton Hershey would periodically conduct his so-called downtown business. Thus, by turns, both Lebbie's and Snyder's offices were for a period of ten years or more known as M.S.'s office at the bank.

Hershey never had an office at the bank. Nor did he, in fact, have an office at the chocolate company or the school either, even though he made almost daily visits to one or all three places and conducted business meetings in all of them when he happened to be in town. In point of fact, Milton Hershey's office in Hershey was any place he chose to hang his hat. The meetings at which he announced or launched his new plans for buildings or products were meetings called wherever he chose. The so-called Hershey office at the bank possibly derived from the fact that Ezra Hershey was the bank president, and he had an office in the Trust Building.

But the home base of operations for the Judge, John Snyder, was in the office on the mezzanine of the bank, next to Lebbie's in the early years, then next to Ezra Hershey's later on. During the expansive years from the late teens to the early thirties of the twentieth century, this was where the Judge performed the duties that earned him another little known title as "governor." But the term was more directly related to the duties performed by a mechanical device. It was never meant to paint him as an executive bureaucrat.

He became a governor by trying to slow down the feverish pace an aging Milton Hershey had seemingly acquired in the boom years of the twenties and the bust years of the Depression.

John Snyder knew Hershey better than anyone else in the world. He probably fought with him more any other person, too, but the intimate knowledge of his man and the constant differences that arose between them were each, in part, a product of the other. The main point of controversy derived from the different means whereby each man sought to put his thoughts into words.

Hershey never wrote anything if he could avoid it. Snyder, on the other hand, was obdurately insistent on getting everything in writing whenever an idea came up for discussion. Hershey had had trouble putting his thoughts on paper from his childhood days of gypsy-like school attendance, but he had no trouble expressing himself orally. His spoken words were usually simple, mostly monosyllabic, crisp, and to the point.

Snyder had gained his early spurs as a law clerk because he had an obsessive yearning and an almost consummate skill when it came to putting words on paper in a way that would make them legal and binding. He thought in legal terms, and he even spoke in the precise and orderly style of a man who was reading from a meticulously prepared script.

The tones of the average Snyder response to a Hershey idea invariably drove M.S. to near distraction. But when Snyder had been given the actual substance of a Hershey venture in order to translate it into a legally binding document, the gemlike precision of his semantic skills really sent the fussy little boss man up the wall.

Hershey wanted things done quickly. Volumewise, he never was much of a speaker, but when he talked, there was a quality of brutal frankness in the bare bones brevity of his chosen words.

Snyder wanted to do things slowly. He took time to think, and he wanted to take the time to make every word stand up for all time and in every possible kind of light.

When Snyder had drafted his legal version of a given Hershey project, he would submit copies to the board members and then he would read from his copy, whereupon the perennial party of the first part and the singularly vocal first person to object would be Milton Hershey.

"What's all that?" he would want to know, and then in exasperation he would add, "I don't understand it."

This became a regular routine, because whenever Hershey told his directors what he wanted to do, Snyder's response was to either tell him he couldn't do it his way—or at all. In Hershey's eyes, every deed, every mortgage, every move to acquire rights-of-way, or, indeed, any and every instance of Snyder's handiwork had been devilishly conceived to hogtie him and thwart his plans. What Hershey believed to have been a simple idea, he then found to have become complicated by Snyder's paper translations.

But it wasn't merely Hershey's objections to Snyder's paper gymnastics that caused this forty year litany of intermanagement squabbling. It seemed to Hershey that every time he proposed anything, Snyder had always been the first of his inner circle who would either try to slow him down or to change whatever it was he had in mind.

He always wound up signing the papers Snyder produced, but only after a raft of arguments, rebuttals, and counterproposals made them acceptable to the concerned parties. One of those former directors, D. Paul Witmer, had a few words about that.

"The final papers didn't become 'acceptable' until the constant debates made the contestants so weary they gave up by deciding to agree so that they could go on to the next project that awaited their attention. And there were always several other plans waiting in the wings."

Witmer's recollections were drawn from the 1930's, almost ten years after he had come aboard the Hershey express, and following the time in which the excellent level of his performance as both builder and planner had resulted in his elevation to executive status. He added something else.

"But John Snyder's influence cannot be measured solely on the basis of the contracts and agreements he drew up. Any number of the things that M.S. launched and completed after Snyder died, still had the unmistakable imprint of the Judge's precision, care, and caution. Even though Hershey had continually balked at Snyder's legal mumbo-jumbo, he eventually seemed to realize that the Judge had once again performed a mighty task in keeping him out of trouble."

Snyder's stand-pat words on that score were, "The best way to stay out of trouble is by not getting into it in the first place."

By consensus, the prevailing sentiment among the Hershey old-timers also points up another effect of Snyder's influence. They contend that the staff lawyer had performed his greatest services by virtue of the Hershey ideas that *never* hit paper, the things that Snyder prevented Hershey from doing.

Two Hershey ideas provide examples of this persuasion. Both of them came about in the early thirties, and both were community related projects. The first one concerned the Community Redemption Center. The second was M.S.'s plan to build a consolidated community church. He outlined the latter plan to Snyder one day, and he prefaced the suggestion by reminding Snyder, "Churches are always in debt, but if all the people would band together and form one big congregation, just think of all the things they could do. And with a membership that big, they could afford it."

The lawyer was so upset he straightaway told Hershey, "It won't work. You can't do it." He explained that the whole idea was not only ridiculous, but that it was inimical to the very reasons why Hershey's own Mennonite forebears had come to America in the first place.

"M.S.," he said, "your Mama and even old Pap would roll over in their graves if they heard that one. But it wasn't only people like the Mennonites in your family who came to America in search of religious freedom. All through the countryside, the Lutherans, the Presbyterians, the Amish, and even the Catholics of this area are descendants of people who came here to escape the pressures of rulers who tried to make them change their beliefs and their orders of worship."

"Milton," he said again, "it won't work, and you can't do it."

Hershey dropped the plan, but then went on to grant separate gifts of $20,000 each to the five church groups in the area. Snyder was happy to draw up the papers for *that* plan.

He did the same thing when Hershey proposed the building of a Hershey Community Granary. In late '33 and '34, Hershey was obsessed with the idea of providing food and clothing for the people he couldn't employ, and he wanted to build a community redemption center to do just that. His idea was to set up an exchange system whereby the center would provide temporary lodging for those without shelter and to also provide food and clothing for those who needed them. As he pointed out, "It wouldn't cost too much money. We can redeem the food, clothing, and shelter vouchers for those who have them. The government will pay for them," he added.

"What about the people who don't have vouchers or food coupons?" Snyder asked.

"Well, Judge," Hershey replied, "you just can't turn people away! We can't let 'em go hungry. If *we* don't help them, *who* will?"

Snyder could not hit back at him for the moment. The simple inborn generosity that dwelt within the breast of Milton Hershey was too innocent and too naive to spear with merciless reality.

At that first meeting, Snyder merely shook his head and promised "to look into it." He waited for some quieter moment to come, a time in which he could point out to Hershey that such a plan would bring a floodtide of homeless and jobless people to Hershey, and that the tens of thousands of those in need throughout the nearby regions of Pennsylvania would inundate even the biggest facility they could build.

The moment came for Snyder to launch his arguments at Hershey in the settled atmosphere of his quarters above the country club. When the lawyer finished, Hershey pursed his lips and shook his head. He then told Snyder he had thought of all those reasons, but he still couldn't shake off the visions of hungry, jobless people.

"If we don't do it, who will?"

Attorney John Snyder left the apartment a disturbed man. He was then in his fortieth year as friend and counselor to Milton Hershey, but he had only this to say to his wife Minnie (the former Minnie Espenshade).

"Somehow, he still wants to do it. He must realize that it can't be done, but you know how he is, and if I don't come up with some kind of alternative to this plan, there'll be no holding him. He'll do it anyway, and it will be a disaster."

But the lawyer's reasoned arguments had accomplished one part of his purpose. They had at least slowed down Hershey's determined plan to get started immediately, and he had agreed to postpone giving D. Paul Witmer and Harry Herr the orders to start building. Meanwhile, the Judge wasn't feeling too well, and he went into seclusion for awhile. He needed rest, and more than that, he needed time to come up with something to either replace the Community Redemption Center idea, or something that would delay the project until M.S. forgot about it.

His withdrawal brought him no peace. Every hour of Snyder's solitude was haunted by one constant reminder: Milton Hershey never forgot anything.

Several weeks passed, and Snyder only broke his absentee skein in order to attend some of the more meaningful meetings of the management board. After several of those, in the summer of 1933, he realized that the overloaded schedule of Hershey projects was beginning to work some of the delay he wanted. The Community Building and The Hotel were nearing completion, the construction company had added a furniture-making plant, and the plans for an arena were being brought front and center. All the while, Cuban business was booming, and Hershey was getting the glint in his eye again. Snyder realized that with the Cuban earnings continuing to rise much higher than expected, Hershey was beginning to feel as though this was the kind of Godsend he needed to build his Redemption Center.

Then, weakened though he was by illness, Snyder got an idea. Right after Labor Day of '34, he made it a point to meet with the Boss to discuss the Sports Arena. The record does not show whether Snyder visited Hershey at the apartment or whether Snyder's illness had by that time progressed to the point where Hershey had to visit him. Whatever the case, the records still show the consequences of that meeting.

M.S. Hershey and his most influential counselor got together sometime following Hershey's seventy-seventh birthday, and it opened on a note that M.S. found refreshing. He had in recent months begun to become increasingly aware of Snyder's frailty, and he was pained by the possibility of open disagreement with the Judge. He also found himself once again in the same sort of situation that had confronted him when his beloved Kitty had fallen into the sad decline that preceded her death. He began to fear that Snyder would also see through any surprising accommodations or anything he might do to give the lawyer the idea he was abandoning a plan merely because he was trying to humor him. Kitty had said, "You must think I'm dying. That's why you always agree with me lately."

So he had chosen to put up a sort of token resistance to her. Now he was faced with doing the same thing with another person, because even in spite of the Judge's opposition, he had become one of Hershey's closest associates and, by then, he was probably the most beloved of Hershey's close friends.

Snyder surprised the boss, not only by appearing to be in brighter spirits than he had been for a while, but also because he opened the talk by announcing an unexpected change of heart.

He told Hershey he no longer objected to the plans that were even then underway for the construction of the Sports Arena. At previous meetings, the lawyer had stalwartly opposed the very thought of spending millions and millions of dollars on a building that wouldn't "have a Chinaman's chance" of making money, or even of supporting itself. But on this occasion, Snyder had obviously changed his mind.

Then, just as Hershey was beginning to warm up to his surprising announcement, Snyder surprised him even more.

"You know," he said, "I've been thinking about the Community Redemption Center you want to build, and maybe that idea can be brought off at a later date, if those Cuban incomes keep coming in the way they are. In fact, this plan for the Sports Arena just might enable us to kill two birds with one stone."

Hershey cocked his head. He was more surprised than ever.

"How come?" he asked.

Snyder went on to tell him that if he really meant to go through with the Redemption Center, they would have to build a much bigger building than anything they had built so far. Then he added, "That sports arena will have to be a bigger building, too, but, you see, if you build one of them or both of them, either would have to be at least some distance from the central area of the department store, the plant, the bank, the Community Inn, and the Community Building."

Then he added that if Hershey went ahead with the plans to clear the ground down back of the park, they could go right ahead with the basic designs for the building. He also reminded Hershey of something else.

"When we start this work, we will be supplying some of the work you wanted to give those jobless and hungry people by building the Redemption Center. This way they will have jobs, and they can earn food and clothing."

Bull's eye. Hershey bought it on the spot. He had been surprised by Snyder's change of heart and by the way the lawyer had dropped his opposition to the sports arena, but he also seemed to have been positively charmed out of his socks by the follow-up in which the lawyer had also decided to quit his objections to the Redemption Center.

There was something else.

The Snyder suggestion that these increased work projects would also provide the jobs to enable workers to pay for their own necessities signalled the very kind of agreement that Hershey had sought for a long time. From even before the turn of the thirties, M.S. had been hard put to spend the constantly rising incomes (mostly from Cuban sugar) in the "make work" projects that eventuated in the building of the Community Building, the hotel and the newly expanded golf links and plant additions. Now he could keep expanding the other payrolls, like those down at the furniture factory and the creamery, and pretty soon he could build the sports arena, which he could either convert or use as a prototype for the Redemption Center when he built it.

If he built it.

Snyder knew Hershey, and the ruse appeared to have worked. But that is merely the half a loaf of assumption. Hershey also *knew* Snyder. When he flashed a happy rejoinder to the lawyer's suggestion, it was because he was happy. Yet, behind the agreeable facade, Hershey also was very conscious that what Snyder had been trying to tell him right along had been right. But he also realized that this newly adopted stance was another one of the Judge's classical moves to make him change his mind, or at the very least to slow him down.

They parted. Hershey came away from the meeting after having agreed to Snyder's plan to build the arena prototype first, then to wait and see before going ahead with the construction of the Community Redemption Center.

But in that fall of 1934 it was obvious to Hershey that John Snyder, his beloved Judge, was not long for this world.

Down through the years, there would be a lot of talk and a lot of stories written about the man who did the paper work upon which the whole Hershey dream was built.

The documentary procession seems almost endless, beginning with the sale of the caramel company in Lancaster, the acquisition of the Homestead in Derry, the naming and land acquisitions of the area that became Hershey, the Deed of Trust of the Industrial School, the establishment of Hershey Estates, the rights-of-way for the Hershey Transit Company, and on and on. He guided not only the acquisitions in Pennsylvania, New York, and Cuba, but he also helped Hershey to engineer the $50,000,000 loan that enabled M.S. to go ahead with his Cuban expansion plans. And Snyder did it in a way that never caused the slightest ripple in the growth of the chocolate company, the school, and the separate entity that would become Hershey Estates.

He had also been, after a typical spate of opposition, the prime draftsman for the International Quality Products company that, by a whisker, had missed seeing the light of day. But if *that* aborted scheme had worked, the biggest grip on the holding company consisting of Hershey, Colgate, and Kraft would have been in Milton Hershey's hands.

The events in motion at the time just prior to his death became notable, too, and they were the subject of many a conversation and many a written account that went to publication in the years that followed.

The Hershey Community Redemption Center was never built. The Sports Arena was. The plan to go ahead with the arena and the other expanded building programs had been wrapped up and expedited shortly after M.S. had concluded his meeting with Snyder in late September, 1934. The very reasonability of continuing his make-work projects had been ably substituted for the Redemption Center plans, and Milton Hershey had come away from the meeting with only one concern.

The Judge was dying, but he, Milton Hershey, would still be alive to continue with the many works and dreams he had always shared with this slow, methodical, and ofttimes disagreeable man. But those disagreements and so many things Snyder had kept him from doing had helped to build the dream and provided him with continuing access to the wealth that was the stuff upon which such dreams are made.

Hershey remembered another Snyder contribution that had almost been forgotten, even though it may have been one of the most important acts the Judge ever performed. The whole incident had occurred many years earlier when Snyder had personally engineered the reclassification of chocolate by the U.S. Department of Agriculture. Until the time of Snyder's documentary presentation, chocolate had been classified as a flavoring for foods and beverages, but the Judge had not been satisfied with that; so, he gathered the nutritional data and the proofs he needed to make the case.

Thereafter, chocolate and cocoa were classified by the USDA as foods, and the man who had hitherto been known as a braking force in the Hershey scheme of things came up with one of the greatest accelerators the company would ever get. There had been a clearly creative side to the Snyder personality, and the one man in town who knew about it and remembered was the man who needed to know the most and was least likely to forget anything.

Hershey looked at the town Snyder had helped him to found and to name. He thought of The Homestead . . . the school . . . the bank . . . the Estates . . . and even the trolleys running up and down the streets. Every last one of those things had come into being because of the carefully selected and meticulously transcribed documents that Snyder's hand had authored.

Everywhere Milton Hershey looked made him feel both good and yet very sad at the same time. Perhaps he would have been justified by feeling as though he were lord and master of all he surveyed; most other people thought of him that way. But the papers the Judge had drawn up spelled it otherwise. Milton Hershey held only temporary control and nominal mastery over the buildings and the wealth-generating entities that stretched out around him and reached to the far horizons.

All of this domain would one day pass into the hands of those who would be charged with the education of needy and underprivileged children. In the meantime, Hershey had been named to the stewardship that John Snyder's Deed of Trust had shaped for him, and the wherewithal to do this had only come about after the Judge had made the kind of agreements and contracts that made it all possible.

These were the thoughts that made Hershey feel good. The sad thoughts came when he realized that he would soon be without the man who had made him *do the good things right* and who had *kept him from doing so many of the wrong things at all.*

On December 20, 1934, the Judge passed away.

Milton Hershey had lost his parents quite a few years earlier, but he chose that occasion to say, "I never knew how it feels to be an orphan until the day John Snyder died."

They called him "The Judge," but he had also served as a mechanical governor, in a sense that he managed to slow down the engine of Milton Hershey's drive. He did his work so well that the engine outlasted the governor.

The Impresario

John Sollenberger was another man of many parts who helped fashion the Hershey story, but he wasn't a builder or a designer of systems. He was the maestro who presented the programs for the park, the theater, and the arena. He was a homegrown Pennsylvania Dutch version of Sol Hurok, and when John Sollenberger wanted to present a particular attraction, it got presented. He, like most of the men that M.S. Hershey picked to perform very important and quite ticklish jobs, was aggressive. In his maestro role for the show business wing of Hershey Estates, his aggressiveness led him to become a skater on thin ice, long before the hockey arena was built.

In the early 1920's, John Sollenberger had been brought in and put in charge of the Hershey Theater. His early responsibilities were about evenly split between scheduling the weekly movie attractions and the peripatetic bookings of theatrical drama groups, operas, and later, vaudeville shows and big bands. Some of these attractions later were staged at the dance pavilion and subsequently they were moved to the arena. As time went by, the same thing happened to John Sollenberger that had happened and kept on happening to nearly all of the men that Milton Hershey put in charge of things.

The jobs grew, and so did the men. It happened with the early birds like Bill Murrie, Harry Lebkicher, and John Snyder; then it went on to include George Copenhaver, Harry Erdman, Sam Hinkle, Joe Gassler, and the hosts of others who were to become the center of an enigma.

Had the town, the theater, the park, the chocolate business, and the school grown because the men grew? Or did each of the men grow because the overall scheme just swept them up and carried them along to greater stature? Then and now, the question persists, and it will probably run off into some shadowy corner of infinity where it will continue to defy resolution.

There was no question in Milton Hershey's mind. He had grown in stature and in capabilities as he increased the size and the volume of the challenges he had faced. In this stance, he found himself in agreement with Fleet Admiral William B. "Bull" Halsey who said, "There are no great men. But there are great challenges that ordinary men like you and I are forced by circumstance to face." By meeting and mastering an ever-growing set of challenges, a man grew in direct proportion to the way he handled the challenges. That was the job, just as it had been Halsey's and Hershey's. As M.S. saw things, the man, his job, the town, the plant, and everything else could grow up together, just as he had done.

But he also knew before he put these men on the track of doing ever greater things that there would inevitably be a series of collisions somewhere down the line. Milton Hershey ran Hershey—town, plant, school, or whatever—and his power was absolute. Consequently, as each of his selected barons enlarged his own personal power sphere, he would also have to make bigger and better decisions. The bigger the decisions, the closer the staff officer came into proximity with the Big Boss's domain.

When big money was involved or a big argument appeared to be in the offing, the case makers went straight to the boss with the choice. Then they stated what they wanted to do and sought his permission to do it. Nobody, but nobody, ever laid a question before M.S. without bringing in a proposal on *how* he intended to handle it. No score was kept on how many proposals were accepted or rejected or changed, but nobody went away without an answer except the guys who showed up *without* solid plans for how they meant to handle the job. They were thrown out.

John Sollenberger found himself at an "open switch" in the early thirties when he came to M.S. with a booking idea. At the time, despite the Depression, just about the biggest name in show business was Rudy Vallee and his orchestra.

On this occasion, John Sollenberger came to the boss with the idea of booking Rudy Vallee, his megaphone, and his band into the dance pavilion for a neat seventy-five hundred dollars for one night.

"Seventy-five hundred bucks!" shrilled the reluctant checkwriter, M.S., in high-pitched tones. "You nuts or something?"

Sollenberger wasn't nuts. He was *ready.*

"No, sir," he replied. "This is the kind of business you charge me with, and I'm prepared to back my judgment in this matter. I'll put up the money, and if we lose it, it'll be my money and any loss will be mine."

Hershey fixed him with a stare that Sollenberger later said felt like a drill.

"What if you're right? What if this Vallee fellow makes money?"

Sollenberger had thought about that, too.

"Why, I'll get my money back and the rest of the proceeds will go into the theater fund as usual."

Hershey cleared his throat.

"See!" he squeaked. "You don't know what you're doing!" Then he told Sollenberger that nobody risked big money when he didn't have it. "And *you* don't have *that kind of money!*" he snapped.

Next he told the theater man that even if he put up his own money, the risk was worth more than just getting his money back. He emphasized that you don't take big risks until you can afford them, and you never take a chance for the sake of merely getting your money back.

Entertainers

Glenn Miller

Sonja Henie

Rudy Vallee

Benny Goodman

Ted Lewis

Joe E. Brown

"I learned that as a young man," he said in somewhat calmer tones. "But do you know what you've suggested, John? If you're right, you'll get your money back, and if you're wrong, you'll lose it."

"I'll still have my job," Sollenberger said, but his voice began trailing off in a squeak of its own. He realized then that by backing this scheme, he could be a loser two ways. He wouldn't only lose his own money, but he would also be showing that he couldn't handle his job, simply by having made a bad choice.

Then he played it back. "I *will* have my job, won't I?"

Hershey grimaced. Then he smiled.

"Of course, John," came the soft reply. "Go ahead and book this guy with a bad case of catarrh. We'll back it just as we always do. Let's see what happens."

J.B. Sollenberger left with a sense of having been atomized and blended. But he booked the act with some trepidations.

Rudy *wowed* 'em!

John Sollenberger went on to become quite an impresario and his orchestral, theatrical, sports, and operatic attractions put Hershey, Pennsylvania, on the map in a whole new way. There were those who said that when "Mohammed (M.S.) got too old to go to the mountain, J.B. Sollenberger brought the mountain to him."

This was evidently meant to explain that once M.S. had reached his late seventies, Sollenberger was assigned to bringing the Boss's favorite kinds of entertainment to his hometown where he could enjoy them.

In part, some of the bookings may have been made to please the old man, but for the most part, J.B. Sollenberger was really more of a true impresario than an apple polisher. He knew what people liked in sports and entertainment as well as M.S. did in confections. J.B.'s forte was ticket sales—and sell them he did.

The foyer of the Cocoa Inn featured a picture gallery of the famous show-biz personalities and the collection of 8 x 10 glossies could have served as a *Who's Who in American Entertainment.* And every one of the pictures featured a personal sentiment from the star who autographed it and they testify to Sollenberger's popularity with the set of performing artists.

His sellouts included appearances in the dance pavilion, the Hershey Theater, the Sports Arena, the Hotel, and, of course, the old Convention Center, the park, and the zoo. He was instrumental not only in bringing big names to town, but he also had quite a hand in bringing new ones up while they were neophytes on their way to stardom. The teen-aged Sonja Henie, two-time Olympic champion figure skater, serves as a case in point. The pixie-eyed, dimpled blonde Norwegian came into the hockey arena to perform her graceful skating artistry just after having attained her eighteenth birthday. She had won the 1932 Olympiad at 13, and the 1936 Gold Medal came when she was 17. She was an early attraction who figured mightily in the growth of ice show popularity that began with the Ice Follies and thereafter led to the inception of its follow-up competitor, Ice Capades. And John Sollenberger had more than a small part in getting the latter group started.

His friendship with celebrities wasn't confined to the Ice Capades, however, and the picture collection proves it. Summertimes he was busy building Hershey's (town) image as a golfing capital, and he was instrumental in bringing in first Henry Picard, and then Ben Hogan, as club pros. The gallery of linksmen who began competing in Hershey after the Hershey Open was inaugurated in 1934 included such greats as Walter Hagen, Sam Snead, Johnny Revolta, Vic Ghezzi, and Byron Nelson.

When the Big Band era came into swing, a really big parade began. The beginnings were made by Vincent Lopez at the dance pavilion, but it wasn't long until the procession ticked off the names of Glen Gray, Glenn Miller, Jimmy Dorsey, Tommy Dorsey,

Louis Armstrong, Benny Goodman, Horace Heidt, Duke Ellington, Hal Kemp, Sammy Kaye, Kay Kyser, Guy Lombardo, and Cab Calloway. Dance band vocalists by the numbers joined the march that included Bob Eberle and Helen O'Connell, Frank Sinatra, Bea Wain, Martha Tilton, Helen Forrest, Ginny Sims, and Harry Babbitt. When Vaughn Monroe brought his "Racing with the Moon" stable to town, they broke all previous records. Much later, cowboy star Gene Autry came to the arena and caused one of the worst traffic jams in Hershey history.

The movie theater, which doubled as the site for stage plays and operatic performances, was to some degree influenced schedule-wise by the personal preferences of the boss. Sollenberger usually got his way on bookings, *but not always*, because when M.S. got word of certain movies being available, he made his weight felt. The Old Man had a thing about some of the stellar attractions, particularly the comedians. He doted on Wheeler and Woolsey, Eddie Cantor, and such, and he was a dyed-in-the-wool fan of Laurel and Hardy. He leaned on Sollenberger at least twice to bring back *Babes in Toyland*, the musical movie version of the operetta of Victor Herbert's starring Stan Laurel and Oliver Hardy.

As he became a real power in entertainment circles, J.B. had theatrical groups with people like Helen Hayes, Paul Muni, the Lunts, and many, many others performing onstage at the Hershey Theater. The operatic performances commanded names like Lily Pons, Gladys Swarthout, Feodor Chaliapin, Lawrence Tibbetts, Paul Althouse, and many others. His radio stars were seen and heard in person with the likes of Lanny Ross, Jack Benny, Bob Hope, Charles Wininger, and a whole host of others.

But J.B. Sollenberger's most unique arrangement would not surface until several years after M.S. had died. It came in the person of the huge Danish operatic tenor from the Metropolitan Opera Company in New York, Lauritz Melchior. The jolly Falstaffian tenor was in town for a Christmas holiday celebration at the Sports Arena when Sollenberger sprang his surprise. It came at a Christmas party held at the hockey arena, and lo! Lauritz Melchior, complete with red suit, white beard, and an oversized bag of toys, showed up as Santa Claus. But the bag was so big they had to have a little helper on hand to carry it for him.

When John Sollenberger witnessed the wide-eyed response of the children, he choked up for a moment and turned away. Several minutes later, he regained his composure just long enough to whisper to one of his companions, "That was the way it was when M.S. was around. *He was the Santa Claus* and I was just the little guy who helped by carrying his bag of toys."

The Soap Shower

M.S. Hershey couldn't stand waste.

Perhaps it was a holdover from the early days of doing without things or the need to make things do that marked the first thirty-five years of his life. Whatever the reason and not discounting Mama Hershey's persistent instructions on thrift, M.S. became like a hawk possessed by the continuing urge to seek out wastefulness and to stop it. He earned the distasteful name of "Snoop" for his habit of sneaking into the most out-of-the-way places and pouncing on the shovel-leaners and water cooler habitues who wasted the most precious of all commodities: *time*.

His restless memory kept reminding him that he had never had enough time to do all the things he wanted to do, and the mere sight of someone dawdling away the precious hours would send him up in smoke. And when he smoked, he fired.

The next item on his list of wasteful targets concerned surplus materials. His main focus was constantly aimed at the cocoa beans that were the source of his chocolate bonanza. Somehow, he couldn't accept the idea of throwing things away, especially when he thought they could be made useful. And this penchant for thrift was really shaken when he studied the cocoa bean and its usable yield in production.

He was rankled by the reports that there was only about a twenty-three per cent yield in chocolate or cocoa from the double fist size cacao pods. His laboratory people had been telling him since the 1920's that the average cacao pod was comprised of twelve per cent shell, eight per cent water, and fifty-two to fifty-seven per cent nibs and usable cocoa butter. The latter percentage represented the flavoring heart of his confectionery bars and the breakfast beverage that had become famous under the Hershey label. This showed an integer of more than twenty per cent of excess cocoa butter.

That wouldn't do. The same lab people who brought him these breakdowns also came with the sorry pronouncement that there was not much to be done for the more than twenty per cent content of the beans represented by bean hulls and water. They said that the hulls had all kinds of nutrients in them, but they also contained a toxic substance, an alkaloid called theobromine, so it couldn't be made into a suitable cattle food. The water yield was just that, water, and there was no use trying to save that.

But the ultimate search for by-product use was concerned with the twenty per cent of each bean represented by the extra cocoa butter. Ever since the previous century, the emollient fatty acids contained in cocoa butter had proven a Godsend for nursing mothers who suffered mastitis. The combinations of blandness, penetrancy, and emolliency contained in cocoa butter were well known. By the mid-twenties, chemist Sam Hinkle and his people were fixing, by crystallization, the refined cocoa butter so that it could be sold in the drug trade.

With the help of the pharmaceutical trade, a whole panoply of rubs and creams for mastitis emerged, and some of the cocoa butter began moving out. Then another use was found to relieve those suffering from hemorrhoids and constipation. The analgesic was in the form of suppositories, and thereafter the sales for cocoa butter began, in a manner of speaking, moving up.

But the burgeoning demand for chocolate bars and breakfast cocoa was building surpluses of cocoa butter much faster than the breast balm and end-users in the suppository marketplace required. M.S. and his chocolate-making confreres were faced with the immutable fact that they were getting twice as much cocoa butter from every bean they shelled and pressed than they could use in the cocoa and chocolate flavoring required for their confectionery items and their syrups and powders for beverage use.

Then Sam Hinkle told M.S., "We can make soap out of it."

There was little for the world to note and even less of it to long remember on behalf of that stirring pronouncement. The antennae of M.S. Hershey picked up the signal loud and clear, and immediately he launched another project.

By the late thirties, Sam Hinkle and his understudy, Elwood W. Meyers, were overwhelmed by the chemical analyses, quality tests, and evaluations the growing chocolate company demanded, so M.S. brought in some new help.

The selectee was Theodore R. Banks, a graduate chemist, and he was brought from Trenton, New Jersey, in 1937 to begin a new soap plant. His previous endeavor had been to study the breeding habits and nutritional requirements of oysters in Delaware Bay. In Hershey he would be called upon to build a vital new link in the chain of enterprises that bore the Hershey name. He would find this calling much more exciting than his oyster studies, but the day would come when he would envy the bivalves that were slumbering beneath the tranquil sands and quiet beaches of Delaware Bay.

He came aboard with no presentiment of the martyr suit they were tailoring for him. The big bucks and the main thrust of the Hershey interests were tied to chocolate—bars, *Kisses*, and beverage bases. In the town, there were all kinds of things happening.

The unions were making the workers restive; the schools, both public and private, were being expanded, and M.S. and his chief expeditor, D. Paul Witmer, were constantly planning new projects and the building of extensions on old buildings, more housing, streets, ad infinitum.

It didn't take Ted Banks long to realize that getting a new product under way, and a new plant in which to produce it, would not be easy. The plant construction was deceptively simple, but that was not necessarily the result of any great enthusiasm for a new soap product. The volumes of surplus cocoa butter were building up at such a rate that the chocolate company was simply running out of space in which to store the stuff. Banks got his new plant because of a pressing need to shift inventory. Nobody, except M.S., cared what he did with the stuff so long as he got it out of the way.

Before the rivets were cold in the new building, Ted Banks hurried over to the upstairs quarters of M.S. with a box full of cocoa butter soap granules. He had set up a laboratory at the Hershey Industrial Junior-Senior High School on Pat's Hill, and he came up with this first in an almost endless line of soap samples. The housekeeper said later that M.S. and Banks spent the remainder of that particular afternoon washing out handkerchiefs and B.V.D.'s with the new cocoa butter soap granules.

Three months later, the new soap plant was completed, and an increasing volume of laundry soap granules began making their appearance. The housewives, first in Hershey and then all up and down the Lebanon Valley from Hummelstown to Cleona, were entreated to try it. The offer was made by offering free samples, and on that basis many of them did try it. Success seemed to portend for awhile, and Ted Banks was beginning to believe he had surmounted his first big hurdle.

He hadn't. Instead of surmounting an obstacle, he found he had hit an open switch; a switch that had been opened for him before he had come to Hershey back in 1937.

His product was new, and so was his plant. Years earlier there had been another Hershey Soap Company in the front of the meat packing plant. The predecessor had used saponified animal fats for its product, and it made use of the animal fats left over, after the needs had been met for quantities rendered and sold as lard. This was another instance of the M.S. directive to make use of everything. It had produced a basic soap very similar to the lye and fat soaps made and used on the farms and homes of the immediate area. Outside of a trickling volume sold in the department store, the animal soap did not sell. But *it was strong*, and it had earned a notorious name for itself as "a hand soap that removed everything from the hands." Including the skin.

Ted Banks reasoned that he needed some big, new push to proclaim that the new item was a cocoa butter soap product. But some short-lived salesman had previously and unconscionably muddied the stream for him by an earlier effort. When the infamous animal soap had run into consumer resistance, it was a case of necessity begetting another invention to meet the need. There had been a cursory, almost dilettante effort to claim that the prior soap was made with cocoa butter. It wasn't, of course, but some earlier pitchman had thereby hung a curse on the product that followed it.

The laundry soap granules were good. They didn't outclean the Fels Naptha, Rinso, and Oxydol products of the day, but they were efficient. And they were much easier on the hands than the soaps their trusting users had tried before. But it wasn't long until cost study figures began to show that the red hands taken from the housewives had wound up by producing an endless tide of red entries on the books. M.S. was quite willing to rid his warehouses of the surplus cocoa butter with a product that broke even, but this one did not come close.

He could always give the stuff away, but the thought was hateful to him. And to Ted Banks. Both of them knew that there were emollient qualities in the base fatty acids contained in cocoa butter that were far superior and more beneficial than anything known to the soapmakers' art of that day. Nevertheless, the laundry soap granules made from cocoa butter were showing a ten cent loss on every box sold. Although increased volume would appreciably diminish the loss by a nickel or so, even if the increased volume were attained, it would only mean they were losing a little bit less on each of a lot more packages. T. Banks likened the routine to a dog chasing its own tail, who speeds up to bite it out of frustration. The ultimate increase in volume would merely substitute pain for denial.

Then M.S. got an idea. Looking up from the page of discouraging cost figures on the granular soap, M.S. beetled his brows and pulled at his moustache.

"We can make a toilet soap," was the pronouncement.

T.R. Banks remembered having made *that* suggestion when he first came aboard, but he was willing to forget the past. Especially the recent past. So he agreed, and they went to work on it.

What Ted Banks didn't realize was that by conducting himself so well during the dismal period of trial and error, he had earned both the respect and the affection of his mentor and employer. There were several reasons for this, beginning with the fact that M.S. had long held a conviction that frequently led him to say, "There's nothing like it," whenever he spoke of cocoa butter. He had used it himself for rashes and burns and all sorts of skin irritations with remarkable results.

Ted Banks shared the same faith, so a common bond was formed because of the belief they shared. Unbeknownst to many people, M.S., despite the opportunity afforded by his "homeboys" at the school, was sometimes still like an affectionate father in search of the son he never had. Ted Banks, on the other hand, was acknowledged to be just about the most likable guy in the junior ranks of the Hershey management team. Even those who were frequently at cross purposes with him admitted that.

In the last two years of the thirties and on into the wartime years of the forties, Ted Banks continued in his dual roles of cocoa butter research director and soap plant operator. He found adventure aplenty, but each of those years seemed to merely bring with it a change of the albatrosses fixed to his neck.

In 1939, Ted Banks and his mentor, M.S., were inadvertently involved in one of the most memorable events that ever occurred in the town of Hershey. The incident came about as the direct consequence of Banks' desire to get samples of the new bath soap out to the public. Both men knew the value of product sampling, but John Sollenberger, the entertainment impresario, came up with a new wrinkle.

He reminded Banks and M.S. that there was an upcoming hockey game at the Arena between the Hershey B'ars and the Providence Reds and both teams were in contention for the Calder Cup that year, for the American Hockey League championship. There would be a sellout crowd for the game, and that meant they would be able to give away more than seven thousand of the four-ounce soap bars. Excursions were bringing in people from all over the area served by the P & R Railroad.

They leaped at the chance, and come Saturday night, the soap bars were given out to patrons entering the arena. A capacity crowd of more than seven thousand, four hundred people was on hand to pick up the free soap samples and to see the game.

Meanwhile a production problem intervened. In the week before the game, both Banks and M.S. were informed that the only soap available in sufficient quantities to offer as samples were pine tar soap bars. They were both unhappy, but the literature and the word was out on the free samples they were going to pass out, so they accepted the inevitable and went ahead with the pine tar sample handouts.

It was a hot contest. In the waning moments of the final period, with the score tied 2 - 2, a referee called a highly disputed and vastly unpopular foul on Hershey's leading wingman. The fans howled. Then they booed. First some of them, then all of them, got up in their seats hooting and hollering. But officials being what they are, nothing was changed. The decision had been made, and the men in the striped shirts nonchalantly skated up and down the ice as they waited for the game to start again.

But for a full five minutes, the crowd would not quiet down. Just as the noise seemed to subside for the merest breath of a moment, a fan threw his bar of soap at one of the ice skating pontiffs in stripes.

That did it.

In less than a minute, a shower of four-ounce, hard-milled tar soap bars began to hit the ice. It also hit the players, the officials, and everything on the arena floor. The players and officials dove for the sidelines and the sheltered exits, but some few of them were caught at mid-ice and didn't make it. When last seen, there were about a half-dozen men fighting for cover under the goalie's nets in the cages at either end of the rink. By the time the shower subsided, these huddled remnants, storm-tossed by torrents of soap, were rubbing bruises not produced by gentleness.

The lather came later. A subsequent count of soap samples retrieved from the arena ice showed that the official's decision was unpopular with some four thousand, two hundred fans. That's how many cakes of soap were counted as having been "returned" in the sampling campaign suggested by J.B. Sollenberger and promoted by Ted Banks with M.S. Hershey's approval.

There was scant happiness shared by the trio of Hershey, Banks, and Sollenberger. M.S. was later said to have been glad that the imbroglio had featured a pine tar soap that hadn't too badly besmirched the name of his pet cocoa butter product. If he was happy about that fact, however, he certainly concealed his emotions exceedingly well.

No record was kept of the exchange that occurred between the three principals who contrived the novel soap storm, but folk rumors still prevail that M.S.'s words to J.B. Sollenberger were short, sharp, hot and crisp. But it would take something beyond the cleansing power of the bath size bars to make the words printable.

T. Banks subsequently regained his usual affability, and in later years when folks brought up the horrendous incident, he'd say "well, nobody can say we tried to *soft-soap* the officials."

Nevertheless, the cocoa butter type of toilet soap was a modest success. It did, at times, break even, but that was about it.

No further studies of the long chain fatty acids in cocoa butter were undertaken because the war intervened. In fact, awesome amounts of surplus cocoa butter were commandeered for the war effort in order to extract the glycerine content needed for explosives. Even though the glycerine only comprised a small percentage of the bulk converted for such extraction, it went anyway.

Down through the years, Ted Banks stuck to his lasts, and he kept right on probing at the mysteries of the butter that comes from cocoa beans. He was still at it when he retired in 1968, some years after M.S. had gone to his reward. But without M.S. Hershey and his faith in that same substance behind him, something more than a luxuriously rich and highly emollient personal soap evolved from his work.

It was no secret that the aging M.S. had come to regard him as one of his favorite people. Ted Banks, just as Abou Ben Adhem, loved his fellow man. He may have washed out on the soap project, but he cleaned up by making more friends than anybody in the annals of Hershey town.

The Greening of Derry

The setting for the jewel that became Milton Hershey's community showcase is mostly emerald green. The ten-thousand acre fiefdom that evolved across the span of years from 1900 is laid out like a checkerboard on which the squares keep changing colors as the passing seasons come and go. In the rural community which sprung up in the fields and on the hills laced by the Spring, Manada, and Swatara Creeks, the beauty is more than incidental to the plan. It is the heart of it.

M.S. Hershey had been a farm boy, and it was in this role that he frequently spoke of himself. He loved to see things grow. Behind a sometimes peppery facade, the bustling tycoon managed to conceal a strange and almost obsessive need to get things started, to nurse them along, and then to watch them grow. The things at the focus of this guiding light were quite varied, for they were extended to include just about everything he touched—people, enterprises, plants, buildings, and animals.

He had come to this place at the turn of the century with the initial purpose of starting a dairy farm, so his first concern was linked to raising the fodder and grains needed to feed milk cows. This was the starting point from which all the other diverse projects seemed to pop up, one after another.

As the years passed and the various parts of the new settlement began expanding a scheme akin to urban sprawl started to emerge. However, in this place and with those people, it would be more appropriate to liken the expansive trend to a kind of rural sprawl. It became mandatory to M.S. Hershey that the small, country town look remain intact; hence up and down the bent-diamond shape that comprised the all-inclusive Hershey scene, the broad brush of the master painter was copiously dipped and lavishly applied in green. Growing things were everywhere. They still are.

None of this just happened. Each plot, each structure, was meticulously fitted to the Pennsylvania Dutch axiom of "a place for everything, and everything in its place." That was the way Milton Hershey wanted it. There was a barroom ballad of the early 1900's entitled, "I Want What I Want When I Want It." Those closest to the enigmatic buzzsaw who became the founder were solidly convinced that the composer must have had M.S. in mind when he dashed off the boisterous ditty.

M.S. had a farm boy's preference for things that were green, but there would be many other colors added to the scheme with the passing years, and many other personalities were called to the backstage area where the scenery paintings had to be done. In all, there were probably more than a dozen such contributors, but one of them left the most indelible footprints for us to trace.

As early as 1905, landscaping plans were drawn up by Oglesky Paul, the landscape architect of Philadelphia. Harry Haverstick was the predecessor of the whole lot of grounds keepers, and he was followed by Harry Erdman, who became the most famous of all. The first Harry (Haverstick) was removed early from the duty roster on perhaps the strangest complaint that M.S. ever lodged against one of his trusted minions. H. Haverstick got fired *because he worked too hard*, and in the records of Milton Hershey, this completely jumped the track of normal expectancy. He loved to work hard, and he expected it from all those around him. Nevertheless, the first man in charge of the overall garden landscaping for the Hershey acreage was fired because he was *put in charge* and didn't *take charge.*

Time and again, M.S. would have his driver stop along a road where Harry Haverstick and his crews were engaged in a new project. Every time it was the same. Harry H. would be on the ground digging, while his men were standing around watching him.

"Dammit, Harry," M.S. would shrill, "why aren't the men working?"

The excuse was always the same. Harry was showing them what to do by doing it himself because he didn't think anyone else could do it right. That set a flame to the powderbox in M.S. Hershey. A dozen men were being paid to do the work, and the man in charge was the only one working. This meant the price was too high, and the work was going too slowly. Time and again, M.S. alighted from his car, blew his high-pitched lid, and departed.

Then, one day, perhaps he snapped a shoestring while tying it, or maybe Tom Black nicked him while he was getting shaved, but on that particular day, M.S. had probably blown off his daily allotted quanta of cordite, and he approached Harry Haverstick without dammits or detonations. He just fired him.

This was before Harry Erdman came onto the Hershey stage, but thereafter virtually all of the scenes, the sets, and the decorations were planned and painted by him. He not only raised nearly every imaginable kind of plant from seedlings in his greenhouses, from tropical orchids to rare Cuban jungle flowers, but he also developed endless varieties of roses and shrubs and miniature trees that made Hershey into the riotously colorful garden spot that it is today.

He was not only an exceptionally gifted botanist when it came to the germination of new strains and hybrids, but he also turned out to be a masterful landscape architect. In years subsequent to the magical works he performed at the greenhouses with tropical plants and every flowering genus from asters to zinnias, he topped the whole act by designing and supervising the construction of the world-famous Hershey Rose Garden. By consensus, from the hundreds of thousands of people who have journeyed to Hershey to view this place, the most often voiced line has been, "These are the most beautiful rose gardens I have ever seen." These expressions have come from folk who have seen the world's best, from Spokane to Shropshire.

Right up front, Harry Erdman was given a blank check. In the early days, he mostly followed the whimsical dictates of his benefactor, but in subsequent years, M.S. turned him loose and in many ways the roles came quite close to being reversed. The projects were germinated in the mind and planted at the discretion of H. Erdman. M.S. just sat back and enjoyed whatever next happy surprise awaited him at the hands of his gifted gardener. So, in a way, Harry Erdman had become the benefactor, and Milton Snavely Hershey came to think of himself as the happy beneficiary.

There was a tight, but invisible bond between these men, borne out of an obsessive inner need that dwelt within each of them to help things grow. It was no secret that in the years from the middle of the Roaring Twenties until his demise twenty years later, Milton Hershey was most happily disposed when walking in the beauteous gardens accompanied by his great, good friend, Harry Erdman.

At best, most of the men who clustered about Hershey through the years regarded themselves as having been most highly rewarded when Hershey treated them as equals or deferred to their judgments, especially when their opinions ran counter to his. Not so with Harry Erdman. In his realm of greenhouses and rose gardens, H. Erdman was monarch of all he surveyed. Not in his mind, for he never wasted a thought on such mundane values, but in the mind of M.S., that's the way it was. And in *that time* and in *that place*, he was the man who could make things happen.

Harry Erdman's tenure ran the gamut for more than thirty years, and he left the brightest, most colorful stamp of all, as his imprint on Hershey.

Harry Erdman's gifts to Milton Hershey were the Milton Hershey Rose and the Hershey Rose Garden. So something of him will remain for so long as people remember and appreciate the nature of beauty.

One red rose and one Rose Garden. Forever.

Changes Behind the Scenes

As the third decade of the twentieth century began dwindling away, something in the Hershey saga had seemingly begun to blur the picture of ambitious and progressive attainment. Beginning with the emergence of the Delaware incorporated Chocolate Corporation in 1927 along with the newly formed Hershey Estates stock company, a need to recognize the changing realities had arisen and lawyer John Snyder was not one to ignore their portent.

No quotes derive from the written record for this period because once again M.S. Hershey kept to the line of being personally articulate while remaining perennially non-graphic. In other words, he gave spoken orders while issuing no written commands. Consequently, across the bridge of years from 1926 to 1936, there were a great many changes made in the scenarios being filmed, but nothing appears on the record to show how the script changes came about.

The activities were several and all were substantial. Down in Cuba the plantations, the refineries, and the transport systems were literally exploding with expanded production of both sugar and profits. In Pennsylvania, Hershey enterprises, i.e., Chocolate, the farms, the school, and the park, were moving along at a lively clip, but there appeared to be a lot of motion for motion's sake, and quite a bit of it seemed to be going sideways. Milton Hershey knew this, of course, for in several instances he was directly the cause of it. But this era proved to be one in which the normally phlegmatic and stodgily methodical John Snyder emerged in a new light. A light in which the record shows him to have been more of a prophet than a pragmatist.

He was instrumental in getting a line straightening of the incorporation for issuance of public stock offerings accomplished in 1927. At the same time Hershey Estates was also incorporated, with the Cuban sugar enterprise included. Hershey also established a trust for the Hershey Industrial School. It held sixty per cent of Hershey Chocolate and one hundred per cent of Estates' stock. Milton S. Hershey, of course, designated himself as administrator of the trust. Even though he was quite alive, he was busily engaged in settling the affairs of his own estate.

The need for change was obvious. Until the late twenties, the Hershey organization looked like a patchwork quilt with some of the patches in motion and some others stitched in place. For example, fellows like Lebbie Lebkicher and Charlie Ziegler were seemingly endowed with free-ranging powers that enabled them to jump departmental fences and make changes almost at will. Meanwhile, William Murrie at Chocolate, George Copenhaver at the school, Ezra Hershey at the bank, and Sam Hinkle at the laboratories were literally rivetted into place.

This scrambled table of organization was all thumbs operationally insofar as procedural guidelines obtained. Fact is, in those days when anyone brought or sent a bill to Hershey, there was clarion call or round-robin inquiries that went out from Ezra Hershey's office, to see which account had the most money in it. In net consequence, incoming bills were paid out of the accounts with the healthiest balances, no matter what they happened to be for. Amusement billposters and programs were frequently paid for by Chocolate and conversely, if the Trust Company account was particularly substantial at any given time, shipping materials, and even ingredients for confectionery supplies used by Chocolate, were paid for by the Trust.

Building costs and property acquisition bills were also drawn from whatever source was better able to pay for them at the time of their receipt. This was the one form of outgoing cash flow that would later arise to slow the hand of Milton Hershey.

With the dually recorded articles of incorporation for Estates and Chocolate put on the record for 1927, lawyer Snyder saw the portent of a growing need to compartmentalize and to streamline the organizational channels of the diverse entities involved. In 1932 he was instrumental in getting Arthur Andersen and Co. called in to conduct an audit on the whole amalgam of Hershey entities. This not only caused more than a smattering of consternation among the players already on stage, but it posed an opportunity which the Andersen people later likened to having been dispatched to a salt mine in Outer Mongolia.

Some nameless pundit once said, "Auditors are like the squads who are sent in after the battle is lost to bayonet the wounded," and it was in this light that several of the old hands at Hershey perceived the Andersen troops. But nothing had been lost at Hershey, either in Cuba or in Pennsylvania, other than a sense of direction. Virtually everything was operationally busy and productive and profitable, and when the Depression came along, instead of the bubble bursting, it just got bigger.

Nevertheless, John Snyder, the lawyer/pragmatist, wanted this particular bubble shaped and protected as it was enlarged and expanded. The corporate guidelines accomplished in 1927 gave some semblance of direction to the line of march. In 1930 with the appointment of P.A. Staples to the Trust Board it began showing a more orderly channel for the enlarged tide of profits flowing in from Cuba. Then in 1932 the Andersen audit and the subsequent "departmentalization" of the various disciplines made the whole previously unwieldy structure more readable and amenable to the snap decisions of Milton Hershey himself. Snyder passed on in late '34, but he had cast the shape of things to come in the building Hershey saga just in time for another curtain to go up.

The first episode appears on the record as an otherwise innocuous account of something which occurred in 1936. But it came about in a year when Milton Hershey was in the midst of his ambitious plan to beat the Depression by spending money on buildings—right then. And all of it started because of a gold shortage. This is what happened.

A little more than a year had passed since the Hershey Theater in the Community Building had been formally opened and dedicated. But in the interim, quite a round of decorative expenses had been authorized for the addition of frescoes, murals, and other classical refinements to the balconies, boxes, and stage appurtenances. It was reported that pounds of 24 karat gold leaf were being applied to the fresco trims and lobby ceilings, and gold by the pound wasn't cheap, even in those days. The consequence of this didn't arise, however, until someone told M.S., "There isn't enough money in the Estates' account to pay those bills."

The announcement was reported to have come while he was engaged in conversation with his Cuban field marshal, P.A. Staples, and aside from the event being noted as "one that upset the Boss," nothing else remains on the actual record regarding the Estates' part in what followed.

Several days later the follow-up took place when the surprise bills were paid by transferring funds from the Hershey Industrial School account. M.S. was able to do this because he held the reins on all the motive power available to him on any Hershey departmental account. Rumor persists that P.A. Staples had influenced Milton Hershey in favor of making a change in the funnels through which outgoing funds were to be applied. Whether or not P.A. Staples had a hand in the actual move cannot be either substantially proved or denied, but the record does show that the channels of outgoing funds for local building programs had been changed.

A whole new conduit would prevail thereafter as Milton Hershey assumed direct control of the funds for building the Hotel, the Arena, and of course the School on the Hill. One other thing changed, too, and that was P.A. Staples' status in the scheme of overall operations. He was made directly accountable to M.S. Hershey and not ever again to Charles Ziegler, President of the Hershey Estates, which was at that time the corporate discipline to which the Cuban enterprises belonged. Meanwhile, the Community Building was deeded over to the Hershey Industrial School and would later serve as a classroom site for school use. The Cuban major domo, P.A. Staples, would return to his Caribbean turf where he would continue writing lengthy daily reports to his mentor, M.S. Hershey. He would not be brought back to Hershey to stay until nine years later when he was summoned home by the boss for higher echelon duties.

In the years that followed the mid-thirties changeover, the personal star of P.A. Staples continued on the rise. But it all came about following the day when they ran out of gold for the Community Theatre fresco and Milton Hershey had dramatically stepped forth to assert himself. And he did it in a manner that remains unmistakably imprinted on the Hershey community.

So the childless Milton Hershey became father to quite a few priceless and tangible things that emerged from one man who commanded the vision splendid. And the *changes* he made *behind* the scenes would one day *become the scene* called Hershey.

*　　*　　*

In 1930, when Elwood W. "Al" Meyers graduated from Lebanon Valley College in Annville, the Depression was well under way, and jobs for graduate chemists were scarcer than those for poultry dentists. Al Meyers remembers going to work as a hod carrier that summer, and he was still carrying bricks three months later when he heard from a friend about a job opening for a chemist at Hershey.

He was on the trolley for Hershey within moments. And, once there he made his application to Sam Hinkle, who then headed the Hershey lab. He got the job, and for the next forty-five years he maintained, "Every day I worked with Mr. Hershey was an adventure." His memories of Milton Hershey are particularly keen.

When Meyers moved into town, his starting salary was twelve hundred dollars a year and he lived at the hotel that was later to become the Cocoa Inn. His rent was four dollars a week, and he remembers his first days in Hershey as being "like moving into another world."

The adventures began when he was given a task of grinding up raisins for use in an experimental Hershey project, and he remembers coming up with a glazed set of rollers that would either get stuck or pass the raisins through unchopped. He took a glazed roller and a mess of unchopped raisins to his boss and asked him what to do next, whereupon he was instructed to take his problem straight to Mr. Hershey.

Over at the Mansion, he presented the tacky roller and the bag of chopped-at, but not chopped-up, raisins to M.S. Hershey. He recalls the shaggy-browed inspection of his evidence and the trace of a smile that crossed Hershey's countenance when the old man handed the grubby components back to him.

"You'll have this," said M.S. Hershey with a sigh. "But how else do you learn about such things? When you get an idea that involves doing something that's never been done before, you've got no choice. You gotta try it to see what happens."

Meyers still believes this attitude played a big part in Hershey's success.

"M.S. was not a trained chemist," he relates. "Fact is, he had little formal education of any kind. But he always said that he had learned what he wanted to know by trying things for himself, and many times after educated people had given up on some of those things. He had the feeling that book-learning sometimes erred by teaching people certain ingredients were not supposed to be mixed with each other. But he said that when he hadn't known about things like chemical incompatibility, he tried various mixtures anyway and frequently found that they were compatible. They *could be* mixed."

He had not known enough not to try. And when he did try something that worked, he frequently wound up with a new process and a new product. Some latter-day food chemists still marvel at the breakthrough he made in his early milk chocolate trials when he found that various balances of cream, whole cream, and even homogenized milk would not provide the characteristic smoothness and shelf life he sought in his products. When he reduced whole milk to a powdered solid and then sweetened it before mixing it with chocolate, cocoa butter and other emulsifiers, he did something that had never been done before. Something that hadn't been tried because textbook chemistry contained neither the guidance nor the prospective promise of success.

Meyers recalls the endless experiments with various barley flours, chopped celery, bananas and all sorts of ingredients intended for use in confections and ice cream.

"Sam Hinkle told me that when M.S. wants you to try something, you try it," he recalls. "He said that even though I may know that some of those trials would fail and would wind up costing the company thousands of dollars, I had to try them anyway. He told me to remember where those thousand dollar orders come from, and *where the money to pay for the failures comes from, too!*"

They came from the guy who hadn't known any better when he tried the new ideas that built a multi-million dollar company out of a new kind of chocolate, made a new way according to his lights.

Perhaps the best-remembered project in Meyers' recollections is the one that had to do with experimental trials that called for bananas and celery. The memory of it brings a smile to his face.

"We were working on a banana-chopping trial when the vanillin thing happened," he relates. "Everyone was watching M.S. as he stood over the mixer where the bananas were being chopped. We were all afraid to say anything, but he had a habit of reaching into a mix and tasting things as they went through. One way the blades would simply push his fingers away if he reached too close, but the other way, well, we'd seen people lose fingers that way."

"What to do? You just don't tell the Big Boss something he probably already knows. But what if he doesn't?

"Well, as it turned out, he didn't reach into the wrong end of the bowl on the banana mix. But the bananas had turned such a nasty black once they were chopped up, that he told us to turn the thing off and quit the project."

As for the celery trials, Meyers remembers that Hershey wanted the celery put through a macerator for a real fine-grain chopping that would produce small particles of celery for flavoring. They had been chopping away at the samples on a late afternoon, and when quitting time came, the particles still weren't small enough. So the lab crew decided to let the macerator keep grinding away overnight, reasoning that the particles would certainly be small enough by the time they returned in the morning. They left, and all they did was turn off the lights and lock the doors. The macerator was still turned on, and so were the blower fans.

Next morning the crew showed up and beheld an indoor winter wonderland. Everything—desks, benches, ductwork, walls, equipment, lockers, glassware, light standards—everything was mantled in garments of snowy white.

The celery in the macerator had turned to flour and having been reduced to a fine powder, it became quite easily airborne by blower action. The surprised crew turned around and beheld Milton Snavely Hershey on an unusually early tour of inspection. He scrutinized the indoor snowscape with all the wonderment of a bushy-browed Alice who'd found herself on the wrong side of the looking glass.

He clucked. Then he stepped into the room and walked around, shaking his head as he looked at this and that. He came back to confront the silently assembled crew and cocked his head to one side in the manner of one who was about to deliver a very meaningful pronouncement.

"Best damn mess I ever saw," said he, and departed.

Chapter XIX

~·~

A Year to Remember—1937

The decade of the 1930's was a time of great change in America. It began with a Depression and closed with an outbreak of what was to become the Second World War. Tin Pan Alley marked the mood of the times by opening the decade with "Buddy, Can You Spare a Dime," switched in the middle years to "Happy Days Are Here Again," then followed a yellow brick road that led to somewhere "Over the Rainbow."

In 1937, the nation seemed to be on its way out of the Depression, since the national income of forty billion dollars in 1932 had risen to seventy billion by the end of 1936. Franklin Delano Roosevelt had been reelected to a second term in the White House, and on January 20th he took office with a huge majority of Democrats in both houses of Congress. His National Recovery Act had been declared unconstitutional two years earlier, and he pledged, "I have just begun to fight." His first move was to go after the "nine old men" on the Supreme Court with a bill to add six new justices and to retire all the men past seventy who were then on the Court.

The move sparked a great deal of dissension, both in Congress and in the private sector. Despite the fact that Roosevelt's party held a clear majority, the Congress turned down his proposal to change the Court. His opponents gathered strength and the Republicans were joined by the conservative Southern Democrats who began to fashion a solid bloc to fight against his plans for sweeping social change.

Within the span of that pivotal year of 1937 a momentary disaffection sprang up between the conservative members of the Congress and the assertive liberal leader in the White House. And the split between the members of the Democratic Congress was to grow until it reached proportions that would later amount to an open breach.

The year 1937 marked an epoch in which a nation that had given evidence of righting itself from the Depression of the early thirties fell into a period of recession that became more damaging to the overall economy than the previous Depression had been. But with the channels of public welfare in operation by that time, the impact on the average working family was less severe.

The town and the working enterprises of Hershey, Pennsylvania, seemed to be floating in a world apart from the want and the dissension that split the ranks of America in early 1937. Sales and employment were booming, and so were individual incomes, as well as community and home-building projects. Over twenty-five hundred people were employed at better-than-average wages by the Hershey Chocolate Company at the beginning of the year, and the combined industrial and community payrolls would expand to over six thousand by the end of summer.

That year in Hershey, beginnings were made on the development of a ration bar for emergency field use by the U.S. Army, because an Austrian corporal with a trick moustache was beginning to stir up a fuss in an awakened and rearmed Germany.

Milk chocolate was the business of the town and the plant and of the people who lived and worked in both. They knew about the Depression. The Harrisburg, Reading and Lebanon papers were full of it every day, and there were people from those towns

219

living or working in Hershey. Just about everyone in Hershey had a radio, so like everybody else they got fifteen minutes of Lowell Thomas each evening before "Amos 'n Andy" came on.

Mary Kershner, a retired schoolteacher who later moved to Lincoln Park, near Reading, recalled something else about those days.

"My father, Samuel Hoover, ran a creamery for Mr. Hershey at Mt. Pleasant, back in the twenties. But I remember when Mr. Hershey used to come by our place in a car driven by his chauffeur, Roy Tice. He always used to try coming around on a Thursday, even after my Dad retired. That was when my Mom made 'schnitz und knepp.' He really loved that."

She went on to tell how he used to tug at her pigtail tresses and tease her. Many were the times he held her on his lap, and he would always leave gifts of chocolate bars and *Kisses*, but they went to her parents because he didn't want to be spoiling her meals.

But most of all she remembered the way the farmers in the neighborhood looked forward to his visits. Many of them were old friends of Milton Hershey's family, and many of them continued to be his friends after the chocolate plant became a prime customer for their milk. Dairy herds had increased over the span of a couple generations, since Milton Hershey had made his plant one of the biggest users of milk in the country. It was certainly the largest milk customer, other than the door-to-door bottled milk dairies, in the Lancaster, Lebanon, and Dauphin County areas.

"We all loved him," she recalled, "because he was such a nice man."

By 1937, the nice man in Hershey was beginning to become disturbed. He knew that demand for breakfast cocoa and chocolate bars was continuing to grow. But as the year began, he also began to notice that there were a lot of envious people putting his works and his community under the eyepiece of a critical microscope.

For a while, there seemed to be a strange lull in the springtime affairs of the town. The only difference in the daily life of the community began when increasing numbers of newcomers appeared on the streets and in the shops and taverns around Hershey. But Hershey and his management team paid them no attention because everyone was working on the new army ration bar or they were completing plans for expansion of the school and the plant. A new stadium was on the drawing boards, too, when one April morning the whole chain of events came to a breathtaking halt.

Hershey had just finished breakfast and was readying himself to get in the car for a drive to the plant. He had become interested in a new formula for a bittersweet bar and wanted to discuss it with the people in the lab. But before he descended the stairs, he was greeted by Abe Heilman from the plant and Sam Hinkle from the lab. They told him he shouldn't go to the plant.

"Why?" he asked. "I want to see about the new bittersweet bar and . . ."

"There's a strike, Mr. Hershey," said Heilman

"A what?" he cried.

The pair told him that the town was filled with pickets and that some of the workers had sat down on the job and were helping to keep people from getting to work inside the plant. It was something new called *a sit-down strike.*

"What do they want?" he questioned. "We're paying them good wages. They have a clean, safe place to work. Why, I've offered them a share in everything . . ."

Then his voice trailed off and he walked out of the room and onto the rear portico.

"Why?" he asked again, as he returned to the room and slumped into a chair.

He looked at the phone for a moment. Then he asked if they thought Bill Murrie, the Corporation President, would be in his office. They told him no, that Murrie had gone to the plant and had been refused entrance before he sent them to the Mansion.

Murrie would join them later at Mr. Hershey's apartment, but he first had to see what was going on and what could be done.

Murrie arrived an hour later with news that was more puzzling than bad. He said that there weren't more than a few dozen employees involved in the strike. Most of the people on the picket line and in the plant were union organizers who had come to town from Philadelphia and New York. When Hershey again asked, "What do they want?", Murrie could only shake his head.

He didn't know.

He told them he didn't believe the union organizers or the striking people *knew* what they wanted. One union man had confronted him with a verbal demand for a minimum starting wage, but the figure he gave was less than the starting salary being paid. Then, he said, the man referred him to someone else who complained about "too much overtime at too little pay." But when asked, "What was too much overtime?", he didn't know. And even the rate being demanded for this disputed overtime was less than the rate being paid.

"Well," said Hershey, "if they don't know what they want, how can we do anything about it?"

Murrie didn't know. The same unanswerables dominated the rest of the conversation and the phone calls coming in shed more heat than light on the subject. For the most part, the biggest concern was about the unshipped merchandise in the storage bins and on loading docks. Then they talked about the incoming milk that the pickets wouldn't let through the gates.

"What a shame!" said Hershey. "That milk will spoil. The farmers have got to sell it every day. What can we do?"

Nobody had anything to suggest, and they parted company until the next day when they met at the bank. Meantime Murrie was told to get the employee representatives and the union heads together for discussion. Next day the group gathered and waited for members of the opposition team, but by noon nobody from the other side had showed up for the meeting. Later that afternoon when they did show up, something else became apparent. This was not going to be a demand for increased wages or shorter hours or better working conditions; it was all tied up with getting a union into the plant. There were also demands for paid vacations and for a possible pension plan, but both of these were far less costly than the plans that had already been offered. Hershey balked.

"Let's be frank, Mr. Hershey. You just don't want a union, do you?" charged one of the organizers, also an employee.

"No," he replied, "I don't. But *do you?* You're an employee, so you should know that what these people are asking for is less than you're already getting."

"Not now," came the sharp reply. "I'm not working for you any more."

"You never were," Hershey replied. "Every man works for himself. But why are you so dissatisfied?"

The rest of the meeting was fruitless, but it became rather uncomfortable for the union representatives. It was apparent that some of the strikers had organized on the basis of a promise that they would be given union stewardship jobs if the strike proved successful. Jobs at not much better pay perhaps, but jobs from which the Hershey management could never fire them. Henceforth, they wanted to work for the union.

Nothing was settled at that meeting. Nor was anything resolved at the two daily meetings which followed, neither of which M.S. Hershey attended. He had departed with word that he would be glad to see any kind of settlement made that most of his workers would agree to; with one exception: no former employee would ever become a union shop steward or a union employee in his plant.

"I'll turn this place back into a cornfield before any of those turncoats go on somebody else's payroll to spy on my people," he said with blistering finality.

The declamation ended M.S. Hershey's part in the discussions and even in the activities surrounding the strike. And the strike itself ended a couple days later when his silent Excalibur became unsheathed.

The dairy farmers from the surrounding areas had been trying daily to get their milk picked up at the way stations and into the plant. All to no avail. The spring sun warmed up the stake trucks and the tank wagons filled with milk cans, so the atmosphere reeked with the stench of milk gone sour and it had to be poured down the sewers. By then it wasn't only the sun that was getting hotter.

Finally, four days after the meeting, the usually peaceful Hershey scene erupted with the force of a pent-up volcano. The crash of noise could be heard much further away than the quarter mile distance to the Mansion. Truckloads of farmers armed with pitchforks and farmers in carts and on foot stormed into Hershey. They gathered in the arena and then headed straight into the plant where they laid strong hands on the strikers, the pickets, and anyone else who tried to bar the way. The fury of the assault was awful to behold. A full scale riot ensued.

Al Meyers, the chemist, was there. "It was terrible! I remember several guys running from the melee with blood-soaked caps and handkerchiefs held to head wounds. One fellow was clasping his midriff where he'd been run through by a knife or a pitchfork. The people were swinging left and right with clubs that dripped with blood . . . It was sickening."

There were dozens of injuries, and later some deaths were attributed to wounds sustained in the riot. Margaret Clark recalled something else.

"We were told to stay away from the plant until the strike was settled, but some of us went down to see what was happening. I guess all of us later wished we hadn't gone. It isn't nice to see your friends, or even strangers, all cut up and bleeding like that. But the one thing I remember being told at the time had to do with something I didn't see; and yet I'm sure it happened."

She went on to relate how a friend of hers who worked at the Country Club had seen Milton Hershey at the foot of the staircase when he received news of the terrible outbreak of violence.

"He was standing at the bottom of the staircase. In those days of the strike, his loyal people gathered around him, staff executives and plant workers, too. They would spend the afternoon together, talking over the news that came by phone or was brought in by eyewitnesses returning from town.

"But someone had stopped him just as he reached the bottom of the stairs and told him about the terrible clash that had taken place. The conversation lasted fully ten minutes, and it was replete with the bloody details, as well as the names of some who had been badly hurt.

"But when he learned that one of the former boys from the school had been hurt, Milton Hershey just stood there, looking out the window, all choked up because of the hurt that had come to one of Kitty's boys. And to him."

The strike was settled, and the boom in Hershey product sales and projects continued. While *nothing seemed to have changed, everything had*. The striking union didn't win because another one took its place, and wages had changed virtually not at all. After union dues were deducted, the take-home pay was somewhat less than it had been, and deductions for a pension took even more. The previously offered pension plan that had been turned down would have cost quite a bit less, with a promise of paying more than twice as much at retirement. But untried, the offer remained unproven.

Those considerations would await later analysis. The most notable things missing were the sounds, like the laughter and banter on the streets and the light-hearted chatter that used to fill the working hours. Now, everything was business—done in silence. And nobody watched the gates to see if Mr. Hershey was coming. He had given up making the rounds.

Communal friendship seemed to have evaporated and the cold steel of businesslike production supervision set in. The Army D ration bar was perfected, and trial contracts were soon to be forthcoming.

Renewed work on the stadium started, and sales on the new *Aero Bar* were up. There was still growing demand for breakfast cocoa and for *Hershey Bars,* plain and with almonds. And a cocoa butter surplus still continued to climb. Through all of it, Hershey took off for one quick jaunt to Cuba, and upon his return stayed out of town and out of sight.

Labor Day rolled around and he didn't even go to the Park for the closing day ceremonies. Nevertheless, his friends and associates at all levels, the Murries and the Blacks and Margaret Clark's girls, all entreated him to come to a special party they were having to celebrate his eightieth birthday. He demurred at first but later relented when they told him, "It will be a private affair; only your friends will be there." So he agreed to come. They told him the party was going to be held at the Murries' home.

The evening of September 13th came, and Milton Hershey dressed early, but he decided to have a snack, just in case the Murries would only have cake at the party. Roy Tice came to his quarters just before seven and offered to help him to the car.

"Cut it out," Hershey said by way of refusing assistance. "I've just been eighty for a few hours. Don't treat me like an old man."

So off they went, but when Tice continued down Chocolate Avenue and turned right instead of left when they passed the plant, the Old Man shouted at him, "Where d'you think you're going?"

Murrie's house was to the left and Tice had quite a time with M.S., and he had an even worse one when he got to the Arena, where a huge crowd and a whole assembly of school bands awaited him. It took the combined entreaties of almost the entire Board of Directors, a smattering of friends, and other well-wishers to get him from the car and into the Arena.

Finally they brought him inside and ushered him to the dais where more than six thousand people roared a welcome and sang "Happy Birthday." Then came an uproar of applause and cheers as the bands played "For He's a Jolly Good Fellow."

It was quite an evening, and virtually everyone there felt sure they had surprised him. They had and they hadn't. In his pocket he carried a sheaf of papers he had worked on for almost a week, a speech he had drafted and reworked a hundred times. Nobody ever knew how he had found out about the party, but later they came to agree that he had somehow learned about it, and he gave every sign of having been prepared for it. He had even written a speech. But he never gave it.

Yet he was not prepared for most of the things which happened that night. For instance, he wasn't prepared to receive the big, beautiful ring they gave him, with eighteen blue-white diamonds and the trademark of a child emerging from a cacao pod. Perhaps he wasn't prepared for the giant orchestra, comprised of the full membership of four local bands, or the boys from the school, marching in their brown and gold uniforms. And, too, there were the public high school boys and girls with their orange and blue and white banners; or maybe he had a special feeling for Hershey Post No. 386 of the American Legion when they rose as a man and saluted him.

A three-foot high cake that measured nearly twelve feet across, and the eighty big candles that shone from it, made a startling centerpiece in the middle of the Arena. All around the cake there were members of the Community Theater Orchestra in their white coats and black trousers. Then, too, the entire speaker's platform was festooned in sprays of roses, chrysanthemums, dahlias, gladioli, and asters. The boys from the school and the men of the American Legion sent along additional bouquets of one hundred roses each, and to each was attached the wish, "May you live another one hundred years!"

Then it came time for the speech he couldn't deliver.

Milton Hershey just stood in the crowded Arena, smiling and whispering almost inaudibly, "These are my people." His eyes were shining with tears held back; they wouldn't come until he returned to the car and he was alone with Roy Tice. He wept on the way back to the Mansion, but this time he asked Roy to help him up the stairs.

"Now I know I'm eighty," were his last words of the evening.

Next day the people who had been at the Arena wakened in a happier mood. Somehow they felt as though some small part of the hurt they had allowed to happen to Milton Hershey had been repaired.

One man remembered that a former strike organizer remarked, "He looks like he's gonna cry," as Hershey hurried from the Arena party.

"Naw," came a sharp rejoinder from someone standing by. "He's no crybaby. He didn't even cry when guys like you turned on him."

But somehow, on the day after the party, the people felt better, at least in the early morning hours. Then the news hit town. After arriving at his apartment on the previous night, Milton Hershey had suffered a stroke and collapsed in his room. He was expected to live only a few hours, or, at best, another day.

The town was stunned. Some people tried to lay the blame on the excitement and its effect on the tired old man. Others recalled that he had appeared to have been ailing for several months, and that happened to be true. It all went back to April and the strike—a time when some of them had behaved like fools.

A shocked silence set in and it lasted for more than a month. But October came and Hershey remained in guarded condition. Meantime, the Army came through with token orders for ration bars. In November, the new *Bittersweet Bar* made its appearance and seemed to be going well. Meanwhile, regular and almond bar sales were still climbing and breakfast cocoa was going strong. The sugar enterprise in Cuba was still booming, but went unnoticed.

Very little news was coming from the Mansion. Hershey had barely survived the first shaky month of being confined to bed, but then there was news that he was now able to dress himself and that he was able to move around the apartment. By late November there came word that he had ventured downstairs into the kitchen and was once again puttering around with the pots and pans. According to the club chef, he was trying some new recipes.

By the time Thanksgiving rolled around, the octogenarian was definitely on the mend, and he was doing much better than merely sitting up and taking nourishment. He shared Thanksgiving dinner with all the trimmings in the company of the kitchen help and service staff at the club. Reports were circulated that he had appeared quite chipper, and yet all the news about him was received secondhand, and that in itself was disquieting.

As December faded and the year drew to a close, almost everyone in the plant and around town, especially those at the bank, the department store and the post office, began to talk about how things had changed and how much they missed him. In other years whenever the holidays approached, Milton Hershey had been a familiar sight as he bustled around town shopping for gifts and, more often than not, he had usually mingled with his people so he could wish them the joy of the season. He had always been especially fascinated by electric trains and mechanical toys. In previous years he had even set up a yard beneath his Christmas tree, replete with trains and mirror ponds, with farm scenes and ducks and geese, perhaps in order to brighten his rooms to match the sounds of holiday cheer that came up from the club rooms below.

As Christmas 1937 approached, he still hadn't put in any kind of appearance at his familiar haunts around town. Almost everyone knew that he had made a better than partial recovery from the stroke that felled him in the wee hours of the morning after his birthday party. But because no one had seen him popping out of the car and into the bank, or cruising the corridors and packing rooms at the plant—*something,* some big part of their daily lives, continued to be missing.

Every once in a while a caller would return from the Mansion and relate how a governor or some other big official, even the President of the United States, had dropped Mr. Hershey a card or a get well letter. Letters and phone calls came in daily from just about every place in the world, but the mail from Cuba was the heaviest of all. And cigars. Now that he had been sharply cautioned against smoking them, boxes of cigars were being stacked up in his rooms like cordwood. The service people at the club carried cigars out of the place by the armful and so did his visitors. But the golf season had folded down for the winter months, and there really weren't many people who visited the club that year. A general feeling of personal chagrin may also have had something to do with the slackened attendance.

Then came Christmas Eve and as the street lights winked on in Hershey, a gentle snowfall began. Milton Hershey had dined downstairs with the club staff, and the workers were getting ready to go home or to Christmas Eve church services. He distributed envelopes with his personal Christmas checks to the entire staff, and he shook hands with each one of them as they departed. Then Roy Tice came by to say good night, after receiving an envelope and a special greeting.

"I thought you'd left, Roy," said Hershey. "You better be on your way before your wife calls."

"She won't call me yet, M.S.," replied the chauffeur. "She went to Harrisburg to take some gifts to her folks. She won't be home until after ten, so I thought I'd stick around here until it's time to go pick her up at the station, if you don't mind."

"No, I don't mind," said Hershey. "Glad to have the company. Why don't you get some of that eggnog from the people downstairs, and grab yourself a box of cigars."

The chauffeur put down his cap and walked over to the big Christmas tree; he looked at the pile of gifts next to the platform on which the tree was standing. In other years it had held a train but now it was full of cards and gifts.

"I liked the train and the yard better," said Hershey, walking by him and heading for the window. He pulled back the drape and watched the snow that was falling outside.

"It's really starting to come down," he smiled. "That'll put a crimp in Ezra and Bill Murrie. They've always been last-minute Johnnies when it came to Christmas shopping. I'll bet they're both over at the store right now."

Tice smiled agreement. Then he walked over to join the boss by the window.

"Say, Mr. Hershey, I've got an idea," he said. "It still isn't snowing too much and I've got chains on the car. How'd you like to take a little ride around town and see what's going on?"

"Hey, that's a great idea," said Hershey, "but don't tell Doc Hostetter. Wait'll I get my coat."

It was only a moment before both men went down the steps and climbed into the warmed and waiting car. When Hershey had settled back in the seat and Roy pointed the nose of the Airflow Chrysler toward the driveway exit, the passenger sat up with a start.

"Hey, hold it!" shouted Hershey. "Is this another one of your tricks, like on my birthday?"

"Oh, no, M.S.," replied the driver, "nobody's expecting us. I promise I'll take just one swing up and down Chocolate Avenue and maybe make another loop down the streets where the churches are. Why, I won't even stop, and I'll have you back at the Mansion in less than half an hour."

"It's the club now," Hershey corrected him. "But you mind me, Roy. None of your tricks. I just want to see people but I don't want them to see me. You understand?"

This was the sharpest speech Tice had heard from him since his September collapse. Nevertheless, he assured Hershey that they would just make a quick tour of the town and look around.

Both men were silent as Tice made the turn down Cocoa Avenue under the gaily lit holiday lights. There was very little wind and the fat snowflakes were lazily drifting downward, sometimes flickering with a sparkle of iridescence when they trailed across the slanting beams of the overhead street lights. There was a band in the courtyard in front of the Community Building and a small group of Salvation Army lads and lassies just outside the department store. Late shoppers were still scurrying about, calling out their greetings. A scene of gaiety, but somewhat subdued, on that Friday evening of December 24.

From the far side of the street came the strains of "Good King Wenceslaus" and a Salvation Army group tootling "Hark, the Herald Angels Sing." As they made the left turn on Cocoa and passed by the Cocoa Inn, another group could be heard somewhere off in the distance as they urged one and all to "Deck the Halls with Boughs of Holly."

Hershey kept himself back in the shadows of the big sedan, fearful that someone might recognize him. After all, everybody in these parts knew the car. And he knew they couldn't just keep going if somebody waved them down. But nobody seemed to notice. He guessed that folks were too busy with their own thoughts of home and family at Christmastime to give any thought to him.

The trip carried them by several of the downtown churches, and it was even more quiet than he expected. Fact is, it was so quiet he actually felt a pang of disappointment. None of the churches seemed to be having any sort of Christmas Eve services, and the back streets were virtually deserted.

"It isn't that late," he said almost to himself. But within the promised half hour they had passed by the Homestead, crossed town, and gone back down the road by the Parkside Apartments to complete the circuit around the Arena. Once more they were heading into the driveway at the Mansion. They pulled up to a side door and Roy got out to help him, with the motor still running and the headlights on.

"Hold it," said Hershey. "You still have plenty of time until you go for your wife. Let the car sit here. You're coming in for a drink and a cigar."

"Okay, M.S.," agreed Tice, "whatever you say."

Hershey began having second thoughts after they departed the car, and the chauffeur kept close by his side as they walked to the side entrance and through the door. Once, in particular, he had a strange feeling when he paused to peer around the back of the building to see if he could get a glimpse of the town lights through the falling snow. But Tice began to hustle him along toward the door.

"Mustn't get a chill," he said, then Hershey began to wonder if he could be running a fever. So far, the night had seemed too warm for snow to be falling.

But they went inside, and as soon as he had reached his sitting room, Tice excused himself and said he wanted to go downstairs to get something. Whatever the something was, Hershey missed it because it came through in a deliberate mumble.

He removed his coat and muffler; then he picked up a cigar and looked at it. He was sitting in his chair still studying the unlit cigar when the chauffeur returned. This time his companion was carrying a tray with a covered casserole and a dusty bottle of port wine. He wheeled out a dropleaf table in front of Hershey's chair and placed the tray and the bottle on it. Then he brought out a pair of tumblers, filling them with port, and made a sweeping gesture as he uncovered the casserole.

"Merry Christmas," he said, and Milton Hershey looked down at a platter of steaming apple dumplings, with a thick cream and cornstarch sauce. Next to schnitz und knepp, this was his favorite.

He thought a moment, trying to recollect whether the dumplings were on the forbidden list from Doc Hostetter, but he was two spoonfuls into the steaming, cinnamon-flavored dumplings before he recalled that the diet forbade only greasy foods. It didn't take long until he'd cleaned up the plate and leaned back to sip the port wine. Then he studied the cigar again.

"Seems a little warm in here, M.S.," said Tice, walking to the French door at the back court portico. "Do you mind if I open this a little?"

"No," Hershey replied. He put down the cigar and got to his feet. Then he picked up the coat and muffler he had draped over a nearby chair and put them on.

"I thought it was kinda warm when we were outside a while ago," he said. "Let's go out on the porch."

The chauffeur nodded and opened the door so Hershey could go onto the porch. He did, and Tice stepped out behind him, clutching his arm as he came through the door.

Hershey looked at Tice, but before he could say anything, a chain of events occurred. First a battery of nightlights went on, illuminating the back driveway. One by one, a whole line of spruce trees lining the driveway was lit with every conceivable color of Christmas light. He blinked in disbelief, just as the singing started.

Off in the shadowy depths that lined the driveway, he heard the sounds of "Silent Night" as, one by one, the assembled choirs from several different Hershey churches had each of its members light a candle and softly break into the words of the beloved old Christmas carol. The volume built as each of the groups reached the driveway and stood holding their candles as they sang.

When they finished, he walked to the edge of the porch and waved to them, but he couldn't say anything. Then the candles were extinguished, and once again the sounds of singing swept upward.

The shadowy forms of several hundred people dissolved beyond the snowswept curtain of the driveway with scarcely a sound. He heard the cars being started to carry them back to town. They had parked the vehicles out on the main road so they could assemble here undetected. Then they tried to make their departures without disturbing him. The driveway lights flickered for a moment, then went off again as he stood at the edge of the portico looking across the silent void of the misted garden.

He heard a faint sound from below, and when he looked down, he saw two huddled figures still standing in the driveway below the portico. The taller one had struck a match and was lighting a candle held by the other small one. By the candle flame he recognized one of the girls from the box-wrapping department with her little son. The boy waved to him and he waved back.

"Merry Christmas, Mr. Hershey," piped the toddler.

"And Merry Christmas to you, son," he responded.

The figures standing below clasped hands and started down the driveway toward the road. Hershey sent Tice to catch up with the mother and son to give them a ride back to town. Then he stood alone in the darkness, looking off into the distance where the twinkling lights made a warm and rosy glow through the mists of falling snow.

The headlights of the Chrysler came on in the driveway below and he saw the departing pair waving again to him as the mother helped the child into the car.

"God bless you, Mr. Hershey," she called to him.

*   *   *

A merry round of well-wishers came to see Milton Hershey in the week between holidays. He was so busy, he scarcely had time for his daily games of Chinese checkers with the nurse, the cook, and the house staff. Toward the end of the weeklong festivities, he importuned the help into allowing him access to the kitchen downstairs where he cooked a batch of fudge for the boys he was expecting from the Industrial School.

The boys came over at twilight on New Year's Eve and serenaded him with one of his favorite selections, "My Hero" from *The Chocolate Soldier*. As a finale, they sang "Auld Lang Syne." Once again, the eyes of Milton Hershey were shining as he slowly climbed up the stairs to his rooms.

He stood before the mantelpiece and looked at the picture of his bride, his Kitty, as she had been in the year they were married.

So much had happened during the past twelve months. A shadow crossed his face when he recalled the strike, but it disappeared as the memories of other events flowed back. He shrugged a bit when he thought back to the birthday party. But he knew the outpourings of love and loyalty he'd seen that night were what his whole life had been about. He brushed a hand across the bushy moustache as he picked up one cherished memento he'd kept from the party. A birthday card that read, "Happy Birthday—from your girls."

He recognized the handwriting, and well he should. For twenty years he had been getting cards from his girls, and he knew which one of them had always been the instigator. Still holding the card, he sat down in his big chair and leaned back.

A distant bell pealed and a faint smile crossed his face as he thought about the dear lady who had sent the card from "your girls."

His mind went back across the span of more than twenty years, and he recalled a prim, bright-eyed slip of a girl whom he had once berated for bringing a box of mice into the plant. He fell asleep with a vision of this one of his girls before him.

Yes, indeed, 1937 had been a year to remember. But it had been the loyal ones like Margaret Clark who had really made it worthwhile.

Chapter XX

⌐·⌐

The Gathering Storm

In the early years of the 1930's, the published record of Milton Hershey's life and times appeared to have been dominated by the turbulence of the Great Depression following in the wake of Wall Street's thundering crash. Throughout the years of 1929 and 1932, M.S. seemed to be gearing up for the personal war he would wage on the depressed economy by the simple means of making and spending more money wherever his operations happened to be.

This was especially true in Cuba where Percy Staples had begun to get the sugar rolling from the cane fields to the refineries after having finished the biggest and most modern rail network on the entire island. Along about this time, the Hershey offices in Havana (handling railroad administration and export/import liaison with the Cuban government) were enlarged to accommodate a venture trading in cocoa.

But these moves, along with the veritable cascade of plans for new buildings in both Hershey, Cuba, and Hershey, Pennsylvania, were begun, pursued, and quite a few of them were pretty well on their way to completion before any appreciable publicity was accorded them. Fact is, virtually all of these turn of the decade plans germinating in the fertile mind of Milton Hershey were kept pretty much under wraps until Alex Stoddart showed up in 1934. But some of them would not have been publicized even had the former New York newspaperman been there to start hammering away at his noisy Underwood.

There were times when Milton Hershey didn't want anyone to know what he was doing, and in those particular times, this stance would have been well-advised, if only for the reason that M.S. himself didn't seem to be too sure about what he was doing. The formation of the cocoa trading company provides a case in point.

It had been about ten years since M.S. had gone bullish on sugar futures and had wound up taking an unsweetened bath. But his fifty million dollar credit from City Bank had helped him get a Cuban bonanza in sugar rolling, and he had managed to escape unscathed from that earlier debacle. So, in the early thirties when the world markets seemed to be going soft on just about every item on the commodity boards, M.S. began casting some fond looks at the cocoa bean market. Meanwhile, with all his staff advisors hopping about at full tilt to keep apace his myriad programs in Hershey, Derry, and Hershey, Caribe, he began dabbling in cocoa futures that hovered between six and seven cents a pound.

Before anyone else paid much attention to this off-stage activity, he was well on his way to doing one of two things. He would either corner the entire cocoa market (which had fallen off an additional two cents and the market price dipped under a nickel a pound), or (when it finally fell under four cents a pound) he was going to disappear beneath a tidal wave of brown beans. Some few experts later reckoned that the saner judgments of lawyer John Snyder and banker Ezra Hershey had prevailed and that M.S., by the middle thirties, had come upon the good sense to pull in his horns. That possibility did, of course, exist, but in the emergence of other factors that were for the most part kept in secret back in those days would now appear to be the real reasons why M.S. Hershey had made some mid-range adjustments in his strategic planning.

One of those influential factors had begun emerging in the headlines of the newspapers he read so avidly every day. Beginning with January 30, 1933, one of the comic opera figures on the European political scene had come out of the wings and into the center stage spotlight. A former Austrian paperhanger from the tiny village of Braunau-am-Inn (across the border from Bavaria) had emerged from the shadows of revolutionary foment and had been named Reichs Chancellor to rule a Germany in disarray. Until then, most newscasters and political pundits in America had dismissed this wild-eyed rabble-rouser with the toothbrush moustache and the unruly shock of hair over the one eye as "some kind of nut."

The nut was Adolph Hitler and Milton Hershey had already heard more about him than he cared to know.

Over on the other side of the world, the Japanese were already in full control of Korea and were making plans to set up a puppet government in Manchuria. All of this had seemed rather far distant from the world of Milton Hershey until December 12, 1937, when the Japanese attacked and sank the American gunboat *Panay* and three Standard Oil tankers in the Yangtze River, nine miles from Nanking China.

The eighty year old former Mennonite had been listening to Lowell Thomas on the radio when that news came on.

"Damn!" he shouted, leaping to his feet and biting the end off his cigar. "They're not going to get away with *that!*"

Ex-Mennonite, man of peace, Milton Hershey, at that instant, was "angrier than I'd ever seen him," in the words of Paul Witmer, who witnessed the incident.

So there it was. The early and middle thirties were rife with the published news of the activities, buildings, expansions, and the like, all undertaken by the dauntless Milton Hershey in his one-man war against the Depression. But behind the headlines, there was the nagging reminder that the world was once again heading toward the brink of open conflict.

Quietly, the somnolent atmosphere of the cocoa trading company seemed to slumber behind the quiet partitions that separated it from the bustling Hershey Cuba Railroad next door. But the five and six cents a pound futures were still being bought up for the years to come, and the cocoa was piling up in warehouses in New York and in Pennsylvania. And, just as quietly, Hershey continued to negotiate for still more of the stuff, some of which wouldn't be harvested off the newly planted trees for another several years.

But there was something more than a shortage of cocoa in the wind, and Milton Hershey had a nose for that kind of thing. He had been all up and down the war torn lands of western Europe, following the close of hostilities in 1918, and he remembered. The toll of the guns had been awesome but another sight had impressed him even more than the shell-scarred fields of Flanders and the skeletized ruins of Cambrai and Rheims.

The people. The hungry people who had survived. They looked heartbreakingly pitiful but, hungry as they were, these French and Belgians had been on the winning side because they had enough life in them to hear the last trumpet call that pealed across the ghostly rows of barbed wire and shell holes.

They still had had some little food when the enemy had none.

God forbid that it should happen again. But a man who had seen these things, remembered, and as a man who had devoted his whole life to making and selling foods, this was no time to forget the hard lessons that history never seems to stop teaching.

Some years later, an Englishman named Sir Neville Chamberlain would ascend to the Prime Ministry of Great Britain, and he would become pictured as an almost ludicrous figure, scurrying about on sunny days and under cloudless skies with his bowler hat and his ever-present umbrella.

Milton Hershey had been working on *his* umbrella back in the days when Sir Neville was still counting pound notes as Minister of the Exchequer. M.S. kept it in a quiet corners of offices in Cuba, New York and Hershey. The gathering storm was on its way.

One day the whole world would see quite a bit of the umbrella.

Motion Behind the Scenes

The Hershey records of 1937 are submerged under an avalanche of significant events, and the headlines from those days still persist in dominating the scenes which only history can properly assay for importance. But aside from the spectacular overlays provided by the strike, the Loyalty Day Parade, the huge 80th birthday party, and then the follow-up drama of Hershey's stroke and his dramatic recovery, there was a whole panoply of other events being set in motion at the same time, even though they were destined to be held in secret for the remainder of the 1930's.

Bill Murrie's personal log never fixed the exact date for the event which started quietly in the background of the tumultuous summer of 1937. But he did make mention of the fact that a young army officer had visited him "on a warm afternoon," and that the initial meeting had consisted of "a discussion about an Army field ration bar that the Quartermaster Corps in Washington wants us to work on."

The pressure of the strike and the union contract negotiations forced the particulars of Captain Logan's visit and the follow-up activities into the background, and another dozen years would pass before they would be brought to light for fuller reassessment. But another line appeared in the Murrie notes, and it was later to provide a key to what may have been one of the most notable contributions ever made by the company that bears the name of Hershey.

The line mentioned, "I called Sam Hinkle and had him come over from the lab to meet Captain Logan. He will handle it."

Samuel F. Hinkle, chief chemist of the Hershey Chocolate Corporation, came over and met Captain Logan, and he subsequently handled one of the biggest jobs anybody in Hershey ever tackled.

Nearly five years were to pass before Alex Stoddart got around to releasing the background details concerning the start of the ration bar development program. By that time Paul T. Logan was a Lieutenant Colonel, the United States had been at war with the Axis powers of Germany, Japan, and Italy for over two years, and Hershey-made field rations were spanning the globe by the tens of millons every week.

The loose ends that had been pulled together by Hershey President Bill Murrie, Quartermaster Captain Paul Logan, and Hershey chemist Samuel F. Hinkle had, by that time, become quite a chronicle. Many of the particulars on the government funded ration programs that had been begun in silence and were thereafter cloaked in secrecy, still deserve better attention than they have thus far received. Even more to the point, the widespread publicity, ballyhoo, and exploitative headlines that subsequently made the Hershey name commercially synonymous with black markets when Hershey bars were the purchasing medium used for everything from illicit sex to Zeiss binoculars deserves a lot better treatment than the half-truths the rumor mills ever gave it.

There are two stories. The first one deals with the ration bar production that wound up commanding over half of Hershey's total output for a period of almost four years.

The second one revolves around the remainder of Hershey's capacity to produce commercial candy bars, and the fact that most of this production also found its way into Army PX's, Navy ship stores, and service canteens and commissaries both at home and abroad. It was this latter item that led more than one cynical scribe to proclaim during the last year of the war, "It begins to look as though the United States forces are spending more of their time trying to sell *Hershey Bars* around the world than they are giving to the determination of who will run Berlin or who will occupy Japan."

And it did look like that.

But looks are deceiving, and half-truths are half again more dangerous than whole, naked lies because they are jacketed to the waist by the cloak of credibility.

The two real stories began with the summer of 1937 when Captain Paul Logan, Bill Murrie, and Sam Hinkle kicked off the initial round of discussions on the Army Field Ration Bar that started this whole skein of incredible events.

This is what happened.

Captain Logan and Sam Hinkle had concluded their first discussion on the new ration bar and the army officer had returned to Washington. Then Sam closeted himself with Bill Murrie and began filling him in on the particulars of what the young man from the Quartermaster Department wanted. But Murrie, harried as he was in those days of shutdowns and union talks, impatiently flagged him to a halt.

"Wait," he said. "Let's call M.S. and see if he wants to hear about this. Maybe this will give him something beside plant troubles to think about, and maybe it'll help get his mind off those other things."

They called M.S. in his quarters above the country club, and he told them to come right over. He was indeed glad for the opportunity to hit the change of pace offered by this new project. Hinkle remembered later that Murrie had been surprised by M.S.'s ready acquiescence to the suggested meeting.

"You know," he told Hinkle while they were driving toward the club, "I don't know what to make of it. M.S. usually shies away from anything that has to do with the government and politicians. But he almost sounded as if he has been expecting this. I can't figure it out."

When the pair sat down with Milton Hershey, Murrie turned the briefing over to Sam Hinkle. Up until that time, he had not given the chemist an opportunity to explain what had transpired in the meeting with the recently departed Quartermaster Captain.

Sam went straight to the point.

He told Hershey the captain had clearly indicated that the Army had a problem. The rumblings from Europe, both in Austria and in Spain, along with the Italian incursions in Ethiopia and the Japanese threats against mainland China, all seemed to point to another global war. At the moment, he said, the Army was short of everything, and even though he agreed that the Navy and the Marines were merely skeleton forces, he also mentioned the fact that "the man in the White House is a Navy man" (FDR having been former Undersecretary of the Navy, there was no secret about that).

Logan then quit talking about weapons and armament preparations. He said that the Army's first need was going to be for emergency field rations. He had told Hinkle, "If war comes, we're going to have to send men all over the world. In the tropics, the Arctic—everywhere." Then he added, "And we're going to have to feed those men. Even if we have to package concentrated foods and drop them from airplanes by parachutes."

Hinkle went on to say that the immediate requirement would call for an experimental ration bar that would weigh about four ounces and contain about six hundred calories. It should contain protein, carbohydrates, sugar and fat, but it should not be too sweet, yet it should be palatable. "About as tasty as a boiled potato," was the way the Captain put it.

Hershey asked Hinkle if the Quartermaster Captain had mentioned chocolate.

The chemist hurriedly assured his boss that Captain Logan had prefaced all his remarks by noting, "In wartime, overseas commodities like sugar and chocolate will be at an all-time premium." Then he had gone on to say, "Of course, the Hershey Company has its sugar interests in Cuba which is only ninety miles away from Florida." Finally Hinkle said something else that he remembered Logan mentioning, and it was something he had expected to come as a surprise to M.S.

"He also said we have a Cocoa Trading Company in Havana, so I guess he figures we can use cocoa butter fats and chocolate flavoring."

Hershey smiled, and Murrie noted the first gleam of enthusiasm he had seen in the eighty year old man's eyes in quite a long time.

"He knew about that, did he?" Hershey mused. Then he sat back and narrowed his eyes, almost as though he were awaiting something that Hinkle had overlooked.

"Oh, yes," Sam responded, his memory jogged by the glinty look. "He said that chocolate would not only be nutritious, but he told me that it would also be a morale booster, too. He said that it would give a lift to men in the field, that chocolate would be like a letter from home, no matter where the men happen to be."

Hershey lowered his gaze. "You've got yourself a good man," he said. "Get started with him right away."

The umbrella that Milton Hershey had kept tucked away in the quiet corner of the Hershey Cocoa Trading Company in Havana was about to be opened.

It would have to cover a lot of people.

Names and Places in the News

Beginning with the outbreak of hostilities in Europe in September of 1939, the experimental production of several types of ration bars had been completed and Hershey was ready to go on line with the output of about 100,000 units per day. But following the lull of the so-called "phony war" that prevailed for the next six months, the threat of American involvement didn't appear to be increasing. Then the offal hit the oscillator.

In rapid succession the Axis triphammer of offensive warfare began to fall, and with every blow Americans started to realize that they were going to get pulled into "a shooting war." The nominal orders for rations had brought daily capacity outputs to something like 150,000 units of the four ounce *Logan Bars* when the European dispatches began popping like a Roman candle. The Russians crossed the Karelian Isthmus and invaded Finland. Then the Germans blasted the French and British at Narvik and took over Norway, and hard on the heels of that, the Nazi Wehrmacht swept across the lowlands to conquer Holland and Belgium, after which they swept into Paris and knocked the French out of the war.

Newly appointed British Prime Minister Winston Churchill and President Franklin Roosevelt met in the mid-Atlantic and arranged a Lend Lease program, and the peacetime pace of the nation was changed. In another year we were not only sending "bundles to Britain," but the men facing Mobilization Day in Washington had enacted a draft and they were busily engaged in ordering the tool-ups for the guns and tanks and airplanes America and the world would need. In Hershey, the four ounce Logan Bars were joined by one and two ounce packets intended for inclusion in the "C" (for combat) ration packets, along with oversized offerings of the four ounce Logan Bars which, when wrapped three to the packet, became known as the "D" (for daily) ration. This unit was intended to furnish the individual combat soldier with the 1800 calorie minimum sustenance needed for a day of fighting or just staying alive.

Beginning in February of 1942, a scant two months after the Japanese hit Pearl Harbor, the Hershey lines went into gear to produce the needed units of the "little D's" (the two and one ounce squares) of chocolate bars that went into C or K packets. Some of the packets (the K's) included the full four ounce bar, but there were other two ounce units that went along with the "C's", and there were some single ounce little "D's" called "E" rations that went into "emergency packets."

Along with all these scrambled designations, the Quartermaster General, Major General Edmund Gregory, issued orders that all QM destined shipments were to be coded so that quantities and ultimate destinations for the rations would be handled under conditions stamped "Confidential." Orders for the various types and quantities to be made and shipped were sometimes numbered and sometimes they were not. Most of them went to the main Quartermaster (U.S. Army) Depot in Chicago. Then other orders were received for shipments to be made to other depots in places like Greenville, North Carolina; Hartford, Connecticut; and Battle Creek, Michigan. Sometimes they stipulated numbers and sometimes they did not. Thus, drawing subsequent totals were made well nigh impossible because so many of these transaction exchanges were coded.

Then the Marines, the Army Air Force, and the Navy got into the act. This resulted in orders for one, two, and four ounce packets under various designations peculiar to the ordering sources, and so more of the rations were sent to San Diego, San Francisco, New Orleans, Philadelphia, New York, and Boston.

Many of these orders were coded, too, insofar as the actual quantities being shipped were concerned. On other occasions, orders would come in for 1,250,000 units, or 700,000 items, but they would be keyed to a letter number which secretly designated whether they were one, two, or four ounce rations. Thereafter, the business of trying to assess just *how many* of *what size* ration bars were made and shipped becomes the enigmatic task of unscrambling an epically proportioned omelet.

There are some memorable evidences of delivered quantities to work with however, and they span the globe from the Philippines to Tobruk, from the North African deserts of Tunisia, Libya, Tripolitania, and Egypt, and there were chilly "wealths" of early prototype bars that fed Finns near Lake Ladoga and accompanied the early draftees sent from U.S. National Guard units in Greenland. The 1940 and 1941 "production volumes" were rated at somewhere in the neighborhood of a half million a week, so there were fifty or more million of these things in motion before Spring 1942 when the automated lines were started. The lines eventually contained seven machines, on three floors of the Hershey plant, each of which would turn out 200,000 (average) units per shift, and there would be three shifts working six and then seven days a week. Eventually, from mid-1944 to the end of 1945, this resulted in seven machines turning out 3,500,000 units *per day for six or seven days a week,* and so the total weekly output was averaging about 24,000,000 units. Thus the 100 week period from 1944 through 1945 turned out more than two billion units. In the period between 1940 and the end of 1943, the total count was something close to half of that, but the all-told quantity surely exceeded three billion.

Impressive as these numbers are (and they have been calculated and tabbed as "reasonable" by former lab chief Elwood W. Meyers and Peter Birnstiel, project production line supervisor), they seem to pale into insignificance when superimposed on the map of the places where they were sent and the missions they accomplished.

Consider the mainstays in the Tropical Bar form that went ashore in Guadalcanal, Makin, Tinian, Saipan, Iwo Jima, Peleliu, and Okinawa with the Marines. The southern elements of U. S. Army Pacific forces carried them into New Guinea, the Hebrides, and the Philippines, and they were the "freezeproof" companions of those "exiles to hell," the Army and Alaskan Scout troops who hit the chill tundra of Attu and Kiska.

They were in North Africa and Sicily, then on to France, north and south, and then on into Belgium, Holland, Austria, Germany, and Czechoslovakia. Along the way, there were "fallout" quantities that mysteriously appeared in places like Pantelleria, Malta, Greece, and even in Poland.

Some of the Russians who met our units at the Elbe in Germany, May 1945, knew about "chokolot" and pointedly offered to trade for them. So the beige and light tan packets of K's and C's and D's showed up almost everywhere, and there was only one thing that these foods which had begun as "the Logan Bars" had failed to do. They had been aimed to match the taste of "a day old boiled potato," but there were by war's end millions of people who thought the ration bars were better than that. They even got into places (in China, Burma, etc.) where people didn't know *what a potato was.*

A great many names became attached to the ration bar chronicle between the late 1930's when the first 90,000 test samples of Logan Bars were sent out for field testing until the end of 1945, when 100,000,000 units were being turned out every month.

Those early samples were the four ounce ration components, and they were sent to soldiers in the Panama Canal Zone, Hawaii, and the Philippines. Early testing was undertaken to determine how well the packet contents would keep under tropical conditions and later the formulas were modified in response to these findings. The first change called for an addition of 150 international units of Vitamin B-1 (thiamine hydrochloride) to be added as preventatives for beri-beri and other tropical diseases. Then when three of the 600 calorie Logan Bars were placed in a single packet, they were designated as United States Army Field Ration D (for daily).

One note of reference to the nutrient value of chocolate was struck several years before the sample ration bars were produced. It happened on July 16, 1938, when Douglas "Wrong Way" Corrigan made a solo flight from Floyd Bennett Field in New York to Bal Bonnell in Ireland. Thereupon, a first ever Hershey ad was run to show that although "Wrong Way" Corrigan had chosen a wrong navigational flight path for a non-stop trip to California, he had carried with him several ordinary Hershey bars that had been nutritionally right for his sustenance. So Corrigan's name became one of the first to be used as a reference point in the ration bar developmental saga, and it popped up in 1938 about the time the first samples were being made. Thereafter, the names of the great, the near-great, and hosts of those who were virtually unknown would take their places in the passing parade of personalities who would be linked to the production, the consumption, and worldwide distribution of the ration bars. The people in Hershey who were charged with making the bars would not gain a great deal of attention for their efforts; in fact, many, and maybe even most, of the people who became subsequently involved in the use and distribution of the bars would never receive public notice about the backstage contributions they made to the project.

Other companies manufacturing either the self-same kinds of rations (according to Hershey specifications) and those who were making other components of the multiple packs of K's, C's, etc. (like ration biscuits, tins of stew, franks and beans, beverage powders, etc.) linked Hershey with Kellogg's in Battle Creek, Michigan, Wilbur Suchard in Lititz, Pennsylvania and the Hartford Bedding Company in Connecticut, and many, many others.

In Hershey, Chocolate Corporation President Bill Murrie was guiding the main linkups between Hershey and the governmental supply agencies, but the brunt of responsibility for getting things done rested squarely on the shoulders of Sam Hinkle. But from the outset of the war until just a few weeks before its end, Milton Hershey was still poking around, watching the works and offering his suggestions until the last bell rang.

World history and, in fact, some world famous names began getting into the scenario that was being written by those "taste as good as a boiled potato" packages that the minions of Sam Hinkle and Paul Logan were grinding out. The names and the events pulled together in the chronicle dealing with this worldwide effort to fight hunger instead of people, began building a treasury of some of the most surprising stories to ever come out of any war in any age. The stories were sometimes as strange and as unpredictable as the man whose company was making the ration packets, and the people who had joined with him to produce them. But, too long hidden, it is time they were dusted off and put into the proper frame of context, if only for the important pages they can add to a chapter in human history where cruelty predominated and sadness prevailed. There was pathos, dignity, and mercy, and there were mysteries and contradictory forces all hidden behind the headlines of those days. But headlines sometimes conceal more than they tell by simply beating on the obvious big things and ignoring the little things behind them. Too often the fascination of big bad things that threaten, distort, or even destroy life tends to conceal the good little things that people do for each other, and they make the very gift of life worth having.

Here are some of the recognizable names drawn from situations that have been too long kept secret.

In April of 1944, M.S. Hershey was midway in his eighty-seventh year, but he was still rather sprightly and he did manage to get around quite a bit. He was generally accompanied by one of his nurses when he went down to the bank or to walk through the plant, but almost daily he went somewhere to "see what's going on." And when the weather was inclement, he got on the phone and kept his hand in and most times his calls went to the production departments where things were being made.

There were several evenings in mid-April of '44 when he stayed up quite a bit later than usual because he wanted to spend some time with several of the men at the Governors' Convention being held at the Hotel. He hadn't frequented the Hotel too much during the war years, mostly because he didn't like the hustle and bustle that seemed to attend the events when the Vichy French legation and its ambassadorial staff had been interned there. But by 1944 they were gone, and his good friend, General Edward Martin, Governor of Pennsylvania was on hand.

Another man had come to the Hotel with Hershey's friend Lowell Thomas, and he was at the convention as the Governor of New York. His name was Thomas Edmund Dewey, a native of Owosso, Michigan, and he had risen to political stature by his racket-busting days as Attorney General of New York. It was this same Thomas Dewey who had broken up Murder, Incorporated and the mobster ring likes of Meyer Lansky and Louis Lepke Buchalter. Then as a consequence of these crusades, he was being touted as the Republican nominee who would oppose FDR in the coming fall election.

The questions posed by the upcoming convention and election were probably discussed, but nothing of political consequence went onto the Hershey record as the result of those meetings. But something germane to the very ration bars that Hershey had developed and was even then producing did emerge from those talks. Somewhere along the line, the state of the war effort came up for discussion, and this provided the launching point for an announcement that was quite surprising to Hershey and to the other locals who were privileged to share it.

The fighting in Italy was going rather badly, and the situation was not easily written off on the basis of the troops or the generalship involved. The Wehrmacht battle forces, even though they had been stripped of their Italian allies, were ably led by Field Marshall Albert Kesselring; but they were outnumbered, outgunned, and they were being attacked by three times their number of combat aircraft and assaulted from the sea by Allied naval forces that completely dominated the Adriatic and the Straits of Messina.

But the German forces not only kept the American Fifth Army and the British Eighth Army pinned down; the Italian partisan forces to the rear of armies on both sides were literally raising more hell with the Allied troop movements than they would have done if they'd remained in harness with the Germans. The problem came up when elements of the Italian Communist Party had risen again, following the demise of the Fascists, and began waging a kind of partisan warfare on their own.

The top Allied intelligence men were called in, whereupon General "Wild Bill" Donovan of the OSS (the Office of Strategic Services) had come forth with a plan. He had told Tom Dewey as Governor of New York that he should help arrange a pardon for known Mafia leader, Charles "Lucky" Luciano.

Dewey didn't like the idea, but his demurrer notwithstanding, Luciano was pardoned and flown to Sicily where he was put in charge of organizing Italian and Sicilian forces to help the Allies against the Germans (and for the real reason of suppressing the anti-Catholic and partisan forces known to be aligned with the Comintern).

Thereafter a false litany of wheeling and dealing by Luciano went onto the record; the racketeer, in fact, *did nothing* to hold the people of southern and central Italy in check while the Allies swept north to Rome and beyond. The real service came from

Pennsylvania Governor Edward Martin, New York Governor Thomas Dewey and Milton Hershey at Governors Convention, Hotel Hershey, 1944

Allied Field Services, the Red Cross, and the GI's themselves, and the help didn't go out in the shape of guns, blankets, and clothing. They went out in beige and brown wrapped packets marked "K" and "C" and "D" rations, and they came from the stores of the United States Army Quartermaster Corps.

But if the names of Thomas Dewey, Lowell Thomas, Wild Bill Donovan, and Lucky Luciano figure strangely in the peripheral lines attached to *The Great Ration Bar Chronicle*, there were quite a few other well-known and unknown people who had a part in the backstage contributions to the play being presented.

When President Roosevelt pledged in 1942 that American industry would meet and exceed the production quotas needed to win the war, most of his contemporaries listened in disbelief. He called for the turnout of 185,000 planes, 120,000 tanks, 55,000 heavy artillery guns, and eighteen million tons of transport shipping. And he called for a "trained military" of ten million men. But American industry, management, and labor went to work, and by war's end every one of those quotas had been surpassed.

The spectacular achievements in armaments and military supplies commanded the headlines of the day. Of course, the interest in the armaments program was one of greater immediacy, so the men, the tanks, and the planes were mustered, shaped, and shipped to battlefronts all over the world in a matter of months instead of years.

Consequently the battles and the fronts got the headlines, for combat is the visible part of warfare that historically provides the most excitement and commands the greater attention. But on the farms and in the American factories that were charged with feeding the combatant and the noncombatant millions caught up in the conflict, another phase of the historical epic called World War II was being wrought in relative silence.

In the ten year period prior to the war, Hershey and many of its counterparts in the fields of industrial hardware and commodity software had been undergoing tool-up programs of automation that were in those days decried as "the labor-saving devices that put men out of work," and they came at a time when the scarcity of jobs was one of the nation's biggest problems. Yet, on the farms and in the factories of the nation, the mass production schemes and tools that increased individual output twofold and more, had progressed in accordance with the tenets of what really motivates a profit system.

Farmers and manufacturers alike, even during the Depression, had remained basically convinced that when goods and services are produced better, faster, and cheaper, the common good was inevitably bound to improve. There was an innate conviction that when more of the good things in life were made both attainable and affordable, the society would have to expand both its job opportunities and the broad base of its individual earning power. Even with something like ten million people out of work, the flame of that inalienable belief in the free enterprise system had not gone out.

During this period in Hershey (both in Pennsylvania and in Cuba), Milton Hershey was one of the leading standard-bearers who had continued to spend, build and expand every facility he had for refining sugar and making confectionery foods. Up and down the length and breadth of America, foodmakers like General Mills, Kellogg, Campbell, Heinz, and myriads of others were retooling and automating production lines. So were automakers General Motors, Ford, Chrysler, Packard, Studebaker, and their counterparts, and so were the steelmakers and the aircraft industrialists. On the farms, newly developed machines were taking to the fields to speedily plow, cultivate, mow, bundle, and wrap the food grains and crops that an expanded need for foodstuffs would require.

But when the explosiveness of war intervened, the goal of an expanded era of free enterprise was postponed. The argument has raged ever since as to whether the dream set aside would ever have been realized, but nobody in his right mind can deny the historic fact that the mass production might of American industry and agriculture was the greatest single factor in winning the war for the allied nations. When Isoroku Yamamoto, the commander of the Imperial Japanese Fleet warned, "We have awakened a slumbering giant," he was reflecting on the great farms, the massive industry, and the virtually unlimited capacity to turn out goods and services that lay behind the men, the planes, the ships, and the tanks that would sweep out of the "arsenal for democracy."

The years Yamamoto had spent in the United States as a Military Attache had shown him that the greatest strength of this nation was *as a producer*. But had there been no belief in the inevitability of an expanded free economy on the parts of the people at Bell, General Motors, Hershey, General Foods, Ford, DuPont, and others that had inspired and sustained their toolups and automation, the Japanese probably wouldn't have attacked Pearl Harbor. They could have stormed into Washington and taken it.

What happened and who was this slumbering giant that came out of the backstage wings and mounted the ramparts to send the food and clothing and other logistical supplies that turned the tide of battle? In small part, Milton Hershey's Chocolate Corporation was an exemplary one of these. He had made his move back in the 1920's; in fact, he had made a series of them.

In Cuba, he had expanded sugar plantations to more than two hundred thousand acres, and then he had built five modern refineries, along with port and shipping facilities along with hundreds of miles of electrical mainline and streamdriven spur railroad lines that would grow into one of the most compact and efficiently run food processing complexes in the world. In Havana he opened a Cocoa Trading Company that was ostensibly aimed at cornering the market, but it had remained virtually silent for more than a half dozen years. When the war came, however, the massive sugar-producing complex was linked up with the ready-made conduit of the Cocoa Trading Company, and they, in turn, fed hundreds and then millions of tons of materials into the maw of the two million square feet of automated production space that he had built into a huge plant that had once been a cornfield in Derry township.

The subsequent output of Hershey's three or four billion ration units, while substantial, became merely companion parts of the flow of tinned stews, beef, and franks, the greaseproof wrapped Logan Bars, the biscuits, the beverage powders, and the innumerable "chunks of this and that" (some hundreds of millions of which were straight Hershey chocolate) were formed up in a main channel of tens of billions of concentrated packaged foods that were sent everywhere in the world.

Sent everywhere from the factories of General Mills, Kellogg's, Campbell, Hershey, Kraft, Heinz, Ralston Purina, W.T. Baker, and hundreds of others.

In combat they evoked comment.

In the Italian heights above the Rapido River, Bill Mauldin of *Stars and Stripes* pictured a GI tapping a tin of C rations on Thanksgiving Day, 1943, and saying, "Tough bird, and even the gravy is cold."

Winter, December, 1944: the 329th Infantry Regiment at the Hurtgen Forest. The men in Pete Adam's squad tore open their K rations and dug into the Logan Bars as one of the men remarked, "They send up hot food in the trucks. When was the last time anybody saw a truck?" An hour later, seven men of that squad had been wounded, and the remainder of them were taken prisoner by an SS Panzergruppe unit. The Battle of the Bulge was on.

On the other side of the world, in the fall of 1942, Richard Tregaskis, who was later to write *Guadalcanal Diary*, was in a dugout with Marines of the famed First Division. A chaplain had come up and was handing out packets to the men who were in the second day of incessant shellfire from Japanese battleships in the offshore Straits of Tassafaronga. A gunnery sergeant was about to thank the padre for what he thought was a prayer book, but the flash of a nearby shellburst revealed the outline of a ration "D" packet.

"Not by bread alone," whispered the padre and ducked.

Thousands of miles to the north, where the icy chill swept down from the Bering Straits and across the cruelly penetrating damp of Attu's frozen beachhead, the forward Army units and the Alaskan Scouts of Col. Lawrence V. Castner (of Castner's Cutthroats) were trying to dig in along the frozen stretches of rocklike tundra. They were pinned down by Japanese gunfire, but the fog was so thick that the backup landing barges couldn't find their way ashore with supplies. Then out of the milky skies overhead came the sputtering drone of an unseen DC-3 from Col. Ted Henderson's makeshift Alaskan Air Reconnaissance Group. A flutter of freezing nylon shrouds wafted to the men, and then an almost indistinguishable thud came to them as one after another of the wire-wrapped Ration crates hit the scaly cliffsides.

One by one the men slithered from cover and retrieved the boxes. Without food or communications for more than two days, they hungrily opened the beige colored packets and tore into them. Before the sounds of tearing paper had subsided, the unlikely sound of muffled laughter pierced the silence. Then another, and another chuckle, until a wave of almost hysterical laughter broke out from all over the rocks and crevices in which the hundreds of men in the ranks of fog-concealed troops were able to read the labels on the packets they were opening.

"U.S. Army Quartermaster Corps. Type D 'Tropical' Ration Bar. Keep From Freezing."

One infantryman turned his frost-bearded face to his companion in the rocky cleft they shared.

"Welcome to Palm Beach."

It was also rather chilly along the Belgian road between Hauffalize and St. Vith when Lt. General George Patton's Third Army trucks rolled down the road the 26th day of December, 1944. Men of the 82nd Airborne and the 12th Division were strung out in snowy foxholes on either side of the road as burly mess sergeants were throwing out "C" and "K" rations to the men they relieved.

One by one the men who had been surrounded for more than two weeks crawled out of their foxholes and, after scooping up the packages, hungrily tore into them.

"Christmas," said one of them between bites, "came a day late this year."

*   *   *

Wherever men fought, the ration bars either showed up with them or they flowed in by the tens of thousands of tons. Then, slowly but surely, the enemy was beaten back. It was the same thing with the planes (DC-3's again) flying back westward from Kunming toward the Karachi and other Indian bases from which they had just transferred "C", "K", and "D" rations. But on that partway backward leg toward "The Hump" (the Himalayas) that these Air Transport Command planes had traversed, there were regiments of Gen. "Vinegar Joe" Stilwell's Tenth Army Engineers, and more than a hundred thousand pick-swinging Chinese "coolies" scratching their way eastward an inch at a time, building a rockstrewn byway called the Ledo Road.

It was the same to men who fought in every theater where the forces of Germany, Italy, and Japan opposed them, but bit by bit in each of those areas the guns would die down and the lines would push forward. Then behind them lay the desolated, shell and bomb wrecked buildings and the pitiful thousands of ragged refugees. The flotsam, the shredded remnants of people driven from cottages, hovels, ghettos, and mansions.

People without homes, people without clothing, pitilessly wrenched loose from all hope, with no place to go and without even the barest scraps of food to eat.

Soldiers, dogfaces, and mess sergeants alike shared the carryables they could snitch from the field kitchens and mobile food supplies, but there was never enough. There were black marketers, too; there have always been that ilk, but they weren't a patch on the ordinary, goodhearted American GI who just couldn't stand the sight of starving children and old people.

It was into these "voids," the behind-the-lines clusters of refugees and into some of the forward areas, and among these notable places were those like Dachau and Auschwitz, Buchenwald, and Belsen. The miserable testimonials that an insufferable glut of bestial bastards had left as their imprimatur on the pages of history. Not on the records of mankind, for they were something less than men.

But out of all this cruelty came mercy, and out of pain came the first tremulous signs of the grace and the compassion it would take to end this suffering. The price that men and women had to pay to be free.

Among the survivors, combatant and non-combatant alike, were some of those who knew what to do with this freedom. The Quakers, American Friends Field Service Committee, the Red Cross, the Salvation Army, and many other secular and non-secular groups banded together in a mighty effort to succor and sustain the survivors of holocausts, Bataan "death marches," and the painful litany of terrible things which had been classically reenacted to very nearly affirm man's kinship with the beasts.

Very nearly, but not quite.

Those who were most distantly removed from affinity with the hordes of bestial scum who had caused all this misery were the very fighting men who had taken up arms to defeat them. In the aftermath of war's end in Europe (Rheims, May 6, 1945) and in Asia (Tokyo Bay, September 14, 1945), the men in the field took up the slack that other agencies and other means would deal with—but later.

In each of the immediate theaters, and in each time and in each place as the guns fell silent, the men in the field took over. It happened in southern Italy, Sicily, the Philippines, in Burma, and in China, and in many of those places these "voids" needed filling a year and more before the war finally ended.

It was in the last year of the war, between the spring of 1944 and September of 1945, and particularly in Europe, that another side of the "balance" story emerged. The so-called balance marks the delineation between the appreciable good name Hershey earned as the consequence of the ration bar (pre-war) development that had gained Hershey's privileged status as co-developer of the Logan Bar, and the other name it got stamped with when Hershey Bars showed up in the black market.

The standardization of Hershey developed products was central to Hershey's designation as prime source contractor. Therefore, from 1940 on it was the Hershey conduit through which cocoa, chocolate liquor, sugar, and cocoa butter (for sweetened) rations were channeled. Hershey was designated prime source not only for many of the finished ration bars, but for most of the Logan Bars produced. Along with this, Hershey also became the central hub for the procurement of sugar (Hershey, Cuba) and for chocolate (Hershey Cocoa Trading Company, Havana). It also became the conduit through which incoming Army, Navy, Army Air Corps, and Marine Quartermaster orders were channeled. Then field guidance was maintained with the other suppliers, and shipments were coordinated for componential (ration bar) parts of each quantity to be packaged and/or forwarded to assembly points in Chicago, San Francisco, Boston, New York, and a dozen other places north, south, east, and west.

By early '44, the Hershey volumes exceeded much more than the fifty percent level of production for war purposes by which the Office of Production Management assigned to it the privileged status under which top priorities for strategic materials (and those in short supply) were assigned. Those priorities applied to the goods needed for commercial production as equally as they did to the goods needed for war production. The goods were essentially the same, and the decision was one that had been deliberately considered, and it was clearly enunciated at the time it was announced. The status and the top priorities granted were the net consequence of governmental policy.

Someone (or some concurring group of someones) who spoke for the combined Chiefs of Staff, the War Department, or for the Roosevelt Administration itself had decided *to show the flag*.

Hershey Bars were chosen as the means whereby the flag would be shown. Nobody in Hershey had even asked for this momentous break, but once the decision was made, just about everybody in Hershey knew what to do with it.

Two byline incidents happened almost immediately following the first substantial shipments of *Hershey Bars* to arrive in the European theater. The first one came from Ernie Pyle, the famous author of frontline wartime dispatches and the book *Brave Men*, and it came when Pyle was in transit from the European to the Asiatic Theater of warfare.

Before departing Europe for the Pacific Theatre (where he would lose his life on Ei Shima) Pyle's last dispatch announced: "This show is finally over, but before bringing the GI's home or shipping them to the Pacific—The Brass has decided to give them a break. Someone in Washington has decided that since they can't bring Mom's apple pies to these tired men while they're waiting, they'll do the next best thing . . . they're shipping in *Hershey Bars*. Someone said it's like 'showing the flag'—but these guys have already done that—all over Africa and Europe. Now it's time we showed them something that has a wholesome 'homey' touch to it. Those *Hershey Bars* were a great choice."

Another incident occurred later in the fall of '44 and it was both briefer and more to the point. A few months after the invasion of southern France (August 1944), an issue of *Yank* appeared in the occupied Port of Marseilles. In three-inch red banner headlines the front page of *Yank* announced: "*Hershey Bars* Arrive in France!" These were typical of the incidents that warmed the hearts of our GI's in Europe.

But in a matter of weeks, the tarnish began to stain the other side of the coin. In the lull before and in the dull void following the Patton dash across Germany, a shameful entry was made on the pages of American history by the black market gangs that went into operation behind the lines in France and in Italy. In the streets of Foggia, in the alleys of Paris, and in the remote towns of Amiens and Trier, the free-booters sprang up, and everywhere it was the same.

American *Hershey Bars*. American cigarettes. American nylons. The greedy one or two in every ten thousand Americans who got involved in it either stole or sold everything they could get their hands on—gasoline, rations, cigarettes, nylons, invasion currency, GI boots, blankets. . . .

The unfortunate consequence of this whole shameful road show was that *Hershey Bars* had quickly earned another top priority. They went straight to the top of the list of desirable black market items. A *Hershey Bar* was worth twice the money a pack of cigarettes brought, and one bar was frequently exchanged for a magnum of champagne. *Hershey Bars* bought Lugers in Paris, Zeiss binoculars in Metz, and a box of them could be exchanged for a Black Forest ornately carved and inlaid German silver clock.

As expected, these ridiculous exchanges and the notorious deals they begat commanded the headlines and they soon became the sum and substance of a lot of letters sent home. Milton Hershey and his following of men and women who had worked so hard back in Pennsylvania were anguished with the dismal evidences of greed that their high purposes had earned in other hands.

One of Hershey's closest confidantes, Paul Witmer, had only this to say about the

Old Man's response to this news about his *Hershey Bars* in the black market.

He had just finished reading a letter from one of his boys (from the Hershey Industrial School) when a radio announcement said, "And meanwhile, the GI Joes are having a ball in Europe. Over there the *Hershey Bars* will buy anything from a case of brandy to a case of something it takes a case of penicillin to cure. How're you gonna get'em back on the farm after they've bought Paree with a *Hershey Bar?*"

M.S.'s eyes shone and he bit his lip. "Oh, my goodness," was all he could say.

There it was. That was, in a word, the crux of it. For it was indeed *his goodness* and *the goodness of his hard-working people* that had gone into the wholesome purpose they had put into everything they made and labeled "Hershey."

Offstage and out of the headlines, thousands of GI's were feeding the ragtag bag-of-bones people who dragged themselves from the stench of Auschwitz, from the disgusting pens of Buchenwold and Dachau. Grimy, sallow-skinned and hollow-eyed survivors of the holocaust reached for the Logan Bars, the Hershey-made "D's" and "C's" and whatever other fragments of food that would once again enable them to put body and soul together.

Nothing about Hershey ration bars showed up in the myriads of headlines and the miles of film footages expended on those scenes of unbelievable misery, showing the terrible travesties committed against the very senses of reason that insult the merest notion of decency. Horror has, regrettably, always furnished better material for headlines than kindness or compassion.

But by hundreds and thousands—holocaust victims and survivors, French, Italian paisanos, Arab, Greek, and Egyptian urchins—lived and breathed to see other and better days because of the concentrated foods that bore the Hershey-made calories and the stamp of Godfearing men among those who made and those who delivered them to where they were needed. Without headlines.

Laurels

More than a score of years would pass following the end of World War II before a recapitulation of the Hershey chronicle of ration bar production would be pulled together by an insider. The man who compiled the report was the man best qualified for the job, former chief chemist Sam Hinkle, who had in the meantime become Chairman of the Board of Hershey Chocolate Corporation.

But in those days, just as in the years when all these activities were taking place and throughout all the years that followed, the bulk of these "inside" figures were compiled without reference to the confidential totals of items shipped or with any recounting of the places to which they were sent or how they were used. Those coded designations that carried QM (Quartermaster) and WD (War Department) orders for units made no differentiation between packages that could have contained a single one ounce bar or a crate that contained a gross or a dozen gross of individual units. The Chocolate Corporation's tax and sales records for the years 1942 through 1945 (included in a latter summary) provide a better handle to the multi-billion unit projections set forth in this piece. The simple arithmetic of taking 72% of the eighty million dollar gross in 1944 derives a war production of $57,000,000 expended for war related unit production. The average base cost per ounce unit was a little more than a penny a piece, and the four ounce unit was less than a nickel. Averaged out at two and a half cents each therefore (which would be high because there were many times more of the smaller units made and shipped), this extended figure would have totalled more than two and a quarter billion units for 1944 alone.

Army Navy "E" Award Ceremony, August 1945

The Sam Hinkle report on the overall period of Hershey toolups and ration related contributions prior to the war is by far the most comprehensive study of what may well be one of the most important period phases in Hershey history, and which certainly has been one of the better kept secrets of the entire Hershey saga. The fact that part of this secrecy was imposed by government ordered procedures during wartime was responsible for the greater part of the concealment thereby contrived. But not all of it was born out of confidentiality, for something of the innate shyness of Milton Hershey had always forbidden him to assume any breast-beating postures for himself, and this penchant for modesty frequently carried over into company policy. Some of it still prevails.

Among the more surprising facts to emerge from the Hinkle report were those contained in the recognition extended to Hershey on behalf of nutrient supplies furnished to the Byrd Antarctic Expeditions, both from 1928 to 1930 and again in 1932 and 1936. Those early days' contributions were frequently spoken about, and so was the Minute Man Flag awarded Hershey employees by the U.S. Treasury Department for their purchases of War Bonds in the summer of 1942. But both the mention of the Byrd project and the Treasury Award were overshadowed by the first Army/Navy "E" Award, made by Major General Edmund B. Gregory on August 27, 1942. The Medical Field Service Band from Carlisle Barracks was there to play a concert on the occasion, and Paul R. Logan, co-developer of the ration bar, by then a full colonel, was also on hand to share the honors. Milton Hershey was there, too, but he only smiled and waved to the crowd. He said nothing.

Perhaps he was thinking about the wrinkles they had been forced to iron out before all this production flow had been attained. Most certainly his thoughts recalled the heavy duty roller equipment they had been denied when access to German producers was cut off just before the war in Europe started. His memory also had to return to the British manufacturers who subsequently agreed to fill those roller machine orders and how this heavy equipment had finally been produced under the severe handicaps of massive bombings and acute shortages of materials and labor supplies. It had taken the combined skills of British workers to construct the machinery, combined with the British Navy convoys that successfully delivered them, and the coterie of British engineers and machinists who had come over to supervise the erection and initial operation of the urgently needed equipment.

Later, it had been the British Navy that once again figured in keeping the Caribbean sea lanes open between Central and South America and the collection points set up in the cocoa storehouses and refineries being put on line by Hershey Cocoa Trading and Hershey Central sugar plants in Cuba.

When M.S. left the reviewing stand after the award ceremonies in summer 1942, he had told Abe Heilman, "There were *a lot of people who helped us get these honors,* but *some of them couldn't be here* today." The scrappy spark in the feisty little man may have been stirring inside him then because he added, "Isn't it funny how much fuss we make over the people *who are still around* when they pass out the medals?"

His thoughts were with those who hadn't made it. He was keenly aware that many more of them never would.

Sam Hinkle remembers the eighty-five-year-old M.S. still hobbling around everywhere he could go, offering words of encouragement to managers and workers alike. The machine shop down in the Hershey Lumber/Crating complex was hard at it, too, for by this time the maze of humming production hardware in the two million square foot plant was being extended, repaired, modified, and reshaped in an endless variety of ways. Changes in government ordered specifications for new item demands were coming in on a floodtide and along with the midsummer 1942 program of accelerated demands came the confidential coding orders that made unit tallies as tough to trace for the Axis spies as it did for plant record keepers and subsequent historians.

The Pearl Harbor bombing had an immediate effect on the community life and the overall appearance of the Hershey town and its plant activities. Military callups were accelarated, and women, youngsters, and those deferred from military service by reason of age or partial physical defects were sought to help fill in on the production lines.

Nobody thought of peaceful Hershey as a hub in the arsenal for democracy, but the per capita involvement of the people from the town, the plant, and the nearby population in war production was higher than it was for Pittsburgh or Detroit, two of the highest in the nation. The youngsters and the 4-F's, along with those whose religious persuasions (Amish, Quaker, Mennonite) exempted them from combat duty, were joined by throngs of volunteers from all over the nearby countryside.

At the plant, Jack Steen, on the package production line, had a whole shift of boys from Hershey Junior College, and there were other shifts of the so-called volunteers (paid, part-time workers, not frozen to wartime permanent jobs and not part of the ranks of regular Hershey workers) who came in on the trolleys from every direction. These included several dozen women (wives of *permanent party* officers and non-coms at Indiantown Gap), as well as students from Lebanon Valley College in Annville, as well as women and over-age (for the draft) men from Lebanon, Palmyra, Hummelstown, Harrisburg, Middletown, and Steelton.

By summer of '42, in a matter of weeks the production lines were restructured and rearranged and the earlier parchment paper and foil wrappings were discarded in favor of heat-sealable cellophane bags adapted for the D bars. After each bar was sealed, the Tropical D's were placed in a brown kraft cardboard box that was glued shut at each end and then submerged in a bath of melted wax. Tests required that after one hour of submersion in water, there could be no seepage in contact with the contents.

The D ration bar formula as established in January 29, 1942, thereafter remained unchanged throughout the war. But the product-making machinery, the conveyor and cutting lines, the pulverizers and the mixers, rollers and packaging hardware had to be reshaped, newly designed, or jerry-built from scraps and previously junked equipment, some of which was scrounged by teams of men searching out the second hand machinery marketplaces. The labor-saving worked by newly fitted conveyor belts and automatic sealing and nailing machines was achieved by the machinists and assemblymen who had mastered their crafts in the better days past, right in Hershey.

M.S. Hershey himself, after a midsummer tour of his plant in 1942, admitted how deeply he had been impressed by the near miracle that had been wrought in the making, the packaging, and the changes without stoppages so smoothly achieved by his people.

When the War Department sent a commendation for this effort on August 1, Bill Murrie, Corporation President, hurried over to M.S.'s apartment at the Country Club. He read the exciting news.

"This is to inform you that the Army and the Navy are conferring upon your organization the Army-Navy Production Award for high achievement in the production of war equipment...."

Hershey was surprised by the mention of his company products as "war equipment," but he said nothing. The letter continued, "This award is your nation's tribute to the spirit of patriotism ... of your plant and your employees ...

"... the Army and Navy will present a flag to be flown above your plant and will give to every member of your organization a pin which they may wear as a symbol of their permanent contribution to human freedom...."

There was more, but Hershey leaned back in his chair and half closed his eyes. Murrie noted the quiet smile that had crossed the Old Man's face, then he left silently because by that time M.S. had fallen asleep.

Milton Hershey would make only one remark in reference to the letter, and it came several days later when he told his nurse, "It was pretty nice of them to send such a letter to a tight-fisted old tyrant, wasn't it?"

He hadn't forgotten the names they had called him in the headlines that had been flying about back in 1937 during the strike. Back during the same summer days when chemist Sam Hinkle and a young captain from the Army Quartermaster Corps had even then been working away on the lab experiments that had started the whole project.

In the midsummer of 1945, following the German surrender, when the war in the Pacific was drawing to a close, some of the production and tax figures were brought to Milton Hershey's attention. The bringing of the figures was arranged more or less on demand by M.S. because Bill Murrie and Sam Hinkle, along with the other management people, had been trying to insulate the eighty-seven-year-old patriarch from the excitement and concerns of those frantic days.

But Milton Hershey would not be insulated. As ever, *he had to know what was going on,* and the more his associates tried to shield him from business and wartime concerns, the fussier and more rebellious he got. The top-level coterie of directors and managers finally heeded the joined advisories offered by D. Paul Witmer and cousin Ezra, who told them, "He gets more upset and more excited by the notion that we're trying to hide things from him than anything else, so let's quit trying to keep things from him."

Hershey had received some other mail earlier on the afternoon that Murrie brought the tax and production reports to his upstairs mansion/club apartment. But M.S. seemed almost disinterested when he went over the balance sheets they had brought him, and after he read through them, he leaned back in his chair and sighed.

Ezra Hershey, out of concern for the way that M.S. had responded to the tax and production volume report, sought to palliate the feelings of sadness that were evidenced in his cousin's eyes.

"Milton," he said in conciliatory tones, "think of all the planes and tanks those taxes are helping to buy. And don't forget, the more of those things we have, the quicker the war will be over."

Hershey turned his head and looked at them. The look told both Ezra and Murrie that they had misread the signs even before the old man said anything.

"Yeah," he said, leaning forward. Then he brought his right hand up, and baring his top row of teeth he grimaced, then leaned forward. Head down for a moment, he rested his forehead on top of the fist of his right hand.

A moment passed in which a shudder seemed to make his whole aging body quiver. Then he turned to the letters on the night table as he reached over and picked up one of them. He handed it to Ezra. His lip quivered as he looked straight at his cousin.

"But all the money in the world won't buy back one of these."

Ezra took the envelope, opened it, removed the letter, and held it between Murrie and himself so they could both read it at the same time.

It was a copy of the standard form used by the War Department to announce the death of another "home boy" from the school.

The work performed by the people of the laboratory staff of Hershey Chocolate Corporation during the war years was never accorded the attention or the credit the efforts deserved. Part of the secrecy came as the consequence of the "wartime wraps" that cloaked virtually all production for the armed forces, and part of it came as the result of the way battlefront news dominated the headlines and the newscasts. But perhaps the biggest reason why these works were so seemingly clandestine and cloaked in silence is simpler than that.

These people were so busy they had no time to pose for pictures.

Throughout the entire span of war years from 1941 to 1945, the Hershey lab ran the plant. They were not only the recipients of the orders coming in (virtually all of which were for products they had formulated), but they were also charged with guiding and monitoring production, quality control, and delivery schedules on the stuff going out, for their plant and for the other plants participating in the contracts for which Hershey had been named prime contractor.

From the chief helmsman, Sam Hinkle, and his good right hand, lab chief Elwood W. Meyers, Bob Bucher, Pete Birnstiel, on down, the lab people worked sixteen, eighteen, and sometimes twenty hours a day. And all too frequently they stuck to their lasts for seven days a week. The rest of the time they worked six full days.

The outfit had been the sparkwheel of Hershey's corporate machinery even in normal times, because the lab had been charged with perfecting the formulations and the production methodology (mixing, grinding, cutting, cooking) of every item Hershey made, but they were also required to assay every one of the raw materials coming in, and they even had to evaluate milk, cocoa, sugar, and virtually everything being stored. Thereafter, they bird-dogged the "batch-mixes" as they proceeded along the production lines, and they were the ones who approved or rejected everything slated to go out.

During the war this same kind of overall responsibility had to be expanded fivefold, and the lab was required to not only set and maintain standards of uniformity and volumes of delivery for the Hershey plant, it also had to monitor and expedite everything its fellow contractors produced. On paper, the verbal recounting of the definitive effort appears quite impressive, but "paper race" figures pale into insignificance when the people who were there look back and remember.

They remember how they got involved in everything; hence the flat declarative statement that the Hershey lab ran the plant is more than merely a provable truth. It is, indeed, an *understatement*. Fact is, the lab not only ran the Hershey plant; it also supervised the systems of refining and shipping sugar and cocoa (hundreds of thousands of tons) and other materials, as it scrutinized every scrap of goods moving in and out of a dozen other plants as well.

Indeed, in Hershey the lab gang was the linkup attached to the lifeline of government orders (and the "specs" that came with them), and this brought them onto the firing line of handling materials in and out of the whole productive network of suppliers, and it hooked them into devising the methodology, designing equipment, setting schedules, along with a list of "required" things that was too long to print.

Secret it was. Consequently, superhuman achievements were submerged and hidden to the point where the surfacing of this very narrative will surprise (as it did among those to whom the proofs and figures were shown) a lot of latter-day executives of the corporation (many of whom were working there at the time).

The consequent effects hold no secrets, for like "truth crushed to earth," they later arose to establish and proclaim the value of what had been done.

When Sam Hinkle later became Chairman of the Board of Directors of Hershey Foods Corporation, and when Elwood W. Meyers was made Research and Development Director of the company, the arrow of effect hit the bull's-eye on the target of credit.

The laurels came late, but they were delivered to the right people.

Chapter XXI

~·~

Kitty's Idea

In November of 1909, the initiation of *Kitty's Idea* to start a school for orphan boys began with a deed of trust drawn up to finance the venture. Thus, the paper part of a dream shared by Kitty and Milton Hershey set the stage for the most ambitious project they would ever undertake.

It was, in fact, a two-part project by the time the following September rolled around. The September first opening of the venture was actually the second part of the project, because four little fellows had already been brought in earlier in the year and established in The Homestead, the birthplace of M.S. Hershey in which George and Prudence Copenhaver served as their newly adopted house parents. So the new venture began by providing a home and house parents for the boys *before* they were admitted to the school in which they would be educated.

The Copenhavers had been installed in the Hershey farm system a year earlier, and this simply presaged the fact of their having been selected as the first two teachers at the school. Both of them were qualified teachers, and their selection was based on the recommendations of a man named Schaeffer, who had been the former head of the Pennsylvania Department of Public Instruction. But their tenure as house parents actually preceded their eventual duties as instructors.

The Homestead was both home and school, but the doors opened on the home first. That fact was and is still a paramount consideration in weighing the values of the Hershey Industrial School, as it was named when it began, or the Milton Hershey School, which it became in 1951, as a place where meaningful training and guidance are provided to enable orphans to lead happy and productive lives.

The Copenhavers and the Hersheys were in solid agreement about the considerations they had to deal with from the start. They knew that the youngsters coming into this new environment would feel strange and out of place, so the first order of business would require them to get to know the boys and to get the boys to know them. This was to become a process whereby the adult teacher/parents and the young student/ residents would have to learn how to live and work together.

As in all his other working experiments, Milton Hershey simply applied the rule of trying things on a small scale to see how they worked. The first four boys were really experimental, and so were the teacher/parents. Once these small scale methods were tried, the second of M.S. Hershey's maxims could be applied.

The second step amounted to taking a look at the experimental results and then enlarging the good things that worked, and getting rid of the bad things that didn't. On the face of it, these appear to be copybook maxims fraught with too much Pollyanna optimism and simplistic reasoning. The societal problems had to be more complex than that. But Hershey was a simple man, and he had learned early to apply simple answers to simple questions. As he saw it, "Things don't get complicated unless we make them that way." In this sense, he found a pair of naturals in George and Prudence Copenhaver, for they were both sure that common sense logic would enable them to separate the problems they faced from the measurable work that needed to be done. The record shows they succeeded.

Perhaps the most meaningful lesson to come out of those first years of children and house parents getting to know each other by learning to live and work together came in the fourth year. By that time, the school had enlarged its enrollment to forty boys. In the interim, George Copenhaver had learned about the typical student. This is what he later told Joe Snavely.

"Coming into the home and the school, we really have two boys under each hat, and so we have the responsibility to fit him for a time when he will become another person and wear another hat. Let's start by taking a look at the first of the two boys under that one hat.

"We begin with the hopeful package of a boy named Daniel. So, as Daniel, we work on the simple process of getting him to learn table manners, to bathe and groom himself neatly, to brush his teeth, to be polite to his fellows and particularly to his elders, and in a general way to be tidy in his habits, truthful in his speech, and to adopt the little mannerisms we seek in a well-behaved child.

"So we have Daniel, the fresh-scrubbed, polite and polished model of a presentable little boy. But that isn't enough, because there is another person under the same hat, and he's quite a different boy. This one we call Danny.

"Well, under the polished veneer of Daniel, this Danny is the 'hooligan' side of the little fellow, and he's itching to grow up too quickly. He's the one who takes the first puff on a forbidden cigar or cigarette, the first drink of an alcoholic beverage, or the first wild wagering with dice and cards for what amounts to becoming a grown-up, a man of the world. But in the image of Danny, if he isn't helped to avoid these things, he's a little boy lost, and he is heading toward becoming a man who will be a loser.

"So we can't polish up the Daniel side of the boy and ignore the Danny side, or we will win the game and lose the series. Our final responsibility is to the person who will eventually be called Dan—the young man who will graduate from the school and leave the home to go out and take his place in the world. And it is with Dan and how he is shaped and cared for, right from the beginning when he is both Daniel and Danny in the same package, that will determine how well we have taught him and how well he has learned his lessons.

"Those of us who are charged with teaching must always be mindful of an early admonition: *Teaching is a learning experience.* Some of the most valuable lessons coming out of the home and the classroom are the ones learned by those whom we charge to teach."

The house parent idea may have begun in the mind of any one of the four principals who launched the program, but it was certainly a plan fitted to the unique personalities of both the Hersheys and the Copenhavers. Seventy years later, the proof of the plan and the people chosen to begin it stands as a model for child care and training that has few, if any, equals anywhere.

*   *   *

One of the most persistently recurring questions about the early school still centers on the fact that it was solely intended for boys. From the vantage point of latter-day observance, contemporary critics wonder what the Hersheys had against girls. Why hadn't the school been set up for boys and girls?

Here we come to the difference that time has always worked in changing social values. Milton Hershey was asked the same question from the outset, and he replied.

"The boys are really two things. First, in an orphan situation, they are less wanted around the house because they don't take to housework and homemaking chores like girls do, mainly because they think of cooking and cleaning and sewing as 'sissy' things to do. The other reason is because the boy is in need of training as a future head of a family and the main wage earner. If he's trained well enough, he can buy a home and support a family, so his wife won't have to work. *Outside the home,* that is."

Thus, just as each of us is a prisoner of the age in which he lives, the Victorian man Milton Hershey was convinced that it was a man's duty to be the main breadwinner and that woman's place was in the home. He addressed his answer to the problem as it existed in his time. But he gave the school a charter flexible enough so it could be changed as needed. The change allowing girls to enter came on November 15, 1976.

Another one of the questions that keeps coming up is borne out of the memories of folks who were around in the twenties and thirties when the football and baseball teams from the Hershey Industrial School were called "homeboys." This is a holdover from the era in which the folks in the surrounding countryside still thought and talked about the place as the Hershey home for orphan boys. Hence, they were homeboys, even though the official name was the Hershey Industrial School.

There are two other stamps carried by the graduates of the old Hershey Industrial School that are frequently observed in conversation, and yet they have virtually never been publicized in the articles written about the school.

They are all courteous, polite, if you will, and considerate. Respectful is the word that comes most readily to mind, and yet it applies to men like Bill Dearden, Chief Executive Officer of Hershey Foods Corporation; Ken Hatt, President of HERCO, Inc.; Joe Gumpher, President of Hershey Trust Company; and Mac Aichele, President of Milton Hershey School.

The other stamp is a credit to the will of M.S. Hershey himself, although it was never expressed in any written code of rules or administrative dictum. It's more the kind of thing one learns from the wives of the men who were former Hershey Industrial School students, particularly the fellows who still think of themselves as homeboys. These guys have earned the name for being so handy around the house, the kind of husband who, in this day and age, has become a rare critter, high on the list of the endangered species.

Somehow it doesn't appear to make any difference whether these former schoolboys were trained for the professions or for the trades, crafts, or commercial fields. Every last one of them is a good man to have around the house when simple things go on the fritz. To some, the matter of performing window repairs or unplugging stopped-up sinks, or the laying of bricks or fixing blown electrical circuits belong to arts lost in ages past. Not so for the homeboys who graduated from the school in M.S. Hershey's lifetime. They are the kind of men a woman wants around the house when shingles blow off the roof, or when the lights go out, and maybe even when a window gets broken.

It all seems too pat, and far too simple. But Catherine Hershey's idea had been inspired by simple needs from the outset, although these considerations seem to have faded in the complexities that followed her assertive request to get this project started.

Even the words she used to announce her idea are still being debated. The early references indicate that she had suggested, "Let's start a *home* for little boys," when she first mentioned the subject to M.S. The latter-day ascription whereby the boys and neighboring townsmen spoke of the student/residents as *homeboys* for the next thirty years tends to confirm that belief. But there is still a fifty-fifty split between this persuasion and the contention that Kitty Hershey had originally said, "Let's start a school . . ."

Credence attends both viewpoints, but the importance of what happened after M.S. took her up on the suggestion far overshadows the importance of the exact words she used to get her idea started. The shadows thickened when lawyer John Snyder prepared the initial Deed of Trust to launch the project, and there is even conjecture attached to that phase of this study. The records tend to show that Snyder had been instructed in 1907 to base his rudimentary charter drafts on the provisions already established by a school set up in Philadelphia before the turn of the century—a boys' school set up by the will of Stephen Girard and known as Girard College. There were elements drawn from the Girard charter contained in the initial 1909 Deed of Trust signed by Milton S. and Catherine E. Hershey; yet that original document remained rather simple even though it also contained unique differences of its own.

The subsequent changes, six amendments in all, came as the consequence of fitting the Trust to the changes in custom and law as they occurred with the passage of time.

The recollections of those earlier times and the reasons why the school got started can better be explained by studying two separate and distinct records which bear on the subject. The first of these is spun off from medical records no longer in existence, if ever they were committed to paper. The second is the record of the Deed of Trust *and* the history of the Milton Hershey School, both of which are inexorably and inseparably tied to each other.

In effect, the first of these records could be considered in the light of the seventeen year span of Milton and Catherine Hershey's marriage. Their childless marriage. The span is from 1898 until 1915, but the most meaningful times occurred between 1899 and 1904, and there are only blank pages to show for what happened in those years.

The point, however, is made up of the unrealized hopes and dreams of Milton and Catherine Hershey to share their connubial bliss in a home of their own and surrounded by their own children. When the century turned and Kitty had failed to conceive a child, their disappointments gave way to dismay. As in all things, Milton Hershey wanted to know the reason why they were childless. And, as in all things, he wanted to know why because he wanted to know what to do about it, for the idea of fixing blame was never as important to him as fixing things.

The year after Papa died in 1903, Milton and Kitty Hershey began a tour of New York, London, and Paris, and each point of call was to a medical center. It is not known if they had at that time arranged for their consultations and medical examinations to be arranged under pseudonyms, but the difficulty of that kind of arrangement under foreign passport regulations seems to preclude the probability. The impetus behind the trips was more than a probability, however, for Milton Hershey had promised both his Papa and Mama a grandson. Following the death of his beloved "Pap," the need to keep this promise to Mama became more of an obsession than a mere wish.

The pseudonym arrangement in the medical consultations probably came about later, and when Bertha Condoni was hired in Vienna in 1908, she was not only believed to have known about the arrangements, but in some lights she was thought to have been hired because she had helped make some of the arrangements.

No records exist, however, if only for the reason that the European doctors would only have known the gender and the assumed names of the patients they examined. If Bertie Condoni knew anything more than that the Hersheys had sought medical help, she revealed *nothing*—not a word about this delicate subject to anyone.

Curiosity, whether inspired by affectionate concern or insatiable morbidity, did arise. The towering Viennese matron blocked all the attempts of intrusive boors and prying busybodies by assuming a stance of hostile stolidity. She may have known the answers as to which of the Hersheys was sterile or she may not. But she did know how to deal with the interrogators.

Consequently, the medical record of a childless marriage is no record at all. But the fact of Milton and Catherine Hershey's knowing that he would be the last of his line *did exist*. There was no way to escape the deadly sting of *that vital statistic.*

The second record, beginning with the opening of the Hershey Industrial School in 1909 tended to erase the first non-record. Thousands of children have shared the loving guidance, the food, the clothing, the shelter, and the excellent schooling provided by the parental generosity of Milton Snavely Hershey and Catherine Elizabeth Hershey.

Now to reconsider the two records to be weighed in the balance. The first was the wish of a couple to have their own children. The second was "Kitty's idea" of a way to remedy the situation when they found their marriage would be childless.

The first record was based on a negative medical opinion. And it is closed forever.

The second record is based on the founding and the growth of a home and a school. It is the record of one of the most positive steps ever taken in the field of educational philanthropy.

It was Kitty's idea. She conceived and gave birth to the most meaningful way in which she could keep her husband Milton from going to his grave childless as the last of his line. The idea and the pursuance of an ideal made them both responsible as the founders of an enduring institution—and more. For the school and the home bespeak the power of what love and care can do when they are brought to bear on the problem of raising and training children. Their testimony stands on the witness of thousands of splendidly equipped young Americans who become "Hershey boys and Hershey girls" when they graduate from this place.

And from the day they graduate they become part of a record that was structured by elements of love from the past and aimed at the hopes and needs of the future.

As Milton Hershey said, "It was Kitty's idea." And it may have been the best one she ever got. There are thousands of others who believe that marrying Catherine Elizabeth Sweeney was the best idea Milton Hershey ever got.

Chapter XXII

><·~

As Memories Serve

The line, "God gave us memories so we may have roses in December," bespeaks a persuasion based on truth and fashioned into poetry. In all probability the line was inspired within the breast of some earlier scribe who had been frustrated by the clinical chill of documentary records and who thereupon sought to come in from the cold by turning to more sentimental values.

Socrates said, "The truth is what we believe," and oral historians have long since found that narratives become more believable and truths become more understandable when the emotional fires of memory are stirred into the lines of stories retold.

Thus we come to a place in the Hershey saga wherein the glowing recollections of his friends and associates have been rekindled again. For we could find no better way to recapture the color and the warmth, the unflinching stubbornness and the sometimes comedic traits that mark this man than in the ways his friends remember him.

These are the often told tales, the fireside reminiscences that keep coming up whenever a group of oldtimers get together to talk about their favorite personality.

As memories serve—this is the picture of "old M.S." *as he was* as . . . painted again and again when those long-ago days are recalled by his friends. These are the roses that come back to warm the December memories of some of those who were nearest and dearest to Milton Hershey.

Goodbye Segis

There are bushels of anecdotes about M.S. Hershey that portray the feisty little guy as a mobile stick of dynamite with an extremely short fuse. Those who loved the man and those who did not, all concur in the judgment that M.S. did pop off quite frequently, and sometimes violently. The delineator that separates his friends from his detractors becomes visible in the differing lights by which the members of each group perceived him. The friends say he frequently became angry for good reasons. The adversary group saw him as an angry fussbudget. Each persuasion was in part right and/or conversely wrong.

One episodic outburst of tempestuous anger occurred in April of 1918, and there was general agreement on all sides that in this particular instance the Old Boy had been justified.

The year marked a time of crisis. In Europe the directives of the German Generals Ludendorff and von Hindenburg were marshalling millions of Germans for a last great offensive on the western front. In America, as in other Allied nations, the civilian populace awaited news of the impending battle that would determine the outcome of the Great War.

In Hershey, people were beset by rumors that German spies had tried to put poison in the reservoirs on Pat's Hill. At the High Point Mansion, Milton Hershey chafed at the bit, awaiting the end of the hated conflict and eager to get his boys home from Europe. He had big plans for them, both in Hershey and in the Caribbean where he had set up a timetable for a new venture in Cuban sugar.

On this springtime afternoon he had made his tour of the bank and the plant, and as he stepped down from the limousine to enter the side door to the mansion, he spotted Lebbie Lebkicher talking excitedly to the chef. This was different. The two men were having a heated discussion at the back end of the driveway, but he simply waved to them and went on his way up the side steps into the house. All he heard was someone shouting the name of his prize bull, *Chocolate Segis Pontiac Al Cartra*, and what a prize he was. This bit of prime sirloin represented a fifty thousand dollar investment.

He continued on his way to the billiard room where he divested himself of his jacket. Then he picked up the newspapers on the table and settled down in a chair. But for a moment after having put on his reading glasses, he let the paper slip down as his mind went back to Chocolate Segis, and he wondered, "Why had Lebbie been talking to the cook about the prize bull?" And the normally cool Lebbie had been excited. *Very excited.*

"Oh, no!" Hershey expostulated, leaping to his feet. But before he took the first step toward the door, Lebbie entered. The oldtimer's face was a mask of white behind the gray sheen of his Van Dyke beard.

There was a brief moment of silence between them, but the reddening M.S. spurred Lebbie from his speechlessness. Then Lebbie droned an awful tale.

Somebody had *axed* Chocolate Segis Pontiac Al Cartra!

By mistake, of course, but of a certainty quite fatally. M.S., stricken, slumped back in his chair. Lebbie kept his distance and went on with the grievous details.

It seems that the cook had called the meat plant and ordered some prime beef. Beyond that, nothing was quite clear other than the fact that one of the men at the abbatoir named Johnny Vassler had been mistakenly given delivery of Chocolate Segis,

Chocolate Pontiac Alcartra
Purchased by
M. S. Hershey, Hershey, Pa.
at Public Sale Corning, N.Y.
Price $10300.00

The Sire of this bull is
King Segris Pontiac Alcartra
#79602   Price $50000.00

whereupon J. Vassler, armed with a sledgehammer, had done a Lizzie Borden on the fifty thousand dollar gold-plate special.

Lebbie seemed for a moment to be poised midway between two extreme persuasions. He had not yet resolved whether to fire all the people on the farm and to kill all the people at the meat plant, or to fire everybody in both places and kill them all later.

M.S. simmered. M.S. boiled. Then M.S. blew up. But Lebbie, by virtue of greater stature and what must have been one of the more classical deliveries of persuasive deterrence, kept Hershey at bay. More importantly, he kept him at the mansion.

In the end it would seem that nobody even got fired, much less killed. But another thirty years passed and both Lebbie and M.S. had gone to glory before cousin Joe Snavely would try to unscramble the puzzle that marked the demise of Chocolate Segis Pontiac Al Cartra.

Johnny Vassler had killed the bull, but he had had no way of knowing that the animal delivered to him was Chocolate Segis. He wouldn't have known the prize bull from any other. His job was to slaughter what was delivered, and that is precisely what he had done. The identity of the specimen rested on the man who had selected the bull and delivered him. When the roll was called down yonder in the meat-packing plant, *nobody* answered to *that name*.

Joe Snavely spun a harmless anecdote concerning a colorful soul named Jakie Schmaltz, whom he later averred to have been the sole target of M.S. Hershey and Lebbie Lebkicher's communal ire. Poor Jakie Schmaltz was fired, according to Joe Snavely's written account, but despite the mournful dialogue of the Snavely narrative, Jakie Schmaltz escaped scot-free for the best of reasons: *He never existed.*

Jakie Schmaltz, as it turned out, was a purely fictional character, a figment-farmer from the fourth estate who dwelt alone within the realm of Joe Snavely's fertile mind. In later years, Snavely would confide that the real responsibility for the errant assassination of Chocolate Segis had been ultimately traced to someone else. The oldtimers who are still around concur in the resolve that it had been none other than Abe Heilman, the longtime friend and co-worker of Hershey's Lancaster days, who had been at fault when the fifty thousand dollar hammer blow fell.

But Abe Heilman was one of M.S.'s loyal Swiss Guard, and as a member of that select group he enjoyed a privilege of rank that was at least a few notches higher than Calpurnia's had been in Caesar's scheme of things. So they fired Jakie Schmaltz, and having been an imaginary product of Joe Snavely's craft, he didn't mind. The only one really hurt by this titanic blooper was Chocolate Segis Pontiac Al Cartra. But unable to speak, he said nothing.

M.S. and Lebbie had quite a bit to say on behalf of the late lamented collection of very prime ribs, but none of their lines ever cooled enough to be put on paper.

A Smoking Hardliner

One of the time honored traditions of the Milton Hershey School had been the continuing practice of awarding each graduate a gift of one hundred dollars at the time he graduated. Back in the middle years of the 1920's the sum of a hundred dollars was something more like a couple thousand dollars in today's currency. In those middle years of the twenties, there were a great many families of three and four persons who had less than that amount of income to live on for a month.

Therefore, it was only natural that the prospective graduates looked forward to getting a hundred dollar gift with just about as much anticipation as they did to the receipt of their "completed attendance" papers. There was, however, a reason why the cash awards were granted. The time of departure from the school was timed for the attainment of one's eighteenth birthday, but the gift was, at least nominally, dependent on conduct. The latter condition more or less implied that the student had to behave himself while in school or else he would run the chance of losing some cold cash before setting out into an even colder world.

In the dozen years after the school opened, there had been about four classes of boys who had received their releases from the school, and all of them had been given the one hundred dollar gifts. Then came the middle twenties and, as Fate would have it, in one of the leanest post-war years, the rule governing the cash award was put to the test. Again by seemingly fateful intercession, the test was caused by a prospective graduate who had been a better than average student and a really outstanding athlete.

His birthday would fall on a Saturday in that fateful year, and that was to be the day when he would be released and get his money. The boy in question had returned with his companions to the student home after having been treated to a movie. There was an amiable feeling of festivity in the air and, like the comic page stripling named "Skippy" contemporary to that era, this particular boy probably "felt so good he just hadda whack somebody or do sumphin'."

He chose to "do sumphin'" instead of "whacking" somebody, and so he produced a forbidden cigar and proceeded to light up and to smoke it.

His fellow students were aghast. They warned him, and one of his close friends even tried to take the lit cigar away from him, but to no avail. The obstreperous smoker was too strong for his well-meaning adversary and managed to hang onto the forbidden cigar. He hung onto it just long enough for the house-father who came to investigate the noise of the scuffle to catch him in the act.

Shortly thereafter, Headmaster George Copenhaver had the culprit and the case brought to him. Being the tenderhearted soul he was, it wasn't long after that when G. Copenhaver called Milton Hershey with an urgent request for an audience. M.S. bid him to "come right on over," then waited, wondering what sort of Friday evening crisis had befallen the usually unshakable Headmaster.

Copenhaver arrived shortly afterwards, but he did not have the culprit with him. He laid out the whole story about how the boy had been caught smoking less than an hour earlier and less than an hour after receiving his course completion certificate.

Hershey waited until the Headmaster finished, then straightaway told him, "Give the boy his 'release'; he's eighteen. But no money. He knew the rules and he broke one. That's all there is to it."

Copenhaver didn't think so. He protested, reminding M.S. again and again how very much that one hundred dollar gift meant in such hard times. But the boss was adamant.

"George," he said, "a rule is a rule. I know how much a hundred dollars means these days, but even a million dollars wouldn't cover the kind of lesson we'd teach this boy if we let him get away with breaking the rules."

G. Copenhaver made the mistake of trying to soften the upshot of all this by suggesting, "Sometimes it doesn't hurt to bend a rule just a little bit."

Hershey blew up.

"You don't bend rules; you bend people. The answer is no, and that's final."

The rule was enforced. The boy was released. But the hundred dollar gift was withheld from him because, "He had not earned it," in the words of M.S. Hershey.

The apparently merciless decision was made quickly known, and there was debate about it for months and even years to come. But not much of the debate, if any, reached the ears of the man who made the decision. Several years later, however, in a visit to an ailing George Copenhaver, he brought up the subject himself.

He explained to his dear friend that there really hadn't been any other course open to either of them back when they had withheld the hundred dollars from the errant smoker. He asked Copenhaver if he had been keeping track of the boy. The pale and stricken Headmaster smiled.

"Yes, I have, Mr. Hershey," he replied. "And I'm glad to tell you he's doing fine. He has done well at his trade, and now he earns more than just a good living. Why, he even has his own shop. I'll bet you didn't know that."

"George," Hershey replied, "there is nothing more than just earning a good living, except maybe the one thing you gotta do first—learn a good lesson when you're young enough."

Copenhaver nodded in silent agreement. Hershey, still smiling, made his way toward the door, but before departing he said, "And that boy learned his lesson. Why, he has 'No Smoking' signs all over his shop over there across the river."

After the surprise wore off, George Copenhaver felt much better. Later on, as this story made the rounds, everyone else around town felt better, too. They felt so good, in fact, that the name of this boy was never mentioned again, no matter how often the story was told and retold.

Another secret, like the one concealing the identity of another boy who would ten years later steal a watch, was kept. But something else, something more, was not concealed.

A Milton Hershey belief: Rules are made to be *kept*. And later, they'll *keep* the *keeper*.

The Sagacious Scribe

Joseph Richard Snavely was a cousin of Milton Hershey, and he became the most prolific of all the Hershey writers. In the course of his lifetime, Joe Snavely worked for forty years in the employ of the Hershey Chocolate Corporation, and he authored a total of five books dealing with the events peculiar to his busy cousin's career.

In chronological order, these publications are titled *Milton S. Hershey, Builder* (1934); "Meet Mr. Hershey" (1937); *Milton Hershey Lives On* (1947); *The Hershey Story* (1950); and *An Intimate Story of Milton S. Hershey* (1957). Some of the subjective articles are repeated in several of Snavely's books, and a number of the studies appear in all of his publications. But, in all, it could truly be said that Joe Snavely worked tirelessly to write down everything he knew about the man who was his personal idol, as well as his friend and relative.

Joe Snavely was a printer and he typeset every word that appeared in the two thousand pages of his published texts about his cousin. He set most of it by hand, one letter, one word, at a time. Much of the work was done in his own print shop that he had set up in the basement of his home on Java Avenue.

The most voluminous text of the five Snavely offerings was *An Intimate Story of M.S. Hershey*, for which he had begun setting type in his home print shop in 1953. He was only partway through the text when Hurricane Hazel struck the Hershey community in October 1954 and interrupted his work.

Power lines came down, roofs were torn off buildings, and trees were uprooted all up and down the Lebanon Valley. The town of Hershey sat like a bull's-eye right in the middle of the storm-wrought desolation. One giant elm on the Snavely lawn had been upended by the furious gale, and the root system had torn a gaping hole in the gas mains beneath the house.

Snavely and his wife Helen had escaped the big blow, but with the power lines down, they were without electricity, and when darkness fell, they were without lights.

That was when Helen Snavely struck a match to light a candle, and an undetected gas leak from the ruptured main did the rest.

The dear lady lost her life in the explosion that followed, and Joe Snavely lost both his legs. Walls and windows throughout the house were smashed by the terrifying force of a rolling ball of fire that burst within that shattered home. It was more than enough to shatter the lives and property of men who may have thought themselves to be more courageous than Joe Snavely, but they would have been wrong.

In the early part of 1956, Joe Snavely wheeled himself into another print shop he had set up for himself. The typeset galleys and the manuscripts he had been working on were gone. His beloved wife was gone, his legs were gone, and virtually every one of his most precious possessions had been swept away. Only the firm resolve to get on with the job remained intact within the courageous heart of Joseph R. Snavely. So he pulled himself into his wheelchair, and he went to work.

In the preface to the book that came off the press a year later, Joe Snavely wrote:

> *I again started with my typesetting. I was seventy-six years of age at that time, and as was to be expected, my typesetting got off to a poor start. I often became discouraged, but I persevered with my objective, and in doing so, I worked ten to twelve hours a day.*

He got it done.

In those latter years of the 1950's, there were quite a few people around Hershey who would see Joe Snavely wheeling himself around his garden on the square-shaped, skate-wheeled platform he had built. He alone tended the flowers in his garden.

A dozen miles up the road in Harrisburg at the J. Horace McFarland Company, the giant letter presses were rolling, and in midsummer of 1957, Joe Snavely's book came into being. Back in Hershey, the roses were in bloom, and the brightest of all these were nurtured by the loving care of a little legless man on a handmade platform that looked like an oversize skateboard. By sheer will and devotion, he had set himself the impossible task of putting one last rose on the grave of his personal idol and his beloved cousin, Milton Snavely Hershey.

Once, long ago, there was a book put together as a testimonial of the faith shared by certain men. One of these appears in the Gospel of St. John (Chapter 15, verse 13), with the lines, "Greater love hath no man than this, that a man lay down his life for his friends."

But what could be said for a man who picked up the tortured remnants of a broken, seventy-six year old body and wheeled himself to a typesetter's job case? A man who would spend his final hours composing one last testimonial to a friend? The friend was dead, so why did he do it?

In a word—*faith.*

The Apostle Paul had this to say about faith in his letters to the Hebrews (Chapter 11, verse 1 and 2),

> *Now faith is the substance of things hoped for, the evidence of things not seen.*
> *For by it the elders obtained a good report.*

Quite a few of the elders and the youngsters of Hershey have received more than a good report from the tireless hands of Joe Snavely. Indeed, there is something of value contained in his demonstration of faithfulness and friendship that should never be lost to the skeptical folks of any age.

It became a lesson that hearkens back to the first book of the Bible, in Genesis, Chapter 6, verse 4, which recalls, "There were giants in the earth in those days."

But this one didn't become a giant until after he lost his legs.

Chapter XXIII

～·～

Twilight

The Hotel Hershey became a many-sided enigma in the lifetime of the man whose name it bears. It began as a pet scheme, and then it became the only one of his many projects he ever thought of as his prized personal achievement. By becoming a source of his personal pride, it differed from all his other works. Perhaps this is why he spent so much of his time at the hotel during the last ten years of his life.

From a purposeful standpoint, the Industrial School represented his most meaningful and conscionable achievement, and, of course, the Chocolate Corporation and the model community that bore the Hershey name, just like the park and the Arena, were early sources of great satisfaction to him. But these enterprises were shared with other men drawn from the host of talents he had chosen to work along with him.

To some lesser degree, this was also true of the hotel and of the perfectionist, Joe Gassler, whom he had chosen to run it. Yet the hotel was quite markedly different because it was his toy, and it was really the only thing that he regarded as a prized achievement. There were quite a few people who thought his obsessive concern with the hotel was far too demanding for a man of his age and declining physical condition.

They were wrong.

Two accounts afford a whole new perspective of the last seventeen years of Hershey's life. One of them is contained in the journal which his personal physician maintained on the daily lifestyle and the physical health of Dr. Herman Hostetter's patient, Milton Hershey. The other account was centered on another ledger which once existed as the diary of Joe Gassler and is now comprised of the recollections of Hotel Hershey workers and the notes collected for the *Hotel Hershey High-Lights,* the hotel news bulletin. These notes remained unpublished because M.S. Hershey wanted that publication to titillate the guests, not to extol the proprietor.

The Gassler diary, just as the Hershey Hotel register books for the period, disappeared. But one salient memory remains in the recollections of M.S. Hershey's friends, and it also appears in the journal of Dr. Hostetter's actual daily accounts of how Milton Hershey spent the twilight hours of his declining years.

The business records, the diaries, the press clipping files, and the memories of those associated with him during this time are all indicative of the fact that Hershey went out of his way to keep just as busy as he had been since his childhood days.

But not so in the twilight hour of evening. After he built the hotel, this hour was set aside for his visit to the small hillock overlooking the pines just below the western entrance. The ritual began a few years after the hotel was finally completed, and the twilight vigil was faithfully kept in summer, winter, spring, and fall, for all the years that Milton Hershey was able to come to the spot and remain alone with his thoughts.

His thoughts and his deer.

On one of his early visits, the straggling remnants of a deer herd had ventured into the sapling grove of recently planted pines while Hershey was munching an after-supper apple. He tossed the remainder of his apple to the ground and walked to a new vantage point in a cluster of sugar pines. He watched as the deer approached cautiously, and saw one of them nip the fragment of apple and eat it.

Thereafter, each evening when he was able to come back to the hill, he brought some apples with him. Later, he had feeders and salt licks installed in the pines so that the deer could feed in the mornings before he came, or anytime they chose.

They say he made these visits repeatedly, as the years passed, and the pines grew taller, and the clusters of wandering bucks and does grew larger. Each evening, the man with the apples would show up like a commuter hurrying to catch a train that was homeward bound.

The deer got to know him and to trust him. As time went by, he had them eating apples from his hand. Back at the hotel, the workers and the guests knew twilight was approaching when M.S. Hershey headed out the back door and made his way to the hillock by the pines.

He subsequently had a chair placed at a midpoint of the half circle of feeders. He would go straight to it and sit down before opening the bag of apples, waiting for the deer to show up. After a few minutes, he would peel an apple from the bag and bite into it. In a matter of minutes, with an interval that seemed each day to be the same, the deer would trickle out of the pines and meander toward him.

He would feed the first deer that came nearest to him, and then he would roll the balance of the apples, one by one, down the slope to the others. Each day, as the sun slowly dissolved beyond the horizon, the deer would eat as he watched.

This quiet glade in the pines was Milton Hershey's sanctuary. There he would come as the soft shades of evening descended and the noiseless scenes of time gone by would flow silently past the windows of his mind and he would recall the names and faces of those whom he had loved so well.

In summer twilight, he would see visions of his beloved Mama. They would become so real that he could almost smell again the fresh baked bread of The Homestead kitchen and little shivers would run through him as he recalled the distasteful memories of Titusville's oily skies, but they were soon dispelled. Somehow the gentleness of Fanny Hershey's loving soul emerged when the soft wings of summer evening once again brought him the inner warmth he always felt when she was near.

The capricious bluster of mid-March brought him memories of his youth and early manhood shared with his venturesome sire. He would smile with an inner feeling of tender bemusement when he recalled Papa Hershey amid a sea of popping tomato juice cans because he had forgotten to add something to prevent the fermentation which made them explosive. He felt warm about Papa, too, for Henry Hershey had spent a lifetime tirelessly pursuing the things he had felt a driving need to dare, to try, and to do. The memories of the straggly-bearded entrepreneur brought no sense of pity for old Henry Hershey, for he had been a man whose times had been filled with adventure and whose latter days M.S. had shielded from want.

But it was when the freshening zephyrs of Maytime brought a scent of blossoms to accompany the glow of a setting sun and the sparkle of the first star to peek through the descending curtain of twilight that he again beheld the sprightly image of Kitty.

The very thought of his "most beautiful lady" brought a glistening shine to his tired old eyes. The bubbling inner feelings of youth would return as her heart-shaped face and impish Irish eyes projected the most beloved image he had ever carried in his heart.

His Kitty. His impetuous, unpredictable, curiously restless, sometimes petulant, and always eager to get-up-and-go-again-anywhere Kitty. Oh, how he missed her! Yet, for all the days of travel and adventure he remembered having spent with her, he seldom pictured her against the palm fronds of the Nile, or as he had seen her in front of St.

Stephen's in Vienna, by Westminster Abbey in London, the Brandenburg Gate in Berlin, or the ice-capped crowns of the purple Tyrolean Alps.

They had seen so much together, but when he recaptured her image in the recollections of a Maytime twilight, she always came back to him in the crinoline polka-dot dress she had worn on the first day he had ever seen her in the little candy shop in Jamestown. The effervescence, the breathless feeling that had come to him with the very first glimpse of his first love, came back to him again whenever the May shades of twilight silently fell on his sanctuary on Pat's Hill.

Whenever kitchen aromas wafted down from the Hotel, the mirror of memory would bring him reflections of Aunt Mattie. The faint scent of anything appetizing carried on the breeze brought with it a picture of Aunt Mattie with her rolled-up sleeves and her busy forearms white-coated with confectioner's sugar. It seemed he always saw the tightly braided strands of gray hair on the top of her head, for she was always bent over, busy with mixing or stirring something in the bowl before her. Dear soul! How mightily, how tirelessly, and how unselfishly she had worked and given . . . and given again to keep him from going under in those early years of fruitless struggle and seemingly pointless work. But she had never been defeated. More than that, she had never once lost faith or given a sign of losing the wellspring of hope from which she dipped so frequently whenever he had need of her. "Oh, Aunt Mattie, if only you could have known what was yet to come, when long ago you left us. . . ." Once again, that sense of warmth would sweep over him and he would be calmed by a haunting inner persuasion. Perhaps *she did know*; perhaps *she had always known.*

In the fall when soft October rains and tints of dismal gray streaked the sky, he would think of Lebbie. Dear old Lebbie, the bearded skinflint, the caustic lone wolf, the aged veteran who had taken a tired and beaten youth to his heart and had given him the snap and substance to start again. In all visions of the thorny old codger who had come to him in the City of Roses so long ago, there also came a sense of shelter. There were times when he could almost taste again the crab cakes and the beef stew that had nourished him on that rainy night in Lancaster. A time when he crawled back from Manhattan, a defeated young man whose own family had slammed its doors on him and left him to go out alone and hungry into that dark and rainswept October night.

Sometimes he would talk to himself. "Good old Lebbie! How thankful I have always been for your help, for yours were the hands that lifted me! You and Papa must be having quite a time of it together. Don't let him mess up the place too much with his popping cans of tomato juice! You keep looking after him just as you always did when you were here."

Sometimes there would be a whole parade of faces from out of the dim and distant realms of an almost forgotten past. He would recall the smells of printing ink and singing children whenever he recalled the giant, blackhatted form of Sam Ernst, hard by his press with sheets of *Der Waffenlose Waechter* tumbling out the news. Then he would remind himself that "The Watchman Without a Weapon" would have no need of a weapon where he had gone.

At other times, he would feel an inner surge of gratitude and respect as he would recall the other Lancastrians, particularly Mr. Joseph Royer, the candy man who had taught him his trade. *How very much he had come to owe that man.* He could still remember his Mama pleading with Mr. Royer for his acceptance as an apprentice with the words, "My son wants to make candy. . . ."

Yes, he had wanted to make candy. Thanks to Mr. Joseph Royer, he had learned how to do it. And he had learned to do it so respectfully that, even at this late date when he recalled his early tutor, it was always as "Mr." Royer.

Flying sparks of memory would spin off the dear old faces of Mr. Decies, the Englishman whose early order of caramels and five hundred pound British sterling note had bailed him out in those early Lancaster days. With this memory he would recall the helping hand of banker Brennemann, who had secured the first really adequate line of credit he had so badly needed to launch a successful career.

So many faces . . . so many memories came back to him here in the evenings spent in this sheltered glade on the lea side of Pat's Hill. How dear they had been to him, and how much closer they seemed as the passing years went gliding by.

Each evening, except in the bitter cold of winter or the bluster of summer storms, the same routine was repeated over and over again throughout the late 1930's and the early '40's. But as infirmity crept up on Milton Hershey in the middle years of his eighties, the time came when he could no longer keep his tryst with the deer, when he could no longer observe that precious half hour of quiet meditation, and the memories that would come to him every day after the just-fed white tails had sauntered away and left him alone with his thoughts to watch for the first evening star to appear.

When his health no longer permitted this twilight tryst and he was unable to spend these moments in tranquil introspection, Hershey made provisions for others to continue feeding his deer. He had come to think of them as children, and in his mind they were as innocent and as worthy of his care as any children had ever been.

There is still food for the deer, and they still come back to that spot on the side of Pat's Hill, but the chair and the little fellow who sat in it are gone. The fawns and yearlings still trickle out of the pines at twilight and come to the quiet glade where their ancestral bucks and doe came to be fed long ago.

Each evening as the sun goes down, some well beloved creature goes along with it, for that is in the natural order of things. When the first star of evening peeps through the descending curtain of darkness, the wishing hour returns. The deer gather again beneath the rim of Pat's Hill. Across the way, where the nightlights illumine the golden crown of Founders Hall, the students cluster together at the same appointed hour. Without knowing it, the deer and the children are keeping a rendezvous that was fashioned for them by hands that have gone to rest.

The chair is gone, and the little man with the great big heart who used to sit in it—he's gone, too. But while he was here, he spent his entire lifetime proving how much he cared for God's creatures. He should rest easy in the knowledge that so many of the good things he came here to do are still being done.

Chapter XXIV

〜·〜

The Harvest Season

In 1940, as Milton Hershey approached his birthday, most of the folks around him believed he was approaching his final year. The white-haired patriarch seemed to have lost interest in the world around him, and for the first time in his eighty-three years he became a recluse in search of sanctuary. But between September 13 of 1940 and the following year when he became eighty-four, the period of self-imposed confinement worked in a way that appeared to have recharged the storage battery of his spirit.

Perhaps some of this renewal could be attributed to a pair of maiden lady nurses whom Doc Hostetter had hired. Miss Catherine Oslansky and Miss Elizabeth Rupp had been hired ostensibly to watch over M.S., but by the end of the year they found themselves watching after him because their patient had not only gotten the urge to be up and around, but by the fall of '41 he was eager to go places and do things again. There was a limit to the time he was able to occupy his busy mind with Chinese checkers and listening to the nurses reading him stories about Sherlock Holmes. Then his patience would snap, and he'd gather up his entourage and head for Atlantic City, New York City, or Saratoga.

Hershey still had business dealings in New York City. Ostensibly, he would seek out his friends H.H. Pike and John Lucas to consult them about a vareity of experiments he was still conducting. The homework phase of those experiments in new kinds of ice cream, chocolate confections, and soap drove the chef in the kitchen of the combined mansion apartment and country club complex nearly crazy.

Hershey still had a knack for keeping things in motion. He would summon Lewis Maurer, former manager of the Hershey Estates Creamery, to the mansion apartment, and confront him with a list of trials for making synthetic ice cream or some sort of high vitamin beverage. Maurer would be told to extract the fats from vegetables for use in ice cream, instead of milk. Then he would be ordered to blend the juices of celery, carrots, turnips, and beets for upcoming flavor tests for a new high vitamin beverage. One such directive produced a dish which combined beet juice, gelatin, and sugar, and it later wound up on the Hotel Hershey menu as red beet sherbet salad. It didn't inspire many orders, but it did start a lot of conversations.

With Maurer fully instructed and with the chef up to his eyeballs in dirty dishes, M.S. Hershey would come to the top of the stairs and yell, "Tell Roy to get the car!"

The effect was instantaneous.

Whichever nurse happened to be on duty would rush to the phone and call the other one with instructions.

"Get packed. We're going *somewhere*."

And that would be it. Within the hour, Tice would be expected to pull up in the driveway, and the Misses Oslansky or Rupp would have to be ready with their things and Mr. Hershey's suitcases fully packed and ready to go. Anywhere.

Sometimes it was to New York City, ostensibly to consult with Mssrs. Pike and Lucas, but it was more likely to end with a trip to the Follies or some musical comedy.

On other occasions, it would be to Saratoga and the racetrack. Hershey would tell Hostetter that he'd "gone to Saratoga to take the waters," but the good doctor would ask him, "What kind of water do they sell at the two dollar window?"

Even when M.S. and his nursing companions stayed in town, he had other things going on beside dish-dirtying experiments and sessions with Sherlock Holmes or Chinese checkers. Every day, he would have lunch with a different set of his cohorts. Early in the week, it was usually Paul Witmer and someone from the school. In the middle of the week, he would have Ezra Hershey and someone else from the bank, frequently young Arthur Whiteman. On alternate days like Tuesday and Thursday, there would be a group from the plant which could run the gamut from Bill Murrie, Percy Staples, Sam Hinkle, Jack Gallagher, to anyone else who may have been working on something that M.S. wanted to know more about.

P.A. Staples was becoming more and more subject to impromptu calls in those days, and the fact of his importance was to become increasingly more evident as time went by and calls became more frequent. But if the star of Percy Staples was on the rise, there were several other luminaries in the Hershey firmament that maintained their constant quality. Joe Gassler would pop in from the hotel just about any time he had a mind to, and Prudence Copenhaver or Minnie Snyder were among those whom M.S. would see whenever they showed up. If perchance a week would pass without either a visit or a phone call, he would seek them out for an afternoon chat. Harry Erdman, the overseer of Hershey's Rose Gardens, was another one of the saints who could come marching in unannounced to see M.S. any time.

Doc Hostetter was the most persistent caller, and when he wasn't around, the young nurses carried out his orders to the letter. He'd personally hired both of them, and every once in a while, this arrangement rubbed the impatient patient the wrong way.

One morning, Nurse Oslansky was in the act of administering medicine for a cold M.S. had picked up when the boss asked for his jacket. She started to comply, figuring he'd felt a chill. Then she had a second thought and asked him, "Do you have a chill?"

"No, I don't have a chill," he said testily. "I'm going out."

"Oh, no, you're not," she countermanded. "Doctor Hostetter said you can't go out of the house until you get over that cold."

"I don't give a hoot what Doc Hostetter said. I want to go out, and I'm going to go out! See?" He was really bristling.

She stood fast and shook her head.

"Get my jacket!" he shouted. "And if you don't get it, I'm gonna fire you!"

She was unmoved, except for her head, which she kept shaking to emphasize her refusal.

"You can't fire me," she said coolly, pulling his shoulders forward so she could slip a cushion behind his head. Then she fluffed the cushion and patted his flushed forehead.

"Doctor Hostetter *hired* me, and only *he* can fire me," she chirped.

A steaming M.S. leaned back against the cushion and muttered, "This is a pretty mess. Not only am I forbidden to get out of this place, but I can't even throw anybody else out either." He growled, "I'm a prisoner in my own home."

Oslansky said nothing, but smiled her agreement. She backed off as the simmering Hershey fidgetted in his rocker. Before reaching the door, she turned back to him.

"Will there be anything else, Mr. Hershey?"

He looked up as he wiped the back of his hand across the bushy moustache. The eyes glared straight at her, then they flickered beneath his equally bushy eyebrows and the growling began to subside. She waited. He lowered his eyes and cleared his throat.

"Bring the Chinese checkers."

Napoleon had submitted to Wellington with far better grace at Waterloo before going off to St. Helena. Hershey would have welcomed a trip into exile. *He couldn't even get out of the house.*

*   *   *

In the early 1940's, when M.S. wasn't winging off to New York, Saratoga, or Atlantic City, he divided his time in Hershey between the bank, the upstairs apartment at the former mansion, and the Hotel Hershey. After his stroke in 1937, he'd quit the habit of nipping up the stairs of the bank to the second floor.

As Arthur Whiteman was to put it later, "His office was in whatever room he chose to sit down. In the early thirties, it was in the place where Judge Snyder held forth in the front of the building. Before that, it had been in the office next to it, the one that Harry Lebkicher had occupied for about ten years, until 1924."

There were reasons for the out-of-town jaunts. New York City usually meant a round-robin tour of the theaters, usually where the musicals were playing. Saratoga was where he followed the ponies. Atlantic City had alternating purposes for his visits that changed with the seasons. In spring and summer, he'd be drumming up business for the park and the theater. But most of the time, and especially across the fall and winter months, he kept hammering away at "Rose Garden Cocoa Butter Soap" sales. The showroom in the Atlantic Avenue boardwalk headquarters had ostensibly been set up to publicize Hershey Park, the theater, and the arena. Then he added another feature attraction to the bill posters and banners that heralded the appearance of famous entertainers in his up-country fiefdom. He installed a washing machine to demonstrate his cocoa butter laundry soapflakes.

One day he overdid the demonstration by putting a whole box of flakes in the machine. Then he got into a discussion with a visitor whom he followed to the door, still trying to make some obscure point before the other party got away. He followed the man out onto the boardwalk and spent another five minutes trying to get in the last word.

The result of his pursuit is not known. Not so the consequence of his soap demonstration while thus engaged. He came back into a room that was ankle-deep in cocoa butter soap suds. Before he could turn off the washing machine, a rising tide of copious foam was beginning to creep up the very walls.

He surveyed the billowing expanse of the indoor snowscape he'd managed to produce, then he sighed as he leaned against the machine.

"And they say my laundry soap isn't sudsy."

*   *   *

By winter of 1941, M.S. had begun to curtail his out-of-town circuit riding. In Hershey, he alternated his residence and administrative seat of power between the upstairs apartment at the club and his tower suite at the Hotel Hershey. This changed after the ambassadorial staff and the consular officials of the Vichy French government were interned in the place.

His most memorable times in the hotel were twofold, one of them coming when he was invited to have dinner with Secretary of State Cordell Hull. This turned out to be an occasion which earned him the Secretary's thanks, in writing, for having been "a most gracious and understanding host."

The most dramatic scene played out in the hotel came on a Sunday afternoon in early December 1941. Frank Edris, career picture framer for the Hershey Department Store and allied interests, recalled that day and the visit he and Harold Hershey shared with M.S.

"We'd come up from Atlantic City in the limousine," Edris reported, "and while we were on the road back to Hershey, the news came over the car radio that the Japanese had attacked Pearl Harbor. When we got to the hotel, we really didn't know what to do.

"Harold couldn't decide whether or not M.S. had heard the news, and he didn't know if he'd still be interested in the theater posters and ticket sales for the Christmas program at the theater. So Harold decided to take the report to the boss, just as he'd been told. If M.S. wanted to talk about the war, it would be his choice, but Harold figured he would be better off if he stuck to doing what he'd been sent to do."

So young Harold Hershey gathered up the poster samples and ticket ledgers and headed for M.S. Hershey's room. Hershey greeted the young man at the door, bid him enter, and spread the material out on a card table before him. M.S. sat down and began grumbling as he seemed to look at the papers, then he snorted as he pushed them aside.

"I won't have it!" he shrilled, bounding to his feet.

All Harold Hershey could do was stand there and look puzzled. He couldn't figure why M.S. was so angry. He'd merely glanced at the sheaf of posters and reports, but that wasn't really what was bothering him.

He put a fist against his lower lip.

"First it was that thing with the Spaniards, just as I was getting ready to expand the plant in Lancaster. Then it was the Germans. They had to get some prince with a feather-plumed hat shot, and then *they* started it, just as I was getting ready to build in Cuba. Now *this!*"

He growled and strode to the radio, snapping it on. "There are more people in that corner of the world than anywhere. And all the good things—the sugar, the flavorings, and the cocoa beans we need—all grow there! Now the Japanese have to go and start something like this."

His deeper concerns and his subsequent prayers would be directed toward things nearer and dearer to his heart. His boys from the school would be marching off again. his people from the town, the plant, the park, and the school—they'd be going away again, just as so many others had done nearly twenty-five years earlier. He would pray for them; he would help their families, and he would do everything in his power to help the war effort. Through it all, his submerged identity as a little boy brought up in a Mennonite home kept streaming into his mind and into his prayers, for he was deeply hurt by the very wrongness of war and the terrible waste of it all.

*   *   *

In the years of the early 1940's, when Milton Hershey was still actively mobile, he developed some rather strange viewpoints on clothing and fashions. He had a fondness for hats that was a holdover from his Lancaster days when his first encounter with real affluence had seen him emerge as a neophyte dandy. The phase lasted a few years, manifesting itself in diamond cufflinks and stickpins. But his Mama's cold-eyed scrutiny and even chillier remarks led him to shuck most of these glittering bits of ostentation. Not so with hats.

He was a two-color pedestrian in his taste for suits: blue and chocolate brown. But in hats he had every shade of tan, beige, buff, and maroon to go with the brown suits, as well as every tint of gray and navy to go with the blue ones. He usually had an average of three or four of the blue ones in service, and an even half-dozen brown ones, but he had better than a dozen hats to go with each of the solid colored suits. After he passed his eightieth birthday, he tried another move to become a stylish trendsetter.

Like the suits, none of the hats were anything other than plain and somber. Until he put the hat on. Then he would turn up the front brim, whereupon he would change into a cross between Lee Tracy and an over-age-in-grade Harold Teen. (Lee Tracy was a movie star of the thirties frequently cast in the role of a newspaper reporter, the kind they called "Scoop" in those days. Harold Teen was a comic strip character who epitomized the collegiate version of a perennial freshman. Both wore their hats with the *brims up*.)

When chided about the incongruity of his appearance in uptilted chapeaux, he said something like, "Would you expect to see an old Mennonite farmer walking around in a hat with the brim down?"

The remark earned no response, despite the fact that most of his close associates could have told him that he had never joined the Mennonite Church, nor had he ever made his living as a farmer. He had earned a kind of privileged sanctuary in the self-styled role of his forebears' heritage, and when he sought refuge therein, nobody who knew him would attack. Privately, both nurses Oslansky and Rupp concurred with Doc Hostetter and Joe Gassler. Hershey's uptilted hat brim had nothing to do with Lee Tracy, Harold Teen, *or* Mennonite farmers. *But it did have a relationship to the movies.*

He had seen Edward G. Robinson and James Cagney in gangster roles. On every occasion, the mobster portrayed could very well have been played by a one-eyed man. The other eye was always covered by a hat brim tipped down. In M.S.'s mind, he wasn't copying anyone when he wore the hat brim flipped up. He simply didn't want to look like the *Little Caesars* who wore them the other way. None of those around him in the forties remembered it, but back during the strike days of spring 1937, some reporter had dubbed M.S. "a penny-pinching *'Little Caesar,'* who ran a one man town."

One man never forgot it, the one who wore his hats with the brims turned *up*.

*   *   *

The "penny-pinching" tag they fastened to M.S. Hershey was fashioned of a mixture derived in equal parts from elements that were both subliminally accurate and patently ridiculous. He would not buy expensive suits; in fact, he had to be bullied into buying any suits at all. He would dock his nurses' salaries whenever they took a day off, even Sundays. But he always saw to it that they got any food their hearts desired, not only at work, but to take home with them in any quantity. He told them, "Get a couple nice dresses, too," whenever they went shopping for new nurse's uniforms. Fact is, whenever he learned that anyone near him was going shopping for a gift or something he knew they especially wanted, he'd say, "Put it on the bill."

He would growl about nurses and other help taking off for the holidays, yet bonuses for holiday observances were paid out so regularly that the staff counted on them.

When they went out to restaurants, he had a fetish against being served with all his food on a single platter. He'd kick up a regular fuss with the maitre d's and waiters, insisting, "I want to eat off the table," which meant that he wanted to pick out the things he wanted to eat because nobody else had the right to put a measured amount of food on a plate and make him eat it. This, as it turned out, was one of the Mennonite family and farm style customs he could have claimed as part of his childhood heritage, but he had hated it as a child, and he kept fighting it all his life.

Telling Milton Hershey what to do at any time in his adult life had been difficult. He came to the point where he adamantly refused to buy suits, so Joe Gassler had to buy the new ones. Then, after vigorously rumpling them and pressing out the creases, he had to substitute them one at a time for the old ones in the closet.

Until his eighty-fifth birthday, M.S. had been, in the words of humorist Irvin S. Cobb, "a hard dog to keep under the porch." But the years began to tell on him, and the nature of things that fascinated him began to show a different kind of picture.

He was never talkative, and he became even more reticent in his latter years. Yet there was nothing he enjoyed more than chatting with friends and talking over old times. But his innate shyness was ever present, and he seldom spoke out in round-robin talks on a given subject until his opinion was sought, unless the topic was some business related to the school or the town. He had some deep-seated feelings and some unassailable ideas about both the town and the school. When his advisors were called to meet with him, they found the plans were already laid out and *he* did the *advising*.

In those later years, Percy Staples was coming up fast on the inside, in the overall scheme of things. This presaged an ultimate contest and came close to open conflict with Bill Murrie, even though Murrie was the highest paid chief executive of the company at the time. Murrie remained the mainstay of the commercial corporate enterprises for M.S.'s lifetime, but it was in the cards for Percy Staples to one day be the man who wore all the hats as board chairman of the School, the Corporation, and the Trust Company. As such, he would ascend to a position closer to the absolute power held by Milton S. Hershey then any other man would attain.

There were waves being stirred by the portent of the impending changes that would be made once the war was over. M.S. pretty much kept his sense of equanimity by saying little and watching his ducks. The duck watching was more than a figure of speech. He'd had a pond built on the back porch of the mansion, with a boardwalk surrounding it and nesting crates for his ducks lining its sides. Whenever the pressures of personal cares weighed down on him, he would hide himself away from the indoor realms of hassles and telephones to slump in his wicker boardwalk chair, brought from Atlantic City, and watch his ducks.

The only comment he made about this new routine came as something of a surprise. One day, he said he never should have built the pond and brought the ducks there in the first place. Then he grumbled something about it having cost him too much. But the facts were otherwise. Doc Hostetter later said that those moments of quiet contemplation with M.S.'s winged paddlers at the back porch pond "had probably extended the Old Boy's life by a couple of years."

When asked why he'd grumbled about the cost of building the pond and installing the ducks, he sprang another surprise.

"Oh, I didn't mean the money," he replied. "Not at all. You see, when I was younger, one of my favorite meals was roast duck. But *I never knew any of those ducks* personally.

"These ducks are different. I spent a lot of quiet afternoons with them, and they all have names. It would be murder and worse to kill them, . . . so now you know why I'll never eat duck again."

In some ways, he reverted to the way he had been as a child, but on most occasions during those final years, he would like to reminisce about the early days. Many of these memories were shared by close confidante Paul Witmer, but most of them went back to days before the builder and planner arrived on the Hershey scene.

As M.S. looked approvingly across the valley, Witmer knew that deep inside himself the boss was saying "Thanks" to Kitty again. Whenever her name came up, that same look came into the old man's eyes.

It happened often, especially when the roses bloomed. M.S. would recall the first roses his wife had planted by the Derry Church school, and he'd walk to the edge of the porch and point to the plot of ground where Kitty had started her first rose garden, right after the mansion had been finished. It had since been moved to Pat's Hill to become a centerpiece in the landscaping jewel wrought by Harry Erdman as the classic Hershey Rose Gardens.

The transplanted memorial to Kitty contained in that plot of roses ofttimes became the Mecca of Milton Hershey's latter-day pilgrimages. Miss Rupp would take him for a leisurely drive through the surrounding countryside, but she assiduously made a point of stopping by the Rose Garden on the way home.

Without a word, M.S. would gather his waning strength to climb out of the car. Sometimes it would take a few moments until he'd regained his breath, then he would turn and wend his way through the lines of roses that were still blooming from the slips Kitty had planted long ago by the side of a newly finished mansion. He would think back to those days as he wandered slowly, hesitant with the infirmities the years had brought him, but refreshed by the wistful aromas, the scented memories of long ago. He would return to the car sometimes giving voice to his thoughts and sometimes remaining silent, but at all times remembering one thing. Sometimes he mentioned it.

"We called the mansion 'High Point,' " he'd say. "And when she lived there with me, it was the high point of my life."

A House By the Side of the Road

In many respects, Milton Hershey seemed to be determined in an effort to confound the crepe hangers who had started chiseling his epitaph at the beginning of the 1940's. His round-robin jaunts to Atlantic City, Saratoga, New York City, and elsewhere seemed to belie the existence of any infirmity, even though he had passed his eighty-third birthday. Even though nurses Oslansky and Rupp, along with chauffeur Roy Tice, were less than half his age, they were still hard put to keep up with him. But all this activity was reflexive. He didn't feel like he was about to die, and he didn't want anyone else to feel that way either.

On his eighty-third birthday, he came away from the lunchtime ceremony at which he had been presented with a rose named in his honor with this remark.

"The American Rose Society named a rose after me, and I can't tell you how proud this makes me. But don't get the idea that we're holding this meeting for someone to put the thing on my grave. This is a birthday party, not a funeral."

He became testy in the face of his expected decline. A pair of events in spring and summer of 1941 seem to indicate the sharpness being honed into the sage who had become a critic. In March, M.S. had his last photo portrait made in Maxine's Studio in Atlantic City, and the proofs upset him.

"Makes me look too old," he gritted.

"But, M.S., you are eighty-three," someone reminded him.

He growled. "I'm almost eighty-four, but that lousy picture isn't even a week old. But you know what? People are going to remember me from the pictures that will be around long after I'm gone. I want to be remembered from a picture taken at a time when I was younger."

The oldtime puncher had become a counter puncher. Later that year, in June, when Bill Murrie and Jack Gallagher told him about the new slogan for the chocolate company he flashed some of his new style.

" 'First in favor and flavor,' " he mused, repeating the slogan aloud. "Yes, well."

His response held all the enthusiasm generally reserved for tax collectors and sticky-fingered kids in boutiques.

Then he fixed Murrie with a flirty look.

"Do you remember the Shirley Temple movie where some big shot radio executive was looking for 'a typical American little girl'? I think it was *Rebecca of Sunnybrook Farm*, but I'm not sure. Do you remember that?"

Murrie wasn't sure, so he said nothing, but he did wonder whether the Old Man was getting dotty.

"Well," M. S. went on, "in the movie, this radio producer wanted to know more about Shirley Temple, who played the part of a little girl who had just been chosen as a most typical American child. Then the agent said, 'She's as wholesome as a *Hershey bar.*' Now *that's my idea of a slogan.*"

He didn't bring up the fact that they hadn't paid anyone to write that line. But Murrie and Gallagher beat a hasty retreat, hoping to get clear of the place before he thought to ask them how much they had paid for *their* new slogan.

In late August of 1942, another picture was taken of M.S. as he showed up to receive the Army-Navy "E" award for the D Ration Bar. He looked both younger and happier in that photo, for it was a proud occasion. Underneath his antiwar sentiments, M.S. was a deep-rooted patriot, and he knew that those ration bars were even then sustaining Field Marshal Montgomery's men as they swept across North Africa in pursuit of a defeated Erwin Rommel's Africa Korps.

He said, "In a war, soldiers aren't the only ones who get hungry. When the guns stop shooting and the bombs stop falling, there are children and women and old folks who will have to be fed in those devastated areas. These people are the innocent ones on both sides, and we've got to keep them from starving. If we don't do something about that, to them it really won't make much difference who wins the war."

The Ration Bars kept going out, and from their stockpiles some of the first needs of the upcoming Marshall Plan were implemented. Even before the war's end, it became evident that there would be a struggle between East and West, Communist Russia and the Western Allies, to feed the people in countries within the political spheres they wished to control in subsequent years. Someone asked M.S. if any of the Ration Bars were going to Russia, and if perhaps the communists were using these American food supplies to influence the people in areas they wished to dominate.

"I don't know," came the reply, "*and I don't care.* You don't ask a person's politics when they're starving. You feed 'em. The life of any child is dear to us, no matter if he is Greek or Russian or German."

The simplistic M.S. again, and he had something else to say about the *Hershey ration bar.*

"If you want to call our ration bar a weapon, that's okay. But we hope it will be used to fight hunger, not people and not political battles. I hate war and you know it, but I hate the thought of starving children ten times worse than that. I couldn't do anything about the war. It never should have happened, but this is different."

His heart was fully in the war effort even though generations of Swiss Brethren and Mennonite forebears had surely convinced him that it was wrong and hateful and wasteful. But throughout the daylight and evening hours, he would sit glued to the radio in his upstairs apartment at the club. He puffed away on a cigar, chugging out impatient jets of smoke when exciting news came in and chomping down hard when reverses were broadcast. To him, it was as though every battle had one of his boys in it. Every casualty report made this childless man feel as though he were the father of every boy who was killed or missing in action.

He put his money where his heart was. Nearly all of his stock dividends and his personal income funds were deposited in war bonds from the day the war broke out until the day he died. Government bonds represented the major source of wealth held in his own name when he passed away, so the peaceloving descendant of Mennonite ancestors chipped in with most of the bucks at his disposal for quite a few of the armaments needed to win the war.

A veritable procession of proud moments came to M.S. during the middle span of the war years, but this did not include an event which occurred on the 17th of November, 1942. The U.S. State Department closed down the Hotel Hershey for several years as they interned the Vichy French Ambassador and his staff at the resort. They couldn't deny M.S. access to the place, of course, but the presence of civilian guards and even the minimal show of confinement spoiled the place for him.

"Who wants to eat in a prison?" was his commentary.

Next year, in October 1943, when most of the internees were released, he went back to the place again, but the feelings he'd had for it had changed. But he still loved to tiff with Joe Gassler, the steely-spined manager. When he sometimes forgot to pick on the white-gloved, bandbox Beau Brummel who ran the place, Gassler would take a jab at him, and that would do it.

Gassler was once asked if he didn't think he should show Mr. Hershey more respect in his declining years.

"Respect? My dear friend, I worship the man! I owe him everything I've got, every memory I cherish. But he likes these squabbles. In fact, sometimes I think it helps to keep him alive. He expects it of me, and these little tiffs are part of it. If I showed even the slightest hint of kowtowing to him or backed off, he'd begin to feel like I thought he was dying. He's been tough, and as long as he thinks he still is, he'll be around. I not only respect him, *I know him.* Does that answer your question?"

The granite hard, steely sharp general manager of the Hotel Hershey was known for the excellent squab he served. He never served *as* a pigeon, however, and that is how he became an M.S. Hershey favorite.

In his middle years, Milton Hershey had acquired a certain fondness for a poem by Sam Foss, published around the turn of the century and titled "A House By the Side of the Road." By the time M.S. reached his eightieth birthday in 1937, he had also been fascinated by an MGM feature series of short subject motion pictures called "The Passing Parade," written and directed by John Nesbitt.

The last line of the Foss poem reads, "Let me live in a house by the side of the road and be a friend to man." The Nesbitt series, "Passing Parade," enjoined viewers to "Come along with us back to yesteryear while we watch 'The Passing Parade.'"

But even in his years as an octogenarian, Milton Hershey didn't want to stay in a house by the side of the road, and he didn't merely want to watch any passing parades.

In his eyes, if there was going to be a parade, it would be coming right down the middle of the road, and he wasn't going to be sitting somewhere off to the side watching it. Until the very end, he believed that for him the only place in a parade was out in front leading it, where he had always been and where he always wanted to be.

Chapter XXV

~·~

Reflections . . . by Birthday Candlelight

Another war had ended on September 2, 1945, and eleven days later Milton Hershey would celebrate his eighty-eighth birthday. On the evening after his memorable ride with Doc Hostetter to the top of the hill over by The Homestead, M.S. sat alone by the radio and thought back across the many years behind him.

Joe Royer had taught him to make candy. Harry Lebkicher had taught him how real worldly riches begin when you find one friend who has the faith and loyalty to stick by you through thick and thin.

Back in the days when he had been on the threshold of his fortieth birthday, the war with Spain came along and caused him to look southward in the direction of Cuba. In a matter of months after that conflict had ended, he and his new bride, Catherine Elizabeth Sweeney, had returned to the lands of the Spanish Main, and there it was that he had found the second leg of his ultimate success. When his chocolate enterprise would totter in a state of equipoise and his model town would hang in the balance as security for a fifty million dollar loan, the canefields of Cuba would sweeten the pot and bail him out.

And it was from the Cuban scene that P.A. Staples would emerge to play a big part in the Hershey saga.

Less that twenty years later, the Hersheys' friends on the mainland of Europe would get into an awful conflict called the Great War. He remembered only the greatness of pain he suffered during that one, for after it broke out in 1914, he lost his beloved Kitty in Philadelphia in 1915. Two years later, he watched as some of his beloved friends and workers marched off to war. When they came home in 1919, he was both pleased and hurt when the returning veterans opened an American Legion Post and named it after him. The hurt was sprung from a feeling which he later said had made him feel a strong bond of kindred empathy with a German-born operatic star named Ernestine Schumann Heinke. The great lyric soprano had lost sons fighting on both sides during the terrible war. Casualty lists from both sides had also claimed the lives of American, French, German, English, and Austrian friends of the Hersheys and of their expatriate companion Bertie Condoni, late of Vienna.

The first two commanders of the Milton Hershey Post 386, American Legion, were Paul Shultz and Paul Zentmeyer, lifetime employees of Hershey.

After another score of years had passed, the madness broke out all over again. Only the numbers had changed. By the time of the second world war, literally hundreds of his workers and townsmen were called away again, only this time they were joined by hundreds of boys from his school. Once again, between wars he had made or maintained friendships with continental Europeans who lived in countries where the call to arms was an absolute requirement. Even though M.S. had no amici or comrades in the Fascist or Nazi ranks, he once again lost friends among the Germans, Austrians, and Italians who fell in battle.

From the battlefronts of World War ll returned former Hershey Industrial School boys named John Aichele, William Dearden, Joseph Gumpher, and Kenneth Hatt. All four of them would eventually take their places in the scheme of things linking the name Hershey to a school, a company, a bank, and a resort/entertainment consortium.

What a terrible waste, he thought, as he sat in his rocking chair in the late hours of the evening when the Second World War formally came to an end. General Douglas MacArthur had stamped finis to another epoch as he terminated the surrender meeting that afternoon on the deck of the battleship *Missouri* in the harbor of Tokyo Bay.

"Gentlemen, these proceedings are closed," was the final pronouncement.

Thereafter, his memories would go back to the days of his childhood and his youth. Back to the well beloved and warmly familiar faces of Mama and Papa, of Aunt Mattie and Uncle Abe, and to the Mennonite heritage that had shaped them—and him.

Neither he nor his Papa had ever become formal churchgoing members of the sect into which they both had been born and within the confines of which both of them had lived the most meaningful and memorable years of their lives. He wondered why he and Papa had been so different from the Mennonite members of the families into which they had been born. He recalled how very much alike he and Papa had been to each other, and this brought him to the realization that the difference had not been a matter of the faith itself, but merely the matter of a name. The Mennonites, just as the Amish, the Dunkards, the Brethren, the Lutherans, and even the Catholics, not only needed a name for their faith, they insisted on it.

His papa and he both believed in God. They prayed, they read the Good Book, and, more than that, they spent their lives doing things for other people. Both of them kept the tenets of the Golden Rule as well as they could, and they believed it because they wanted to. But neither the father nor the son would join a church, because the rules puzzled them. There was an innate streak in both Hersheys that forbade either one to join a church with rules he knew he couldn't keep and with creeds he couldn't understand. In their simplistic view, the complications interposed by punitive rules and confusing doctrines became like a wall between them and God as they knew Him.

These thoughts had often been brought home to Milton Hershey, man and boy, by his dear departed Mama. They would return to him even more frequently during the summer and early fall of 1945.

When September 13 rolled around in 1945, M.S. gathered himself for the big events scheduled in his honor. Of late, he had been a late sleeper, but on the morning of his eighty-eighth birthday, he was up and around and ready to go when the first shafts of daylight came into his room. By the time Nurse Elizabeth Rupp came by for the day watch, he was all dressed and ready to go.

The nighttime nurse departed after wishing M.S. a happy birthday, and it then became Miss Rupp's chore to make him eat breakfast. Even though it was not yet eight in the morning, he was already chafing at the bit to be off to The Homestead. The birthday party wasn't scheduled until six p.m. that evening when he would share dinner with his directorial friends and business associates.

The help had trouble restraining him. They pointed out the hour was not yet eight in the morning; they reminded him he had not yet taken his pills, and he hadn't even had breakfast yet. The nighttime nurse returned with a gift, and sometime after eight-thirty, Roy Tice came by with Mrs. Hugh Seavers, another of M.S.'s part-time nurses. They brought him a slice of cake with his coddled egg, oatmeal, and hot milk breakfast.

A single candle was placed on the slice of cake, and a mixed choir of Nurses Rupp and Seavers were joined by Roy Tice and the club chef from belowstairs to sing "Happy Birthday" to him. He grumbled a bit, then smiled, but he said nothing. The members of this informal group of songsters later became divided on the reasons behind his speechlessness. Most of them believed he simply couldn't talk because he had been overwhelmed by this show of affection. Roy Tice thought perhaps M.S. had been so keyed up because he was looking forward to getting out of the house and being once again in the company of his friends.

The chef was of another persuasion.

"He knew he was going to be treated to roast squab on toast, and I'll bet he lay awake all night just thinking about it."

Roast squab was on the menu, as it turned out, and roast squab had been denied his frequent requests on the dietary orders of Doc Hostetter, not because the squab itself posed any problem, but because of the side dish of lavish mounds of potato filling swimming in gravy that M.S. insisted on with his favorite squab.

Whatever the reason for his silence, the coterie of morning companions did manage to get his mind back into the room where he was and back to the breakfast he hadn't eaten. He found voice again and began demanding fried sausage and home-fried potatoes "to go with these *'curdled'* eggs." He lost that argument, too, but they took some of the heat off his brow by bringing in a whole trove of gifts and birthday cards from his well-wishers.

Then he was all for opening the gifts and reading the cards, but these were withheld until he'd suitably polished off the orange juice, oatmeal, and coddled eggs set before him. He made dilatory attempts to continue grumbling, but a brightness of eye and the appearance of flickering smiles betrayed him. He was happy.

Later, he was even happier when they began opening the gifts and cards for him, but one rose-colored envelope caught his eye.

"Hold it!" he said, putting up his hand. *"That pink envelope—give me that one."*

The ceremonial routine came to a halt as he was handed the envelope, and he tore it open and adjusted his glasses to read the card. The hand with the card dropped to his lap, and he cocked his head sideways with a tiny grimace and then the hint of a smile, as he adjusted the frames of his glasses on the bridge of his nose. A single tear trickled down his cheek.

"It's from Margaret," he said, half-choking on the word. Then he sniffed. "From Margaret, and my girls."

The Margaret in question was Margaret Clark. The card was the twenty-fifth one she'd sent him, and, as usual, it was signed. "From Margaret Clark and your girls." Of all the people Milton Hershey had ever known, including dear old Lebbie Lebkicher, not one of them had been a more loyal friend than this one. There was no question about that. None dearer to his heart than kindly, appreciative, humble, and adoring Margaret Clark.

He snapped out of it after a while and went back to reviewing the procession of gifts and the mountain of cards that piled up on the table by his chair. Then he got out of his chair, against orders, and took an hour or so of incoming phone calls from well-wishers without having them cleared by anyone. He fought off the ten o'clock remonstrations to take a midmorning nap. Even after they'd pried him away from the telephone, M.S. waved off the opposition and ordered them to let some of the downstairs help come up to see him.

Hershey stayed at it until just before lunchtime, and they had trouble getting him to eat his soup and salad. But that wasn't a patch on the difficulty that came when they tried to make him lie down for his afternoon nap. He finally flopped across the bed from twelve-thirty until about an hour later. Then he was up and at the phone again. By that time, Ted Banks came over with another batch of cards from the plant, so he stayed busily undeterred for most of the afternoon.

By the time Miss Rupp announced that she and Roy Tice were ready to take him to The Homestead for dinner, he'd been busily and continually engaged in round-robin exchanges for just about four straight hours after his midday nap. He assented to the notice of departure without a word, but on the way to the door, he made a stop by his night table.

He folded a rose-colored envelope into the pages of the well-worn Bible he kept at his bedside. For all the bustle and sprightly exchanges he had shared throughout the day, he was still clutching Margaret Clark's card in his hand nearly eight hours after he'd first opened it.

"Now." he said, "you can take me back to the room where I was born."

The old Homestead was his destination, and it nearly became the scene of a fight. He opened the door to these differences when he tried pushing off Miss Rupp's attempt to help him into the limousine.

"Let me go," he growled, "and when we get over to The Homestead, I'm gonna walk into that place under my own power."

This represented the second round of a disturbance in which Miss Rupp and Roy Tice had already lost the opener. Doc Hostetter had wanted M.S. to confine his mobile activities to a wheelchair, but the Old Boy refused. He told the good doctor that the day he would start going around in a wheelchair would be the day after the doctor brought him a pig that could sing. Hostetter had ordered a wheelchair for him despite this instruction, but it had been tucked away belowstairs at the club, no doubt awaiting the debut of the porcine vocalist that could make it viable in the eyes of M.S.

The vociferations subsided by the time the trio of riders reached The Homestead. No hands were put upon him, and no wheelchair had been brought along. They pulled up at the front door, and the guest of honor alighted with an air of cool austerity that simply amazed his travel companions. A broad grin wreathed his face as he greeted his hosts, but they'd broken a rule, too. Earlier instructions had been for them to be seated around the table where the dinner was to be held until M.S. showed up. But before the car came around the driveway, someone had noted its arrival at the cutoff, and they'd all hurried outside to greet the boss.

The spontaneity of the greeting momentarily refreshed M.S., but the hour and a half that followed clearly began to tell on him. He took turns speaking to every one of the men seated around the table, and he made it a point to bring up the particular subject he had discussed with each of them the last time they had shared a private conversation.

Clockwise, from his left side at the table, he had P.A. Staples, Ezra Hershey, P.N. Hershey, W.H. Ernest, O.E. Bordner, J.J. Daniel, and Harry N. Herr. To his right were William F.R. Murrie, D. Paul Witmer, Charles F. Ziegler, Arthur R. Whiteman, John B. Sollenberger, and Abe Heilman.

He had his roasted squab, and he enjoyed it. He enjoyed being with the thirteen men who had shared most of his successful business ventures with him. There wasn't a man seated around the table who didn't feel that his own personal success had been the direct consequence of the hard work and the genius of the man whose birthday they were observing.

M.S. departed, but there wasn't anyone left at the table who didn't realize that this had been the last time they would ever share a birthday party with their good friend Milton Hershey. There wasn't a cold heart in the crowd nor a dry eye in the house.

The big, bluff frame of Bill Murrie shook with spasms of quivering, and the nether lip of iron-jawed Percy Staples trembled. The eyes of both were bright with tears held back. The glitter of other ambitions and all thought of contention had dissolved when their little friend departed. In parting, they held hands, rather than shaking them. For a moment, they clung to each other, speechless with an inner feeling that they had

Clockwise, from his left side at the table, he had P.A. Staples, Ezra Hershey, P.N. Hershey, W.H. Ernest, O.E. Bordner, J.J. Daniel, and Harry N. Herr. To his right were William F.R. Murrie, D. Paul Witmer, Charles F. Ziegler, Arthur R. Whiteman, John B. Sollenberger, and Abe Heilman.

finally found the only common bond they would ever share with each other.

Their differences would rise up again, but at that moment the prospect of winning anything had lost all meaning for both of them. They were about to lose someone who could never be replaced.

There are no words to describe what happened after M.S. left the room. Nobody said anything. Nobody could.

Gone, not Gently . . .

When Dr. Herman Hostetter prevailed on Milton Hershey to submit himself to round-the-clock nursing care back in 1941, he had not only won a big concession from M.S., but he also introduced the first, and perhaps the only form of orderly record-keeping for later use in compiling the Hershey saga. The letter writing career of Milton Hershey had been closed with his final entreaties for money addressed to Uncle Abe Snavely back in the early 1880's. Thereafter, his chronicle was mainly built on the articles that appeared in local and national publications.

M.S. kept no diary at any time in his life, and when he had attained enough stature to warrant press coverage, such coverage was frequently distorted locally or woven from the whole cloth of some remote scribe's imagination. Then, in 1941, along came Doc Hostetter and his coterie of nursing companions to change all that. The good doctor immediately instituted a medical log. Henceforth, Milton Hershey wouldn't be able to brush his teeth, smoke a cigar, or go to the bathroom without having it wind up on the record. The nurses were charged with reporting his every symptom and his every move, around the clock and every day.

By gaining access to the private letters and the credible memories of some of the men and women who shared the last five years of Milton Hershey's lifetime, a meaningful pattern becomes clearer and something of value emerges. The following chronicle represents an exercise in which the nurses' medical entries were matched to the memories of those who shared the final days of Milton Hershey's lifetime.

A compilation of the last year of entries in the medical log shows the one line that was most often repeated—"Patient fussing with his hands." This notation was sometimes phrased as, "His hands bother him again," or, "Patient rubs irritated hands," and even, "Today he scraped hands with scissors blade to stop itching."

Next comes another observance which tends to show the difference between the social chats and the business talks that marked the procession of Hershey's daily visitors. On the social side, the times when he would reminisce or just plain gossip with the visitor, the name most frequently encountered was that of Paul Witmer. It was Witmer with whom he took his daytime rides or spent quiet afternoons on the porch.

John Zoll, at that time Personnel Director for the Corporation and also a Hershey Justice of the Peace, was another social companion and one of those who would spend two or three hours at a time with M.S. Ted Banks who ran the soap plant and the cocoa butter experimental trials was also the labor relations boss for Estates, but his time with the Old Man was also more of the sociable kind rather than the business type.

The visitors who came in as Witmer, Zoll, or Banks departed recall that M.S. was "more seemingly satisfied and at ease" following Witmer's visits. They also said he smiled more after Zoll's or Banks' conversations. He was heard to laugh out loud most often in the presence of these two, and this honor was also shared during the less frequent sojourns of Alex Stoddart, the publicity man.

Harry Erdman, the gardening and rose-growing wizard, was one of the more frequent visitors who would spend more than a mere dilatory hour with M.S. He was also among those who would accompany the boss on his mid-afternoon rides. Quite a few of these discussions were about business, however, because M.S. was still spending a great deal of time working on garden expansion and landscaping plans that projected ten years into the future and beyond.

Strange to relate is the frequency of the visits made by cousin Ezra Hershey, especially in the days of late summer and early fall of 1945. Ezra, of course, was Corporate Treasurer, as well as M.S.'s closest surviving relative, but no meaningful notes show the substance or the mood of their discussions. Virtually all of the visits with cousin Ezra lasted less than a half hour when he was accompanied by others, and they averaged about fifteen minutes when he came alone.

P.A. Staples and his wife had returned from Cuba in the summer of '44, and both of them were frequent visitors, although Mrs. Staples always came with her husband, never alone. Bill Murrie came frequently, too, often in the company of other executives.

An interesting progression of events show up on the medical log for October 1945. On the first of October, P.N. Hershey, James Bobb, and P.A. Staples had lunch with M.S. from noon until one p.m. Then Bobb and P.N. Hershey departed, and Percy Staples stayed until three p.m., when he left.

Then the record reads like this:

4:00 to 5:00 P.M.	—John Zoll visited with M.S.
5:00 P.M.	—Mr. Staples called on business
6:00 P.M.	—Dinner—ate well. Rx yellow tablet; liquid Rx tz ii
7:00 P.M.	—Soaping and scraping hand
7:10 P.M.	—To Mr. Murrie's home
7:30 P.M.	—Returned home with Mr. Murrie
8:05 P.M.	—To theatre to see opera
11:00 P.M.	—Returned home. Buttermilk.
11:30 P.M.	—Visited by Dr. Hostetter

The doctor stayed twenty minutes and left just before midnight. M.S. stayed up and played cards until two a.m., but the record notes "a slight coughing spell." He went to bed and slept intermittently from three to five a.m., from six to seven, and then from seven-thirty until eleven, when he had breakfast. But interspersed notes of "coughing" appear throughout these entries and continue until noon. Mid-morning, he had the nurse rub Vick's ointment on his chest.

The next entry shows M.S. at 11:30 a.m.: "Breakfast. *Ate well.*" Then he "read his mail and scraped his hands." He took his medicine and then he went to lunch with Mr. Staples, Mr. Murrie, and Ezra Hershey. The lunch was held at the apartment, or it would have been otherwise noted on the record. This was the only time Murrie and Staples were in the company of each other and M.S. since the birthday party. Nothing appears concerning their discussion, and all three of them were gone by one p.m.

M.S. Hershey's afternoon carries notes that he "soaped and scraped at his hand" twice, once at one-thirty and again at two-fifteen, but then he went out for a ride at four p.m. and "had dinner—Oyster bar—at 5:45." The only other meaningful note from that evening is "very nervous" throughout the familiar entries on "working with hands," plus the card playing, checkers, apple game, and evening medicines.

But he didn't turn in until one forty-five the following a.m., after which "patient coughed a little, slept, got rubbed with Vick's salve, and slept again until 10 a.m." Early morning note states only "had good night."

October 4th was noteworthy from the standpoint that it followed the only day that Doctor Hostetter did not call on him, but marked the first day in which he would begin seeing a series of other doctors, in addition to Hostetter. The record shows that Dr. Bealor called on M.S. at seven p.m.

Dr. Hostetter was back in to see him between ten and ten forty-five that evening, and they had milk and ice cream together. He slept off and on until he took a steam bath in late morning, after which he had lunch with Ted Banks. Banks left at one-ten, and Bill Murrie came in and talked with him until two p.m. Then he "fussed with hands" until "Miss Rupp came in and played 'the apple game' with him until six" and he had dinner.

Doctor Bealor's visit on October 4th presaged a period in which a strange series of medical couplings began appearing. The log shows a visit by Dr. Horn from two-fifteen until three-thirty p.m. on the seventh of October. Then came dentist Dr. Cooper on the eighth, followed by a Dr. Fowler on the morning of the twelfth and Dr. John Atlee, Jr., on the evening of the twelfth. In the interim, the record notes the recurrence of "rapid pulse" and "frequent coughing."

It is clear that Dr. Hostetter spotted the signs of another oncoming bout with the chronic bronchitis that had bothered Hershey all his life, so he took no chances. The doctor was fully cognizant of his patient's weakened heart. Hence he sought second and third opinions on the digitalis regimens he had prescribed for M.S. To a man, each of the consulting medicos conferred with him and concurred both on his diagnosis and the medicines he prescribed.

But on the late afternoon and early evening of October 6th, however, M.S. had confounded Hostetter's orders by checking out of the apartment at four p.m. and going to the Hershey Hotel barbershop for a shave and a haircut. He capped off the visit by staying at the hotel and visiting with Mr. and Mr. Staples between five and six p.m., after which he returned to the apartment for dinner. During this period and thereafter, the notes indicate "increased coughing and rapid pulse" with alarming regularity. When Doc Hostetter learned about this ill-advised trip, he put aside his gentle manner and gave M.S. quite a lecture.

Next day, Dr. Hostetter spoke to Dr. Horn, who was scheduled to see M.S. after lunch, and he learned some disturbing news about a close friend of Milton Hershey's. Both Hostetter and Horn decided against telling M.S. that his good friend Minnie Espenshade Snyder, Lawyer John Snyder's widow, was desperately ill. Hershey had known her since 1895, before he had hired Snyder or had even met Kitty.

Hostetter had another reason to get upset when he walked in and caught Hershey smoking a cigar. He read him out again, but save for a sheepish attitude and a slightly rapid pulse, nothing more transpired, according to cousin Ezra who visited him in the interim, once with Bill Murrie on the eighth. On Saturday, the ninth, Mr. and Mrs. Staples came over to watch movies with him.

Next day, Sunday, cousin Ezra came with devastating news. Minnie Snyder had died. Hershey's dearly beloved friend was gone, and he was so upset he cried himself to sleep. On the medical records for this period Hershey was noted to have "coughed in his sleep." Noting that M.S. talked to no one for the next twenty-four hours, Ezra later said he believed "M.S. was really sobbing, not coughing." He added, "The old fellow really didn't want to talk to anyone."

This even applied to Doc Hostetter, and one nurse noted, "Patient doesn't cough in his sleep when Dr. Hostetter is here." The nurse would later wonder "if he really had been asleep when the doctor was here."

By October 12th, the sleeping intervals became shorter, the coughing started to become more frequent and violent, and then he began showing streaks of blood in his sputum. To Hostetter, the combined rapidity and the weakening of pulse indicated an onset of myocardial distress, along with a sudden elevation in the patient's temperature. The doctor ordered an ambulance and had M.S. admitted to the Hershey Hospital, where he was immediately installed in an oxygen tent.

The time was 8:45, Friday, October 12, 1945.

Milton Hershey had fallen prey to the medical catchall which in those days was called "complications." His heart was failing him. He was in deep pain and fevered, with a temperature of 102 degrees F., as a consequence of lobar pneumonia. The medical records show round-robin ministrations of digitalis for heart, aspirin for the fever, penicillin for the pneumonia, and morphine for pain.

In the late morning, around ten a.m., after his admission, his former Nurse Oslansky came to see him. He peeped out from the oxygen tent and said, "I'll bet you never expected to see me this way—under glass." These were his last words, and he was smiling when he spoke them. A few minutes later, he fell asleep. At ten a.m. on the following day, he died.

M.S. had entered the hospital on Friday, October 12th, and with all life signs notwithstanding, he had been brought in bucking at the traces, fighting against the unthinkable notion of death. Until the last few moments following his former nurse's visit, his entire stance could have been expressed by the lines of Dylan Thomas' poem:

> *Do not go gentle into that good night*
> *Old age should burn and rage at close of day*
> *Rage, rage against the dying of the light.*

But thousands of miles to the east, those lines were being deleted from the final stanza of the Welsh poet's composition called "Poem in October," and the "Do not Go Gentle" poem wouldn't be published until 1951. The rhapsodist had closed his folio on the "Poem in October" he'd finished with another line that more closely matched the tenor of Milton Hershey's final thoughts:

> *. . . heaven stood there then in the summer noon,*
> *Though the town below lay leaved with October blood.*
> *Oh may my heart's truth*
> *Still be sung*
> *On this high hill in a year's turning*

These lines were written at virtually the same moment Milton Hershey passed through the veil that marked his entry into the Promised Land. He knew about promises; he had been keeping them all his life. The people in "the town below" would remember him and his "heart's truth would still be sung on this high hill" for many another "year's turning."

He departed, leaving one tiny patch of this world a good deal brighter for his having been there. His life had come and gone in buildings a few hundred yards from each other, but the eighty-eight years between had been witness to some vast changes in the landscape and the economic well-being of the area. Milton Hershey had come into the world a simple child believing, and he left it to join the Maker of the greatest promise of them all with his faith renewed and quite intact. But he did not "go gentle" into any good night.

He went at mid-morning, and he went smiling.

The End

The Timeless
HERSHEY
ALBUM

Come, count the faithful shining faces
brightening the byways of olden places:
They flow like golden grains of sand
and fill the hourglass bowl anew
with memories of the precious few
Who shaped the substance of a vision grand.

. . . the faithful shining faces . . .

Milton S. Hershey
Founder

Born September 13, 1857, at Derry Church, Pennsylvania, he returned to the place of his birth where he labored to make his dreams for a whole new way of life come true.

His products, his town, his school and his park were all forged out of the ideas he had and the work he shared with the people he loved.

He was one of a kind.

Catherine E. Hershey
Wife

Born Catherine Elizabeth Sweeney, July 6, 1872, in Jamestown, N.Y., she was the daughter of Michael W. and Catherine (Maloney) Sweeney. She was married to Milton S. Hershey at the Rectory at St. Patrick's Cathedral, New York City, on May 25, 1898. She loved to travel and to entertain, and because she loved children, the Milton S. Hershey School is known to have been *Kitty's Idea*.

Fanny B. (Snavely) Hershey
Mother

Born Veronica Buckwalter Snavely, September 4, 1835, in Pequea Township, Lancaster County, Pa. Daughter of Mennonites Abraham and Elizabeth (Buckwalter) Snavely, she married Henry H. Hershey and became the mother of Milton S. Hershey.

This timid, gentle and cautious lady devoted her every energy to helping her only son to "make good."

Henry Hershey Hershey
Father

Born Henry Hershey Hershey, January 4, 1829, at the Homestead, Derry Church, Dauphin County, Pa., he was the son of Jacob Hershey and Nancy (Hershey) Hershey. He wed Veronica B. Snavely, January 15, 1856, in the parsonage of Holy Trinity Lutheran Church, Lancaster, Pa.

The adventurous sire of Milton Hershey was certainly the biggest influential force in his son's life.

William Henry Lebkicher
Friend

Born September 10, 1845, at Lancaster, Pennsylvania, "Lebbie" Lebkicher joined Milton Hershey in Philadelphia in 1876 and remained with him until the venture failed.

The crotchety bachelor met Hershey again when he returned to Lancaster from New York in 1885. He put up his meager savings and helped Milton Hershey in a whole new start. In later years he would become a Bank Board Member and Vice President, and Vice Chairman and Board Member of the Hershey Industrial School. (Now Milton Hershey School)

Matilda Snavely

Aunt

Born on some unspecified date in 1832 on a farm southwest of Lancaster, Aunt Mattie was the older sister of Milton Hershey's mother, Fanny Snavely. She had an elementary education, but she also had an inordinate wealth of love for her younger sister's only boy. She remained a Mennonite maiden lady for her whole life and she spent most of it working or putting up the money to help her beloved nephew.

John Snyder

Lawyer

Born April 13, 1863, in Lancaster, Pa., he was the son of Edwin E. and Margaret C. (McLane) Snyder. He graduated when he was 15 from Lancaster High School at the top of his class.

Snyder joined Hershey before the turn of the century and thereafter became the legal draftsman for virtually the whole string of commercial, institutional and personal ventures undertaken by Milton Hershey.

George E. Copenhaver

Headmaster

Born April 15, 1877, in Berrysburg (Dauphin County), Pa., he graduated from Berrysburg Seminary and attended Penn State College. Married to Prudence May Daniel, he became the first Superintendent of Hershey Industrial School and served from 1909 until 1938.

George Copenhaver was a man among men, but to the boys in the school he was more like a saint. They all loved him.

William F. R. Murrie

President, Chocolate Company

Born March 25, 1873, at Mann's Choice (Bedford County), Pa., William Franklin Reynolds Murrie graduated from Bedford High School at age 16 and became a telegrapher. Milton Hershey hired him away from Weaver-Costello in Pittsburgh in 1895 and brought him to Lancaster as plant supervisor.

He headed Hershey Chocolate for forty years and was president of the Cocoa and Chocolate Mfg. Association for twenty-five years. His contacts were innumerable.

Joseph Royer Royer

Confectionery Mentor

Born March 5, 1836, on a farm in Manheim Township (Lancaster County), he was the son of Joseph and Catherine (Royer) Royer.

Joseph Royer earned a commission in the Union Army during the Civil War. He was mustered out of service in June, 1865, after which he bought the Whiteside property on West King Street in Lancaster. His shop known as Royer's Confectionery and Ice Cream Parlor was where the 14 year old Milton Hershey began his apprenticeship as a candymaker in 1871.

John B. Sollenberger

Entertainment and Amusement Manager

Born June 13, 1897, in Silver Spring Township (Cumberland County), Pa., John Sollenberger was educated in the public schools and attended the Harrisburg School of Commerce.

John B. Sollenberger was taught the ropes by Charles Ziegler and quickly demonstrated his aptitude for the entertainment business. He subsequently made Hershey, Pennsylvania one of the most popular tourist and entertainment centers in the nation.

Harry Neff Herr
Chief Engineer

Born March 30, 1868, near Lancaster, Pa., Harry Herr earned a degree in Civil Engineering from Lehigh University.

When told he was being retained to submit plans for a new community in Derry Church, Dauphin County, he asked Milton Hershey, "Where's that?"

Thereafter, Herr designed or planned the factories, streets, the water and power plants, the streetcar lines (Hummelstown-Palmyra and Campbelltown-Lebanon), as well as sewer systems for the place called Derry Church that became Hershey.

Prudence May Copenhaver
Head Mistress, Hershey School

Born September 18, 1881, in Berrysburg (Dauphin County), Pa., Prudence May Daniel was married to George Copenhaver. Shortly after their marriage, they were chosen as the first two house parents and teachers of the Hershey Industrial School.

She was a vital counterpart to her husband at the school and a dear friend and confidante of Milton Hershey.

Charles Franklin Ziegler
Hershey Estates President

Born August 17, 1884, in Lancaster, Pa., Charlie Ziegler had attended the Duke Street School in Lancaster and Pennsylvania Business College. In his youth he had mowed the lawns for the neighboring Hershey family in Lancaster.

Charles Ziegler worked his way through different jobs in the Hershey complex, serving at various times as a Director on the Boards of Hershey Bank, Hershey Industrial School (now Milton Hershey School), Estates, Foundation and Trust Company. he became the first Manager of Hershey Estates and was its President from 1935 until 1949.

Percy Alexander Staples
Heir Apparent

Born March 31, 1883 in Portland, Maine, Percy A. Staples was the son of Charles A. and Marie (May) Staples. He graduated from the Episcopal Academy and Massachusetts Institute of Technology.

He became the heir apparent to Milton Hershey in the middle 1940's and Board Chairman of the Chocolate Corporation, School, Trust Company, and Foundation.

Margaret May Clark
His "Girl"

Born December 11, 1893, Derry Township, Pa., daughter of Joseph Clark and Catherine (Sanders) Clark. Margaret Clark quit school at the age of fourteen to go to work at Hershey in 1908.

Nobody in Hershey history was more faithful and devoted to M.S. (always *Mister* Hershey to her) than Margaret Clark.

Abraham T. Heilman
Plant Manager

Born in 1876 in Shillington, Pa., Abe Heilman was educated in the public schools of Cumru Township. He entered the employment of Milton Hershey before he was twenty.

He finally earned the title of Plant Superintendent at the Chocolate Company, but in the interim Abe Heilman had been dispatched to any place a problem arose, at Milton Hershey's direction.

Joseph Gassler

Hotel Manager

Born in Koblenz, Switzerland, in the late 1880's, Gassler came to the U.S. in 1903.

He assumed management of the Hotel Hershey when it opened in September, 1935, where he shared residence with his wife, the former Annie Josephine Smyth.

Samuel Forry Hinkle

Chief Chemist

Born June 9, 1900, Columbia, Pa., attended Columbia High School and graduated from Penn State College in 1922 with a degree in Chemical Engineering. He arrived in Hershey in 1924 and was hired as Chief Chemist and put in charge of materials analysis, forerunner to quality control.

Among his notable achievements during M.S. Hershey's lifetime was the development and the production engineering that enabled Hershey to become prime contractor for WWII ration bars.

David Paul Witmer

Builder

Born March 6, 1894, son of David Witmer and Fanny Elizabeth (Garber) Witmer in Elizabethtown, Pa., he attended public school in Elizabethtown and Stevens Trade School, Lancaster County, Pa.

During his tenure as builder (1926–1959) every major construction job in Hershey bore the personal trademark of D. Paul Witmer. He became Milton Hershey's advisor and confidante, as well as his good right arm, in anything that needed building or planning.

Ezra Frantz Hershey

Treasurer and Bank President

Born September 1, 1879, Lancaster County, Pa., son of Elias H. and Elizabeth (Frantz) Hershey, he was Milton Hershey's cousin and the only blood relative to become an executive in the businesses associated with the Hershey name.

Ezra began working with Milton Hershey at the Lancaster plant before the turn of the century, and when he came to Derry Church a few years later, he was named Treasurer of Hershey Chocolate.

Harry L. Erdman

Horticulturist

Born in 1890 in Erdman, Pennsylvania, Erdman served thirty-five years as Chief Horticulturist for Hershey Estates. He built the Hershey Rose Gardens and became President of the American Rose Society.

Harry Erdman also planned the rose garden for the Eisenhower Museum in Abilene, Kansas, but his proudest achievement was the Milton S. Hershey Rose, first grown in 1940.

Herman Harrison Hostetter

Physician

Born November 22, 1895, in Cleona, Penna., son of Jacob and Emma (Wolfe) Hostetter, he was the personal physician and devoted friend of Milton Hershey.

He arrived in Hershey in 1918 following his graduation from Lebanon Valley College in Annville, Penna., and worked in the chocolate factory. Following a year teaching school and four years at Jefferson Medical College in Philadelphia, he returned to Hershey in 1924 and then became M.S. Hershey's personal physician.

. . . the byways of olden places . . .

Chocolate Avenue - 1915.

As the last pages of the Gay Nineties spun off the calendar to make way for the twentieth century, Milton Hershey found himself on the threshhold of a whole new way of life. He would be forty-three years old on September 13 of the year 1900, and he had a lot of living behind him. Thirty years earlier, he'd gone through the separation of his parents, the death of his little sister Sarena, and a failed apprenticeship with Sam Ernst, the printer in Pequea. At fourteen, he'd begun learning to become a candymaker with Joe Royer of Lancaster. This course he didn't fail.

Thereafter, he started his own candy ventures in Philadelphia and New York— and both of them had failed, even though he had help from his Mama, Fanny Buckwalter Snavely Hershey, and from her sister Martha (Aunt Mattie), and her brother Abe (Uncle Abraham). Meanwhile, his Papa, Henry Hershey, remained conspicuously mobile, moving in and out of the scene on an unscheduled basis that would warrant the name gadabout, laid on him by the distaff side of the Mennonite Snavely Family.

But young Milton survived all that, and then he returned to Lancaster in 1886 to make a go of things. The "go" included a Lancaster Caramel Company that he built up and sold a dozen years later for a million dollars, a move which led to the realization of three dreams.

First, he married Catherine Elizabeth (Kitty) Sweeney, twenty-four year old Irish colleen from Jamestown, New York.

Second, he took his ready cash and used it to buy up the land and buildings of the old Hershey Homestead in Derry Church.

Then he started his third dream on its way to fulfillment by journeying to Denver and bringing Papa back to where he could be installed in residence with Mama. The last part of this aim would go amiss, but a start had been made.

Thus, the three dreams had found partial fulfillment, because they comprised a trio of accomplishments that brought him to a new threshold at the turn of the century. Now he could go back again to the Homestead he'd left when he was a six-year-old boy. Now he would have his Mama, his Papa, and his beloved young bride all together, or at least they would all be in the same place. It was the place where he'd been born, and it was the dearest spot in all the world to the man who would become famous as an industrialist, an innovator, an educator, a philanthropist, and a human being. He was Milton Snavely Hershey, a shy, Pennsylvania Dutch farm boy, who was destined to be a man in motion from the day of his birth on September 13, 1857, until the day of his death, October 13, 1945.

Along came the turn of the century, when he took part of his money from the sale of the Lancaster Caramel Company and set out to see the world with his new bride. But she cut the trip short in Mexico City and brought him back to Pennsylvania with the admonition that "he wasn't meant to stay away from business."

Milton Hershey had already brought Papa back from Denver and had installed him at the Homestead in residence with his close friend and business associate, Harry Lebkicher. By that time, the little family had entered the dairying business at the Derry Church site with a company-owned herd of Holsteins.

This is where he would make it happen. This would be the place where he would make a new start with his loved ones, friends and family gathered around him. And this time, he would have enough money to make his scheme work.

The Homestead, as he saw it, would provide the hub for several new ventures in which he would have all the milk he needed in the dairy business and an expanded plant devoted to making milk chocolate.

His plan to get Mama and Papa reconciled to living together in the Homestead was shot down early by Mama. So with Henry Hershey and Harry Lebkicher moved into the Homestead, M.S. and Kitty made frequent trips to Derry Church in an effort to ascertain what their next move would be. Mama stayed in Lancaster for the moment. Meanwhile, the original plan was still to enlarge the Lancaster plant and subsequently to add other chocolate producing mills in Mt. Pleasant and Reading. But initially the Derry site had been primarily intended as the place that could fill an expanding need for fresh, whole milk.

Then one day after touring the valley, as the Hersheys were making their way back to the Homestead, Kitty asked Milton to stop the carriage. On a little rise about halfway down the hill from some newly-acquired quarry sites, she asked, "Why don't you build a new chocolate plant right here?"

Everything he needed was there in the rolling valleys, where the corn and oats would provide feed for the dairy cattle and where the cows, in turn, would yield all

The Chocolate Factory - 1903

the milk he would need for an expanded venture in milk chocolate. And from there, where they stood, the Hersheys had a good view of the railroad track of the Philadelphia and Reading Line; the lines of transport for incoming tonnages of sugar and cacao beans were readily available. So right there, on the spot, Milton Hershey came to the same conclusion that many another wise man had reached before him: the obvious and most logical answers are ofttimes the ones which are most easily overlooked.

His resolve to follow Kitty's suggestion was made quickly, but in later years he would often wonder why it had taken him so long to make up his mind. There hadn't been much going on in the rolling meadows and sequestered vales that lay between

The first construction workers begin work on the plant - 1903

Skylight frames await installation as the factory nears completion.

the broad Swatara and the trickling currents of the branches of Spring Creek. In fact, there were only a half dozen farms scattered between the Homestead and quarry on the east and the Hockersville Post Office on the west.

Over at the crossroads to the north was the tavern that the Zentmeyer family ran for the Haefner Brewery in Lancaster. Across the railroad tracks to the east was the old Presbyterian Church that had been there for more than a hundred and seventy-eight years.

Every other spot was dotted with fields of corn and oats, with green patches of fruit trees and the truck gardens of scattered family farms. These were homes of people who had been friends and neighbors of the Hershey clan for well over a hundred

View of the chocolate factory from Chocolate Avenue - 1905

Papa Hershey (far left) and Lebbie Lebkicher (in straw hat) and early work force.

years, since Isaac, than Jacob Hershey, had settled there.

Kitty's reminder surprised him because it was so obviously right. Without knowing it, she was to repeat this practice of suggesting just the right thing at the right time on several more occasions throughout the few brief years they shared together.

*   *   *

Much of the land needed for the new venture already belonged to the Hersheys when Kitty made her suggestion. Nevertheless, once the decision was made, Milton Hershey followed up by buying everything in the area he could lay his busy hands and idle dollars on. It wasn't until March 2, 1903, that ground was broken for the new plant site in Derry Township. The place was officially listed as Derry Church in deference to the Presbyterians who had put their stamp and their place of worship there so many years earlier; this applied to the five-hundred acre tract that Milton Hershey had already begun planning as the site of a new town where his workers would live.

The Daniel Schlesser family had been moved into the Homestead to assume management of the new venture in February 1898. They were on hand to greet Papa Henry Hershey when he returned with Milton from Denver. Thereafter, everyone came under the supervision of Mama Hershey, who was brought over from Lancaster to assume command of the household chores. Then Aunt Lizzie, Henry Hershey's sister, was brought in to help in the kitchen. Even though this lady was crippled, she hobbled about on crutches to help sister-in-law Fanny run the place. Both Mama and Aunt Lizzie shared the displeasure of the Reformed Mennonite Church, which frowned on their being separated from their husbands.

With this bustling camp under the generalship of Mama, the Catholic bride, Kitty, stayed well clear of the command post. But she accompanied her husband Milton on his daily rounds of the ever-expanding beehive. She knew the signs. He was already working on future needs to enlarge and equip a plant and a workers' paradise, even before the first shovelful of dirt for the experimental milk plant had been dug in the

A view of the original Hershey homestead farm shortly after the turn of the century.

YMCA, later the Hershey Men's Club.

meadow across from the Homestead.

The buildings would require a lot of stone, and the newly imported Italian quarry workers were carving it out of the newly acquired land. The transportation of sugar and cacao bean supplies was arranged when M.S. made a deal with the P & R (Reading) Lines. He failed in his initial effort to have the company build a freight and a passenger siding spur on his land. But after that demurrer, he came up with a right-of-way that ceded the land to them for both a passenger and a freight station. The freight-siding came first, of course, but the idea of a passenger station was accepted with a wink and some smiles. Later, the wink became a blink of astonishment, and the smiles subsequently broadened into masks of surprised satisfaction.

One by one, the buildings went up, first for the plant and then the testing kitchen. The streets of the new town were laid out, and a parade of exotic names came into being: Java . . . Para . . . Ceylon . . . Chocolate . . . Cocoa . . . Trinidad . . ., and along with them came the need for a post office, a fire company and a school.

The Haefner House, an early landmark in Derry Church and a favorite meeting place for Henry Hershey and Lebbie Lebkicher.

For the people awaiting signs of what would be another company town, there were more winks that were later exchanged for astonished blinks.

The first six houses that went up on what was to become Areba Avenue didn't look like company houses. They were larger and nicer than that. However, they all looked alike, and that is where the assertive Milton Hershey angrily stepped forth.

"I won't have this!" he exploded.

Which was his way of telling the builder that, in this town, no two homes were to look alike. He wanted different shapes, different colors, and he wanted them landscaped differently, surrounded by shrubs that were also different.

"The people who live in these houses will be different," he said, "and they will own them. How are you going to get people to live in houses that look alike? They won't buy them. You've got to give them something they want to buy, something they'll be *proud* to live in. Let's give 'em what they want."

Something different.

Hard rubber tires and open cabs gave the early milk drivers lots of jolts and fresh air.

Chocolate Avenue - 1915.

The McKinley School Building, soon after it was built (later replaced by the Community Building).

Chocolate conches lined up in early plant photo.

Employees keep a careful watch on the wrapping machines.

Crowds, parades and general festivities were the order of the day, as Hersheyites celebrated Hershey's 10th Anniversary - 1913.

*Post Office and Tea Room on first floor, Men's Club on second floor -
about 1919.*

And so it went in a continuous line of one building scheme after another—commercial buildings, domestic residences, schools, and all the other projects which confounded the prognosticators of that day, and still manage to bewilder some of the more uninhibited community planners of this one.

Some anecdotes continue to persist from the times when this tiny village made its burgeoning way forward in the name of progress and expansion. One of the stories centered on the contest the new community planners decided to run when the town had grown large enough to merit the location of a post office. The new town needed a name, so the prize of a hundred dollars was announced, and the competition began, under the guiding hand of lawyer John Snyder.

The hand became a bit shaky as the judge reviewed the outstanding entries gleaned from thousands of suggestions submitted. Such glowing entries as *Beansdale, Cocoahirsh, Chococoa City, Etabit, Hersheycoco, Hustletown, Qualitytells, St. Henry, St. Milton, Thrift,* and *Ulikit* came quickly to light and were even more speedily consigned to anonymity in a file replete with seltzer bottle caps. Finally, Snyder decided to award the prize to Mrs. T. K. Doyle, a Wilkes-Barre lady, for the name Hershey-Koko.

Milton Hershey told Snyder he could make the presentation personally in Wilkes-Barre, but if he, Snyder, thought they were going to name his town Hershey-Koko, he, Snyder, should stay in Wilkes-Barre.

The lawyer responded by asking, "Did you call it your town?" Hershey said he did, so Snyder said, "Then why don't we call it *Hershey*?"

Hershey smiled.

"It's already been done," he said. Then he went on to tell Snyder that a Hershey Trust Company charter had already been granted by the state of Pennsylvania, and the address was listed as "Hershey, Pennsylvania." The date of the charter was April 27, 1905.

Snyder was taken aback. "But what are we going to do about this woman?" He pointed to the entry selected as a winner.

"Pay her," said Hershey. "She won your contest, y'know, so you owe her the money."

Snyder shook his head. "But we're not going to use her entry. We can't now, not with that charter and all."

Hershey remained unruffled. "It makes no difference," he told the flustered lawyer. "We don't have to use the name she submitted, but she did win your contest, so pay her. She earned it."

The Chocolate Company - 1925.

Bustling activity along Chocolate Avenue - about 1915.

Snyder, erstwhile known as "Judge," was still puzzled. Nevertheless, he agreed. Then he said something about the name not being official until the first piece of mail addressed to the new post office was received. He left, beseeching some unseen power for curses to be brought down on the heads of the people who had roped him into becoming the judge of a contest.

The first mail for the new Hershey Post Office arrived on the P & R five-thirty p.m. train from Harrisburg on Wednesday, February 7, 1906. Exactly four weeks later, Milton and Kitty Hershey decided it was time for them to get a new mailing address. Hence, a new project appeared on the books of the Hershey Improvement Company entitled "New Homestead—Hershey Mansion." But the site for it had been chosen years earlier when M. S. leased three acres of land from the Imboden family on April 3, 1903.

At that time, the grassy knoll across Spring Creek from the new factory site was known as Imboden's Woods, a name that would be changed to High Point after the mansion was built. Artisan, stone masons, laborers, and carpenters descended on the site; more than fifty of them began digging, hacking, sawing, stone-cutting, and wood-planing.

The completed Mansion without the formal gardens - 1909.

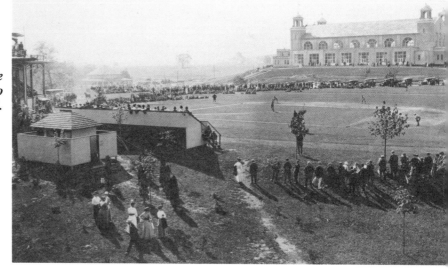

A baseball game in the shadow of the Convention Hall drew a large crowd to the Hershey Athletic Field - 1915.

Home of the Hershey Men's Club - about 1920.

Two recent customers stand outside the Hershey horse-shoeing and blacksmithing shop.

The old Central Theatre (McKinley Building).

Hershey football, town team - 1914.

Their work resulted in a good-sized, but unpretentious, building that looked more comfortable than grand. It was indeed spacious, but its primary claim to majestic splendor was a large cut-glass torchier that Hershey had purchased at the Columbian Exposition in Chicago back in 1893. There were also more than a dozen oil paintings from the Holland Galleries in New York, but they were more scenic than classic. They carried titles like "Puss in Mischief," "Maids Playing Ladies," "The Moorish Jewel Seller," and "Wash Day in Brittany." The names of the artists are not in the records.

Hershey's aesthetic side dictated that there be several fireplaces scattered throughout the building, in the main drawing room, the library, which eventually became a billiards room, and in two or three of the upstairs bedrooms. He loved to dream away a late evening sitting before the fireplace. But his practical side ruled out the fuss and bother of woodchopping, log-toting, and sweeping up ashes. So the fireplaces that illumined his reveries were designed to contain the flames and to emanate the desired heat, but they were all fired with gas logs.

After nearly three years of building and decorating, fitting the garden landscaping into the structural motif, M.S. Hershey and bride finally strolled out one evening to look at the dream castle and the artisans' handiwork and gave it their seal of approval.

The Mansion's decor was the height of contemporary fashion.

Mr. Hershey purchased this magnificent torchier at the Columbian Exposition in Chicago in 1893.

The first Hershey Volunteer Fire Company (notice the horse-drawn fire engines - with the horses).

Car barns of the Hershey Transit Company. These trolley cars carried workers to and from the plant and picked up milk from local farmers.

Hershey Trust Company - early 1920's.

The Hershey Cafe decked out in its summer awnings.

Hershey town band.

*   *   *

Another legend was born on the thirty-first of August, 1905, when the Hershey Volunteer Fire Company was organized. It didn't receive its charter until the eighteenth of February in 1907, but it managed to record two fire alarm calls on the day it opened. The first one reported a fire at company president William Murrie's home, and the other one came from the Homestead.

A kaleidoscope of events followed the deed of trust that Milton Hershey had set up on November 15, 1909, to establish the Hershey Industrial School for orphan boys. This, too, was Kitty's idea.

On September 1, 1910, the first four boys were enrolled at the school, and the Hershey Department Store opened later the same month.

Hershey Improvement Company store under construction. Later Department Store; later yet, Cocoa Inn.

The "Hershey Girl." An early advertising poster.

Hershey Trust Company Interior - 1930.

Another view of Chocolate Avenue looking east.

Convention Hall - 1917.

The Hershey Department Store (formerly the Chocolate Press) - about 1930.

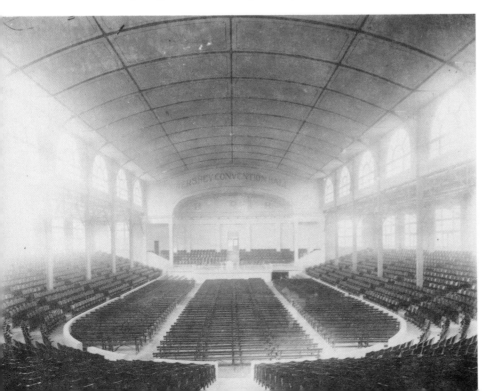

*Interior view,
Convention Hall.*

Hershey Industrial School students "bloom" in Mansion gardens.

The following year, the factory floor space was increased to eighteen acres. Then, in quick progression, there followed the opening of the Kinderhaus at the school, and charters were granted to the Hershey Water Company and the Hershey Power Company.

On the twenty-eighth of June 1914, the Hershey Trust Company building was scheduled for dedication and occupancy, but that had to be postponed because of some unpleasant news from Europe. So the dedication date was moved to the thirteenth of July. By that time, the populace realized that the assassination of Franz Ferdinand, Archduke of Austria, and his wife Sophie in Sarajevo had really been important enough to cause the earlier postponement.

The people of Hershey came to see their first community Christmas tree in December of 1914, and most of the folks gathered there simply prayed that the war in Europe would soon come to an end.

On the twenty-fifth of March, 1915, the entire community was stunned by the news of Kitty Hershey's death in the Bellevue Stratford Hotel in Philadelphia. Once again, community prayer services were held in the square, and in churches throughout the town people gathered to pay their last respects to the beloved lady.

Milton Hershey remained in Philadelphia for some time after his wife's interment at Laurel Hill Cemetery. For the next several years, even though expansion and new enterprises occupied his time, Hershey withdrew from public view until April of 1917. Then a monument was erected and dedicated on the Hershey family plot in the Hershey Cemetery where Mrs. Catherine Hershey was reinterred; and Milton Hershey again began taking an active interest in business and community affairs.

In the meantime, the zoo had opened and the Chocolate Company unveiled a visitors' bureau. The first meeting of the Consolidated Hershey High School Alumni Association was held and a new water treatment plant was constructed.

But as the war in Europe came to an end, Milton Hershey was off to Cuba, where he was starting a sugar mill and intended to build a railroad. At the end of 1918, three days after the war ended in Europe, Milton Hershey formalized the gift of his

The Mansion quickly becomes a tourist attraction - 1913.

Derry Township public school.

Hershey Chocolate Corporation stock to the Hershey Industrial School. At the time, the stock was worth sixty million dollars, but the actual gift was not announced publicly until 1923.

*   *   *

The village of Hershey continued its "boom town" expansion after the war, even though it was visited, in February of 1918, by a tremendous fire loss of more than five million dollars which destroyed the cocoa storage department of the Chocolate Corporation.

Change swept across town and countryside as the returning soldiers from France opened the Milton S. Hershey American Legion Post No. 386 in a loft over the fire company station. Charter members Paul Shultz and Paul Zentmeyer were instrumental in getting the new post started; Milton Hershey helped things along by providing a grant for a prospective drum and bugle corps, although this group wasn't officially chartered until ten years later.

Then the whole town was saddened on March 11, 1920, when Milton Hershey's mother, Fanny B. Hershey, died in her eighty-fourth year. Up until the last year of her life, this lace-capped Mennonite matriarch had still been busily engaged in hand-wrapping the silver foil *Kisses* for her son's "new chocolate business" across the street.

Hotel Hershey and rose garden.

A Pennsylvania State Police Training Academy and a remount station were located in downtown Hershey, and the modern sewage disposal plant came on the scene in 1924. In the following year, the Hershey National Bank was chartered, and a junior-senior high school building was added to the Derry Township school system. Over at the Chocolate Corporation, a new confection named *"Mr. Goodbar"* was added to the line, but most of the salesmen didn't hold out much hope for its survival in the marketplace.

In 1927, the Hershey Chocolate Corporation was incorporated in the state of Delaware, and stocks were listed on the New York Stock Exchange. The Fanny B. Hershey Memorial Building was dedicated in September of that year, and William F. R. Murrie was named President of the newly incorporated Hershey Estates, which included the park, the bank, the zoo, the department store, the Convention Hall, the utility companies, and various other community building programs and enterprises.

As the Roaring Twenties ended, a nationwide Depression commanded the headlines in the other world that lay outside the place of sanctuary called Hershey. A park golf club was opened, a new park swimming pool was built, and the Hershey Estates opened a new dairy. The former home of Dr. Martin L. Hershey was renovated into a new Hershey Museum in 1930. Later the museum was moved to a building next to the arena, and the original building was occupied by the Hershey Post of the American Legion.

The first ice hockey game was played in the Ice Palace on February 17, 1931. The name "Ice Palace" was given to the former Convention hall, a building that was later connected to the Hershey Sports Arena and one that currently houses the museum.

By the second or third year after the Hershey Bears began competing in the Eastern Amateur Hockey League, Milton Hershey had become an ardent fan of the sport. One evening, he made a last-minute decision to visit the old Ice Palace and cheer for the hometown team in a particularly crucial game. When he arrived at the ticket office, the house was sold out, and he not only couldn't get a seat, he couldn't even get into the place. All the standing room had been sold out, too.

"I won't have it," he said on his ride back to the mansion. But his angry call to master builder D. Paul Witmer had to await the morrow. Witmer had bought his ticket early, and on that evening he was at the game.

At breakfast next morning, plans were made for the giant new Hershey Sports Arena. The instructions were clear and simple. It was to be big, but no posts or columns inside to obstruct the view.

It didn't come into being until 1936, just before Christmas, but in all the time between, M.S. Hershey reminded the builder Witmer, "Just see that it's big enough so a guy can get a seat, even if he shows up late." Not a word about a specially reserved box for M.S. Hershey, because M.S. Hershey didn't think like that. As in almost everything else, he reasoned that if something was big enough to serve anyone who was interested, there would be room enough for him, too.

He thought of himself as a person who was only entitled to the same consideration that he extended others. He was not a self-centered man. And, in that sense, he was different.

*   *   *

When the New Deal arrived following the 1932 election, the country had reached what is supposed to be the pit of the Great Depression, and almost everyone looked to Washington for direction. Not so in Hershey.

A lawn party at the Hotel to celebrate M.S. Hershey's 79th birthday. (Mr. Hershey is at the center of the round table wearing a white suit.)

Community Building - 1933.

Theatre in Community Building - 1933.

Hershey Store Company (later the Hershey Inn).

Hershey Chocolate Corporation windowless office building - 1936.

Hershey railroad station with Hershey Chocolate Corporation in background - 1936.

A lot of pump-priming legislation was enacted to put new blood into the public works engendered by social legislation; yet commercial and private dwelling construction ground to a virtual standstill. But again, not in Hershey.

Down in Cuba, the sugar mills were humming right along, and in Chocolate Town, although the confectionery and cocoa business wasn't booming, the Pennsylvania enterprise was doing better than just hanging on. In the mind of Milton Hershey, this was just the right time to apply the principles he had adhered to ever since he had been a little boy. He figured people needed work to do, so he would give them work, and that meant jobs. They needed money, so he would make money and he would spend it. That meant security, the only kind of security he ever understood. For him, to be afraid to work and take chances with either time or money was sinful, in almost the same sense that gamblers are prone to say, "Scared money never wins."

As he saw it, scared anything could lose everything.

The new breed of social planners scoffed at this simplistic attitude and sat back to watch him run his model plant and town, along with his crackpot ideas, off the cliff to financial ruin.

He started with one after another multimillion dollar project—building a new Community Building in 1932, and Hershey Hotel in May 1933.

Hershey Industrial School - about 1930.

Hershey Industrial School, Senior Hall cafeteria - 1935.

Although the Community Building was begun first, the inclusion of a hospital and theater held up its formal dedication until Labor Day of 1933, which followed the formal opening of the Hotel Hershey. Another hospital for the town and Industrial School was later built over beyond the Homestead on Route 322, and the several hundred yard distance between those buildings would figure in the birth and death entries to mark M.S. Hershey's life span.

Then he announced the beginning of a great new golf tournament, the Hershey Open, to be played on the expanded links of the Hershey Country Club. The Hershey Hotel would be opened with a dedicatory address by Lowell Thomas, the famous radio newscaster, and the Hershey golf links would go on to hire such famous pros as Henry Picard and Ben Hogan. Virtually every famous pro, beginning with Walter Hagen, Gene Sarazen, Sam Snead, Byron Nelson, Vic Ghezzi, Johnny Revolta, and so many others, would come along to contend on these internationally famous links.

In 1934, it appeared to his open-mouthed detractors that he had finally come to the edge of the precipice. His ambitious project of building a senior high school that

Hershey Industrial School, Christmas program - 1912.

Dedication of Fannie B. Hershey Memorial School Building (Milton Hershey, aged 70, first row, fourth from left).

would serve both the Industrial School boys and the boys and girls of the public school system in Derry Township was turned down by the Pennsylvania State Board of Education. Off the record, he was told that the paternalistic disciplines and moral codes peculiar to his private school would not be workable on the same premises where students were being educated with public funds. They said his school would have to make several concessions in keeping with some vague notion of what constituted public morality.

This translated into terms diametrically opposed to his own beliefs. To his critics, it mattered only that this feisty little man with his high-pitched voice had finally bitten off more than he could chew. The high school was built, and it contained facilities for both boys and girls, even lavatories, locker rooms, and classrooms specially set up for sewing and cooking instruction.

There were no girls in his school at that time, and he didn't have half enough boys of high school age to warrant the staffing and operation of such an overly large and much too expensive place. Now, they chortled, let's see what he's going to do about that. He rocketed ahead to open and staff the school.

Entrance to Hershey Park - early 1920's.

In the sector of spiritual enterprises, he bequeathed each of five Hershey churches with twenty thousand dollar grants and set up a special M. S. Hershey Foundation for educational purposes. Hard on the heels of that, he built a big new windowless Hershey Office Building to help administer both a sugar business in Cuba that was bursting its seams and an expanding confectionary business in Hershey, Pennsylvania, that was still doing better than merely waging a fight for survival.

He followed this by building and opening the Sports Arena, just after opening one of the beautiful new rose gardens. All of these endeavors, to anyone with any notion of what a dollar was worth, clearly ran in the face of what was believed to be economically feasible. This was the era in which the term "fiscal responsibility" was coined by politicians who always talked about it at election time, but who never mentioned it when it came time to levy taxes or budget lavish spending funds.

Of all the energetic working and spending programs his critics had doomed to failure, not one failed. Those who predicted the failures could not understand it. And even those who had joined with him to make these ventures work found themselves too busy to explain. Thereby, they helped cause another kind of unforeseen trouble.

A train load of visitors arrives at Hershey Park - 1915.

The Hershey Tea House was a favorite meeting and eating spot for many of the town's residents.

A full house at Hershey Park amphitheater - 1909.

An afternoon boat ride on Hershey Park Lake was a "proper" way for young ladies to spend leisure time.

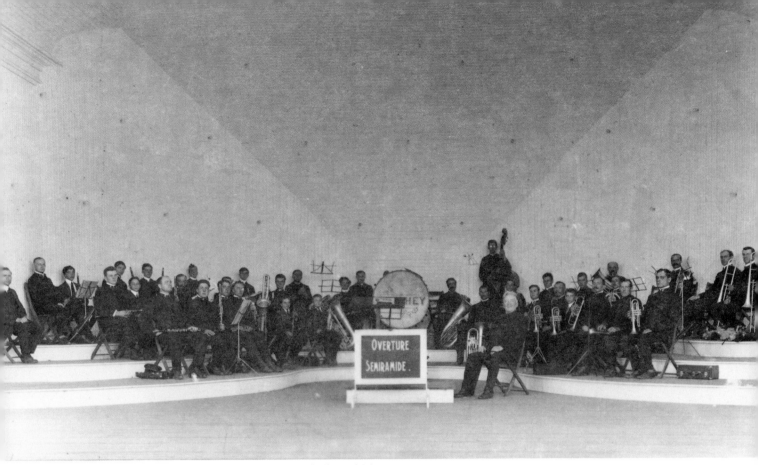

Hershey band in concert at park band shell - 1914.

Getting ready to enjoy a band concert in the park - 1916.

In 1925, Hershey Park pool drew as many spectators as swimmers.

The water slide was one of the main pool attractions - 1916.

Swimming Pool, Ballroom (left), and Hershey Park Golf Club (top) - 1930's.

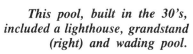

This pool, built in the 30's, included a lighthouse, grandstand (right) and wading pool.

Ice Palace (old Convention Hall) - 1931.

Exterior of Convention Hall - 1925.

After riding the carousel (right) park visitors boarded the miniature trains (left) - about 1917.

Dancers swing and sway in the Hershey Ballroom - mid 1930's.

Hershey Sports Arena - 1936.

Ice hockey at the Sports Arena - 1936.

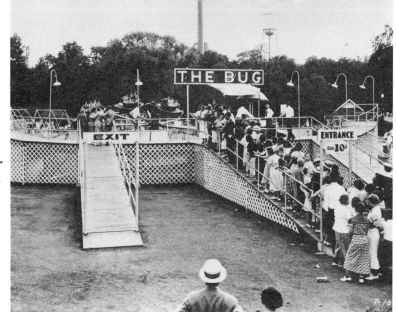

"The Bug" was popular about 1940.

"The Comet," roller coaster, built in the 1940's.

"Wild Cat," roller coaster built in the 1930's.

Some union people who had set themselves a round-robin circuit to unionize private business elsewhere put Hershey on the same target with the automakers in Detroit and the garment makers in New York. The C.I.O., using essentially the same shop representation teams, appeared on the Hershey scene. There followed a sitdown strike in April 1937, and on the seventh day of that month, the farmers, who were being deprived of their daily earnings via milk sales to the company, told the strikers to get out. The sitdowners refused.

So the farmers armed themselves with cudgels and pitchforks and threw them out. The Pennsylvania State Police, a short block down the street from the scene of the action, were held on stand-by alert, awaiting a call from the sheriff's office. They had not been called when the original trespass had been made by the union people, nor were they summoned in time to prevent the violence that erupted when the farmers stormed the building.

It wasn't pleasant, and yet in a way it was unavoidable.

The Hershey Community Building Theatre.

Hershey Open - 1936. From left, Byron Nelson, Frank Welsh, Sam Snead.

The C.I.O. hierarchy and the liberally oriented U.S. Department of Labor had been misinformed as to the true nature of what the workers wanted when they framed their joint plan of action. But they didn't learn about that mistake until later. By the time they realized this error, it cost the C.I.O. the representation contract it sought, and the subsequent unionization of the plant fell to the A.F. of L. by default.

The point that "tyrannical private interests," in the form of Milton Hershey and his management team, had accomplished this "workers' paradise" by slave wages and cheap labor simply wasn't true. The so-called exorbitant profits of the whole corporate entity were largely gained in Cuba. In Cuba, tremendous profits were being made, and a big part of those profits was being spent right there. For in Central Hershey, Cuba, just as in Hershey, Pennsylvania, there was a model village, an orphans' school; and the wage and working conditions down there were by far the best on the whole island. In fact, they were better than they were in a number of places in the United States.

In both places, Hershey built and Hershey spent, and Hershey made possible thousands of jobs to people on the continent and on the island called the Pearl of the Antilles through another gem of reasoning. "There are no money problems you can't work your way out of." This was the simplistic rule that the scoffers decried and, because they failed to comprehend this maxim, they very nearly destroyed it.

The strike proved to be an enigmatic lesson and a painful disappointment to Milton Hershey. He withdrew in seclusion throughout most of the spring and summer of that year. His plant workers held a Loyalty Day Parade on April 20, 1937. Then, on September thirteenth, his birthday, they had a big party for him at the Arena. Late that night, following the festivities, he had a stroke and very nearly died. So Milton Hershey further withdrew from things for a while.

Throughout this disruptive period of the late thirties, and into the early forties, the march of buildings and enterprise in the bustling Pennsylvania town continued. In 1938, the Hershey Soap Company came on the scene and a junior college was opened. The Chocolate Corporation introduced a *Krackel Bar,* and the "Hershey BEARS" played their first professional hockey game in the Sports Arena. An outdoor stadium was built to hold 16,000 spectators for football and track events. In 1939, a baking and experimental candy shop was opened to commemorate

Loyalty Parade - April 20, 1937.

World War II Field Ration D bars.

Milton Hershey's eighty-second birthday. The next year on his birthday, a beautiful new rose was named after the man who had tried so long and so hard to bring a little more beauty and happiness into the lives of those who had chosen to share his dreams.

In August of 1942, the Army and Navy E. Award was given to Mr. Hershey for the *Hershey Ration D Bar* that had sustained the embattled men who had gone off to fight in defense of the individual rights they held so dear to themselves and the rights which they wanted to preserve for all Americans.

These rights were eloquently expressed by the moral codes and the dutiful ethics of a hardworking Pennsylvania Dutch farm boy who had grown up to be a fearless, tough-minded man, but a man whose generosity had room for everyone whom he could reach out and touch.

Presentation ceremonies awarding the Army-Navy E to the Hershey Chocolate Corporation - August 27, 1942.

On October 13, 1945, the final curtain came down for the little guy who had fashioned this twentieth-century Camelot from the raw cornfields, quarries, and dairy lands of Derry Church. The former Hershey Hospital (now the Health Center of the Milton Hershey School), just down the road from the expansive M.S. Hershey Medical Center of the Pennsylvania State University, still stands in eloquent, though silent, testimony to the man of so many parts who died there. For he was indeed the living example of what can be done by someone who holds tenaciously to the proven moral values of the past, and yet who manages to shape the future into the functional and realistic form that his courageous optimism holds for it.

Hershey's fourscore and eight years were almost equally divided between the last forty-three years of the Victorian nineteenth century and the first forty-five years of the bustling twentieth century. But throughout all the eighty-eight years, he gave daily proof of a belief in the simple tenets of cleanliness, truthfulness, dedication, and generosity with which he had been endowed. Yet he was positively relentless in wresting every golden drop of promise from every passing day that marked his journey into the future that endlessly beckoned him.

M.S., Kitty and friends in the Mansion gardens.

In the early days of collecting the memorable events that some of Milton Hershey's oldtime friends still recalled sharing with him, we chanced to mention the title we intended using for the book. The very suggestion of calling Milton Hershey "one of a kind" brought a smile to the face of Paul Shultz, who happened to be the man being interviewed at the time.

"I can see old M.S. now," said the former Chocolate Company salesman and early Hershey Post Legion Commander," and maybe you don't know this, but a lot of people did call him one of a kind to his face back in the good old days."

Shultz nodded his head in the manner so patently mastered by kindly and world-wise octogenarians.

"Yep,"he continued, "I can still see the bushy, iron-gray brows going up and those bright blue eyes twinkling as M.S. would ask in that high-pitched voice of his, 'Isn't everyone?'."

View of Highpoint Mansion from atop the chocolate factory - about 1918.

Down through the years of constant change . . .
. . some Hershey memories remain the same . .

The millions of people who have walked the streets, the midways, the corridors, and the garden pathways of Hershey come away with the feeling that they have visited a model American community. For more than half a century, this place has won renown for the structures, the landscaping, and the strangely unique array of rose gardens, parks, schools, golf links, and buildings, both commercial and residential. These things always seem to be changing, and yet the spiritual outlook of the people continues to remain intact.

Since 1903, when the first ground was broken for the new plants and homes that have sprung up in this "cornfield," there has always been some kind of building program underway. One after another edifice has become a bank, a retirement condominium, or a school. The mushrooming business places have done just that—they've continued to be built and the community keeps on growing. Today, many a new building stands where once there was a printing plant, a lumber yard, or a fire house that has long since disappeared. Yet, in the words of the old French adage, *Plus ca change, plus c'est le meme chose*—"The more things change, the more they remain the same."

Here, only the structural scene has changed, because the pervading sense of optimism and the enthusiastic way of life still prevail just as they have from the beginning. The clean, wide streets, the gently rolling hillocks, so green in summer and white in winter, the marble halls and the shining facades, have either mellowed and blended into the background, or they have given way to the newer, larger, and more beautiful structures that replaced them.

Thus, Hershey Pennsylvania, has become a showcase of both shadow and substance. But only the visible substance—the earth, the brick, the clay, the steel—has changed. The physical structures that once figured in a man's dream of a model town

keep changing, improving, growing. From this ongoing scheme of continual change, the physical dimensions of the community have emerged.

But one thing has not changed. The shadowy forms of those who came here at the turn of the century and built the stage for all this—they are still here, too. Somewhere off in the wings, hidden from sight in the backstage area, is the spirit of Hershey past, and here the bristling energy of the feisty little guy who started all this still hustles and bustles about.

When you walk by the Homestead, you can almost hear Mama Hershey busying herself in the kitchen and fretting about the way her men folk, son Milton and husband Henry,"are still out there in the shop, tinkering away, while their supper is getting cold."

The wispy form of Kitty Sweeney Hershey is still flitting about the halls of High Point Mansion, for "Judge" Snyder and his wife and Bill Murrie and spouse are coming over to visit, and Milton isn't home yet.

Down at the bank, Harry Lebkicher and Ezra Hershey are pondering over a pile of notes that mark another string of "M.S.'s extravagances," like a zoo, a park, or a school.

Yes, these are the shadows behind the substance that become the Hershey community. The landscape keeps changing as new structures are shaped and fitted into the hard rock things which have emerged from the dreams of long ago.

The dreamer has long since gone to rest.

But the spirit of the man who made all this possible is alive and well, and still directs the play from backstage.

The wordly substance of the buildings may change, but the indomitable spirit of the bustling little guy who shaped it will always be part of those who live and work here.

Some things change, and some things remain the same.

*But with it all . . . .
there still remains the
substance of a vision grand*

Hershey Foods Corporation Corporate
Headquarters, formerly Highpoint, the
residence of Milton and Catherine
Hershey.

Hershey Chocolate Plant.

Milton Hershey School Students.

The Rotunda at Founders Hall, Milton Hershey School.

Hershey Community Theatre.

Hershey Museum of American Life

The Milton S. Hershey Medical Center of The Pennsylvania State University.

Hersheypark's sooperdooperLooper.

Ice Hockey at Hersheypark Arena.
Hotel Hershey and Hershey Garde

Hershey Entertainment and Resort Company Corporate Headquarters, formerly Parkview Manor.

Hershey Foods Corporation Corporate Administrative Center, formerly the Community Center.

It was late on the afternoon that World War II ended . . .

when Milton Hershey and Paul Witmer had motored around the town to take part in the joyful celebrations of victory. Then they headed for the hilltop behind the old Copenhaver farm and got out of the car. A deepening silence set in as they stood together watching the darkening streaks of twilight descend on the rooftops of the distant village.

Hershey finally broke the veil of stillness as he inclined his head toward the misty panorama spread out below them.

"Someday," he intoned in words that were balanced between his quizzical and wishful inner feelings, *"someday,* maybe one of our Home-boys will come down the hill from the school and take charge of the whole works down there."

Both the question and the wish were to be answered within the span of less than thirty years after he first put them into words. For no less than five of his boys would come down that hill, and each of them would rise to take command of one of the various enterprises that had by then been gathered under the world-famous name of Hershey.

The planter had gone to rest. History merely awaited these five of his beloved Homeboys who would see to the harvest assured.

Arthur R. Whiteman (retired)

Born 7-6-09 (Wentworth, North Carolina).
Milton Hershey School (1913-27), Alumnus
of the Year (1954, Finance). Education -
Beckley Business College, American Institute of Banking. Key Positions/Offices -
President of Hershey Estates (Now Hershey Entertainment & Resort Company),
Hershey Trust Company, Hershey National Bank. Director of Hershey Foods
Corporation, Milton Hershey School, Hershey Trust Company, M.S. Hershey Foundation.

William E.C. Dearden

Born 9-14-22 (Philadelphia, Pennsylvania).
Milton Hershey School (1935-40), Alumnus
of the Year (1964, Marketing). Education -
Albright College, Temple University, Harvard University. Key Positions/Offices -
Vice Chairman of the Board and Chief Executive Officer, Chairman of the Board of
Hershey Foods Corporation, Chairman of
the Board of Hershey Trust Company and
Milton Hershey School, Director of M.S.
Hershey Foundation.

Joseph S. Gumpher (retired)

Born 1-16-19 (Progress, Pennsylvania).
Milton Hershey School (1925-35), Alumnus
of the Year (1957, Finance). Key Positions/
Offices - Vice President of Hershey National Bank. Treasurer and President of
Hershey Trust Company. Director of Hershey National Bank, Milton Hershey
School, Hershey Trust Company, M.S. Hershey Foundation.

John M. Aichele

Born 9-4-21 (Carlisle, Pennsylvania). Milton Hershey School (1935-39), Alumnus of
the Year (1974, Business Affairs, Education). Education - Shippensburg State College, Pennsylvania State University. Key
Positions/Offices - Executive Vice President, President of Milton Hershey School.
Director of Hershey National Bank, Milton
Hershey School, Hershey Trust Company,
M.S. Hershey Foundation.

Kenneth V. Hatt

Born 12-20-23 (Mohnton, Pennsylvania).
Milton Hershey School (1933-41), Alumnus
of the Year (1962, Business). Key Positions/
Offices - Executive Vice President of Hershey Estates (Now Hershey Entertainment
& Resort Company). President and Director of Hershey Entertainment and Resort
Company. Director of former Hershey Estates, Milton Hershey School, Hershey
Trust Company, M.S. Hershey Foundation.

His deeds are

his monument.

His life is

our inspiration.

Bibliography

∿·∿

AUTHOR'S NOTES: Preface to the source credits and acknowledgments offered on behalf of this text

First—HERSHEY'S, HERSHEY'S KISSES®, KISSES, MR. GOODBAR®, and KRACKEL® are trademarks of Hershey Foods Corporation and have been used with the permission of the owner.

Second—The careful reader will note certain variances between factual narrations appearing in the general text of the book as against certain of the chronologically ordered sequences depicted in "The Timeless Hershey Album" (at the end of the main text). No disclaimer is offered, for although these narratives may differ in their specific content, they were drawn from different sources and such drawing was done from different time frames. Therefore, while the mainstay narration of the general text was the product of hundreds of personal interviews (as well as bank, court, and governmental documentary files), the "Album" chronology was elicited from the press clippings (compiled by the Archives), and for a considerable part they represent a compendium of press releases originally issued by one of the publicity departments within each of the Hershey disciplines, i.e., Hershey Chocolate, Hershey Estates, Hotel Hershey, Hershey Press, et al.

Special Mention

The art and design work on the main text was furnished by Jere (Jeremiah) L. Gabrielle, an Art School Cum Laude Graduate of Syracuse University a half century ago. Varying styles which alternate betwixt the baroque and the neo-Victorian predominate in the sketches and full-color illustrations. We have chosen this style to project the scenes and the physiognomy of M.S. Hershey as typical of the man and his times. The motifs are "old-fashioned." And, after forty-five years of working together, so are Jere and I.

Credits Due

The compilation of a personal biography on a man who virtually never wrote a letter or kept a diary or made speeches during his triumphant years would have been well nigh impossible without privileged access to the records and memorabilia assembled during his lifetime. Consequently, the first credit for this book must go to Harold S. Mohler, former Board Chairman of Hershey Foods, who provided the vital assists that gained us access to the materials and gave us the wherewithal to organize and collate the basic files from which these materials were drawn.

Co-dwelling in the same executive headquarters, we received some wonderful tape-cutting assists from Bill Dearden, former Vice Chairman and Chief Executive Officer, now Chairman of the Board of Hershey Foods, and from former General Counsel, Sam Schreckengaust. The *in vivo* guidance counsellors' contributions made by Arthur Whiteman, Joseph Gumpher, John Aichele, Earl Houser, Ken Bowers, and Dexter Koehl were largely responsible for the screening which made this text provable as well as believable. Some extra special measure of thanks must go to the insightfully humane contributions of Arthur Whiteman and Joseph Gumpher as well as to my perennial buffer Ken Bowers. From the former two I learned *the reasons why* that made this text understandable, and by the latter I was given a shield which kept me alive long enough to make the whole thing printable.

But along with these contributions there were the myriad "connections" provided by four gentle women: Marge Kokal (Hershey Foods, Public Relations Office), Marie Daniels (Hershey Trust Company), Joanne Gibble (Hershey Foods receptionist), and Nellie Huber (HERCO Headquarters). They remain anonymous, but made the priceless contributions which gave far more impetus to this project than mere thanks or adulation can cover. Other vital "assists" were provided by the meaningful bits and pieces poured into the entire effort by a tireless group of cordial contributors. Danny Steiner (of Steiner Studios, Annville), along with Ruth Hack (of the Milton S. Hershey School, Farm Office), as well as Susan Graham and Paul Hoch (both of Hershey Foods), and Don Struke (formerly with Hershey Foods) were instrumental in supplying design sketches, photographs, copy distributions, interview "leads," and inputs of personal guidance that helped to weld the many parts of this book into a unitized structure.

From the historical and archival expertise of Miss Eleanor King (the Milton Hershey School Archivist, retired) and Jane Stacks (current School Archivist) we were furnished with the clinical perspectives and a quality of candor that frequently attained levels of being surgically merciless. Indeed, it was King who helped shape the earlier collections and compilations of Dr. Paul Wallace upon whose base frame much of this finished text was structured. And subsequently, in turn, it was she who guided and documented "The Milton Hershey Story," the previous version of a text that was previously published by Random House and copyrighted by the Milton Hershey School.

In the round-robin interviews, studies, and discussions covered by the four-year search and selection routine necessary to these compilations, a large measure of thanks must go to Al Meyers (Elwood C. Meyers, former Research and Development Director, Hershey Foods), to Sam Hinkle (former Chairman of the Board, Hershey Foods) to Joanne Hostetter Thomas (daughter of Dr. Herman H. Hostetter, Hershey's personal physician), and to Pete Birnstiel (former Assistant Lab Director of Hershey Foods) who lent their personal contributions to whatever there is of vibrancy and authenticity in our efforts to recall things as once they were in Hershey. George Booth, former "Homeboy" and HERCO Real Estate Manager, along with his fellow worker Lindsay Spencer, placed a feeling of warmth and camaraderie in this scribbler's heart by performing so many kindnesses and by going out of their way so many times to help this entire effort. There were, of course, and still are hundreds of others whom we sought and who were either personally interviewed by myself or by Earl and Dolly Ibach, who researched and catalogued the tons of archival materials to which we were provided access. These efforts ultimately became the main structures from which we bound together the wealth of random splinters that ultimately became the mainstay of the book itself.

All of which brings us to . . .

Credits Overdue

This exercise of extending my sentiments of personal gratitude is not without some tearful reminders, for some of the best help I received was provided by the dearly and recently departed.

I shall always be mindful that I was privileged to share a bit of time with some of the finest people with whom I was blessed to become acquainted. They include my longtime friend Paul Shultz, and they call back the memories of such dearly beloved folks as Margaret Clark, Jim Bobb, Mom Gordon, Elsie Ziegler, Konrad Hartmann, Frank Edris, Paul Zentmeyer and, of course, J. Paul Witmer.

In the years to come, whatever success may be enjoyed by this book will in large part be due to the input of these grand and gracious personalities.

They were easy to love.

For myself, I can only say that each of them must surely appear on the "guest list" of those who dwell in *the better place* to which I hope to go when the roll is called up yonder for me.

When they were *here,* they not only shared a dream, they helped to fashion it into a town and a way of life that became the spiritual blood and bone and the structural brick and clay that eventually became the real place called Hershey, Pennsylvania.

So it was that I arrived at the immutable conclusion that Milton Snavely Hershey became *one of a kind* because he shared a lifetime with some very precious people whom God saw fit to gather around him.

Source Credits

The base frame for this book was largely drawn from the prior compilations gathered by Dr. Paul A.W. Wallace, Professor of English, Lebanon Valley College, in the middle and late years of the 1950's. Subsequent to the initial Wallace effort, a joined work entitled "Milton S. Hershey," co-authored by the same Dr. Wallace and Katherine B. Shippen, was copyrighted in June 1959 and published by Random House for the Milton Hershey School. The entire content of the latter (co-authored and copyrighted) publication was elicited from the text of Dr. Wallace's former compilations. Our permission to use materials garnered from both works was granted by the Milton Hershey School and the M.S. Hershey Foundation Trust to whom they belong.

The source data elicited from previous compilations and publications were too numerous for cross-indexing in this bibliograph of credits. Indeed, many of these anecdotes were already in the public domain prior to the Wallace and Shippen copyrighted texts. Consequently, we have chosen to proclaim this *blanket acknowledgment* for the priceless assistance gained from our distinguished predecessors.

Two other authors, Joseph R. Snavely and Dr. Herman H. Hostetter, also published previously copyrighted texts on the life of Milton Hershey. We have, therefore, noted the names of the source publications in each instance where such narrative facts were elicited from those earlier texts. Permission to use these stories was granted by the heirs of the original copyright owners, i.e., Milton H. Snavely, son of Joseph R. Snavely, and Joanne Hostetter Thomas, daughter of Dr. Herman H. Hostetter.

Index of Interview Sources

1. Peter Birnstiel, ch. XX
2. Charles Bikle, ch. XVIII
3. Robert S. Black, ch. VIII, XIV
4. Tom Black, ch. VIII, XIV
5. James Bobb, ch. XXV
6. George Booth, ch. XVIII
7. Art Bowman, ch. XV
8. Amos Brandt, ch. VII
9. Theral Brehm, ch. XVIII
10. Margaret Clark, ch. IX, XIX, XXV
11. Clyde Ebersole, ch. XII
12. Frank Edris, ch. XVIII, XXIV
13. Dr. Thomas Fox, ch. VII
14. Kathryn "Mom" Gordon, ch. IX, XIX, XXV
15. Joseph Gumpher, ch. XXI, XXV
16. Harry Hartman, ch. XVIII
17. Konrad Hartmann, ch. XII
18. Dr. J.O. Hershey, ch. XXI
19. Dr. Martin Hershey, ch. VII, X
20. Sam Hinkle, ch. XIII, XVIII, XIX, XX, XXIV
21. Mary Kershner, ch. XIX
22. Eleanor King, entire
23. Earle Markley, ch. XXI
24. Robert McCafferty, ch. XX
25. Elwood Meyers, ch. VII, XIII, XVIII, XIX, XX
26. Miss Violet Pierce, ch. XXV
27. Kathryn Oslansky Pugliese, ch. XXIV, XXV
28. Mrs. Hugh Seavers, ch. XXV
29. Robert Coleman Schaeffer, final picture
30. Paul Shultz, ch. XXV
31. Irvin W. Slesser, ch. XX
32. Joseph Snavely, ch. XIV, XXI, XXII
33. Alex Stoddart, ch. XVIII, XX, XXV
34. Monroe C. Stover, ch. III
35. Joanne Hostetter Thomas, ch. IX, XI, XV, XVI, XXIII, XXIV, XXV
36. Harry Tinney, ch. VII
37. Richard Uhrich, ch. XII, XX
38. Paul Wallace, throughout
39. Arthur Whiteman, ch. XVIII, XXIV, XXV
40. D. Paul Witmer, ch. XVII, XVIII, XX, XXIV, XXV
41. Paul L. Zentmeyer, ch. XXV
42. Elsie Ziegler, ch. V, XVI, XVIII, XXV

*Note: The persons listed above provided the information which appears in the chapter text shown next to their names. Where precise page locations were deamed meaningful, the listings were added to the final index on pages 354-355.

Footnote Documentary (Chapter XIX, pages 219-228)

The New York Times: April, 1937

The reckless leaders of labor who have called sit-down strikes in many parts of the country ought now to find in the affair at Hershey a warning of the familiar truth that violence breeds violence. They ought also to find a useful reminder of the fact that the interests of an important third party are involved in these attempts of theirs to settle an industrial dispute through a resort to force. The third party is the general public: typified, at Hershey, by the farmers who lost a market for their goods. But some part of this general public, and usually a larger part, suffers similarly whenever a labor union resorts suddenly and without warning to the new method of the sit-down strike. In their own interest the discoverers of this new method will do well to remember that, after all, they represent only a minority of the organized labor movement, and that the organized labor movement is in itself only a small minority of the whole rank-in-file of people gainfully employed in the United States.

The Philadelphia Inquirer: April, 1937

It is a curious anomaly that the dispute and the violence at Hershey should have taken place in a community where every conceivable consideration has been given the workers' comfort and happiness. This "industrial dream city," with its model factory, magnificient community house, theatre and sports facilities, is, in effect, the people's own enterprise. The sit-downers were striking not against a "soulless corporation," nor against "vested interests," They were striking against their own community and, in a real sense, against themselves.

When the worst violence of the year occurred in The Dream Town of Hershey, Pennsylvania, the following statement was made as the joined response of Representatives Robert E. Woodside, Jr. and William E. Habbyshaw, Assemblymen, from Dauphin County:

MR. SPEAKER AND MEMBERS OF THE HOUSE:

Last week when Mr. Habbyshaw and I introduced our Hershey Strike Resolution, we did so first to prevent a collapse of the milk market in Pennsylvania, which would have been inevitable had the strike continued much longer, and secondly to prevent the violence which happened last Wednesday when the strikers were driven forcibly from the plant.

We do not condone violence. But before we criticise the farmers for settling this strike in their own way we should remember the facts. We should remember that there was being thrown upon the market over 350,000 qts. of milk a day, that the collapse of the milk market was imminent, and that nearly $15,000 a day was being lost to the farmers at a time they could least afford it. Above all we cannot forget that during all this time the Governor was keeping a very discreet silence concerning the entire situation.

Had the Governor made any effort to meet this problem, the violence would not have occurred. The responsibility for all lawlessness that occurred at Hershey rests with the Governor and not with the farmers or any other group.

One acquainted with the situation cannot help but conclude that had the Governor merely opened his mouth he could have persuaded the strikers to permit the operation of that part of the plant which would have made possible the use of the farmers' milk. There was a close connection between the Governor's followers and the strikers. Meetings of the Union were held in the rooms of the Democratic Clubs in the vicinity. The Democratic Senator from the District spoke at one of the first meetings which was held. The theme song of the strike was "We cannot be moved, the Governor is back of us." Telephone calls were made from strike leaders directly to the Governor's office, keeping him informed of the situation. But, through it all our Governor mimicking Washington, kept a discreet silence, while the farmers suffered.

It is interesting to compare the quality of the courage that existed among the farmers with the official cowardice at Harrisburg. Prior to the time that the violence occurred, it had been announced to the group of farmers that the strikers had machine guns in the building. Although in fact false it was believed at the time. With their own eyes they saw and faced guns, knives and other weapons which apparently were going to be used on them should they enter the building. In spite of this, determined to do what in the opinion was right, they entered the factory and gave it back to its owners so that they and their fellow farmers would not be threatened with financial ruin. Was it the farmers or the officials of Pennsylvania who disgraced the Commonwealth.

The farmer is the backbone of the American civilization. No laboring man knows more about labor. No man arises earlier, puts in more hours or works harder than the farmer, no brow perspires more profusely. No man is in a position to appreciate the problems of labor more than the farmer. On the other hand he is a business man who must buy, sell and employ. All farmers own property and appreciate that a property right is a human right which must be respected. Their opinions and their rights are entitled to the greatest respect. When they were denied a market for their milk, they were deprived of an income of $15,000 a day; when their milk industry was threatened with ruination, they had a right to expect the Governor of this Commonwealth to be active in assisting them in solving this problem. When that help was not forthcoming, they took it upon themselves to solve it in their own way.

It doesn't go down well with the farmer to be called a disgrace to the Commonwealth for solving a problem which the Governor should have solved. The farmers of this section, peaceful and law abiding as any group of citizens in the County, did not want to deal with this problem. But just as their ancestors the famous Paxton Boys of 1775 were provoked to violence by their ruler George the III of that day so the farmers were provoked to violence by our ruler George the III of this day.

The Governor's attempt to hide behind the skirts of the Sheriff is childish. His own Attorney General furnished him with an opinion that he could send in his police. The way the Governor and the State Democratic party has stuck their nose into all manner of local problems, it is amusing how when the issue gets hot they pass the buck.

The Governor knew of the situation. All the County knew. The Governor even had telephone calls from the strikers which strangely he referred to the Lieutenant Governor who under the Constitution and laws of this Commonwealth has nothing to do with law enforcement.

The Governor cannot hide behind the fact that his subordinates have now secured an agreement. The fact is the Governor permitted the violence. The fact is the Governor made no effort to solve the problem as it related to the farmers.

Although the violence was unfortunate and not to be condoned, considering mob psychology and the feeling that existed, it is fortunate that there were no more serious injuries. We must remember that feeling ran high among those who appreciated what the great philanthropist had done in the community, We must remember that feeling ran high against certain of the strikers who Mr. Hershey had educated. We must remember that the community realized that Mr. Hershey had given away even the roof over his own head in his unselfish effort to build a model community. Why pick on the farmers who in addition to their own losses had their keen sense of justice aroused?

The Governor has permitted anarchy in the coal regions and he permitted it in Hershey. That the "disgrace to the Commonwealth" should only appear to him when the farmers step in to the scene is to the rural communities most reprehensible.

Violence breeds violence. Even the Governor should know that you cannot sow the seeds of anarchy and reap orderly government.

Index

MILTON HERSHEY ... *believed*

that the meaning of life is found in the work one does. He was convinced that truth is better than a lie and that clean is better than dirty. He insisted that loyalty was the very keystone to friendship and he counted the friends he had made and kept as his life's most cherished possessions.

He never joined a church. But even though he wasn't much for reading books, the well-worn pages of his bedside Bible provide a silent testimonial to his one most notable exception. And, at least once every day, he would stop whatever he was doing and take time to say his prayers.

His ways were eccentric and sometimes they were maddeningly erratic. But his vision was phenomenal and he had a stubborn grasp of common sense values that helped him to pile up an astounding wealth of epic accomplishments.

Somehow, even though he lived by the Golden Rule, his ways were most times strangely mysterious to his fellows. And while he may have chosen to live in accordance with some unspoken creed, it would seem that the Prophet Isaiah had someone like Milton Hershey in mind when he wrote the following lines several thousand years ago:

> *Everyone follows after rewards, and they judge not for the fatherless,*
> *nor does the cause of the widow come into them, which justify the*
> *wicked and grind the faces of the poor. . . .*
> *He hath sent me to bind up the broken hearted as one whom his*
> *mother comforteth, so will I comfort you . . .*
> *Yea, they may forget, yet* **will I not forget thee.** . . .

Milton Snavely Hershey went to his reward thirty-five years *after* he had set up his monumental trust for homeless little boys. But the world had to wait for quite a long time before it would learn that he had been early to put his treasure where his heart had always been.

He did not forget. He will not be forgotten.